LIBRARY OF
RELIGIOUS AND PHILOSOPHICAL THOUGHT

PRIMITIVE CHRISTIANITY

VOL. II

PRIMITIVE CHRISTIANITY

ITS WRITINGS AND TEACHINGS IN THEIR HISTORICAL CONNECTIONS

BY

OTTO PFLEIDERER, D.D.

PROFESSOR OF PRACTICAL THEOLOGY IN THE UNIVERSITY OF BERLIN

TRANSLATED BY

W. MONTGOMERY, B.D.

VOL. II

REFERENCE BOOK PUBLISHERS, INC.
CLIFTON, NEW JERSEY
1965

Published 1965 by
Reference Book Publishers, Inc.

Library of Congress Catalog Card Number: 65-22085

Printed in the United States of America

CONTENTS

THE GOSPEL OF MARK.

THE GOSPEL OF LUKE.

THE ACTS OF THE APOSTLES.

THE LUCAN WRITINGS.

THE GOSPEL OF MATTHEW.

THE PREACHING OF JESUS AND THE FAITH OF THE FIRST DISCIPLES.

PRIMITIVE CHRISTIANITY

SECTION II.—HISTORICAL BOOKS

THE GOSPEL OF MARK

CHAPTER I

The Work of Jesus in Galilee

(Mark i. 1–ix. 50)

The Gospel of Mark must be taken as our point of departure in describing the historical literature of primitive Christianity, for it is without doubt the earliest of the Gospels which have come down to us, and a principal source of those which followed it. Its order of narration, which is in itself perfectly clear and simple, has also, in the main, been closely followed by the Gospels of Luke and Matthew; and where one or the other temporarily departs from the order of Mark we can in every case recognise, as will be shown later, an arbitrary interruption and dislocation of an order previously present, which can be no other than that which lies before us in Mark. Similarly, the accounts of incidents and discourses in Mark bear for the most part (with the exception of a few later interpolations which do not affect our judgment of its general character) the unmistakable stamp of genuineness, of self-evident clearness and accuracy, of well-rounded coherence and completeness. In contrast with this, the divergences, abbreviations, and insertions of the other two Evangelists betray their derivative character by the very fact that they can often only be fully explained by a reference to the primary form of the narrative in Mark, quite apart from the many traces of later motive which are found in the content of these alterations and additions. As the proof of this statement will have to be given in the later discussion of the three Evangelists, we may here proceed at once to the description of the Gospel of Mark, in the course of which we shall, however, cast occasional side-glances at the narratives of the other two Evangelists, in so far as these give parallel accounts to those of Mark; although these are not necessary for the understanding of Mark, since, as we have said, Mark's Gospel is perfectly intelligible in itself. It is the first attempt which has come down to us to present the gospel of Jesus as the Christ, which Paul had proclaimed as a theological doctrine, in narrative form as a history of the life and sufferings of Jesus. While, on the one hand, it is certain that this narrative embodies very early traditional material, on the other hand it is equally clear that it betrays the influence, affecting the conception of particulars, of the great teacher Paul, of whom the author of this oldest Gospel had probably been an immediate pupil.

The author begins his historical presentation of the gospel of Jesus Christ with a short introduction (i. 1–13) which recounts the preparation for the work of Jesus by John's baptism of repentance, the dedication of Jesus to His vocation by baptism and the reception of the Spirit, and His temptation in the wilderness. As Paul at the commencement of the Epistle to the Romans (i. 2) described his gospel of Jesus Christ, the Son of God, as the fulfilment of the prophetic promises, so Mark sees in the advent of John, the preacher of repentance, the fulfilment of the prophecy concerning "one crying in the wilderness" and commanding to prepare the ways of the Lord.[1] While John, who in his ascetic appearance is the antitype of Elijah, baptizes with water as the symbol of the moral purification of repentance, and points to one stronger than he, who, coming after him, shall baptize with the Holy Spirit, Jesus comes from Nazareth and causes Himself to be baptized by John: immediately Jesus sees the heavens opened, and the Holy Spirit like a dove descending upon Him, and hears a voice from heaven, "Thou art my Son, the beloved, in whom I was well pleased." Even though the interpretation of this narrative in the sense of a purely subjective vision would not, so far as the wording of the passage is concerned, be quite impossible, that would hardly correspond to the narrator's view, according to which Jesus became Son of God, in the supernatural sense which this phrase always conveyed to Greek and Roman readers,[2]

[1] The quotation of Mal. iii. 1, combined with Isa. xl. 3, has perhaps been interpolated into the Gospel of Mark from Luke vii. 27 (=Matt. xi. 10).

[2] *Cf.* Wrede, *das Messiasgeheimnis in den Evangelien*, p. 72 f. Dalman, *Worte Jesu*, p. 236 f. (E.T. 283 f.): "A Greek would always be disposed to understand ὁ υἱὸς τοῦ θεοῦ in the proper sense of the words. . . . The Synoptists' manner of thought is Greek.

precisely by the fact that at His baptism He received into Himself the Spirit which came down from heaven, the real possessor of all wonder-working powers, and thus became Himself a superhuman, miraculous being, an instrument of the Spirit, as He thenceforth showed by His miraculous acts. How literally the Evangelist conceived this relation to the Spirit as a being possessed and impelled by it, he immediately makes manifest in the ensuing section of his narrative: "And immediately the Spirit driveth him into the wilderness; and he was in the wilderness forty days being tempted by Satan, and was with the wild beasts, and the angels ministered to him." The mention of the wild beasts recalls the legends of Samson's fight with the lion, of Daniel in the lions' den, of the poisonous serpents when Israel was journeying through the wilderness: here, as there, the beasts are the symbols and embodiments of spiritual powers hostile to God, which the Son of God conquers by the miraculous power of the Divine Spirit.

After this brief introduction the Evangelist begins the first part of his history by giving a picture of the Galilæan ministry of Jesus. He tells how, from its small beginnings in and about Capernaum, it gradually extended its radius, until at length it crossed the borders of Judæa; how, as Jesus' influence on the people grew, the opposition of His adversaries grew and intensified likewise; how Jesus gave to the inner circle of His disciples deeper revelations concerning the Kingdom of God, and sent them out, as a test, on their first missionary journey; and how, at the close of His Galilæan ministry, belief in Him had reached such a pitch that the Galilæans recognised Him as the Messiah. From this central and culminating point of the Gospel history the eye of the Evangelist turns to the sufferings which lay before Christ, which form the subject of the second part of the Gospel story.

If we follow the course of the narrative in somewhat greater detail, the first thing that strikes us is the Pauline form[1] in which Mark states at the outset the content of the preaching of Jesus—its thesis, so to speak: He came into Galilee preaching the gospel of God, namely, "The time is fulfilled, the kingdom of God[2] is at hand, repent ye and believe the gospel" (i. 14 f.). Here, as in Paul's teaching, faith in the message of salvation sent by God is the first demand. And just as Paul ascribes to the word of the Gospel, when it comes as a call to individuals, a divine power to produce the obedience of faith, so the Evangelist shows how the two pairs of brothers, turning from their nets at the call of Jesus, which was charged with spiritual power, became His permanent followers and disciples. As those who were first called had

[1] With τὸ εὐαγγέλιον τ. θεοῦ cp. Rom. i. 1, xv. 16; 1 Thes. ii. 2, 8 f. With πεπλήρωται ὁ καιρός cp. Gal. iv. 4. With πιστεύετε ἐν τὸ εὐαγγ. cp. Gal. iii. 26; 1 Tim. iii. 13.

[2] This expression may as a rule be kept, since we are accustomed to it, but it is inexact and misleading. For βασιλεία τ. θεοῦ properly betokens, not a kingdom in our sense as a territory ruled over—a land and people belonging to God: such a kingdom could surely not "come near unto us." It means, rather, the rule of God, *i.e.* His possession and exercise of rulership, and the resultant condition upon earth, which the pious are granted to experience as "life" and happiness. This will be more fully discussed below in the section on the preaching of Jesus.

their homes in Capernaum, there was a natural reason why Jesus should commence His public activity as a teacher in the synagogue in that place.

Of Jesus' first appearance as a teacher, and of the immediate impression and effect which it produced, Mark suggests a very vivid picture (i. 21 ff.), which naturally gives rise to the conjecture that it is based on the recollections of an eye-witness (Peter). The hearers were amazed at His manner of teaching, which had such a very different ring from the traditional scholastic wisdom of the scribes. It was new and individual, the word of a man who derives his authority to teach, not from the heads of the Schools, but from God Himself, a teacher by the grace of God. It was, as we might say, the impression of inborn religious genius which the hearers received from the first discourse of Jesus, and they recognised in it something fresh and distinctive (original) in contrast to the traditional teaching of the Schools. And that was immediately followed by a demonstration of the healing power of Jesus' word. There was among the audience in the synagogue "a man with an unclean spirit" — as we might say, one mentally and nervously deranged. Under the tremendous impression of the word, and of the whole personality, of Jesus, he fell into a state of painful excitement, which Jesus calmed and cured by speaking to him; whence it was concluded that even the unclean spirits were subject unto Him. When, later on the same day, Simon's mother-in-law, who was sick of a fever, was healed by the touch of Jesus' hand, His fame as a worker of miraculous cures was complete, and He was so thronged by those who sought healing that on the next day He left the house before dawn, and withdrew into solitude to pray; then He made with His disciples a tour through the surrounding districts, everywhere preaching and healing. It is clearly evident in this narration that the rôle of a wonder-worker was by no means sought by Jesus, but rather was forced upon Him against His will by the people. He sought to withdraw Himself from it, and repeatedly forbade those who were healed to make it known in such a way as to attract attention; but that was of course useless, the numerous cases of wonderful cures could not be concealed, and confirmed the people in their belief in the wonder-working power of Jesus—a belief which had indeed solid grounds, if only we do not understand by wonders absolutely supernatural "miracles." That this popularity with the multitude would provoke the opposition of the official guardians of religion was to be expected, and Mark immediately proceeds, in the second and third chapters, to relate a whole series of occasions on which this opposition appeared, first in a veiled and then in overt, pronounced, and sharper fashion. That the Evangelist, in grouping these occasions together, is following an order of subject-matter is of course obvious, but that gives us no reason to doubt that occasions of incipient opposition began to occur soon after the commencement of Jesus' public ministry, and were frequently repeated. Moreover, all these narratives bear so unmistakably the stamp of reality that it is impossible, except from a prejudiced point of view, to see in them mere symbolical embodiments of the ideal opposition between the teaching of Jesus and the official religion of Judaism. The very first of these narratives is, in Mark (ii. 1–12), of an especially graphic character; while in Matthew's abbreviated version the vividness has, to a large extent, gone out of it. In this case offence was taken at the fact that Jesus declared to the sick man the forgiveness of his sins, in which he was to see the cause of his sickness. The Scribes found in this saying a blasphemy against God, since only God could forgive sins; but Jesus refuted them by the practical proof of healing the sick man, for that implied that the Son of Man must also have power on earth to forgive sins, since He could give practical demonstration of His power to remove the sickness which was the consequence of sin. "The Son of Man" here signifies no more than "Man": it is the literal translation of the Aramaic *barnascha*, which is the standing expression for "Man"; and herein lies the point of Jesus' words, namely, that forgiveness of sins takes place not only at God's throne of judgment in heaven, as the Jews supposed, but that even man on earth is authorised to manifest the Divine will of love, not only in healing sickness, but also in the forgiveness of sins. A reference to the Messiah would only obscure the significant force of this saying, and would, besides, have been quite unintelligible to His opponents; that, on the other hand, the saying was understood by His hearers with reference to man in general, is shown by the conclusion of the narrative in Matt. ix. 8: "They praised God, who had given such authority unto men." (We shall have more to say on this point when we come to treat of the Messianic consciousness of Jesus.) Again, when after the call of the tax-gatherer Levi, Jesus sat at meat in his house "with publicans and sinners," the Scribes, who belonged to the strict legalistic party of the Pharisees, were offended. But Jesus explained to them that, just as the physician is called to serve the sick, not the healthy, so He felt it to be His vocation to call[1] not the righteous but sinners to share in the salvation of the Kingdom of God. Further ground of offence was given to the legal zealots by the fact that the disciples of Jesus, in contrast to the disciples of John and of the Pharisees, did not practise the pious usage of fasting. So far as regarded the special case of His disciples, Jesus met them with the answer that for them, in their present mood of joyful exaltation, fasting would be as unseasonable as for the friends of the bridegroom on the marriage-day. That is the simple sense of the image in verse 19, which is not to be allegorised as if Jesus intended to represent Himself as the bridegroom of His people, *i.e.* as the Messiah. But even the Evangelist has interpreted the image as an allegory, and on this assumption adds (ii. 20), "But the days shall come when the bridegroom shall be taken away from them, then shall they fast in those days." That is evidently a prediction of His death which is put into the mouth of Jesus, and which in this connection is

[1] This is the simple sense of καλέσαι in Mark (as in Paul). Luke, on the other hand, by adding εἰς μετάνοιαν, narrows the sense of the word, while Matthew has interpolated (ix. 13) a thought which is foreign to the context.

hardly probable. The suggestion[1] that some similar saying of Jesus, perhaps an allusion to the death of the Baptist and the consequent fasting of his disciples, underlies the account, must remain problematical. To this defence of the practice of the disciples in not fasting the Evangelist adds the two parables of the new patch on the old garment and the new wine in the old wine-skins (v. 21 f.), which both express the same thought, that the new spirit of Jesus could not be conformed to the old ways of Jewish piety: a saying of unassailable genuineness, in which Jesus' consciousness of the unique character of His spirit as a reformer declares itself in the clearest fashion. But clear as is this point of the double parable, every attempt to interpret the details in an allegorical fashion is involved in insoluble difficulties, as is shown by the curious controversy among exegetes as to whether the purpose is to defend the not-fasting of the disciples of Jesus, or the fasting of the disciples of John and the Pharisees, or, finally, both. Even the presupposition, which might seem to determine the interpretation, that this double parable must find its explanation in the foregoing controversy about fasting, is itself very questionable.[2] The thought of the parable is so general that it extends far beyond the special case; the protest against half-heartedness and false compromise might have been spoken on many other occasions (*e.g.* vii.

[1] Jülicher, *Gleichnisreden Jesu,* p. 188. Menzies, too, *The Earliest Gospel,* p. 87, questions the genuineness of this allegorical trait, and adds the remark: "The Early Church practised fasting, and our narrative as it stands furnishes a warrant for an observance which Jesus had not encouraged in His own lifetime."

[2] Jülicher, *ut sup.*, p. 199.

1–23 or viii. 15), and only have been placed here by Mark. But even if it was originally spoken in this connection, its width of meaning is unduly narrowed by confining it to the special case of the fasting customs of the disciples of John and of the Pharisees. This application is indeed quite impossible in the concluding words which Luke here adds (v. 39): "No man having drunk old wine straightway desireth new, for he saith, The old is good." Is that intended to excuse the conservatism of the Jews or Jewish Christians, with its disinclination to anything new? But how little that would agree with the preceding defence of the new spirit of the Gospel and rejection of all weak compromises! This saying has therefore found its place here only in consequence of the loose association of ideas suggested by the mention of old and new wine, since we find similar associations of ideas not infrequently in Luke.

There follow next two narratives in which the freer conduct of the disciples, and of Jesus himself, upon the Sabbath provoked the opposition of the Jewish rigorists. In the first case it was the disciples' plucking the ears of corn as they went through a field, in which, of course it was not the action as such, but the fact that it took place on the Sabbath, which gave offence to His opponents. Jesus refers His questioners first to a case in the history of David which showed that the breaking of a ceremonial ordinance was justified by imperative need, and then He adds, once more, a general assertion of the widest scope: "The Sabbath was made for man, and not man for the Sabbath; therefore the Son of Man is Lord also of the Sabbath" (Mark ii. 27 f.). This saying is an appeal to natural moral feeling, and at the same time to healthy common sense, according to the judgment of which the good of man is the ultimate end in view, of which every statutory command is only a subordinate means, the value and the application of which are therefore to be determined by the higher regulative principle of that end—a saying which lays the axe to the root of the positive legal religion, according to which the enacted ordinance as such is of paramount validity. It is to be noticed here that the lordship of the Son of Man also (even) over the Sabbath is not a consequence of the special Messianic dignity of Jesus,[1] for in that case the logical connection between verses 27 and 28 would be severed, but of the dignity of man in general, as the highest end of creation, whose well-being takes precedence of all mere legal ordinances. The Son of Man is therefore here, just as in verse 10, simply man in general. The apocalyptic-Messianic significance of the phrase is only found, in Mark, from the predictions of the passion (viii. 38) onwards. The second conflict about the Sabbath was caused by a cure wrought by Jesus in the synagogue. The narrative, which in Mark (iii. 1–6) is remarkably lively and graphic, shows the increasing self-consciousness of Jesus; for He no longer awaits the attack of His opponents but anticipates it with the question: "Is it right on the

[1] In Matthew, however, this certainly seems to be the case, since he has omitted the saying in Mark ii. 27 ("the Sabbath was made for man," etc.), and substituted for it the proof from the service of the priests in the Temple, the force of which lies in the thought that in Jesus the Messiah there was present something greater than the Temple. But who does not see in this argument something forced, which betrays its secondary origin from theological reflection?

Sabbath to do good or to do evil, to save life or to kill?" Thus He narrows down the controversial question to an alternative which admits of no evasion; He recognises no third course between the fulfilment of duty by doing good and the transgression of duty by not doing good, for the omission of a possible work of love is in itself an evil-doing which cannot be justified by any Sabbatic ordinance. Thus healthy moral feeling condemns the perverse legalistic religiosity which exalts the ceremonial ordinance above the obligations of love; and that this perversity should give itself out as the loftiest piety evokes, according to Mark's dramatic narrative, the holy anger and the profound grief of Jesus over the hardness of heart of His opponents.

After such encounters as this it is quite intelligible that the opponents, on their part, soon advanced to an uncompromising rejection of Jesus' ministry. There were, as Mark tells us (iii. 22 ff.), Scribes who had come down from Jerusalem, perhaps for the very purpose of taking cognisance of Jesus' work; and these delegates of the hierarchy declared the cures wrought by Jesus to be nothing less than works of the devil, with whom He was in league. Jesus meets that in the first place by pointing to the inconsistency of this reproach, since it assumes a division and consequent destruction of the kingdom of the demons (contrary to the Scribes' own theory). The conclusion to be drawn from the driving out of the demons was rather that He had overcome the Lord of the House of Darkness. In the next place, He reminds His opponents how deep was the guilt which they drew upon themselves by this accusation, since while all other guilt could be forgiven to the sons of men,[1] it was not so with blasphemy against the Holy Spirit, *i.e.* the deliberate hardening of oneself against the impression of the Holy One, and the misrepresenting of His influence as its contrary, as the opponents of Jesus had done in referring Jesus' works of healing to the influence of an unclean spirit. At the same period as this conflict, which signified that Jesus had broken with the hierarchy of His nation, Mark records an encounter of Jesus with His relatives which similarly resulted in a severance of the restraining ties of family. According to Mark iii. 21 and 31, the mother and the brethren of Jesus sought to call Him away from His activity as a teacher, and to take charge of Him, saying that He was out of His mind (ἐξέστη). Jesus refused, saying, as He cast His glance over the disciples who stood about Him: "Behold my mother and my brethren! Whosoever doeth the will of God, the same is my brother and sister and mother." This account, which is given in its entirety by Mark only, is in several respects worthy of notice. It is unanswerably clear evidence of the fact that of a supernatural birth of Jesus His own mother knew nothing, for otherwise she could not possibly have so completely failed to recognise the higher vocation of her Son, as is implied by her thinking Him out of His mind. But even the Christian community cannot, at the time when our Gospel was written, have known

[1] Out of this phrase *τοῖς υἱοῖς τῶν ἀνθρώπων* of Mark the other Synoptics have made the statement that even blasphemy against the Son of Man can be forgiven, only not that against the Spirit —a distinction of which Mark knows nothing, and which is in actual contradiction with the context.

anything of the birth-story of the later tradition, for otherwise the Evangelist could not have so innocently reported the mistake of Jesus' mother. The later Evangelists have clearly recognised the inconsistency of this statement of Mark with their story of Jesus' birth, and for that reason suppressed the former; as, however, they report His refusal to see His relatives without the explanatory motive given in Mark, the conduct of Jesus appears in their narrative to be characterised by a causeless rudeness and harshness. Their description of this occurrence is therefore evidently an abbreviation due to dogmatic considerations, and is consequently obscure as compared with the complete and perfectly intelligible report of Mark.

While antagonisms thus increased in number and intensity, the multitudes who flocked to Jesus grew so large that it became more and more difficult to influence and teach them in an orderly fashion. It became obviously necessary to choose out of the multitude of adherents a narrower circle of disciples to be constantly with Jesus. For this purpose Jesus withdrew himself, as Mark (iii. 13) reports, from the seashore, where the multitude thronged Him, to the higher ground above it,[1] and called one and another to Him at His free choice. In this way He appointed twelve to be His permanent companions, and also with the intention that they should act as His messengers and emissaries in

[1] It is in this sense that τὸ ὄρος in Mark is to be understood; there is no reason here for a symbolical mountain. In Matthew, however, "the mountain" no doubt acquires the symbolical significance of the second Sinai, for it is there not the scene of the choice of the disciples, but of the giving of the new law.

extending the sphere of His teaching and work. Almost immediately after this choice of the inner circle of disciples, Mark represents Jesus as beginning His teaching regarding the coming of the Kingdom of God—a teaching clothed in parables, which were no doubt spoken to the people in general, but were only interpreted to the inner circle of disciples, since it was only to them that the "mystery of the Kingdom of God" was to be communicated, while to those without it was only to be given in parables, that they might not see, nor hear, nor be converted (iv. 11). The Evangelist sees therefore in the parables a secret and esoteric method of teaching, for the understanding of which a special interpretation was necessary which was not accessible to all. This conception arose from the traditional confusion of the parables with the allegories of the apocalyptic writings, from which they are nevertheless quite distinct. The parables of Jesus are not secret allegorical teachings, but universally intelligible graphic presentations of experiences which Jesus Himself had met with in His work as a preacher, and of the practical inferences which He drew from them. As He looked back upon His work up to this point the painful conviction forced itself upon Him that its success was small, the progress of His cause slow, its beginnings still almost imperceptible. But He did not allow this to discourage Him, but recognised that the cause of this modest success was in the nature of things, since the spiritual seed of His word was subject to the same conditions and laws of growth as the natural seed. As not every grain of corn which the sower sows comes up, or at any rate reaches maturity, because many meet with hindrances in unfavourable soil, so the word, the proclamation of the gospel, does not find everywhere alike receptive hearts. And as the husbandman, when he has put in his seed, can do nothing more, but must wait with patience the gradual sprouting, growing, and ripening of the grain, so in spiritual things everything must have its time, and nothing can be forced or hastened. And, however imperceptible the beginning may be, something great may yet grow out of it, as from the minute mustard-seed there grows the great mustard-plant. These are all thoughts of the simplest kind which naturally presented themselves to the mind of Jesus in looking back upon His past experiences; from the perception that in these experiences exactly the same laws and sequences of the world-order were manifested as are observable in nature in general, He drew for himself and His followers a lesson of patience and of courageous confidence. But the Evangelist, looking back over the intervening period with the experience of the non-success of the gospel among the unbelieving Jews in his mind, could only explain this, in agreement with Paul (cp. iv. 12 with Rom. xi. 8), as due to Divine fore-ordination, and therefore believed that Jesus used parable with the purpose of not being understood by the people; and, accordingly, that the parables in general were so obscure and mysterious that even the disciples could only understand them by the aid of a special interpretation. He therefore himself adds this explanation, allegorising in traditional fashion the individual traits, keeping the allegory, no doubt, within modest limits, but at the same time going beyond the simple force of the original meaning.[1] Next comes a two-fold warning to the disciples in regard to their calling as teachers. The light whose brightness had dawned on them was not to be restricted to their narrow circle, but was to be set upon a lamp-stand, to be made the common possession of all through the freest proclamation of the truth; but in order to be qualified for this duty they must themselves take heed to (direct their attention upon) that which they heard: according to the measure with which they measured it should be measured to them again, "for to him that hath shall be given, but he that hath not, from him shall be taken away even that which he hath" (iv. 24). Everything depends, therefore, upon steadfast attention, and upon making practical application of that which is heard; for it is by that alone that understanding of the secrets of God is won, and, in consequence, the light of truth successfully spread abroad.

On the evening of the same day which had become memorable to the disciples through the first sermon of the Master, Jesus crossed, as Mark recounts (iv. 35–41), in the boat from which He had addressed the multitude who stood on the strand, to the other side of the lake. As they were crossing, a storm arose while Jesus was asleep. The disciples, in alarm, awake the Master; He rebukes the storm, and it is stilled, and He then blames the disciples for their little faith; but they are dismayed in the presence of this Man

[1] *Cf.* on this point the admirable work of Jülicher on the parables of Jesus, also the commentaries of Weiss, Holtzmann, and Menzies, on Mark iv.

to whom the wind and the sea are obedient. This narrative may be based on an historical reminiscence of a stormy crossing in which Jesus by His calmness and trust in God shamed and calmed the trembling disciples, somewhat as Paul did in the storm in Acts xxvii. 22 ff. But out of this reminiscence the idealising imagination has made a miracle of omnipotence, partly suggested by some Old Testament imagery—phrases such as Nahum i. 3 ff., "The Lord hath his way in the whirlwind and the storm. . . . He rebuketh the sea, and maketh it dry"; Ps. cvii. 25 ff., "He commandeth and raiseth the stormy wind which lifteth up the waves thereof. . . . They trembled and cried to the Lord in their trouble, . . . and he commanded, and the waves were still." The story of Jonah, too, offers a striking parallel. "There arose a mighty tempest in the sea, so that they thought the ship would sink. . . . But Jonah had gone down into the hold, and was asleep. . . . Then the shipmaster came to him, and said, Why sleepest thou? Arise, call upon thy God, that we perish not!" (And the servant of the Lord was confident in God's help), "then the sea ceased from its raging. And they feared greatly." The idea of these pictorial expressions and narratives is always the same: to the pious man who is in alliance with God, even the elements are serviceable. When the religious imagination sees this idea embodied in a memorable experience of the disciples and their Master, what happens is that it embellishes and idealises the occurrence almost involuntarily, and gives it the character of an actual miracle. In this particular case we can clearly follow the various stages of the process. In its simple form, as it is first told by Mark (iv. 36 ff.), the actual facts contain nothing impossible (the miracle lies only in the causal connection which, in the judgment of the narrator, subsists between the word of Jesus and the stilling of the storm). In the related narrative of Jesus walking upon the water (vi. 45–51) the miracle has already been considerably heightened, and the same miracle-story undergoes a still further development in the form given to it by Matthew, where (xiv. 28–33) Peter tries to imitate Jesus in walking on the water, but in doing so, being overcome with fear, is in danger of sinking, and is only kept above the water by the saving hand of Jesus. Here the allegorical and poetic character is immediately obvious, and we thus perceive in these three sea-pictures the tendency of religious tradition to a progressive idealising and allegorising of historical reminiscences.

The narrative of the cure of the possessed man at Gerasa (v. 1–20), which follows on that of the stilling of the storm, is perhaps a similar case. The picture of the madman is so vivid, his behaviour at his meeting with Jesus, and after his cure, is psychologically so probable, that there is no sufficient reason for holding the whole story to be an allegory, whether of the conversion of the heathen world in general, or, as has even been held, of the Apostle Paul. But with this in itself entirely probable story of the cure there has been bound up a clearly mythical, and possibly allegorical, trait; viz., that the legion of demons by which the man supposed himself to be possessed not only went out of him, but entered into a herd of swine and hurled them into the sea. Here the conjecture readily suggests itself that we have an allegorical representation of the apocalyptic idea that the demonic powers of unclean heathenism, overthrown by the superior might of the word of Jesus, are delivered over to the abyss of hell,[1] where they belong (*cf.* Apoc. xii. 9, xx. 2 f.). In particular, we might think of the overcoming of the orgiastic Cybele-worship which had its special seat in Syria, to which Gerasa belonged, and in which the uncleanness of foul unchastity was associated with mad raging and raving. The origin of the narrative as we have it is perhaps to be conceived in some such way as that the cure of a madman performed by Jesus in the Peræan district was at a later time thought of by the Church as a symbol of the overcoming of orgiastic heathenism by the missionary activity of Paul in Syria, in which the uncleanness of the cult overthrown by the Gospel gave rise to the image of the herd of swine, which became inwoven into the symbolic narrative of Jesus' miracle of healing; so that the narrative in its present form is probably to be con-

[1] According to Luke viii. 31, the demons begged that Jesus would not command them *εἰς τὴν ἄβυσσον ἀπελθεῖν*, for which Mark v. 10 has the unintelligible *ἵνα μὴ αὐτὰ ἀποστειλῃ ἔξω τῆς χώρας*. The latter may have arisen, according to the probable conjecture of Nestle, from a confusion of the Syriac word תְּהוֹמָא = abyss, underworld, with תְּחוּמָא = boundary, borders. Here, therefore, Luke seems to have followed a more accurate translation of the common Aramaic source than Mark. A similar confusion of טוּרָא = mountain, with טַוְרָא = far, perhaps underlies the Matthæan variant *ἦν δὲ μακρὰν ἀπ' αὐτῶν* (viii. 30) for the Marcan and Lucan *πρὸς (ἐν) τῷ ὄρει*. Dalman, however, *Worte Jesu*, p. 52 (E.T. p. 66) explains the difference from the different geographical presuppositions of the Evangelists as to the scene of the occurrence.

sidered a mixture of historical reminiscence with poetic allegory.

Again, the narrative of the raising of Jairus' daughter and the healing of the woman with an issue does not appear to me to be mere poetic symbolism, because, especially in the original account in Mark, it has a very graphic and natural character, and no single feature occurs in it which is impossible. That the sick woman felt herself to be healed by the touch of Jesus' garment, and that Jesus at the same time felt that power had gone out of Him, could only appear mythical to one who had given no attention to the whole domain of magnetism and of the cures based upon it. We have, in my opinion, a further proof of the originality of Mark in the very fact that he, more than the others, in particular than Matthew, who loves the supernatural, represents the cures of Jesus as effected by a physically communicated power which streamed, in a way that could be felt, from the healing to the suffering organism. How could we properly conceive these cures—which, nevertheless, no sensible person will hold to be nothing but myths—otherwise than in the way described by Mark? In any case, we have obviously no reason, from the point of view of rationalism, to doubt the originality of Mark and prefer the much more pronounced supernaturalism of Matthew's narrative. In the case of the Jairus story, how natural is its progress in Mark compared with the manifold improbabilities in Matthew! According to the latter, Jesus was from the first entreated to raise one who was dead; in the former, on the contrary, only to come to the aid of one who was grievously ill, news of whose death first meets Him as He is on the way. But that she was really dead when Jesus came and raised her up, Mark nowhere says. The reserve of his narrative leaves the possibility quite open that the child was only seemingly dead, and at the touch of Jesus was strengthened and rose up (ἀνέστη); whereas the two other Synoptists speak unambiguously of an actual raising of the dead, and in so doing show that their representation is a clumsy retouching of the more delicate picture drawn by Mark. Finally, we may call attention to the simple realism with which Mark closes his narrative: "And he told them they should give her something to eat." That can hardly be interpreted allegorically; and we may therefore the more confidently find in this little touch, which Mark alone has preserved, a trace of historical reminiscence.

Mark goes on to tell of Jesus' visit to His own village, Nazareth (vi. 1–6), where His townsmen, in the well-known fashion of the vulgar, were offended at the superior spiritual greatness of one who had gone forth from among themselves. That the same feeling encountered Him in His own family is expressly mentioned by Mark (vi. 4; οἰκίᾳ), and is quite in harmony with his earlier narrative (iii. 21). When, in this connection, he adds that Jesus could there do no mighty work, or miracle, he exhibits once more his own rational view of Jesus' miracles of healing, namely, that they were conditioned and mediated by the receptivity of the sufferer and his environment; Matthew no longer understood this, and therefore changes the not being able to do the wonders into a (deliberate) not doing of them. Luke, again, has quite unhistorically placed the account of the rejection at Nazareth at the beginning of Jesus' ministry, and in that way, as also by the discourse which he represents Jesus as delivering on this occasion, made it an allegorical type of the rejection of Christ by Judaism. In Mark, however, it has not this character, but is simple history.

There follows next the account of the sending forth of the Twelve, of their work and their return; but before the latter there is inserted, to fill in the intervening pause in the history of Jesus, the episode of the death of John the Baptist (vi. 7–13, 14–29, 30). Here, too, the originality of Mark's account is everywhere manifest. The instructions which are given to the disciples for their journey are in Mark quite simple and appropriate to the situation. Luke introduces a few small alterations, and adds, besides, a parting charge of some length at the sending forth of the Seventy Disciples, which he alone recounts. Matthew, like Mark, records only the sending forth of the Twelve, but in doing so gives a set of instructions pieced together from various sources, and adapted not so much to the actual situation as to the later circumstances of the Church. Besides giving this long discourse of instruction, which goes far beyond the immediate purpose of the sending forth of the disciples, Matthew has forgotten to give any report of the activity, and of the return, of the disciples, and, in order to return to the framework of the Marcan narrative, adopts the singular expedient of reporting, instead of the return of the disciples to Jesus to give an account of their work (Mark vi. 30), the coming of the disciples of John with the news of the death of their master (Matt. xiv. 12), and fails to notice that the death of John is only inserted here by Mark parenthetically, having taken place at a much earlier point in the historical order, and that it is therefore impossible that the disciples of John could only now have brought word of it.

After the return of the disciples, Mark next relates (vi. 31 ff.) that Jesus, in order to give the disciples some rest from the growing pressure of the multitudes, withdrew by ship with them to a retired spot; but that the multitudes, going by land, outstripped Him, so that when He disembarked He found them again gathered together upon the shore, and now, from sympathy with this "flock without a shepherd," gave Himself to them once more, and taught them many things, until evening came upon them. Then, to the spiritual food of instruction in the gospel, Jesus added in the evening miraculous food for the body, satisfying five thousand men with five loaves and two fishes. This miracle-story must have had a very prominent place in the oldest legendary strata, for Mark gives a twofold version of it (viii. 1–9 is the same story in a slightly different form), and on another occasion it is expressly called to remembrance (viii. 19 f.). Accordingly, Old Testament types, such as might be found in the manna, and still more directly in the feeding of a hundred men by the prophet Elisha with a few barley loaves (2 Kings iv. 42) will not alone suffice to explain it. We must assume that some direct interest of the primitive community was a contributory cause in the formation of the legend. What this interest was, the account itself very clearly shows. When we observe that the meal took place in the evening, at the close of a discourse, that the people reclined at it in orderly ranks and companies

(vi. 39 f.); and when we listen to the familiar words "He took the loaves, and blessed them, and gave thanks" (viii. 6), "and broke, and gave to the disciples, and they did all eat," we recognise clearly the allusion to the Lord's Supper, or to the Love-feast of the Church, with which the Supper was originally one. This reference has been made explicit by the Fourth Evangelist in the doctrine of the Lord's Supper which he has attached to the story of the feeding of the multitude (John vi. 51–58). The oldest ecclesiastical pictures of the Lord's Supper, too, point, by their customary five loaves and two fishes, to the present narrative as representing the typical celebration. With this agrees also what Justin Martyr reports regarding the function of the deacons as the distributors of the Love-feast. This is precisely the rôle which is played in Mark's account by the disciples, who distribute the bread, after the Lord has blessed it, among the ranks of the people. From this point of view the lively interest which the oldest tradition shows in this story can well be understood; it was much more than mere dogmatic interest in a specially striking miraculous act in the past, merely as such: it was a unique practical interest which here came into operation, the great importance of which for the Early Church is evidenced by the Acts of the Apostles also. The question at issue, in all probability, was whether the poorest members of the Church must content themselves at the regular evening assemblies with the word of exhortation and go home hungry, or whether at the close of the sermon there should take place a common meal, provided out of the resources of the community. The latter was demanded by brotherly love, and also served the purpose of binding the community together; on the other hand, those who prudently calculated the slenderness of the resources available might point out that they would by no means suffice for so many. "Send away the people [after the sermon] that they may eat in their own houses" (viii. 3, vi. 36), so counselled the practical men. "We are moved with pity for the people, if we send them hungry and tired to their homes; give ye them to eat" (vi. 37, viii. 2), responded those who had the courage of faith; and in urging this they may well have recalled the wonderful blessing which sometimes made small gifts, if provided by faith and love, suffice to satisfy many—not only in the legends of sacred history, but also in the enthusiastic gatherings of the Galilæan disciples during the full tide of Jesus' work, the memory of which might well linger on in the tradition of the community as the typical model for its later Love-feasts. It is in this, therefore, that the significance of our present story lies: it is intended to exhibit the practice of the primitive community of providing out of the common funds, at the Love-feast, bodily sustenance for all its members, as having been undertaken in Jesus' name and with His authority, as a work of love willed and blessed by Him. In the typical brotherhood-meal of the disciples of Jesus, which was consecrated by His blessing, it is intended to be made manifest that even the slender offerings which pious love makes in His name for the benefit of the community bring rich blessing and good to all. As a poetic and allegorical expression of these religious and ethico-social ideas, which are of the highest significance for all periods of the life of the Christian Church, but in the Early Church had a position of quite central importance, the story of the miraculous feeding of the multitude has an abiding significance for us; indeed, when we remove it from the region of the purely supernatural and understand it in the light of the ethical ideals which animated the actual Church-life of the earliest Christianity, it becomes thereby only the more interesting and important.

The feeding of the five thousand is followed, both in Mark and Matthew, by the story of Jesus' walking on the sea, in reference to which we have seen above that it is a further allegorical development of the story of the storm on the Lake, with its miraculous features still further enhanced. Then follows, after a summary notice of the flocking of the people to Jesus, and of the many cures which He did, the account of a controversy concerning ceremonial purity with the Pharisees and with certain Scribes who came down from Jerusalem (Mark vii. 1–23). These champions of tradition had taken offence at the fact that the disciples of Jesus ate bread with "unclean," that is to say, unwashed, hands, thus neglecting the tradition of the fathers. Jesus meets them first with a comprehensive rebuke: applying a passage from Isaiah, He characterises their pious zeal as a hypocritical lip-service, paid with a heart far from God. Then He points out to them, by a single example, that they do not hesitate to invalidate the command of God in subordinating the duties of the Fourth Commandment to their own ordinances regarding the gift to the Temple. Up to this point Jesus' attack does not seem to be directed against the Mosaic law but only against the traditions of the Pharisaic schools. But here again we find a generalisation of His reforming polemic, similar to that which we noticed in the case of the controversies regarding healing upon the Sabbath and fasting. Solemnly, before all the people, Jesus gives utterance to the declaration that nothing which enters into a man from without can defile him; only that which goes forth from a man, namely, evil thoughts which proceed from within, out of his heart, can defile him or make him unclean. By this saying He establishes the principle of inwardness, of the spiritual and moral valuation of a man, which goes beyond mere opposition to the Pharisaic system of observances, and must, in its logical consequences, lead to the discrediting of the Mosaic ceremonial law. Whether Jesus himself consciously intended this inference to be drawn is another question, and in view of other well-authenticated sayings to which we shall have to give careful attention at a later point, it can hardly be answered in the affirmative. It is the way of all heroes and reformers, and more especially of religious reformers (think, for example, of Luther!) to give utterance, in the loftiest moments of their struggle against old abuses, to thoughts of which the subversive significance is still hidden even from themselves, and which go far in advance of the more conservative mood of their calmer days; thence come the manifold contradictions in the life and thought of the men whose spirits are the battle-ground of two ages of the world's history.

This public manifestation before all the people of the breach between Jesus and the ecclesiastical authorities of Judaism seems to have been the cause of His withdrawing for a time beyond the borders of His country. Immediately after this controversy Mark narrates a journey of Jesus into the territories of Tyre and Sidon (not merely to their borders, as it is in Matthew's account), which was then continued into Decapolis, and concluded with a return to the sea of Galilee. Of this journey Mark tells two peculiar miracle-stories, the healing of the Syrophœnician woman's daughter and of the deaf mute (vii. 24–37). The peculiarity of the former is partly that it is the only case of healing at a distance which Mark reports (Matthew and Luke give the similar cure of the nobleman's servant at Capernaum), partly, and more especially, in the fact that it is only after some resistance on the part of Jesus that the cure is won from Him by the humble faith of the heathen woman. When Jesus answers the request of the Syrophœnician woman by saying, "Let the children first be filled: it is not meet to take the children's bread and cast it to the house-dogs," He expresses thereby the consciousness that He is called in the first place to work among Israel, and that He must not think of work among the heathen until He has fulfilled His task among Israel. In the answer of the woman, however, there lies the thought that even the unclean heathen may be allowed some share at least in the abundant blessing intended in the first place for Israel. We may undoubtedly see in this narrative a symbol of the attitude of the primitive community towards the question of the Gentiles: it permitted, indeed, to the Gentiles a partaking in the Messianic blessings, but only on condition that they humbly recognised the prerogatives of Israel. The narrative, therefore, certainly has its source in early tradition, and it is not improbable that the recollection of an historical incident in the life of Jesus lies at the basis of it; but exact knowledge on this point is not possible, any more than in the case of the story which follows, of the deaf and dumb man, or the similar story of the blind man at Bethsaida (viii. 22 ff.). In the case of these cures, peculiar to Mark, distinguished by protracted manipulation and progressive stages of success, it is best to leave it an open question how much is legend and how much history.

Scarcely had Jesus returned from His tour through the territories of Tyre and Sidon and Decapolis, when the Pharisees again approached Him; this time with the demand that He should show them a sign from heaven (viii. 11). What they meant by that was perhaps an appearance of light in heaven, such as, according to the tradition of the Jewish schools, was to accompany and authenticate the appearance of the Messiah. Whether this demand was seriously meant, or was only intended to discredit Jesus in the eyes of the people, it at any rate shows that in the authoritative circles people were beginning to attribute high significance to the person and the work of Jesus, and to pay serious attention thereto. According to Mark's account, Jesus simply refused to accede to the demand, declaring emphatically that assuredly no sign should be given to that generation (viii. 12). From this it is evident that Jesus did not consider His cures to be actual miracles in the sense in which the sign which they demanded would have been so, and that He considered the doing of actual miracles not to belong to His vocation, and therefore, also, not to be an object of faith. But as the later Church could not dispense entirely with the proof from miracle, Matthew (xii. 40) points here to the miracle of the resurrection as an antitype of the deliverance of Jonah.

After this attack of the Pharisees, which raised the question of the legitimacy of His work, Jesus withdrew again, this time to the district of Cæsarea Philippi, which lay to the north of Galilee. The more the conviction forced itself upon Him, in consequence of the experiences which have just been detailed, that He could not hope to maintain peaceful relations with the authorities of His nation, and could not, therefore, count on producing a direct effect upon the people as a whole, the more desirable did it appear to assure Himself of the confidence of His disciples, and to make His relation to them clear. He asked them, therefore, in the first place, whom the people held Him to be, and then, whom they themselves held Him to be? Peter answered: Thou art the Christ. Thereupon Jesus warned His disciples that they were not to tell any man anything concerning Him, namely, that He was the Messiah (as Matthew and Luke rightly explain). This may appear remarkable, if we consider that a hidden Messiahship is a self-contradictory idea. If, then, Jesus forbade unconditionally the making known of His Messiahship, we should be obliged to draw the conclusion that He himself refused this rôle, which was universally understood to imply the exercise of sovereignty over God's people Israel.[1] But that would be difficult to reconcile with His conduct at His entry into Jerusalem, when He openly accepted the homage offered to Him as Messiah by the troops of pilgrims, or with His question about the Davidic sonship of the Messiah, or His discourse to His disciples at the Last Supper.[2] Our choice, therefore, seems to be limited to one of two methods of explanation: either Jesus was already, at the time of Peter's confession, convinced that He was the Messiah, and accordingly tacitly accepted this confession, but imposed upon His disciples a temporary reserve, in order not to provoke a premature outburst of the popular Messianic hopes[3]; or He was not at the first conscious of His Messiahship, but preached only the coming of the Kingdom of God, without reference to His own person; then, when His Messianic vocation was declared by others, especially by His own disciples, He did not at once take up a definite attitude towards this idea, whether of acceptance or rejection, but left in God's hands the question what place in the new order of things was destined for Himself, awaiting its solution from the Divine ordering of circumstances.[4] On this assumption the imposition of silence upon His disciples at this critical moment would be easily explicable. Whatever may be the case in this regard—we shall return to the matter in a later connection—it is in any case certain that it was

1 So Martineau, *The Seat of Authority in Religion*, p. 352.

2 The reference is doubtless especially to Luke xxii. 29, 30.—Translator.

3 So Holtzmann, Keim, and most of the authors of Lives of Jesus.

4 So Brandt, *Die evangelische Geschichte*, p. 476 ff.

thenceforth for Jesus a fixed principle that He must, in order to fulfil His Divine mission, bring about a decision in favour of the Divine Kingship in the central citadel of the hierarchy, without heeding the dangers which, according to all His previous experiences, were certain to confront Him upon this path.

This resolve to enter upon the decisive and dangerous journey to Jerusalem was first communicated to the disciples immediately after Peter's confession. That is the one point of historical certainty in the predictions of the passion, the first of which is inserted by all the Evangelists at this point, and which are subsequently repeated with manifold variations. The form of this prediction, however, as regards the more definite features of the suffering and death, and more especially the rising again after three days, is derived not from historical recollection, but from the earliest Christian apologetic, which sought to remove the offence of the cross by means of this *vaticinium ex eventu* put into the mouth of Jesus. Against the historicity of so direct a prediction of the death and resurrection there is to be noted (1) the obstinate refusal of the disciples to understand; (2) their complete surprise at the catastrophe, and their flight when Jesus was arrested; (3) the entire absence of any such expectation on the part of the women who brought the materials for embalming the body of Jesus; (4) most of all, the behaviour of Jesus at the Last Supper, in Gethsemane, and on the cross, and in general His whole conduct at Jerusalem makes the impression that He journeyed thither, not in order to die, but to fight and conquer, and that in looking forward to the conflict His own death presented itself not as a certainty, but, at the most, as a possibility, much as in the case of a general on the eve of a decisive battle, or of Luther on the way to Worms. A further confirmation of the assumption that in the predictions of the death and resurrection which are related in the Gospels we have, not literal history, but early Christian dogmatic, lies in the fact that the subject of these predictions, both here and in the subsequent cases, is regularly designated the Son of Man, which in this connection can only mean the Messiah. Now, the same expression occurs in one or two earlier passages (ii. 10, 28, and iii. 28 in the plural) in the mouth of Jesus as an expression for man in general, quite in conformity with the standing significance of the corresponding Aramaic locution *barnascha*; but it is highly improbable that Jesus used the same expression at one time in the sense of man, at another in the sense of Messiah—to do so would have been to court misunderstanding. This being so, we must seek some other explanation of the Messianic use of the expression. The explanation is apparent in the apocalyptic utterances in xiii. 26 and xiv. 62, which both point back to Daniel vii. 13, and of which the first belongs to that Gospel apocalypse which, as we shall see later, dates from the time of the Jewish war. From this we naturally conclude that the Messianic significance of the expression "the Son of Man" is derived from the early Christian apocalyptic, which is closely connected with the Jewish, and that it was originally used in the Early Church as a designation of the Messiah-Jesus as exalted to heaven; the next step being its application to Jesus as in the process of becoming, through

His death and resurrection, the heavenly Messiah; and finally it reached its widest extension of usage as a *terminus technicus* for Jesus the Messiah even during His earthly life. Accordingly, I hold it to be highly probable that "the Son of Man" was never a Messianic self-designation of Jesus in any sense whatever, and that, therefore, all the passages of the Gospels where this sense is unmistakably present do not belong to the oldest tradition, but are derived from the apocalyptic-dogmatic terminology of the Early Church. In the case of the predictions of the passion this result has already been arrived at, on the grounds noticed above, and this will be confirmed later in the case of other sayings: the Messianic characteristics predicated of the Son of Man point as clearly as does the title itself to the reflective, dogma-building consciousness of the Early Church, and not to the consciousness of Jesus, as its original source.

When Jesus told the disciples of His resolve to bring His cause to a decisive issue in Jerusalem, in spite of all the dangers which such a course involved, Peter, as Mark tells us, took Him aside and began to remonstrate with Him, endeavouring, evidently, to dissuade Him from this rash purpose (viii. 32). But Jesus turned from him with the sharp rebuke, "Get thee hence, Satan, for thy thoughts are not the thoughts of God, but of men!" Matthew has added, by way of explaining the severity of the "Satan," "Thou art an offence unto me," that is, a temptation to be unfaithful to His divine vocation. Luke, from loyalty to Peter, has entirely suppressed this scene; it certainly belongs, however, to the oldest tradition, and has perhaps also influenced the Matthæan account of the Temptation (*cf.* Matt. iv. 10: ὕπαγε, Σαταvᾶ). The picture there given has first here its historical reality, for in the counsel of the disciple, well-meant as it was from a human point of view, the temptation presented itself to Jesus to abandon, from fear of suffering, the path set before Him by God, and to conclude, on a basis of compromise, a treaty of peace with the world-powers. Instead, however, of allowing Himself to be shaken in His heroic resolve by their persuasions, Jesus now endeavoured (verses 34 ff.) to raise His disciples to the height of a resolution like His own, prepared for the sacrifice of self and wholly resigned to the will of God: "Whosoever will follow me, let him deny himself and take up his cross. For whosoever will save his life, the same shall lose it; but whosoever shall lose his life for my sake and the gospel's, the same shall save it. For what shall it profit a man to gain the whole world and lose his own life? Or what shall a man give as a ransom for his life? For whosoever shall be ashamed of me and of my words in this adulterous and sinful generation, of him shall the Son of man be ashamed when he shall come in the glory of his Father with the holy angels." In this saying (verse 38) the apocalyptic language of the Early Church can easily be detected—if only in the surprising change from the first to the third person, which sounds almost as if the coming Son of Man were a different person from the speaker. That is not, of course, the Evangelist's meaning; the fact is rather that, when these words were put into the mouth of Jesus there was still a certain hesitation about making Him speak of His own return, due to the influence of the well-grounded recollection that He had never Himself so spoken when on earth. As the Church only spoke of the "Coming," not of the "Coming-again," of the Son of Man (*i.e.* the heavenly Messiah), this way of speaking was maintained even when Jesus Himself was represented as the speaker, and the consequent linguistic inconsistency is a clear proof of what has been urged above regarding the apocalyptic origin of the designation Son of Man. Even in the foregoing sayings (verses 34–37) the form seems to have been influenced throughout by Pauline language,[1] but in content they are probably genuine sayings of Jesus. This is more doubtful in the case of ix. 1, "There are some of those that stand here who shall not taste of death until they see the coming of the kingdom of God with power (the mighty rule of God)," in place of which Matthew has (xvi. 28) "until they see the Son of man coming in his kingdom." In the latter, more definitely apocalyptic, form the saying is certainly not from the lips of Jesus: it would be more possible in the less definite parallels of Mark and Luke. But what makes even this seem doubtful as a saying of Jesus is not so much the early coming of the Kingdom of God—before the disappearance of the whole of the then living generation — but rather its late beginning after the disappearance of the majority of those then living, whereas Jesus was at that time endeavouring to bring about the immediate establishment of the Kingship of God in Jerusalem, and

[1] With verse 34, *ἀράτω τὸν σταυρόν*, cp. Gal. ii. 19, vi. 14; with 36, *κερδῆσαι* and *ζημιωθῆναι*, cp. Phil. iii. 7 f.; with 37, *ἀντάλλαγμα*, cp. 1 Cor. vi. 20; with 38, *ἐπαισχυνθῇ*, cp. Rom. i. 16.

sayings such as Luke xii. 32, xxii. 16, 18, 29 f. make it appear that the decisive moment is close at hand.[1]

When historians and biographers reach a crisis and turning-point of their narrative, they are accustomed to pause and indulge in reflections intended to throw into relief the significance of the moment, and of the further development of the history which follows from it. This is precisely what Mark does, but he gives his reflections not directly in the form of his own thoughts, but clothes them, after the fashion of antiquity, partly in the form of discourses put into the mouth of his hero, as we have just seen in the case of the section viii. 31–ix. 1, but partly also in the form of allegorical pictures, which declare themselves at the first glance as ideal representations, portraying, not real occurrences, but religious ideas clothed in the garb of apocalyptic visions and the poetic imagery of the Old Testament. Ideal stories of this kind meet us at the outset of the Galilæan ministry in the vision at the Baptism, and again now at its close in the Transfiguration upon "a high mountain," as the ideal scene of this ideal picture is described, with appropriate vagueness (ix. 2). The materials out of which the Evangelist has composed his narrative can be indicated with some completeness. The motive which underlies the whole is the dogmatic idea of Paul in 2 Cor. iii. 7–iv. 6: whereas the brightness upon the face of Moses at Sinai was only temporary, Christ, as the risen Lord, the Spirit, is the abiding manifestation and reflection of the brightness, *i.e.* of

[1] *Cf.* Menzies, *Earliest Gospel*, p. 173; Jesus could hardly have deferred the Coming (of the Kingdom) to a time when most of His disciples should have died.

the glory and truth, of God. Of this glorifying and exaltation of the risen (spiritualised) Christ above Moses and the prophets the Transfiguration is the ideal anticipation. The details, however, of the pictorial representation of this idea are taken from Old Testament legend, especially from the story in Exodus xxxiv. of the transfiguration of Moses on Sinai. From the very beginning it is evident that the narrative is a companion-picture to the story of Moses: as Moses goes up with his three comrades, Aaron, Nadab, and Abihu, to Mount Sinai, which is covered for six days by the cloud in which the brightness of God is concealed, before God reveals Himself to Moses; so after six days, Jesus, with the three disciples who were His most constant companions, goes up to the Mount where the revelation takes place. As Moses then beheld the brightness of God, and the reflection of it made his own countenance shine, so Jesus was transfigured into the heavenly "body of glory" in which He manifested Himself after His resurrection, and into which those who are His shall also be transfigured in the future (2 Cor. iii. 18, iv. 6; Phil. iii. 21). Again, as in the Apocalypse of Enoch the garment of God is brighter than the sun and than the snow, so in Mark's narrative the garments of Jesus become "exceeding white, so as no fuller could whiten them." Then appeared Elias and Moses talking with Jesus: they are the two representatives of the Old Covenant; as such they are present as witnesses at the exaltation of Jesus to be Lord of the New Covenant, and, as the first-fruits of the Old Testament people of God, offer Him their homage. Peter, however, misunderstands this appearance of the Old

Testament witnesses, supposing that henceforth all three (Law, Prophets, and Gospel) should dwell together, and in this association of the Old and New Covenants there seems to him to be assured "a beautiful life," the ideal life of the Christian, so to speak—just as this was, in fact, the opinion of Peter and of the Jewish-Christian church. But this aspiration of Peter was based, in the judgment of the Pauline Evangelist, on a want of knowledge due to timorous faint-heartedness—just as Paul judged the conduct of Peter at Antioch. To correct this misunderstanding, the truth of the gospel is now made known to the disciples by a voice from heaven: "This (that is, Jesus, and He alone) is my Son, the Beloved, hearken unto him." The pronouncement of God that Jesus is His Son and Beloved, which the Evangelist has already given at the Baptism in the words of the Psalmist, is here repeated, with the addition of the command to recognise Him henceforth as the sole authority of the new People of God. That before this new authority the highest authorities of the Old Testament, like Moses and Elias, must give way, is then immediately made manifest by their sudden disappearance, so that the disciples, who a moment before had wished to build tabernacles in which these witnesses might dwell permanently along with Jesus, now suddenly saw themselves left alone with Jesus. Would it be possible to symbolise more clearly the thought of 2 Cor. iii., that the glory of the Old Covenant faded before the abiding glory of the Lord who is (the) Spirit? When the Evangelist next proceeds to make Jesus give the disciples, as they are coming down from the Mount, the charge to say nothing of this vision to anyone until the Son of Man should be risen from the dead, adding that the disciples obeyed this injunction, and questioned among themselves what the "rising from the dead" should mean: we have in this a very instructive piece of Early Christian apologetic. Its object is to explain how it came about that it was only after the death of Jesus that His disciples began to understand and proclaim His higher, more than earthly glory, whereas He had Himself previously revealed it to them. This difficulty the Evangelist seeks to explain by means of the command put into the mouth of Jesus; but by making the disciples themselves, by their question, betray their previous ignorance regarding the resurrection, he shows clearly the true state of the case—that the disciples, before the death of Jesus, and even afterwards, until the events of the Easter-tide, had no inkling of the resurrection of Jesus as about to take place, and that, therefore, neither the prediction nor the anticipatory representation of the resurrection at the transfiguration, actually took place. No doubt such discussions regarding the fact and the significance of Jesus' resurrection took place among the company of disciples, but not before Jesus' death. The ultimate belief of the Church (which grew out of later experiences) is therefore here referred to a saying of Jesus (Menzies, *Earliest Gospel*). The same apologetic interest is served by the question of the disciples which follows upon the story of the Transfiguration —the question regarding the traditional expectation that Elijah would come as the Fore-runner of the Messiah (ix. 11), which Jesus answers in the sense that Elijah had already appeared, and that the Jews had rejected him with high-handed wilfulness, and that, for that reason, the Son of Man had not found a people prepared and ready to receive Him, but must suffer many things, according to the Scriptures. That by this Elijah the Fore-runner is meant John the Baptist, Mark allows us to guess, while Matthew makes the statement explicitly. Without doubt this discourse springs from a controversy between the first Christians and their Jewish opponents, and Mark brings it in here because he has spoken in the foregoing narrative of an appearance of Elijah.

The Old Testament model of the story of the Transfiguration continues to exercise its influence on the narrative which follows. As Moses (Exod. xxxii. 17 ff.) when he came down from Mount Sinai found the people in great excitement, in connection with which Aaron was not without guilt, and as Moses thereupon waxed very wroth with him and with the people, so Jesus (ix. 14) when He comes down from the Mount of Transfiguration finds the people in dispute with those of the disciples who had been left behind, because they had been unable to heal an epileptic boy; He reproaches them for this as a faithless generation, and explains to the father of the boy that to the believer all things are possible. When he thereupon announces his desire to believe, and begs for help (indulgence) for his still imperfect faith, Jesus drives the evil spirit out of the epileptic. From the earliest times the contrast has been remarked between the scene of suffering at the foot of the mount and the scene of transfiguration on its summit, and no doubt the contrast is designed by the

Evangelist, in order thereby to symbolise the thought that sick and helpless humanity, torn by the demons of sin, can only be helped by the glorious power of the Son of God, which alone can avail to break the tyranny of sin, upon the sole condition of faith.

The last Galilæan discourse to the disciples, which Mark recounts in ix. 33–50, is occasioned by a dispute among the disciples as to which should be greatest, to which he immediately attaches the second announcement of the passion, as though he desired to show how far the minds of the disciples still were from taking in the thought of the suffering Messiah. Jesus set a child in the midst, not so much as a type of humility (which is the turn Matthew gives to the incident) as in order, by Himself caressing the child, to impress upon them the principle that the humbler brethren, such as were aptly typified by this child, must be treated in a loving and brotherly fashion, and no offence must be given to them by high-handed and selfish conduct. To this saying about the giving of offence there is attached a further saying about offences—those, namely, which have their seat in one's own members and their functions. The connection of these verses (43–48) with what precedes is, it must be admitted, effected in a quite external fashion by means of the term "offence," which is common to both. Similarly, no natural connection can really be shown between verse 49 and the verses preceding;[1]

[1] In consequence of this want of connection, the original sense of these sayings can no longer be determined; what the commentaries have to say upon the point is not very satisfactory. Probably the later Evangelists found themselves in the same case, and have therefore omitted this saying.

it seems as if the Evangelist had brought in here, on the strength of the external association of ideas (πῦρ), some isolated sayings which were current in the tradition, unless indeed one prefers to think of them as additions and interpolations from another hand; verses 38–40 (from Luke ix. 49 f.) are certainly of this character, since these verses obviously interrupt the continuity of thought between verses 37 and 41.

THE GOSPEL OF MARK

CHAPTER II

The Final Conflict with the Authorities

(Mark x. 1–xvi. 8)

After the Pharisees' demand for a sign and His disciples' confession of faith in His Messiahship, Jesus regarded His work in Galilee as completed. He considered that the time was now come to bring His cause to a decisive issue in Jerusalem itself, the focal point of the national life; and for this the customary Passover-pilgrimage offered the most suitable occasion. Of the occurrences of the journey Mark has told us but little (chap. x.), while Luke has made use of this journey to introduce the long section peculiar to his Gospel. The question of the Pharisees regarding divorce (x. 2) gave Jesus occasion to correct the ordinance of the Mosaic law in the direction of the ethical idea of marriage, founded upon the ordinance of God at the creation; in this case increasing the stringency, as in others He mitigated the hardness, of the positive enactment, but always in accordance with the same fundamental principle of the exclusive validity of ethical truth, based upon the nature of things (*cf.* ii. 28, vii. 8–23). All these sayings equally bear the stamp of genuineness—that regarding marriage is moreover witnessed to by Paul as a saying of Jesus. To the discourse about the sacredness of marriage is very appropriately attached the beautiful story of Jesus' love for the children; He blessed the children, and rebuked the disciples for refusing to let them come to Him, since it was just for such as these, *i.e.* for children and those of childlike spirit, that the Kingdom of God was destined, adding the beautiful saying, "Whosoever doth not receive the kingdom of God like a child can never enter into it"—a saying which is indeed in harmony with the inner meaning of the Pauline doctrine of salvation, but has in its simpler form an advantage over the dogmatic theory of Paul. For this reason a saying such as this—and there are many such sayings in the Gospels—is no more to be explained from Paulinism than from Judaism, but is the genuine expression of Jesus' own childlike purity of spirit. There follows next the narrative (x. 17–27) of the rich man (Luke speaks of him as "a ruler"; Matthew, as "a youth") who asks Jesus what he must do to inherit eternal life. Jesus first directs him to keep the commandments; then, when he professes his righteousness in this respect, meets him with the challenge to sell all his possessions and give to the poor, in order that he may have treasure in heaven, and to come and follow Him. His inability to respond to this challenge gives Jesus occasion to make the general remark that it is hard for the rich man to enter the Kingdom of God, but that what is impossible with men is possible with God (by means of the strength which He imparts). If this narrative is historical, as we have no reason to doubt, it shows that Jesus shared in the views regarding voluntary poverty and alms-giving which prevailed in pious circles among the Jews; indeed, He goes beyond this in holding the possession of wealth to be in itself an almost insuperable hindrance to partaking in the Kingdom of God, and He sets up, as a consequence, the principle, "Whosoever forsaketh not all that he hath, he cannot be my disciple" (Luke xiv. 33). Matthew has omitted this saying, and, consistently with this, he weakens, in the narrative we are considering, the unconditional demand for the renunciation of all property into a conditional one, "*If thou wilt be perfect*, then go and sell thy possessions," etc.; in place of which Mark and Luke have, "One thing thou lackest, go and sell all that thou hast," etc. Obviously, Matthew's version is a softening of the original rigorism, and already points in the direction of those "counsels of evangelical perfection" which facilitated in Church morality the compromise between the high-pitched ideal and the actual conditions of social life.

The saying about the danger of riches gave Peter occasion to point out that they—in contrast with the rich man who had just gone—had left all to follow Jesus. Mark does not tell us that he asked what would be the reward of this sacrifice (x. 28), but Matthew (xix. 27) does, probably taking this question concerning reward from the answer of Jesus (as in xix. 20). The answer, moreover, is different in the two cases. In Mark, Jesus promises to everyone who for His sake and the Gospel's has left house, family, or possessions, that he shall, even in this present time, receive, along with persecutions, an hundredfold, and in the world to come, everlasting life. Luke and Matthew have, instead of an hundred-fold, the indefinite "manifold," and omit "with persecutions"; Matthew also omits the distinction between the present and the future world, because the period when the reward is to be bestowed is thought of simply as that mentioned just before, the renewing of the world at the Parousia. If the words "with persecutions" in Mark stood originally in this connection, they evidently refer to a condition of the Christian community preceding the complete coming of the Kingdom of God, in which Christians would still have to bear persecutions from without, but, through the solidarity of their brotherly love, should find ample compensation for all the sacrifices which they had made, as was actually the case in the Apostolic Church (*cf.* Acts ii. 44, iv. 32; 2 Cor. viii. 13 ff., ix. 8 ff.). As Jesus, however, expected the commencement of the Kingdom of God in the near future, and all His promises are connected with this event, doubts arise as to the originality of the Marcan version, which is also uncertain from the point of view of textual criticism.[1] The promise of reward for all disciples who have made sacrifices, which is common to all the Evangelists, is preceded in Matthew by a special promise for the Twelve who were Jesus' followers in the most literal sense—that at the Renewing of the World (παλιγγενεσία, used, here only, for the commencement of the Kingdom of

[1] In Cod. D, verse 30b runs (after καιρῷ τούτῳ·) ὅς δὲ ἀφῆκεν οἰκίαν καὶ ἀδεφὰς καὶ ἀδελφοὺς καὶ μητέρα καὶ τέκνα καὶ ἀγροὺς μετὰ διωγμοῦ, ἐν τῶ αἰῶνι τῶ ἐρχομένῳ ζωὴν αἰώνιον λήμψεται, "but whosoever hath left, etc., *with persecutions*—*i.e.* amid persecutions—shall receive in the world to come eternal life."

God), when the Son of Man shall sit upon the throne of His glory, they themselves shall sit upon twelve thrones and judge (rule over) the twelve tribes of Israel. The form of this saying is obviously influenced by the apocalyptic language current in the Early Church, but it has a parallel which quite agrees with it in purport in Luke xxii. 28 ff., the genuineness of which, in its Lucan context, hardly admits of doubt. The words which close this section in Matthew and Mark, "Many first shall be last, and the last first," are repeated by Matthew at the close of the following parable of the Labourers in the Vineyard; in which connection it was originally spoken, it is impossible to say.

As the second prediction of the passion was followed by a dispute among the disciples about precedence (ix. 33), so there follows now upon the third prediction of the passion another dispute (x. 35), caused, in this case, by the ambitious request of the sons of Zebedee that they might sit on the right hand, and on the left hand, of Jesus in His Kingdom of Glory.[1] Jesus points these men, who were so eager to rule, to the cup and the baptism of His passion,[2] which it was needful first to share with Him; while to sit on His right hand and on His left was not for Him to give, but should be given to those for whom it had

[1] Matthew, in order to free the sons of Zebedee from the reproach of ambition, represents the request as made by their mother, but betrays in the answer (xx. 22) that the brothers themselves are to be thought of as having made it.

[2] The latter rests, according to A. Meyer (*Muttersprache Jesu*, p. 85) upon a mistaken translation of the Aramaic טְבַל = dip the morsel into the bitter sauce, as was customary at the Passover. This would then give the same sense as the drinking of the bitter cup.

been appointed by God. In interpreting this saying, however, we are not to think of the Pauline doctrine of predestination, but simply of the Divine providence. Further, it is to be noticed that in this answer Jesus does not negative, but tacitly accepts, the presupposition of the disciples that the Kingdom of the Christ will be a new social order, with thrones of honour and rule, and distinction of rank; which agrees with Matt. xvi. 28 (= Luke xxii. 28 ff.), and is opposed to the modern spiritualisation of the thought of the Kingdom. But there is, nevertheless, an essential distinction, as Jesus proceeds to teach His disciples, between His Kingdom and the kingdoms of the world, in the fact that greatness in the latter depends upon selfish power, in the former upon unselfish love which renders service to all: "Whosoever will be great among you shall be your servant, and whosoever will be first among you shall be the slave of all." The visible embodiment in the example of Jesus of this greatness and rule resting upon serviceable love is then pointed out: "For even the Son of Man came not to be served, but to serve, and to give His life a ransom for many" (verse 45 = Matt. xx. 28). In Luke the parallel to this saying is found in the discourse at the Last Supper in the simpler form: "I am among you as he that serves" (xxii. 27). It is very probable that the latter is the original form of Jesus' saying, which has been modified by Mark from the point of view of the Pauline theory of redemption and expiation; in the original form, as preserved by Luke, the "service" of Jesus consists in the manifestation of His unselfish love by His whole fulfilment of His vocation, which is directed to the procuring of salvation for His followers: according to Paul and Mark, on the other hand, it consists in the sacrifice of the life of the Messiah, who has come just for this very purpose of redeeming sinners by His death, as a sacrifice of expiation in the room of many, from the curse of the law, from sin and death (*cf.* Gal. iii. 13; 1 Cor. vi. 20; 2 Cor. v. 21; Rom. iii. 24 f., viii. 2 f.). That this theory was far from the mind of Jesus, is proved by all His teaching concerning the free love of God for sinners, which forgives those who are penitent and humble, and, on their part, desirous of forgiveness; by His own forgiveness of sins; and by parables such as those of the Prodigal Son and the Unmerciful Servant. How could He, if He Himself had seen in this sacrifice of death the means of expiation required by God as the ransom of sinners, have prayed in Gethsemane that this cup might be removed from Him? How could He have had, when dying, the sense of being abandoned by God? This theory first arose, and could only arise, when the unexpected and baffling fact of the death of Jesus upon the cross was made the subject of apologetic and dogmatic reflection, with the object of explaining away the offence of the cross by bringing it under the point of view of a divinely ordained means of salvation; and such explanation was only possible on the ground of the belief that the crucified Jesus was the Son of Man of apocalyptic expectation—that is, the Son of Man who through death and resurrection had been exalted to be the heavenly Messiah. Thus in verse 45 the designation of the *subject* as the Son of Man is connected in the closest possible fashion with the *predicate* of the surrender of His life as the ransom for many; both spring from the mind of the Church, as influenced by Paul, not from the original self-consciousness of Jesus.

Towards the close of this journey, after Jesus had passed through Jericho, Mark recounts yet another miracle of healing—that of blind Bartimæus (x. 46).[1] It is the last of his stories of healing, and the only one which takes place on Jewish soil. Mark alone gives the name of the man who was healed; he was called the son of Timæus, that is, the unclean (or the blind?). In this unfortunate man, who was blind and a beggar, we may perhaps see a type of the poor, religiously blind and morally debased Jewish people, despised by the Pharisees in their bigoted pride; which others passed by proudly and with reproaches, but which Jesus calls to Him and bids take courage and rise up; which hastens in all its nakedness to Jesus, and through faith in Him is healed of its spiritual blindness: this does not mean, however, that the Evangelist intended this narrative to be understood as mere allegory.

Of the entry of Jesus, with the company of Passover pilgrims, into Jerusalem Mark gives us the simplest picture. It is true, the statement that the animal which Jesus used for His triumphal entry had never been ridden before by any man, is doubtless an unhistorical reflection of the Evangelist; if, however, Matthew seems to have the advantage in omitting it, he allows

[1] Matthew has two blind men instead of one, combining the healing of the blind man at Bethsaida (Mark viii. 22 ff.) with that at Jericho. In doing so, he has omitted the significant name of the blind man of Judæa.

himself, on the other hand, to be misled by a too literal interpretation of the passage from Zechariah (ix. 9) into the odd representation that Jesus rode upon two beasts, the she-ass and her foal, at the same time. Whereas, moreover, according to Mark it was only the company of Passover pilgrims which had accompanied Jesus from Galilee which hailed Him as "He that cometh in the name of the Lord," and hailed with Him the Kingdom of David, *i.e.* the Messianic Kingdom—a representation which doubtless rests on an historical basis; Matthew, on the other hand, pictures the whole city as being powerfully excited at the entry of Jesus—which is doubtless unhistorical. Immediately after His arrival in the city, Jesus went, according to Mark, to the Temple, and looked round upon all things, as was natural to one entering it for the first time; but there was no time left for any action on this day of His arrival; it was now late evening, and Jesus went back with His disciples to Bethany, where He lodged for the night (xi. 11). The next day He went again to the Temple, and began to drive out of it (that is, out of the Fore-court) the traders, whose chaffering seemed to make God's house of prayer a den of thieves. This vigorous act of attempted reform—which has much the same significance for the origin of Christianity as Luther's nailing up of his theses against the sale of indulgences had for the origin of Protestantism—stirred up the ecclesiastical authorities at Jerusalem to aim at the destruction of the bold reformer; but they recognised that, for the moment, there was an obstacle to the carrying out of their designs in the favour with which Jesus was regarded by the people (xi. 18). From this report of Mark, which commends itself by its clearness and historical probability, Matthew diverges in several particulars. According to him, it was on the very day of Jesus' entry into Jerusalem that the cleansing of the Temple took place, and it was not this bold act, but the cures which He proceeded to work in the Temple, and the praises which were offered to Him by the children, which roused the wrath of the hierarchy (xxi. 15); similarly, on the next day, it was not about the cleansing of the Temple, but about His teaching in the Temple, that they took Him to task, and demanded by what authority He so acted (verse 23). Anyone can see how much less probable this account is than that of Mark.

The episode of the barren fig-tree is related by Mark in two parts: first the cursing of the tree on the way from Bethany to Jerusalem, then, on the next day, the perception of its consequent withering. To this are attached some maxims regarding the power of faith and of believing prayer (xi. 12–14, 20–25). Matthew, with his usual habit of abbreviating, has combined the two parts of the narrative, so that in his version the withering of the fig-tree follows immediately upon the cursing, and the miracle therefore appears to be made still greater (xxi. 19). Luke omits this narrative at this point, and gives instead, on an earlier occasion (xiii. 6 ff.), the corresponding parable of the unfruitful fig-tree, in which God's patience with the unfruitful Jewish people, and the judgment which threatens them, is typified; obviously this parable is the foundation of the story in Mark, the latter being nothing more than a dramatised version of the parable. It may remain an open question whether Luke, rightly recognising the allegorical significance of Mark's miracle-story, altered it into a parable, or whether the same thought was already current in the tradition in a dual form, the parabolical and the dramatic, so that Luke in adopting the one would naturally reject the other. In this instance the Gospels have themselves preserved, alongside of the miracle, a parable embodying the idea which gave rise to the miracle-story; it is thus of the highest interest as a decisive justification of the general principle of interpreting miracle-stories allegorically.

On the day after the cleansing of the Temple Jesus went into the Temple again and "walked round about" it (presumably to observe the result of His reforming act of the previous day). The ecclesiastical authorities put to Him the question by what authority He did these things, *i.e.* what sanction had He for His coming forward as a reformer at the cleansing of the Temple (for it is only to this act that the question in Mark can refer, not to His authority for teaching in the Temple, of which Mark says nothing, though Matthew and Luke refer to it). Jesus answers this question with the counter-question regarding their opinion upon the baptism of John, whether it was from heaven or from men, based upon a Divine mission or upon human caprice. The embarrassment in which this question involved His assailants shows how admirably this counter-stroke was calculated to disarm them.

Immediately after this abortive attack of the hierarchs, the Evangelist makes Jesus proceed to attack them by describing their guilt, and their final rejection, under the figure of the unfaithful and murderous husbandmen, who maltreat the messengers of the owner of the vineyard, and finally slay his son, in order to get possession of the "inheritance" for themselves, after which the lord of the vineyard finally comes himself in order to destroy them and to give the vineyard to others (Matt.: "to a people who will bring the fruits thereof"). In the form in which it lies before us, this narrative is no ordinary parable, no story of everyday occurrences setting forth a law of universal application, but a transparent allegory referring to the Jewish theocracy, the administrators of which, as they had from of old ill-treated the prophets, the messengers of God, so now, finally, would slay the Son of God, Jesus, the Messiah, in order to secure for themselves the permanent lordship over the people of God; but so far from succeeding in that, they would themselves be broken upon this stone which they had rejected, but which God had raised to be the headstone of the corner. It is obvious that this cannot be the authentic account of a controversial discourse of Jesus, though it may well be based upon utterances of His, the form of which, however, we cannot now recover from its allegorical transformation. The allegory can only be understood as "a product of early Christian theology"[1]—an indictment of the Jewish hierarchy by the Christian Church, as having filled up the measure of their guilt by the rejection, in Jesus, of the son and heir; and in this the Christian conviction that Jesus was this son and heir is assumed to be the motive of the conduct of the hierarchy

[1] Jülicher, *Gleichnisreden Jesu,* p. 406.

(whereas it was just this that they disbelieved). The pronouncement, however, that the vineyard, *i.e.* the government of the people of God, should be taken from them and handed over to others may well be a saying of Jesus (*cf.* Matt. xv. 13), and may have been the point of a simpler parable lying at the basis of the allegory. Whether the Matthæan version also —that the vineyard should be given to a people who would render the fruits of it—is intended to express the same thought, the fall of the hierarchy, or the further thought of the rejection of the Jewish nation in favour of the Gentile Church, is doubtful; but the latter is certainly the more probable interpretation. As a result, the Evangelist tells us, of this polemic, the hierarchs, who felt it as a blow against themselves, desired to arrest Jesus, but from fear of the people left Him still at liberty. In these circumstances it was a well-calculated stratagem on the part of the rulers to endeavour, by the catch-question regarding the tribute money, to bring Jesus into conflict either with the Roman Government or with the people (xii. 13–17). Jesus saw through their device, and cut the noose which was intended to ensnare Him with the well-known words: "Render unto Cæsar the things that are Cæsar's, and unto God the things that are God's," by which He meant that the religious-social revolution involving the fall of the hierarchy, to which He looked forward, would have nothing to do with the political domination of Rome—an ideal view which was destined to make shipwreck upon hard realities, but which nevertheless contained the true and profound principle that religion should be kept apart from politics.

After thus disposing of the Pharisees, Jesus was approached by the Sadducees with the doctrinal question regarding the resurrection, the irrationality of which they endeavoured to prove by the imaginary case of the seven brothers who had successively married the same woman, and whose claims to her consequently came into conflict at the resurrection (xii. 18 ff.). Jesus first corrected the erroneous view of the resurrection upon which this objection was based—the assumption, namely, that it would be a mere continuation of the earthly, corporeal existence, including the marriage relation, whereas really the risen would be like the angels in heaven, and therefore would enjoy a higher form of existence, freed from the earthly body. He then bases the certainty of the resurrection, understood in this sense as a continued life in heaven similar to that of the angels, upon the passage of Scripture (Exod. iii. 6) where God is described as the God of Abraham, Isaac, and Jacob; for, since God is not the God of the dead but of the living, this implies the continued existence of the Patriarchs, and therefore of the dead in general. The Sadducæan denial of the resurrection is thus shown to be an error which has its roots in ignorance of the Scriptures and of the power (omnipotence) of God (xii. 24, 27). That reminds us of Paul, who in 1 Cor. xv. 33 f. similarly reproaches the Corinthians who doubted the resurrection with error and ignorance of God. It is noticeable, too, that the more spiritual conception of the resurrection which is here opposed to the Sadducæan view essentially agrees, in its contrast with the grosser imaginations of the Pharisees, with the teaching of Paul in 1 Cor. xv. 35–49.

In immediate succession to these controversies Mark places a conversation of a friendly character with a Scribe, who asks Jesus, not (as in Matthew's version) by way of entangling Him, but with an earnest desire for instruction, which is the greatest commandment (xii. 25). Jesus designates as the greatest the command to love God with the whole heart (Deut. vi. 4 f.), with which, however, He immediately combines the commandment to love one's neighbour as oneself, the latter also being drawn from the Mosaic Scriptures (Lev. xix. 18); but whereas in the original context neighbour is used in the restricted sense of fellow-countryman, on the lips of Jesus it receives the wider meaning of fellow-man in general, as is clearly evident in the parable, recorded by Luke only, of the Good Samaritan. The Scribe is delighted with Jesus' answer, and repeats it with the addition that the fulfilment of these two commandments is worth more than all sacrifices. Jesus recognises from this his insight, and gives him the honourable testimony that he is not far from the Kingdom of God (xii. 34). Matthew passes over in silence this conclusion of the conversation, though he was well acquainted with it, as he shows by bringing in at a later point Mark's closing reflection (xii. 34; Matt. xxii. 46). The omission of this saying, in which the essence of all piety and morality, for man as man, is set in contrast with the externality of the Jewish system of religion and worship, is no sign of greater originality, but rather of a narrower ecclesiastical standpoint.

After these discourses, in which Jesus answered various questions which were put to Him, He now (xii. 35 ff.), on His part, puts the significant question,

How did the Scribes come to maintain that the Messiah was the Son of David? Had not David himself, filled with the prophetic Spirit, called him his Lord? How came it then that he was, according, it must be understood, to the opinion of the Scribes, his son? There can scarcely be any doubt as to the meaning of this question: Jesus intends to show that the current opinion of the Schools regarding the Davidic sonship of the Messiah was based upon an error which was opposed to David's own words. But what can have caused Jesus to raise this question? It certainly cannot have been a purely theoretic interest in a question of the Jewish Schools; rather, the point at stake for Him was the very practical question whether one who was not a descendant of David could be destined to be the Messiah and be recognised as such. And from this we may well draw the conclusion that in those days Jesus was deeply occupied with thoughts regarding His Messianic vocation, and that He saw in the opinion current in the Schools and among the people that the Messiah must be a son of David a serious obstacle to His recognition as Messiah. That, however, would not have been the case if He had known Himself to be a scion of David's race—for in that case the popular opinion would have been particularly favourable to His aims, and He must rather have used it than opposed it; or if He had intended to be the Messiah, not in the generally current sense of a King of the People of God, but in a quite different, purely spiritual sense—for in that case the question regarding the correctness or otherwise of the traditional opinion regarding the Davidic sonship of the Messiah would have been quite indifferent to Him. The fact that it was not thus indifferent to Him, and that He sought to invalidate the opinion by an argument from Scripture, seems to me to imply two presuppositions: (1) that He did not know Himself to be a son of David, and (2) that He nevertheless cherished the thought that He was destined to be the Messiah, not in a purely spiritual sense, but in the traditional sense of the term, namely, as the theocratic Head of the People of God, who should take the place of the existing hierarchy (*cf.* verse 9). It is further to be remarked that this meaning of the question can only be inferred from the version of Mark and Luke; whereas in Matthew the possibility is not excluded that the Davidic sonship of the Messiah is taken for granted as certain, and the question is directed to the point, how, on this presupposition, the Messiah could nevertheless at the same time be David's lord. The solution of the question could then only, in accordance with the meaning of this Evangelist, lie in the fact that Jesus, the Messiah, was indeed, on the one hand, the son of David, but on the other, in a supernatural sense, the Son of God. This is the sense in which the Church understood it, and it is very possible that the Evangelist Matthew had it in mind[1] in narrating the incident. But that that cannot have been the meaning of Jesus is obvious; the sense which He attached to the question must be inferred from the more primitive version in Mark.

While the discourses of Jesus during these days in

[1] *Cf.* Holtzmann, *Komm.*, 3rd ed., p. 277 f. The analogous setting in contrast of Son of God and Son of Man in Matt. xvi. 13, 16, is in point here.

Jerusalem which have been reported by Mark up to this point bear in a high degree the marks of genuine historical reminiscence, it is otherwise in the case of the long concluding eschatological discourse in Mark xiii. Genuine sayings of Jesus may well have been worked up into it, especially in the exhortations at the close; and the prediction in connection with which the Evangelist introduces it, of the destruction of the splendid buildings of the Temple, may well be derived from Jesus Himself. The speech as a whole, however, is not historical, but is a composition artistically worked up from material of various kinds by the Evangelist, or perhaps already in the source which he used. Two of the different component parts can be clearly distinguished: in the one (verses 5 f., 9–13, 21–23, 28–37), the hortatory interest is paramount, the Christian community is warned against temptations and exhorted to faithfulness and vigilance; in the other (verses 7 f., 14–20, 24–27), the discourse speaks partly of wars, and natural calamities of a general character, partly of a period of severe distress which would come upon Judæa, and with which was to be immediately connected the coming of the Son of Man in glory upon the clouds of heaven. The latter portion forms a well-connected whole, a miniature apocalypse, composed of three scenes: "Beginning of Sufferings," great "Distress," the "End." The connection of these apocalyptic sections is broken by the insertion of the hortatory sections in a way which shows clearly that the latter have been interpolated by another hand into a well-articulated whole to which they did not originally belong, being, recognisably, additions of a different origin and aim.

Turning our attention first to the apocalyptic sections of the discourse, we find the middle section (14–20) of special importance for the determination of its origin. The words of verse 14, "When ye see the abomination of desolation standing where it ought not—let him that readeth give heed—then shall they that are in Judæa flee to the mountains," are generally understood as a reference to the destruction of Jerusalem, and of the Temple, by the Romans under Titus; but this is certainly wrong. How could it be said of the destruction of the Temple that it "stood where it ought not"? And what sense would there be in an exhortation to flee after the destruction of the city? Even if the exhortation to flee is thought of as directed to the Christians in Jerusalem, it could only have a meaning before the destruction of the city, say at the commencement of the siege; in that case we should have to understand by the "abomination of desolation standing where it ought not," not the destruction, but a desecration of the Temple, which might perhaps be referred to the reign of terror of the Zealots, who defiled the holy place by the blood shed in civil strife. Although I myself formerly gave this explanation,[1] I am obliged to admit that it now seems to me improbable on several grounds. After all, this expression, "When ye see the abomination of desolation standing where it ought not," is hardly more suitable to the wild doings of the Zealots in the Temple than to its destruction by a Roman army. The expression is derived from Dan. ix. 27, xii. 11,

[1] "Über die Komposition der eschatol. Rede Matt. xxiv.," *Jahrb. f. d. Theol.*, xiii. p. 135 ff.

in the Septuagint translation, and there signifies, without doubt, the setting up of an idol in the Temple, so that a similar meaning in the present passage also is certainly the most natural. Now, it is true that nothing of that kind really happened in the war of Titus, but ever after the year 40 A.D., when the Emperor Gaius formed the design of setting up his statue in the Temple at Jerusalem, the fear of such a desecration kept the Jews in a constant ferment of excitement, and produced the temper from which sprang constant attempts at insurrection, long before the campaign of Vespasian. Mommsen[1] says in reference to this: "After that fateful edict [of Gaius] the apprehension that another Emperor might give a like order was never set at rest." Accordingly, he describes the situation thus: "We are accustomed to date the outbreak of the war from A.D. 66; it would be equally, perhaps more, correct to fix on the year 44. After the death of Agrippa there was never any cessation of the fighting in Judæa, and besides the local feuds in which Jew was at strife with Jew, the fighting was constantly going on between the Roman troops and the men who had taken to the hills—the Zealots as the Jews called them, or, as the Romans designated them, the brigands. In the streets of the towns the patriots openly preached war, and many followed them into the wilderness, while the peaceable and prudent who refused to do the like had their houses set on fire by these bands of outlaws. When this was the prevailing temper, signs and wonders could not fail to occur, nor men to come

1 *Römische Geschichte,* vol. v. pp. 520, 527 (=E.T. *Provinces of the Roman Empire*, vol. ii. pp. 194, 203 f.).

forward who, whether deceivers or self-deceived, used them to rouse the masses to frenzied excitement. Under Cuspius Fadus, Theudas the miracle-worker led his adherents to the Jordan, assuring them that the waters would part before them, and overwhelm the Roman cavalry who were in pursuit. Under Felix, another thaumaturge, known as the Egyptian, promised that the walls of Jerusalem would fall down, like those of Jericho at the trumpet-blast of Joshua; on the strength of which promise 4000 dagger-men followed him to the Mount of Olives. It was just this irrationality which made the danger. The great mass of the Jewish people were peasant-farmers who ploughed their fields, and pressed their olives, in the sweat of their brows, villagers rather than townsmen, of small education and unbounded faith, in close relations with the freebooters of the mountains, and full of reverence for Jehovah, and of hatred against the unclean foreigner. Such was the war—not a struggle between one power and another for the mastery, not even, properly speaking, a struggle of the oppressed against their oppressors for the recovery of freedom; nor was it due to the rashness of statesmen: it was fanatical peasants who began the war, who waged it, and who paid the price with their blood." It is, as it seems to me, to these conditions of the last decade before the destruction of Jerusalem that the brief apocalypse in Mark xiii. transports us. It has nothing to do with the Christians of Jerusalem and their flight from the city: rather, it is the Jewish peasants in the villages of Judæa who are called on to flee (14 ff.) to the hills, the signal being a new desecration of the Temple such as had been planned by Antiochus Epiphanes and the Emperor Gaius, by the fear of which the Jewish imagination was at that time goblin-ridden. That the event which was to give the signal for universal flight must at the time when the apocalypse was composed have already occurred—as is generally assumed—is an unfounded presupposition which there is nothing in the text to oblige us to adopt: it is quite sufficient to assume that among the peasant population, to whom the watchword is here given, it was a subject of lively apprehension, as was actually the case in the years of growing Jewish fanaticism which preceded the destruction of Jerusalem. To this period also are appropriate all the other warning signs which are indicated in this passage—wars of the peoples, where the reference is probably in the first place to the Parthians; earthquakes (Laodicea in the year 60, Pompeii, 62) and famines (under Claudius and Nero); the appearance of wonder-workers who should mislead the people, giving themselves out to be prophets and Messiahs (such as Theudas and 'the Egyptian'); and, as regards the fearful sufferings, there is historical evidence for these some time previous to the siege of Jerusalem, due to the increasing severity, provoked by constant Jewish risings, and the misrule, of the proconsuls of the time, and, finally, to the campaign of Vespasian with which the war began: moreover, the "great affliction such as has never been in the earth" is one of the standing formulæ of Jewish apocalyptic writings (*cf.* Dan. xii. 1; 1 Macc. ix. 27; Assumption of Moses, viii., etc.). If we have found in the first sections no reason to think of anything but a Jewish apocalypse, the same applies to the last section

(24–28). The picture of the cosmic catastrophes is based on prophetic imagery, and the coming of the Son of Man from heaven is sufficiently explained by Dan. vii. 13. The writer of a Christian apocalypse could hardly have failed to indicate that the coming Son of Man was the crucified Jesus coming *again* (*cf.* Apoc. i. 7); the complete absence of any such indication confirms the impression which we have already received, that we have before us in the apocalyptic sections of this discourse a brief Jewish apocalypse which was circulated broadsheet-wise in Judæa in the seventh decade of the first century. The Christian communities of Judæa would naturally be obliged to take up a definite attitude in regard to a publication of this kind; the more nearly it seemed to touch their own hopes, the more difficult it was for them to ignore or repudiate it. Accordingly, the simplest thing was to turn this Jewish apocalypse into a Christian one, by inserting such exhortations as appeared appropriate to the position of the Christians at the time. It was of the first importance to warn the Christians against the seductive influence of those perverters of the people who might seek, by some kind of Messianic claims, to alienate the Christian Jews from the Church of Jesus and win them for the national movement (verses 5 f., 21 ff.). And whereas the Jewish apocalypse found the sign of the end in the general, and especially the political, situation of the outer world, the Christian redactor directs the attention of his readers to events within the Christian community, especially the persecutions which it experienced at the hands of Jews and heathen, exhorts them to patience and loyalty, and shows how even these adverse occurrences only served to further the cause of Christ by contributing to the extension of the preaching of the gospel throughout the heathen world, the completion of which must precede the coming of the end (9–13, 28 f.). Accordingly, the Christian redaction sets in contrast with the fanatical Jewish expectation of the Messiah the exhortation to patient waiting, to courageous witness-bearing and loyal acceptance of suffering in the service of the Lord Jesus, whose coming is certainly to be looked for in the near future, within the lifetime of the existing generation, but without the definite period being known with certainty, as, indeed, Jesus Himself had not claimed to know it.[1] It is this practical exhortation to watchfulness and dutiful preparedness that constitutes the essential point of distinction between the Christian redaction and the Jewish apocalypse on which it is based.

The account which follows of the events of the last days at Jerusalem is in Mark (xiv. and xv.) of great vividness, and doubtless rests for the most part on authentic tradition, which does not, of course, exclude the possibility that here, as in the earlier course of the Gospel history, some legendary elements have found their way in, and some apologetic and

[1] Verse 32, *οὐδὲ ὁ υἱός*. This description of Jesus as "the Son" in an absolute sense is unique in Mark, and in the other Synoptics occurs only in the Christological hymn in Luke x. 22 (= Matt. xi. 37). Seeing that it obviously implies a fixed terminology, we must "suppose an influencing of the text by the linguistic usage of the Early Church," or regard the words "not even the Son, but only the Father," as an interpolation. (Dalmann, *Worte Jesu*, p. 159, E.T. 194.)

dogmatic motives of Pauline origin have exercised a modifying influence upon some of the details. Of the two later Evangelists, Matthew here follows Mark very closely, while Luke has many divergences in these sections. The opening incident in the story of the Passion, the anointing at Bethany, in the house of Simon the leper, is omitted by Luke, because he has anticipated it at an earlier point, in the story of the anointing of Jesus by a penitent woman in the house of Simon the Pharisee (vii. 36–50). The close of the story of the anointing, in which this action is described as an anticipation of the anointing of the body of Jesus for His burial (*i.e.* of the embalming of His body) and the promise is given that she shall be held in honoured memory wherever the (Matt.: "this") gospel is preached in the whole world (8 f.), is subject in several respects to the doubt which attaches to the historicity of this saying. The word "gospel," which on the lips of Jesus always signifies the glad tidings of the nearness of the Kingdom of God, seems here to be used already in the later sense of an "evangelical history"; and that the preaching of it throughout the "whole world" should be assumed by Jesus Himself hardly agrees with sayings such as Matt. x. 5 f., 23, xv. 24, xvi. 28, according to which Jesus' horizon was still limited to the people of Israel. Therefore verse 9, at least, must be regarded as an addition of the Evangelist, who desired to commend the woman-disciple who anointed Jesus to the honourable remembrance of the Church.[1] But the preceding

[1] It is, however, surprising that he does not name her. Is it possible that he did not know her name; or did he, perhaps, refrain from mentioning it from modesty, because it was his own mother,

remark also, that the anointing was an anticipation of the embalming of the body of Jesus, can only be understood as an interpretation of the act which grew up later in the Church, not as its actual purpose. For how could this woman-disciple have possessed such a foreknowledge of His death while the other disciples had, to all appearance, no inkling of its likelihood? And even assuming that she had such a premonition, is there any probability that she would have given expression to it in this peculiar form, contravening, as it did, not only custom, but even natural delicacy of feeling? Anyone who, discarding prejudice, tries to think himself into the historical situation must inevitably find that very improbable. What, then, can have been the original purpose and significance of this anointing? We can only make conjectural suggestions, and among these the most obvious would appear to be that it was intended as a consecration to the Messianic Kingship,

Mary? She, according to Acts xii. 12, owned a house in Jerusalem, which she placed at the disposal of the community of disciples, in its early days, as a place of meeting; she was therefore in such circumstances as to be well able to afford the outlay which is so accurately described in vv. 3 ff. Moreover, in John (xii. 3) the name of the woman is Mary—there identified with the sister of Martha mentioned in Luke. Further, in the narrative in Luke x. 41 f. also, Mary is defended by Jesus against the censure of others, and receives distinguished praise, though no doubt on a quite different occasion, having no connection with the narrative of the anointing, which Luke has given earlier and in a different form. It is not, however, on that account impossible that the Mary in Luke who sat, rapt in adoration, at the feet of the Lord is identical with the Johannine Mary who anointed His feet, and that both are further to be identified with the unnamed woman-disciple of the Marcan story of the anointing, and that this was in reality the well-known Mary, the mother of Mark.

in which the faith of this enthusiastic disciple in the immediate commencement of Jesus' Messianic rule found an extravagant expression which is quite in accordance with the excited, confident mood of the company of disciples, as shown even in the dispute about precedence at the Last Supper.

In striking contrast with this loyal disciple's deed of faith stands the betrayal by the disloyal disciple (verse 10 f.). In the original form of the narrative in Mark and Luke, the motive of the betrayal is not necessarily avarice (that is first implied in Matt. xxvi. 15). It is therefore possible to suppose some other motive, such as that he was alarmed by what seemed to him the dangerous turn that events had taken with the Messianic anointing, or, on the contrary, that events were not moving rapidly enough for him, and he wished to prevent any further hesitation by bringing about an open conflict. These are possible hypotheses, but certain knowledge is here not attainable.

The preparations for the Paschal meal are next described, in verses 12–17, in such a way that it is difficult to say how much rests upon recollection, how much is legendary addition, influenced by Old Testament examples (1 Sam. x. 2 ff.; Gen. xxiv. 14). The very difficult critical question, too, whether the meal was really, as the Synoptic Gospels, in contradistinction to John, represent it to have been, a proper Paschal meal, or whether this conception of it first arose in connection with the Pauline theory of the foundation of a new covenant,[1] I will not

[1] The arguments advanced by Brand (*Evang. Geschichte*, pp. 283–304) in favour of this explanation are at any rate worthy of notice.

venture to decide. In the first place, Mark, who is followed by Matthew (Luke alters the order), represents the betrayal "by one of the Twelve" as foretold by Jesus with the addition: "The Son of man goeth, as it is written of him [Luke: as it was determined (by God)]: but woe to that man by whom the Son of man shall be betrayed!" These words obviously have their source in that apologetic reflection by means of which the Early Church endeavoured to do away with the offence of the cross; it is to be noticed also that this *vaticinium ex eventu* is further elaborated in Matthew and John, increasing in definiteness and consequent improbability. Then, during the supper, Jesus took a loaf, and, after giving thanks, brake it and gave it to the disciples with the words: "Take ye, this is my body." And, taking the cup, He gave thanks, and gave it to the disciples, and they all drank thereof. And He said unto them: "This is my blood of the covenant which is shed for many. Verily, I say unto you that I will drink no more of the fruit of the vine, until the day when I drink it new in the kingdom of God" (verses 22–25). In this narrative only the distribution of the bread (verse 22) is common to the Evangelists, and is therefore to be regarded as the kernel of the story, of which the historical evidence is certain. The subsequent distribution of the wine is given, indeed, by Matthew in exact agreement with Mark, but with the explanatory addition "which is shed for the forgiveness of sins"; in Luke, as we shall see below, it is wanting in the original text, and is replaced by a passage borrowed from 1 Cor. xi. 24 f. If this circumstance is itself sufficient to give rise to doubts regarding the authenticity of the distribution of the wine as reported by Matthew and Mark, these are accentuated by the following consideration. The saying in verse 24 contains a clear reference to the death of Jesus, which is described as a sacrifice of atonement, for the forgiveness of sins, and as a means to the making of a new covenant, the counterpart to the former making of the covenant at Sinai, at which Moses sprinkled the people with the blood of the sacrifice, saying, "This is the blood of the covenant which Jahweh makes with you" (Exod. xxiv. 8). Now the thought that the death of Jesus is the sacrifice of atonement with a view to the establishing of a new covenant is no doubt the cardinal dogma of the Pauline theology, but is quite foreign to the thought of Jesus, who certainly never intended to annul the old covenant resting on the giving of the Law to Moses (*cf.* Matt. v. 17 f.), but only to overthrow the Jewish hierarchy (Mark xii. 9), and who was so far from looking forward to His death by violence as a necessary God-ordained means to the fulfilment of His mission, that even at this Last Supper He gave expression in quite unambiguous terms to His confident hope of the immediate victory of His cause—for it is only of that, and not of a condition of blessedness in the other world, that the well-authenticated saying about ere long drinking the fruit of the vine new in the Kingdom of God (verse 25 = Matt. xxvi. 29 = Luke. xxii. 18 and 16) can naturally be understood ; as also the promise given at the same time to the disciples, that they should share the reign of Jesus, and eat and drink at His table (Luke xxii. 29 f. = Matt. xix. 28). In view of these sayings, it is scarcely conceivable that Jesus, in giving the wine, should have pointed to His bloody death and the atoning significance which it bears in the Pauline theory; and it is quite certain that any such indication would have been wholly unintelligible to the disciples, who, in the sequel, were completely taken by surprise by the catastrophe. And even of their subsequently recalling these words of Jesus there is nowhere any trace. In the love-feasts of the company of disciples it is always only the breaking of bread that is spoken of; the cup, with its symbolism of death, remains (apart from Paul) completely out of sight, and the feeling with which the community celebrated these love-feasts was not one of solemn commemoration of Jesus' death, but of a joyous celebration of their brotherly unity (Acts ii. 46 f.). From all this follows, as it seems to me, the inevitable conclusion that the saying regarding the symbolism of death (verse 24) has its roots in the Pauline theology, and is put into the mouth of Jesus by Mark, the follower of Paul. From this it follows, further, that the well-authenticated words at the giving of the bread, "This is my body" (verse 23), can originally have had no relation to Jesus' death, but only meant, "In partaking of this symbol of my body, that is, of my *life*, you unite yourselves with me and with one another into *one body*," that is, into one indivisible whole (*cf.* 1 Cor. x. 17). It was therefore simply the conclusion of a covenant of loyalty by partaking in common of the religiously consecrated food, corresponding exactly to the ancient, and therefore universally intelligible, idea of a "sacred communion" which underlay all religious feasts, especially sacrificial feasts, and made them into a means of religious and social union.

On the way to Gethsemane, Jesus utters, according to the Evangelist, a last prediction of the Passion: "Ye shall all be offended, for it is written, 'I will smite the shepherd, and the sheep shall be scattered,' but after I am risen again I will go before you into Galilee" (verses 26–28). The passage in Zech. xiii. 7 runs, in the original, "Smite the shepherd, and the flock will be scattered"—an appeal of God to His faithful people to smite the ungodly king, and therefore by no means a Messianic prediction. Jesus cannot, then, have used it as such, as He could not have identified Himself with an ungodly king, and, moreover, did not expect defeat, but victory. Therefore this saying (verse 27 f.) must be a *vaticinium ex eventu*, based upon the fact that after the arrest of Jesus the disciples scattered and fled like a shepherdless flock, and that it was only afterwards, in Galilee, that they attained to faith in the resurrection of Jesus. Luke has omitted these words, since they did not harmonise with his story of the Easter week. What has been said of the prediction of the offence of the disciples in general must apply also to the more specific prediction of Peter's denial (verses 29–31).

The scene which follows, Jesus' agony of prayer in Gethsemane, must be in the main, at least, historical, since it can hardly have been invented by tradition, as it shows Jesus shrinking with natural human emotion from the perilous decision which lay before Him, desiring that the bitterness of His cup of suffering might be removed, but bowing to the will of God in childlike submission; giving herein the example of acceptable prayer, which submits all personal desires to the will of God. At the same time, this scene is yet another proof that the preceding predictions of the suffering, the dying, and rising again of Jesus are not historical; for, assuming that they were so, the agony in Gethsemane would not have been possible. In matters of detail, too, some legendary traits may have slipped in—the double separation, first from the rest of the disciples and then from the chosen three, recalls the sacrifice of Isaac in Gen. xxii.; the three withdrawals for prayer recall the three temptations; the address "Abba, Father" is known to us through Paul as the form of invocation of the Greek-speaking Christians (combining the Aramaic word with the Greek translation). Again, the antithesis "the spirit indeed is willing, but the flesh is weak" (verse 38) is specifically Pauline, and is not found elsewhere in the language of Jesus.

The procedure at the arrest of Jesus is narrated in the simplest form by Mark; in the parallel narratives there are additions designed to show how easily Jesus could, if He had wished, have escaped from His enemies, and therefore how entirely of His own free will He submitted to His sufferings. Peculiar to Mark is the brief notice (verse 51) of the young man who followed Jesus after His arrest, and only escaped being arrested himself by leaving his light garment in the hands of his pursuers. Is it possible that this young man was Mark himself? That would explain the interest of the Evangelist in preserving this unimportant incident.

In his account of the trial before the Sanhedrin Mark reports, as false witness offered against Jesus, the assertion that He had been heard to say, "I will break down this temple made with hands, and within three days I will build another made without hands" (xiv. 58). In Matthew the saying runs more simply, "I can break down the temple of God, and within three days build it up" (xxvi. 61). Luke omits it here, but brings in a similar saying at the trial of Stephen: "Jesus of Nazareth will destroy this place, and change the customs which Moses hath given to us" (Acts vi. 14). As this saying is alluded to again in mockery by the onlookers at the Crucifixion, the "false witness" may, after all, have had some genuine saying as its basis.[1] But how the saying of Jesus actually ran, and on what occasion it was spoken, we do not know (Mark's version doubtless includes his interpretation of the metaphor, which has a more simple form in Matthew), and it is therefore useless to advance any opinion regarding its original sense. It certainly cannot have referred to the destruction of the Jewish religion (*cf.* Matt. v. 17), but at most to a purification of the Temple-worship from sensuous ceremonial, like the saying which John (ii. 19) attributes to Him on the occasion of the purification of the Temple.

When Mark, and Matthew following him, represent Jesus, in replying to the solemn adjuration of the High Priest, as not only acknowledging Himself Messiah, but also adding the assurance that they

[1] Noticeable in this connection is the reference in the recently discovered fragment of the Gospel of Peter, verse 26: "We disciples hid ourselves, for they hunted us as criminals and men who sought to burn the Temple." A charge of this kind against the disciples must have rested upon some saying of similar import to that referred to in the "false witness."

should see the Son of Man sitting on the right hand of Power, and coming with the clouds of heaven, suspicion regarding the authenticity of these words is aroused, not only by their apocalyptic character, but also by the circumstance that none of the disciples was present at the examination before the Council, and therefore none was in a position to give accurate information regarding the words spoken on that occasion. This gap in their actual knowledge, tradition must have filled up from the consciousness of the Church, attributing to Jesus the Messianic expectations current in the community. In the case of the charge in verse 58 the matter stands rather differently, since this was current among the people also (xv. 29), and would therefore naturally come to the knowledge of the disciples.

Of Peter's denial, Mark and Matthew give the original account, which Luke amplifies by representing Peter as recalled to himself not merely by the cock-crowing but by a look of Jesus. This is possible in Luke's order of narration, in which the denial precedes the examination before the Council, but is not consistent with the original and more probable order, according to which the denial took place outside, in the court below, while Jesus was at the time in the judgment-hall above. The alteration is quite in harmony with Luke's tendency to an emotional portrayal. The trial before Pilate, too, is described in a simpler fashion by Mark than by the two later Evangelists, who introduce various discordant traits. Luke (xxiii. 6 f.) represents Jesus as sent by Pilate to Herod, and as being mocked rather than tried by the latter—an improbable episode in which we may perhaps see an imitation of the submission of Paul's case to the Jewish king Herod Agrippa. Matthew keeps in general closer to the Marcan scheme, but expands it by the introduction of three episodes of obviously legendary character—the fate of Judas the traitor, of which two versions were known to tradition (Matt. xxvii. 3–10; Acts i. 15–20); the dream of Pilate's wife (xxvii. 19); the hand-washing of Pilate in solemn token of his innocence, whereupon the whole multitude declared that they took the guilt of Jesus' blood upon themselves and upon their children (verse 24 f.). That is hardly the language of a superstitious multitude, any more than the other is the language of a Roman official.

As Jesus was being led away to be crucified, Mark tells us (xv. 21), one Simon of Cyrene, the father of Alexander and Rufus, was pressed into service to bear His cross. This identification of Simon, which is peculiar to Mark, may be naturally explained by supposing that at the time when Mark wrote the two sons of this man were still alive and known to the community; later, this personal notice had ceased to be of interest, and was therefore omitted by Luke and Matthew. Before the Crucifixion, Mark relates further, drugged wine was offered to Jesus, but He refused it. It was a customary act of humanity, the object being to stupefy the sufferer; and Jesus doubtless refused it for the very reason that He did not wish to be rendered unconscious, but to suffer with full consciousness—a small but characteristic trait, for the preservation of which Mark deserves our gratitude. In Matthew quite a different turn is given to the incident—the drugged wine becomes a mixture of vinegar and gall, which Jesus, when He had tasted it, refused to drink, evidently because of its nauseous taste. The drugged wine of the original narrative was offered with good intentions; how came Matthew to make it into the curious and repulsive mixture of vinegar and gall? Obviously he was led astray by the pictorial expression in Ps. lxix. 22, "They gave me gall to eat and vinegar to drink." In order to represent this as literally fulfilled in the case of Jesus, he has altered the historical statement in the document which he was following, undeterred by the improbability of this new version of the incident.

At the last, according to Mark and Matthew, about the ninth hour, Jesus uttered, from the cross, the cry of distress of Ps. xxii. 22: "My God, my God, why hast thou forsaken me?" then, with a loud cry, died. Luke omits the cry of distress, but gives instead three other sayings, to which John adds three more. Of these seven sayings of the Gospels as a whole, only that reported by Matthew and Mark seems to rest upon genuine reminiscence. In favour of its genuineness are, the Aramaic wording; the curious misunderstanding of the bystanders, who thought that Jesus was calling for Elias, which could scarcely be invented; and, more especially, the consideration that the cry of despair, conveying the sense of being abandoned by God, is, from the point of view of the Christian faith, so strange that it could hardly have been put into the mouth of Jesus if it had not been given by the tradition; it is just this strangeness which has caused it to be left out by Luke and John, and other sayings given in place of it. But if this cry of distress of the dying Jesus is historical, it is yet another piece of confirmatory evidence that Jesus had not expected to meet death at the hands of His enemies, but hoped to the last to be delivered by God, that all the predictions of His death given by the Evangelists are unhistorical, and, finally, that Jesus did not think of the Messianic kingdom as a heavenly kingdom, nor as a spiritual kingdom to be established on earth when He returned from heaven, but simply as the realisatian of the prophetic ideal of the Reign of God in a religious-social reorganisation of the Jewish people. It was only when this hope was destroyed by the combined resistance of the hierarchic and worldly powers that the faith of the community of disciples rose to the ideal of a new Kingdom of God of super-earthly origin and character, to be founded by the heavenly Messiah, or "Son of Man," and already, in a measure, present in His miraculous spiritual operations. This transformation was the fruit of the death of Jesus, and showed itself first in faith in the resurrection.

As, at the commencement, and at the climax, of Jesus' work in Galilee, ideal scenes are introduced by the Evangelist, in which the significance of the moment is expressed in sayings and symbolical incidents; so now, at the close, he adds a series of ideal scenes in which the foundation of reality, on which his presentation of the fate of Jesus at Jerusalem has in essentials hitherto been based, is more or less completely abandoned. When he represents the veil of the Temple as being, immediately upon the death of Jesus, rent from the top to the bottom (xv. 38), that is an allegorical expression of the thoroughly Pauline idea that through the death of Jesus the wall of partition is done away which separated the world of sinners from the Holy of Holies, the gracious presence of God (Rom. v. 1; *cf.* Heb. x. 19 f.). When, further, the Gentile centurion, on hearing the death-cry of Jesus, breaks out into the confession, "Verily, this man was God's Son," we are to see in this first Gentile confessor the representative of Gentile Christianity in general: in this confession of Jesus Christ as the Son of God the Divine voices at the Baptism and Transfiguration find an echo which is to resound throughout the world.[1] Again, when we read that a wealthy councillor, Joseph of Arimathæa, begged the body of Jesus from Pilate, and laid it in his own (the parallel accounts say "new") rock-hewn grave, the fact that this narrative is flanked on one side and the other by ideal scenes makes it natural to suppose that here also we are in the ideal realm of legend or allegory, the suggestion perhaps coming from the thought in Isa. liii. 12, that he who was reckoned with the transgressors (Mark xv. 28) should receive his portion with the great. The climax of these ideal closing scenes is formed by the story of the Resurrection, of which, however, only the first half is preserved to us in Mark, the narrative of the visit of the women to the grave, the appearance there of the angel, and the indication of Galilee as the place where the disciples should see the risen Jesus; with the flight of the terrified and trembling women

[1] *Cf.* Brandt, *Ev. Gesch.*, p. 266 ff. "The wording of the confession is not what a Gentile would have said in the given circumstances, since it presupposes Jewish-Christian monotheism. In this the Christian author betrays himself. It would have been better art to make the centurion say, "This is a god, or a favourite of the gods!" (p. 269).

from the open grave (xvi. 8) the genuine text ot Mark comes to an end. As this can hardly have been the original conclusion, while what follows is manifestly not genuine,[1] it is to be supposed that the original conclusion has been lost. Whether this was due to some mischance, or whether the Church allowed this conclusion of the earliest Gospel to fall away, because it no longer served the interests of her faith (as the statement in iii. 21 has been dropped in the later Gospels)—who can tell? Perhaps we may find a hint as to the genuine conclusion of Mark in the recently discovered fragment of the Gospel of Peter, which has in verse 57, exactly as in Mark xvi. 8, "the women fled (from the grave), filled with fear," but then, in 58–60, proceeds to narrate that the disciples, when the Feast was over, returned to their homes, full of trouble at all that had occurred; Peter, Andrew, and Levi, however, went with their nets to the sea (the Lake of Gennesareth). Here the fragment unfortunately breaks off, and leaves us again uncertain as to the remainder of the story, which presumably included an appearance of the risen Jesus to the three disciples mentioned. It is possible that

[1] Verses 9–20 were unknown to the earliest Greek Fathers, are wanting in the best MSS., and in others are at least marked as doubtful. Besides, their spuriousness is clear from internal evidence. The charge to the disciples in verse 7 is not obeyed in the sequel; instead, a series of appearances in Jerusalem is mentioned, which make the journey to Galilee, to see Jesus there, superfluous. Instead of the two Marys of verse 1, it is now only Mary Magdalene who is spoken of, and she is described in the same way in which she is designated earlier only in Luke. Finally, the appearances of Christ here brought together are obviously taken from the three other Gospels, and form, in fact, a kind of harmonistic abstract of the appearances.

there was a similar narrative in the lost conclusion of Mark. However that may be, the Gospel of Peter certainly agrees with Mark in ignoring any appearances of Jesus prior to the return of the disciples to Galilee; the older tradition which is represented by both excludes, therefore, the whole of the appearances reported by the later Gospels to the women, and to the disciples, at Jerusalem.[1]

[1] *Cf.* Brandt, *Ev. Gesch.*, p. 316; Holtzmann, *Komm.*, 3rd ed., p. 182; Harnack on the Gospel of Peter, in *Texte und Untersuchen*, ix. 2, 32.

THE GOSPEL OF MARK

CHAPTER III

ORIGIN AND DISTINCTIVE CHARACTERISTICS

WE have already, in our survey of the contents of Mark's Gospel, frequently had occasion to make the remark (and we shall find further confirmation of it in the sequel) that this Gospel, where it differs from the other Synoptics in parallel passages, can almost always lay claim to priority, and accordingly is to be regarded as the earliest of our canonical Gospels. Its early origin is indicated not only by the greater naturalness and historical probability of its general order of narration, but also, and more particularly, by certain traits which are peculiar to its presentation of the person of Jesus. He is here, as in the speeches in Acts, the Son of God in virtue of His reception of the Spirit at His baptism; it is with this that the Gospel story begins, not with the birth and childhood of Jesus. His mother and His brethren have no inkling of His higher vocation (iii. 20, 31). His miraculous power is not unlimited, but is conditioned by the faith of men (vi. 5 f.), and also works partly by natural means and gradual stages (vii. 32 f., viii. 23 ff.), and is therefore not wholly removed from the analogy of other miracle-workers of that period.

And like the power, so, too, the knowledge of Jesus appears not yet unlimited, for, according to xiii. 32, even the Son knows not the day and hour of the Parousia, but only the Father. Further, this Gospel is rich in minute touches which portray the human emotions of Jesus—displeasure and impatience, anger and love. Jesus was angry with the leper who interrupted Him in His work of teaching (i. 42); at the healing on the Sabbath (iii. 5) He looked round upon the censorious bystanders with anger, vexed at the hardness of their hearts; when the Pharisees asked for a sign (viii. 12), the want of understanding of "this generation" wrung from Him a sigh of dejection, and, immediately thereafter, the disciples' slowness of apprehension evoked an impatient complaint (verse 17), which was repeated soon after at the healing of the epileptic boy (ix. 19); when the disciples wished to turn the children away from Him, He was indignant with them, and He showed His love for the children by tenderly caressing them (x. 14 f.); on the young man who asked about the way of life He looked with a glance of affection (x. 21). In general, the softer traits, on which Luke lays special stress in his portrait of the Saviour of sinners, are left in the background, and so is the legalistic conservatism of Matthew's picture of Christ. The Marcan Christ is, above all, a heroic reformer, who, from the first, does not seek to avoid a conflict with the ruling authorities, but almost seems deliberately to provoke it; who does not shrink from a breach with His own family, but, in words of stern resolution, makes it decisive (iii. 31); who, after taking the critical resolve, bent His steps towards

Jerusalem prepared for battle, an object of astonishment and awe to the disciples who followed Him in fear and trembling (x. 32); who then, in Jerusalem, opens the campaign against the ruling powers by the revolutionary act of cleansing the Temple, the true significance of which can be recognised in Mark alone; who bluntly announces to the hierarchs their coming fall (xii. 9), and, by implication, defends His claim upon the Messianic sovereignty against the objections urged by the wisdom of the Scribes (according to the Marcan version of the question regarding "David's Son," xii. 35 ff.); who frankly and decisively acknowledges this claim before His judges, but, for the rest, meets all charges with the silence of a heroic resignation; who, finally, dies with a cry of despair upon His lips, feeling Himself abandoned by God—the truly human hero of the most awe-inspiring tragedy in the history of religion. In all this the reality of the historic Jesus and His reforming work is brought before our eyes with a distinctness unequalled in the other Evangelists. Renan[1] is wholly right in his verdict when he says: "The precision of detail, the originality, the picturesqueness and vividness of this first narrative, are never afterwards attained. A certain realism gives sometimes a rather hard and sometimes a bizarre effect, which the later evangelists have removed. But as an historical document Mark has a great advantage. The powerful impression which Jesus left behind Him is here preserved in its completeness; we see Him here in the reality of life and action."

The tradition of the Church ascribed this Gospel

[1] *Les Évangiles,* p. 116

to Mark, that is, indubitably, to the John Mark who is known to us from Acts, the Pauline Epistles, and the First Epistle of Peter. According to Acts xii. 12, his mother, Mary, lived in Jerusalem, and her house was the meeting-place of the young community. It was through Barnabas, whose nephew he was, according to Col. iv. 10, that he was brought into relations with Paul (Acts xii. 25). He then accompanied Paul and Barnabas on their first missionary journey, but left them during its course, for which reason Paul refused to take him with them on their second journey (xv. 37). Later, however, he seems to have been reconciled with Paul, for we find him again among Paul's companions in Col. iv. 10, Philem. 24; even summoned to Paul's side (in the probably genuine fragment of a letter which is preserved in 2 Tim. iv. 11), and that, moreover, with the honourable description that he is useful in the service of the gospel. On the other hand, however, the tradition of the Church made Mark the constant companion and interpreter of Peter. That is in harmony with the statement in Acts xii. 12, according to which Peter was well known in the house of Mark's mother, and with 1 Peter v. 13, where Mark is called the son, *i.e* the disciple, of Peter. As the "Babylon" from which this letter is dated probably means Rome, it has been suggested that we have here a confirmation of the tradition which makes Mark the companion and interpreter of Peter at Rome. But not only is the sojourn of Peter at Rome and his death there doubtful, but it is also most improbable that Peter was the author of this letter, as we shall see later. Equally problematical is the tradition that Mark, in composing his Gospel, followed Peter's sermons, as Papias asserts that he heard from John the Presbyter (according to Eusebius, *H.E.*, iii. 39). For it is inherently improbable, in a high degree, that the teaching of Peter in his discourses could have referred to all the details of the life of Jesus, His miracles, journeys, and controversies; the description of the missionary preaching of the Apostles given in Acts is quite different, and certainly much nearer to historical reality. To this, moreover, must be added that the tradition sets Mark in progressively closer and more definite relations to the authority of Peter the further removed it is from Apostolic times. According to Papias and Irenæus, it was only after the death of Peter that Mark wrote his Gospel from memory; according to Clement of Alexandria, it was in his lifetime, but without his co-operation; according to Eusebius, it was with the direct approval and, to a certain extent, with the ecclesiastical sanction of Peter; finally, according to Jerome, he wrote at Peter's dictation! "Obviously, men looked round for an Apostolic authority for the Second Gospel, and found it by first combining 1 Peter v. 13 with the supposed sojourn of Peter at Rome, and then by making the relation of the direct author to the indirect ever closer. A later tradition sought to attain the same end in another way, by making Mark, as well as Luke, one of the Seventy Disciples, in direct contradiction to the evidence of Papias (and to Luke i. 1)" (Holtzmann).

If, in view of this, we must hold the details of the tradition regarding the relation of Mark to Peter to be unhistorical, the question still remains whether it may not, nevertheless, contain a kernel of fact. When we observe with what surprising exactitude and vividness Mark's Gospel pictures the circumstances of Jesus' first appearance in Galilee, and then, again, of the closing days in Jerusalem, the conjecture is naturally suggested that this surprisingly detailed knowledge may be based on the direct tradition of the earliest disciples, and in particular on that of Peter—in the case of the story of the Passion we might even suppose it the report of an eye-witness, for the conjecture that the brief notice (xiv. 51) of the young man who fled, which is peculiar to Mark, refers to an experience of the author's own, has some claims to acceptance. At the same time, alongside of the possibility of a direct oral tradition communicated by Peter, we ought not to leave out of account the other possibility, that the author may have taken his material from a written source. This cannot, of course, have been one of our present canonical Gospels; so long as it was sought in this direction, the priority and originality of Mark indubitably held its ground. But that does not exclude the possibility of a source prior to the canonical Gospels. That there must have been another source besides Mark from which Matthew and Luke derived that part of their common material which is not in Mark, is in any case certain. The question naturally arises whether, perhaps, the same source which must be assumed in the case of Matthew and Luke was also available for Mark, so that his Gospel would be, in that case, only the earliest Greek redaction which has come down to us of an older original Aramaic

Gospel? This question is still the subject of controversy; the answer to it depends mainly upon exact philological investigation of the relation of our Greek text to the Aramaic, and on this point the views of the linguistic experts are up to the present somewhat divergent. At the same time, we may draw attention to one or two points which seem to favour the hypothesis of a documentary, and, moreover, of an Aramaic, source for the Gospel of Mark. Among these are, in the first place, the frequent occurrence of Aramaic words in this Gospel,[1] which is most simply explained on the assumption of an Aramaic source. Further, it is significant that the expression "the Son of Man" is, in this Gospel only, twice found in the sense which its Aramaic use suggests = man in general (ii. 10 and 28; *cf.* also iii. 28, "the sons of men"); the Messianic significance is confined, so far as this Gospel is concerned, to the apocalyptic portions of the second part, which are influenced by dogmatic and apologetic considerations, whereas in the later Gospels this prevails from the first as the sole significance. Further, in at least a few cases[2] the conjecture that a misunderstanding

[1] Βοανηργές, iii. 17; *ταλιθὰ κούμ*, v. 41; *κορβᾶν*, vii. 11; *ἐφφαθά*, vii. 34; *ἀββᾶ*, xiv. 36—here only in the Gospels; ἐλωΐ, ἐλωΐ, *λαμὰ σαβαχθανεί*, xv. 34.

[2] On v. 10 and x. 38, *cf.* above, pp. 21 and 50. The phrases, too, δύο δύο (vi. 7), *συμπόσια συμπόσια* (vi. 39 f.), εἷς κατὰ εἷς (xiv. 19), *μιᾷ τῶν σαββάτων* (xvi. 2), are distinctly Aramaic, as Wellhausen remarks (*Skizzen und Vorarbeiten*, vi. 188 ff.). He sums up his investigation in a statement which deserves close attention: "The traces of the Aramaic originals of the Gospels have been progressively diminished and obliterated by continual stylistic correction, but they have not been entirely destroyed; and the vestiges which remain speak clearly enough."

of the Aramaic underlies the Greek text has much probability. In connection with these observations, too, the generally Hebraising character of the language with its simple paratactic structure, which in itself would not be surprising in a Palestinian writer who was only moderately versed in the Greek idiom, takes on a greater significance. The hypothesis that he had a written source to follow in addition to oral tradition, seems also to be favoured by the doublets — the two stories of stilling the storm (iv. 36 ff. and vi. 45), and the two stories of feeding the multitude (vi. 35 ff. and viii. 1 ff.)—for it is clear that these are only variants of the same narrative, which must therefore have come to the author from more than one source. Finally, we have to take into account the relation of the apocalyptic discourse in Mark xiii. to that of Matt. xxiv. Comparing Mark xiii. 14 ff. with Matt. xxiv. 15 ff., it is unmistakably evident that Matthew has preserved the more original form (see further upon this point below). In this passage at least, therefore, Mark must have used a written source which was still accessible when the Gospel of Matthew was written. Could this have been only a fly-sheet containing an apocalyptic discourse, and have been preserved so long purely for its own sake? Is it not much more probable that an apocalypse belonging to the time of the Jewish war, which can be recognised in those passages, was from the first worked up together with the eschatological discourses preserved by the tradition of the Christian community, and came into the hands of our Evangelists in this form only? On the latter assumption it follows that a Gospel which contained the apocalyptic discourse of Mark xiii. (= Matt. xxiv.) must have been used even by Mark. In view of all these considerations, there is a preponderant probability in favour of the existence of an Aramaic Gospel prior to Mark's Gospel, which was used as a common source by him and the later Evangelists. But if this is the case, the question arises how we are to explain the fact that Mark has omitted so much of this original Gospel which Luke and Matthew have inserted? To this we can only answer that he seems to have been guided in his choice of material by his own and his readers' interests. He wrote for Gentile Christians, and he desired to confirm them in the conviction that Jesus of Nazareth, in spite of His rejection by the Jews, had been proved by God, by means of signs and wonders of all kinds, especially by the miracles at the Baptism, the Transfiguration, and the Resurrection, to be the heavenly Messiah and Son of God (Rom. i. 4); and that by His victorious struggle with the Jewish hierarchical and ritual systems He had set up in the place of the old material temple a new and super-sensible one in the community of the believers in Christ, and had established a new covenant through His blood which He shed for many (x. 45, xiv. 24, 58: *cf.* Rom. x. 4; 2 Cor. iii. 6 ff., v. 17 ff.). It is the fundamental thought of the Pauline gospel, that Christ, as the Son of God in virtue of the Spirit of Holiness, is the end of the Law for all who believe, which our Evangelist desires to illustrate by means of a selection of the doings and sayings of Jesus. And it is undeniable that his selection is admirably adapted to this end In the first place, the remarkable and numerous collection of miracle-stories is thoroughly suited to the taste and the needs of Gentile readers, who saw by preference in just such imposing miracles as these, signs which inspired faith in the Divine mission and dignity of the Lord Christ. Of the discourses of Jesus, he selects those which centre round His struggle with the hierarchs and legalists, whereas those that have to do with the inner life of the Christian community are more sparingly used, while those, finally, which maintain a conservative attitude towards the Jewish law and Jewish national aspirations are carefully suppressed. The very fact that Mark used as one of his sources this Aramaic Gospel, which, to judge from Matthew, certainly contained passages of this kind—and it seems very probable that he did so—makes his anti-Jewish choice of the material of the discourses the more remarkable a proof of the Pauline Gentile-Christian spirit and aim which inspired the composition of his Gospel. We have noticed, moreover, direct allusions to specifically Pauline methods of thought and expression—we may recall, for instance, the phrases of the first sermon of Jesus, "The time is fulfilled, and the kingdom of God is at hand; repent ye, and believe the gospel" (i. 15; *cf.* Gal. iv. 4); the pessimistic and predestinarian version of the aim of the parables (iv. 12 ff.; *cf.* Rom. xi. 8); the various Pauline echoes in the exhortations which followed on the first announcement of the Passion (viii. 34; see p. 38); the story of the Transfiguration (ix. 2 ff.), in the Marcan version of which we recognised a running commentary on the Pauline thoughts of 2 Cor. iii.; and finally the two passages (x. 45 and xiv. 24) in which the Pauline doctrine of the atoning significance of the death of Christ seems to be introduced into the gospel story for the first time (pp. 52, 75). In the face of all these unambiguous indications, it is difficult to understand how the assumption of Pauline influence in the Gospel according to Mark can be described as an arbitrary and absurd hypothesis.

As regards the author of the Gospel, we have found in the preceding investigation no reason to doubt the correctness of the Church tradition of the authorship of John Mark. On the contrary, his dual relationship to Peter on the one hand and Paul on the other fits exactly the author of a Gospel in which the oral and written traditions of the primitive community are worked up together under the guidance of the ideas associated with Pauline Gentile Christianity. The time of writing is most probably to be placed in the decade following the destruction of Jerusalem. For the place of writing, Rome is sometimes suggested and sometimes Alexandria: the frequent use of Latinisms is in favour of its having been addressed to Roman readers; it is in any case to be assumed that the readers were Gentiles, since it seemed necessary to the author to explain Jewish customs.

On the question whether we have in the canonical Gospel of Mark the original writing of the author or a redaction by a later hand, Renan very justly remarks: "The Gospel of Mark offers the appearance of being a complete unity, and, setting aside certain details in which the manuscripts differ, and those little retouchings which the Christian writings almost without exception have undergone, it seems not to have received any considerable expansion since it was first composed. The characteristic feature of the gospel was, from the first, the absence of a genealogy and story of the childhood—if there was any gap which cried aloud to be filled, in the interest of Catholic readers, it was this, and yet men refrained from undertaking to fill it. Many other peculiarities too, which from the apologetic point of view were unacceptable, were not removed. Only the account of the Resurrection shows evident traces of mutilation. The best manuscripts break off after xvi. 8, ἐφοβοῦντο γάρ. It is hardly to be supposed that the original text concluded in so abrupt a fashion. Probably there followed something which conflicted with the traditional representation. That was removed, and then, later, the conclusion was replaced by various versions, of which none had sufficient authority to oust the others."[1] This hypothesis certainly seems to me more probable than that which has lately been advanced, viz., that Mark was prevented by some accident from finishing his work—after all, it is only a matter of a few verses.

[1] *Les Évangiles*, p. 120.

THE GOSPEL OF LUKE

CHAPTER IV

The Stories of the Birth and Childhood
(Luke i. and ii.)

The author (we may provisionally call him Luke) prefaces his work, according to the usual practice of Greek authors of his day,[1] with an introduction written in classical Greek, and to the following effect: "Seeing that many have endeavoured to compose a narrative of the events which have come to pass among us, as they have been handed down to us by those who from the beginning were eye-witnesses, and servants of the word, I have resolved that I also, after tracing the course of events from the beginning, would draw up for you, most excellent Theophilus, an orderly narrative, in order that you might have a firm conviction regarding those subjects on which you have received instruction." From this introduction we infer (1) that the author had not been himself an eye-witness

[1] There is, between the introductions of Josephus to his *History of the Jewish War* and to the first and second books of his polemic against Apion, and the introductions which Luke prefixes to the Gospel and the Acts, so marked an affinity in thought, phraseology, and wording, that the direct influence of these writings upon Luke is not to be doubted. *Cf.* Krenkel, *Josephus und Lukas*, pp. 50–60 and 145.

of the events of the gospel history, but knew them only by the report of others; (2) that already, before his time, many had embodied the evangelical material in written form, but that these, also, had not themselves been eye-witnesses, but had drawn only upon (oral) tradition derived from those who had been so; (3) that Luke hoped to surpass his predecessors by striving after greater completeness and exactitude, and a more orderly arrangement of the narratives; (4) that in so doing he was aiming at the practical end of helping to confirm his Gentile-Christian readers, of whom we must regard Theophilus as the representative, in the certainty of their faith.

Luke desires to set forth all things in order "from the very beginning," as he tells us in his preface. Accordingly, the baptism of John, which serves Mark as his point of departure, does not suffice him. He prefixes a preliminary narrative regarding the birth of the Baptist, and of Jesus, in order to exhibit the significance of each, and their relation to one another, as already, at and before their earthly appearance, grounded in the Divine fore-ordination. In the story of the birth of John the particulars are taken throughout from Old Testament types—in fact, from the births of Isaac, Samson, and Samuel. As these three heroes of Hebrew legend and history were born to their aged parents after many years of childless marriage, through the special grace of God, and were thus marked out from the first as notable men of God, so it was in the case of John the Baptist. As the birth of Samson was announced to his mother by the appearance of an angel or "man of God" of awe-inspiring aspect (Judges xiii. 3, 6), and as the promise of motherhood was given to Hannah in answer to her prayers (1 Sam. i.), so the birth of a son in answer to his prayers was announced to Zacharias by the angel Gabriel (the name means "Man of God"), whose appearance struck him with fear (Luke i. 12–20). And as in Isaac's case the name, and in Samson's his vocation to be an ascetic, dedicated to God, (Nazirite), and an instrument of Divine deeds of deliverance for Israel, were announced at the time of the promise of their births, so it was also at the promise of the birth of John the Baptist; and, indeed, in words which are taken almost exactly from its historical pattern in Judges xiii., except that the prediction in regard to Samson that he should be dedicated to God from his mother's womb here takes the higher form that John should be filled with the Holy Spirit from his mother's womb. Again, the oracle which announced the destiny of Samson to be the political deliverer of Israel here takes the form (with allusion to Malachi iii. 1 ff.) that John, in the spirit and power of Elias, would convert the people, and prepare them for the coming of the Lord to deliver them—an announcement by which his mission as the Fore-runner, to prepare the way for the Messiah, is definitely determined in advance. The doubt of Zacharias and the punishment of it by temporary dumbness recall the similar doubt of Sara and the rebuke which she received. "The miraculous character of this story of the birth of the Baptist contrasts significantly with the absence of miracle in his whole work, to which John x. 41 bears witness. This birth-story seems, therefore, to be merely the reflection of another, to which the Evangelist now passes on" (Holtzmann).

In the sixth month after the events just referred to, as Luke proceeds to narrate, the same angel Gabriel was sent by God to Nazareth in Galilee, to a virgin named Mary who was betrothed to a man named Joseph, a descendant of the house of David. To the maiden, who was alarmed at the appearance and salutation of the angel, Gabriel says, "Fear not, for thou hast found favour with God, and, behold, thou shalt conceive, and shalt bear a son, and shalt call his name Jesus. And he shall be great, and shall be called the Son of the Highest; and God the Lord shall give unto him the throne of his father David; and he shall rule over the house of Jacob for ever, and of his kingdom there shall be no end." This promise, with its allusions to Old Testament prophecies (2 Sam. vii. 13 ff.; Isa. ix. 5 f.), has reference, therefore, to the Messianic kingship of Jesus over the house of Jacob, that is to say, the Jewish people, and it is only in the sense of a title of the theocratic king (as in 2 Sam. vii.) that the promise here, "he shall be called a Son of the Highest," can be intended. Now we should certainly find it quite intelligible that at the prophecy of so great a destiny for her future son, Mary, the child of humble parents in an obscure Galilæan village, should be greatly astonished; we are therefore the more surprised by the sequel (verse 34 f.), where the betrothed maiden shows no astonishment at the exalted destiny of the son who was to be expected from her approaching marriage, but is astonished, rather, that she shall have a son, seeing that she "knows not a man." There is no reason in what precedes for this question (verse 34), and it can only be explained as an abrupt introduction to the new prophecy, entirely disparate from the foregoing, which next appears (verse 35): "The Holy Spirit shall come upon thee, and the power of the Highest shall overshadow thee, therefore that holy being which shall be born of thee shall be called the Son of God." What is promised here is no longer, as in verse 32, that the son who is to be expected in the course of nature from the approaching marriage of Mary with Joseph should be the theocratic "Son of God," *i.e.* the Messianic king, but that, while still a virgin, she should become in a supernatural fashion, by the miraculous power of the Holy Spirit, the mother of a son who, for that very reason, should be called the Son of God in a wholly unique, supernatural, physico-metaphysical sense. The question, however, necessarily presents itself whether this new thought, the promise of the supernatural Son of God in verse 35, can have stood in connection with what immediately precedes and follows in the original document?

In reference to this question, we have to take into account the following considerations. In the story of the childhood there is repeated mention of the parents and of the father of Jesus (Joseph) (ii. 27, 33, 41, 48), in such a way that, were it not for i. 34 f., we should not suppose that there had been anything unusual in the human parentage of Jesus. In ii. 33 we are told of the surprise of the parents of Jesus at the prophecy of Simeon; in ii. 50 their failure to understand the words of their son is spoken of in a fashion which goes almost as far to exclude the possibility that Mary knew anything of a supernatural origin of her son as does her supposition (Mark iii. 21) that her son was beside himself. The genealogy in Luke iii. 23 ff. and Matt. i. originally implied the fatherhood of Joseph—the words "as was supposed," which cut the genealogical thread at the decisive point, are a later interpolation, designed in the interests of the same dogmatic end as the alteration of the original reading in Matt. i. 16 (see below). Especially significant is the story of the baptism in iii. 22, where the heavenly voice, according to the certainly original reading (preserved in Cod. D), took the form, "Thou art my Son, this day have I begotten thee." Here, therefore, it is the baptism which is thought of as the moment in which Jesus is made the Son of God by the communication of the Divine Spirit. He who wrote this narrative cannot also have thought of the Divine Sonship of Jesus as mediated by the Holy Spirit, and cannot, therefore, have written the two verses i. 34, 35. Similarly, we find in the Acts of the Apostles, written by the same author, many allusions, indeed, to the anointing of Jesus with the Spirit at His baptism, but not a single reference to His supernatural origin. The fact that this is elsewhere without exception the case in both the Lucan writings leads, in my belief, to the inevitable conclusion that the Gospel of Luke originally contained no story of the supernatural origin of Jesus, but that this story arose later and was interpolated into the text by the addition of verses i. 34 f. and of the words ὡς ἐνομίζετο in iii. 23.[1] Of the motives which

[1] Compare the able discussion of this question by Hillmann in his essay "die Kindheitsgeschichte nach Lukas" (*Jahrb. f. prot. Theol.*, 1891); also Harnack, *neutest. Zeitschr.*, 1901, 53 f.

gave rise to this legend we shall have to speak later.

Luke then (i. 39 ff.) brings together these two so highly honoured mothers, in order, by the reverential greeting addressed to the mother of the Messiah by her elder friend, to typify the subordination of John to Jesus, which Matthew has exhibited in a similar way at the first meeting of the men themselves (iii. 14). This occasion is immediately used by Luke in order to express, through Mary, as the typical representative of believing Israel, the hope of redemption which had always been the soul of the religion of this people, and at the same time to show how spiritually gifted was the mother from whom, according to the Divine appointment, the highest religious life of mankind should spring. The model for Mary's song of praise was taken by the Evangelist from the song of Hannah, the mother of Samuel (1 Sam. ii. 1–10), whose history had also hovered before his mind when writing of the announcement of the birth of John the Baptist. One reason why this pattern may have seemed to him especially suitable was that it gave strong expression to an idea with which he was peculiarly in sympathy—the offer of salvation to the poor and lowly. Yet another hymn is put by Luke into the mouth of Zacharias the father of John, on the occasion of the birth and naming of the child (i. 67–79); of this, too, the burden is the prophetic hope of the redemption of Israel in its political as well as in its ethico-religious aspect, and the preparation for the fulfilment of it by John as the Fore-runner of the Lord. Thus the Evangelist, beginning at the very beginning, leads on through the fore-court of the faith and hope of Israel to the manifestation of the Saviour.

In chapter ii. is recounted the birth of the Messianic child, which has been so solemnly announced in the preceding chapter. That the Son of David should be born in David's town of Bethlehem seems to be demanded as appropriate to His destiny as theocratic king. But what reason could be assigned for this, when it was notorious that the home of Jesus was far away from Bethlehem of Judæa, in Galilæan Nazareth, where also the Evangelist had represented the mother of Jesus as dwelling at the time of the Annunciation (i. 26)? In order, in despite of this fact, to make the birth of Jesus occur in Bethlehem, the Evangelist had to make the mother of Jesus travel before his birth to the Davidic town of Bethlehem, and it was important, therefore, to find an historical occasion for this journey. Here our author's acquaintance with the history of the time came to his aid; it was not, however, sufficiently thorough to save him from chronological error, but went just far enough to enable him to make a free use of well-known historical circumstances in the interest of his own philosophy of history. Thus, he knew of a census which the Syrian Governor, Publius Sulpicius Quirinius, carried out in Palestine when it was made a tribute-paying Roman province—a proceeding which, as the first of its kind in Palestine had caused ill-feeling among the Jews and had provoked the rising of Judas of Galilee, and therefore would doubtless still be remembered in Jewish circles in the time of the Evangelist (*cf.* Acts v. 37). In this historical event Luke found a welcome motive to explain the journey of Mary with Joseph, her betrothed, to David's city of Bethlehem, and at the same time an opportunity to bring out clearly the interconnection of the birth-story of Jesus the Saviour of the world with the great world-policy of the Emperor Augustus. It was certainly an ingenious idea, and reflects the greatest credit upon the literary skill of the Evangelist. Only, we must not judge his skilful "history-with-a-purpose" by the strict standard of historical reality. For with this the Lucan narrative comes, at several points, into direct conflict. The census of Quirinius took place at least six, according to another reckoning, ten, years after the birth of Jesus, and has therefore been ante-dated by Luke with the object of supplying a motive for the journey of Mary to Bethlehem; moreover, the census was for Palestine only, not for the whole (Roman) world. Further, even supposing that this census would fit in point of time, it could not really have caused the journey of Mary and Joseph to Bethlehem, since the Roman Government always, as might have been expected, had the enrolment of the population which was laid under tribute made at the houses of the individual citizens, never cited them to present themselves at their ancestral town. Finally, that this journey to the city of David had to be made not only by Joseph, who alone could be concerned by the taxing, but also by Mary his betrothed, especially in the difficult circumstances in which she then was—that fills the measure of improbability to the height of actual impossibility. That which, however, purely from the historical point of view would be inexplicable, becomes completely explicable when we take into account the literary purpose of Luke, to supply an explanation of the birth of Jesus at Bethlehem, and to do so, moreover, by indicating a causal connection between it and a well-known historical event such as the census of Quirinius.

That a writer of the sensibility and imagination of Luke should glorify the birth of Jesus by poetically ideal pictures, will seem natural enough to everyone. The contrast between outward humility and spiritual greatness which runs through the whole life of Jesus, as through that of the community which He founded, is symbolised in the story of His birth by the contrast of the miserable stable, in the manger of which the child found His first resting-place, with the splendour of the heavenly glory which shone over the shepherds (in accordance with Isa. lx. 1 ff.), and of the heavenly hosts who proclaimed joy for all, glory to God in the highest, and peace for men of good will, as a consequence of the birth of the Saviour. The representation, too, that it was poor shepherds who were permitted to be the first to hear these good tidings and to be the first to offer their worship to the Saviour is a skilful touch which is in harmony not merely with the traditional rôle which shepherds play in the history and legends of Israel (Patriarchs, Moses, David, Amos), as of other peoples, but also with the especial sympathy of Luke for the poor and lowly, as the heirs by preference of the Divine promises.

Eight days after the birth of Jesus there took place the circumcision, and subsequently, at the time appointed by the Law, the presentation of the child in the Temple at Jerusalem. On this occasion it happened that a godly man of prophetic gifts, named

Simeon, to whom it had been revealed that he should not see death until he had seen the Lord's Christ, came to the Temple, impelled by the Holy Spirit, just as the parents of Jesus brought in the child. He took Him in his arms, blessed God, and said, "Now lettest thou thy servant depart, O Lord, according to thy word, in peace; for mine eyes have seen the salvation which thou hast prepared before the face of all peoples, a light to lighten the Gentiles, and the glory of thy people Israel!" The parents were astonished at the words; and Simeon blessed them and, addressing the mother, said, "Behold, this child is set for the fall and rising again of many in Israel, and for a sign that shall be spoken against—yea, a sword shall pierce through thine own soul also—that the thoughts of many hearts may be revealed." An aged prophetess also, named Anna, gave thanks to God, and spoke of the child to all who waited for the redemption of Jerusalem.

That for this whole series of pictures of the childhood the author cannot have had historical materials before him, is self-evident. But that does not mean that he composed them quite freely, but that he worked up for his purpose legends which had come to him from various quarters, the origin of which reaches back far into pre-Christian times, and which perhaps belong to the common stock of western Asiatic folk-lore, for we find the same legends, with a remarkable correspondence in some of the details, worked up in the story of the childhood of the Indian saviour, Gautama Buddha.[1] He, too,

[1] On this point reference should be made to the very thorough discussion of these parallels, and of others which will be mentioned

is miraculously born of the virgin Queen, Maya, into whose immaculate body the heavenly light-essence of Buddha entered. At his birth, too, heavenly spirits appeared, who sang the following hymn: "A wonderful, incomparable hero is born; Saviour of the world, full of compassion, to-day thou extendest thy good-will to all the ends of the earth! Let joy and peace come to all creatures, that they may be still, lords of themselves and happy!" He, too, is brought by his mother to the temple to perform the legal usages, and there they are met by the aged hermit Asita, who had been impelled by a presentiment to come down from the Himalayas. He prophesied that this child would be Buddha, the deliverer from all evils, and should lead men to freedom, light, and immortality; then he wept for sorrow that he himself would not live to see the coming time of deliverance (note the contrast between this and the Christian version, in which the pious seer passes away in peace, because he has seen in faith the

later, in the writings of Rudolf Seydel, *Das Evangelium von Jesu in seinem Verhältniss zur Buddhasage* (1882) and *Die Buddhalegende und das Leben Jesu* (second edition by Martin Seydel, 1897), where further information will be found regarding the sources. Seydel believes that he is able to prove a direct dependence in many points of the Christian upon the Indian legend, *e.g.* in regard to the presentation in the Temple, the reasons for which are more natural in the Indian narrative than in the Lucan, since in Judaism the presentation of children in the Temple was not demanded by the Law, nor can it be shown to have been a custom. At the same time I should like to remark, with reference to all these parallels, that a direct dependence of the one on the other does not seem to be a necessary assumption, since it is much more probable that ancient and widely current myths formed the *common source* from which the materials were taken for the formation of Indian as well as Christian legend.

coming of the time of salvation). These prophecies of the seer Asita are followed by further blessings from aged women, and the narrative closes with a brief statement of the daily advance of the royal child in mental and spiritual excellence, and in physical beauty and strength—just such as Luke makes in regard to Jesus (ii. 40 and 52).

The conclusion of this preliminary history is formed by the story of the twelve-year-old Jesus in the Temple (ii. 41–52), in which the art of the Evangelist has blended together elements of very various origin into a so well-conceived whole that most readers even now take it for actual history. In the first place, the occasion for the journey of Jesus to Jerusalem was suggested by the story of the childhood of Samuel, who was in a similar way brought in early boyhood by his mother to the Temple, and there became aware of his high vocation. Just as it is there narrated of Samuel's parents that they journeyed yearly to Shiloh in order to make an offering to Jahweh, so it is here of the parents of Jesus that they went up yearly to Jerusalem to the Feast of the Passover. The remark, too, which Luke makes at two different points, before and after the story of this visit to the Temple (ii. 40 and 52), regarding the bodily and spiritual growth of Jesus is couched in a very similar form to that regarding Samuel in 1 Sam. ii. 26: "The boy grew on, and was in favour with God and man." In the further course of the story we have to distinguish three different elements: (1) Jesus' sitting among the teachers in the Temple; (2) the losing of the child; (3) His self-justification in answer to His mother.

For each of these elements parallels can be produced in which the narrator may have found the pattern and suggestion of his composition. With the sitting of Jesus in the Temple among the teachers may be compared what Josephus tells us regarding himself in his autobiography (chap. ii.); as a boy of only fourteen, he distinguished himself above all his contemporaries by his insight, and was praised by all for his love of knowledge, since the chief-priests and principal men of the town constantly came together in order to get accurate information from him regarding the problems of the Law. Here the vain Josephus represents himself as a youthful teacher, whereas in the Lucan narrative the meaning is doubtless only that the boy Jesus was desirous of learning from the teachers in the Temple, a difference which only emphasises the close affinity in point of subject-matter between the two stories.[1] That the boy Jesus was lost by His parents owing to His zeal for learning is a further and by no means necessarily connected trait, the suggestion for which must be sought elsewhere, in the legends of the East and of the West. In the story of Buddha[2] it is told how, on the festival of the dedication of ploughs, as all the people were streaming out to see the great spectacle, when the king himself, with a golden plough, drew the first furrow, the boy Gautama was lost, and was anxiously sought by his friends, until at length he was found under a sacred tree, where he sat wrapt in contemplation in the circle of wise and holy men. Suetonius tells of Augustus that when he was a little infant he

[1] Krenkel, *Josephus und Lukas*, p. 81 ff.

[2] Sacred Books, xix. 48 f.; *cp.* Seydel, *Buddhalegende*, 25.

one day disappeared from his cradle, and after long search was found in the highest part of the house, lying towards the sunrise, the region of his father Apollo.[1] Amid all their differences, these legends have this in common with the Lucan narrative, that the boy, conscious, as it were, in anticipation of his high vocation, withdraws himself from his ordinary surroundings, is anxiously sought, and is at length found in a situation which corresponds to his mysterious relationship to a higher world and his destiny to higher ends. To this must be added, in the case of the Buddha-legend, the special parallels in regard to the occasion (a high festival) and in the surroundings in which the boy is found (circle of teachers, wise and holy men). Can all this be mere chance? Finally, however, the Evangelist adds yet another significant trait, in a sense the point of the whole, and for this he finds the suggestion, not in extraneous legends, but in the historical material of the gospel tradition. In Mark iii. 21, 31 f., he read that the mother and the brethren of Jesus had desired to come to Him in order to take Him away from the circle of His disciples, thinking that He was out of His mind. Jesus, however, refused to see them, saying, "Who is my mother, and who are my brethren?" Then, looking round upon His disciples, He said, "Behold my mother and my brethren!" In this form the narrative appeared unacceptable to Luke, since he was unwilling to attribute to the highly favoured mother so grave an error (ὅτι ἐξέστη). He therefore alters the time and the motive of the search. Instead of seeking, as in Mark iii. 32 ("Behold, thy mother and

[1] *Octavius*, xciv.

thy brethren are without seeking thee "), her grown-up Son, with the mistaken purpose of snatching Him away from His life-work, in Luke the anxious mother seeks her boy with the best intentions, and addresses to Him the deserved reproach, "My child, how couldst thou so deal with us? Behold, thy father and I have sought thee sorrowing." But although His mother's seeking of Him has here a quite different motive from that in Mark, there follows here, just as there, an answer from her Son in which the contrast of His higher religious consciousness with common human opinion comes to decisive expression: "Why seek ye me? Knew ye not that I must be in the things of my Father?" The implied rebuke of the limited understanding of the parents, which in a real history would be actually offensive, finds a simple explanation in the fact that it is the Lucan counterpart of that rebuff which Jesus, according to Mark iii. 33, no doubt administered, but in quite different circumstances, and with very different cause. Then, too, the further remark (Luke ii. 50), that the parents of Jesus did not understand the saying, betrays also the influence of the Marcan account of the mistake of Jesus' friends—of the contradiction between this remark and the story of the miraculous birth we have already spoken.

THE GOSPEL OF LUKE

CHAPTER V

From the Appearance of the Baptist to the Close of Jesus' Work in Galilee

(Luke iii. 1–ix. 50)

Whereas chapters i. and ii. contained only legendary stories of the childhood, for which we need not seek any historical background, in chap iii., with the appearance of the Baptist we find a firm historical foothold. At the outset there is a sixfold determination of the time of the appearance of the Baptist: (1) the fifteenth year of the Emperor Tiberius, (2) the proconsulship of Pontius Pilate in Judæa, (3) the rule of Herod the Tetrarch in Galilee, (4) that of his brother Philip in Ituræa and Trachonitis, (5) the rule of Lysanias in Abelene, (6) the high-priesthood of Annas and Caiaphas. The mention of Lysanias is an anachronism, since the only known prince of this name died in the year 36 B.C. (Josephus, *Ant.*, xv. 4. 1), and the occurrence of a later Lysanias is only an inference from this passage in Luke. Again, the mention of the two high-priests, Annas and Caiaphas, is an error, since there was always only one ruling high-priest, and during the proconsulship of Pilate Caiaphas alone held this office. Annas had held it earlier, and was still held in high respect in the time of his successors. Luke may have known his name from tradition, and have been led to set him alongside of Caiaphas by the influence of Josephus, since the latter frequently speaks of several, and especially of two, high-priests in conjunction.[1]

The "baptism of repentance" which Mark tells us that John proclaimed becomes in Luke a definite preaching of repentance, addressed first to the people in general, and then more especially to the publicans and soldiers. That the latter, who were for the most part, if not exclusively, heathen, should have crowded to the Messianic baptism of repentance is hardly probable, and is doubtless to be ascribed to the friendly attitude towards soldiers which Luke constantly displays in both his writings—in the case of the centurion of Capernaum in vii. 2 ff., in the case of the centurion Cornelius at Cæsaræa in Acts x., and the centurion Julius in Acts xxvii. The exhortations which he represents the preacher of repentance as addressing to the soldiers remind one very much of similar exhortations which frequently occur in Josephus (*B.J.*, ii. 20. 7; *Vit.* xlvii.). Another feature of this account which is peculiar to Luke is the remark that the people were in expectation, and were wondering whether John might not be the Messiah. Here, as often elsewhere, he desires to supply a definite occasion for a saying which had been preserved by tradition (iii. 16). The announcement, recorded by Mark, of "one stronger than he" who should come after John and should baptize with the Holy Spirit, is expanded by a reference to the decisive judgment of the Messiah, in

[1] Krenkel, *Josephus und Lukas,* p. 98 f.

which the chaff shall be separated from the wheat and burned with unquenchable fire; and to this the expression is perhaps also to be referred, "He shall baptize you with the Holy Spirit and with fire," though it is possible to see in this an allusion to the descent of the Spirit at Pentecost in the appearance of flames of fire (Acts ii. 3).

In the narrative of the baptism of Jesus by John, Luke, with the epic realism which is constantly to be observed in him, represents the Holy Spirit as descending "in bodily shape" upon Jesus. The voice from heaven, however, according to the doubtless original reading which has been preserved in Cod. D, runs exactly as in Ps. ii., "Thou art my Son; this day have I begotten thee." This clearly expresses the significance of the miracle at the baptism for the consciousness of the earliest Christianity—by the communication of the Holy Spirit at the baptism, Jesus was exalted to be the Son of God in the sense of Messiah; and with this agrees also the saying in Acts x. 38, that God anointed Jesus with the Holy Spirit and with power, which can only be referred to His dedication to His Messianic vocation at His baptism. According to this older view, therefore, Jesus was not the Son of God as being supernaturally begotten by the Spirit of God, for such an one would not have needed a further special communication of the Spirit at His baptism, and it could not first on this occasion have been declared to Him, "Thou art my Son; *this day* have I begotten thee." It was just on account of this discrepancy with the later legend of the miraculous birth that the necessity was early felt of altering the original wording of the voice at the baptism to the form which we find in the traditional reading, but which derives no confirmation from the oldest Patristic quotations (Justin, Clem. Al., Constit. Ap.).[1]

At the first appearance of Jesus, Luke inserts a genealogical table which, through seventy-seven steps (reckoning in the first and the last), traces the lineage of Jesus through David and Abraham to Adam, and ultimately to God. By so doing he attains the double purpose of showing Jesus to be not only the Son of David (Rom. i. 3), but also the "last Adam" (1 Cor. xv. 45) and the anti-type of the first Adam (Rom. v. 14). On the historicity of the names it is not possible to lay much stress, since Luke, probably from dislike of the historical Davidic dynasty, with its many unworthy kings, turns aside from the main line of descent, and follows an obscure collateral branch of the royal house. Moreover, it is not to be overlooked that there is a serious break at the very beginning of the list which really robs the genealogy of all significance. If Jesus was only apparently (ὡς ἐνομίζετο) a son of Joseph, the descendant of David, then the whole aim of the genealogy would be rendered nugatory. These two words, therefore, cannot originally have stood in the text of this genealogy; they are evidently an addition by the same hand which made the original story of the birth into a supernatural one (see above on i. 34 f.), and therefore wished to correct the assertion of the fatherhood of Joseph. The wholly different genealogy which Matthew gives shows, moreover, that many attempts were made in the earliest

[1] *Cf. Zahn. Einleitung*, ii. 356 f.

community to confirm the Messianic claims of Jesus by gathering together the names of legendary ancestors. How far removed an apologetic of that kind was from the mind of Jesus, any one may recognise who has understood the meaning of Mark xii. 35–37.

A further piece of early Christian apologetic is to be found in the detailed story of the Temptation which Matthew and Luke attach to the short notice in Mark i. 12 f. in such a way that the juncture, though skilfully made, is still clearly perceptible. For while Luke, like Mark, says that Jesus "was driven about by the might of the Spirit in the wilderness, being forty days tempted by the devil," he then adds an account of three temptations which took place, not in the course of these forty days, but only after the termination of them, the first temptation being caused by the forty-days' fast of Jesus. Mark says nothing of this; on the contrary, his words, "the angels ministered to him," are to be understood in the sense that they provided Jesus with miraculous nutriment, just as the Israelites in the desert were fed with the miraculous manna, and Elijah with the bread which the ravens brought. This older form of the legend rested on the presupposition that the miraculous help which an Elijah experienced could not have been wanting in the case of Jesus the Messiah. But how was this presupposition to be reconciled with the fact that Jesus had lived, not in Messianic splendour, but in humility, poverty, and renunciation, and that His followers were for the most part poor men, who had to struggle anxiously for their livelihood? It can well be understood that this contrast of the actual reality with the assumed power of working miracles and the glory appropriate to a Messiah might easily become a ground of doubt to Jewish Christians, and be used by opponents as a reason for refusing to believe in the Messianic claims of Jesus. This objection the Evangelist (whether Luke or one of his "many" predecessors) has put into the mouth of the devil in the form of the challenge "If thou be the Son of God, command this stone that it be made bread." Jesus answers by quoting the words of Deut. viii. 3, "Man shall not live by bread alone"—meaning, in this connection, "the idea that the Messiah is to provide earthly benefits is based on a low and unspiritual way of thinking." The second time, the devil takes Jesus "up"—whether upon a mountain or into the air is not stated—and shows Him all the kingdoms of the world in a moment, and tells Him that all this power and glory shall be His if He will worship him. Jesus repels him with the words of Deut. vi. 13, "Thou shalt worship the Lord thy God, and to Him only shalt thou make supplication." Here, too, the aim is to meet the doubt concerning the Messiahship of Jesus which arose from the presupposition that the Messiah must be a political ruler. That, the evangelical apologist intends to say, Jesus certainly might have been if He had worshipped the prince of this world, and had aimed at Messianic sovereignty by the godless methods of violence such as are usual among the world-powers; but He repudiated this ungodly method and remained firm in His obedience to God, in the confidence that afterwards—so we may doubtless, on the basis of Phil. ii. 6 f., expand His thought—He should, as His reward for being faithful unto death, be exalted by God to be the heavenly Messiah and Lord over all the world. Moreover, a temptation of that kind once really presented itself to Jesus, on the occasion when Peter endeavoured to hold Him back from the path of suffering (Mark viii. 32); and it often assailed the young Christian community, since by worshipping the images of the gods or the emperor they could buy their peace with the heathen world-power of Rome. In the third temptation, the apologetic idea is not quite so clearly apparent as in the two earlier ones. The proposal of the devil that Jesus, confiding in the promised protection of the angels, should throw Himself down from the pinnacle of the temple, betrays the same Jewish presupposition that the Messiah must exhibit the most astounding miracles, as is evidenced in the authentic demand of the Pharisees for a sign which is reported in Mark viii. 11. Whether the special form of miracle here imagined was determined by the recollection of the fate of the martyr James,[1] who was hurled down from the Temple (Euseb., *H.E.*, ii. 23), or of the ill-starred attempt at flight by Simon Magus at Rome, or some other similar incident, we cannot tell. In any case, the presupposition that the Messiah must prove His claim by a work of magic is here, as in the case of the historical incident (of the temptation by Peter), rejected by Jesus as the sign of an unspiritual frame of mind, which proposed to tempt God. Thus the polemic against the false Jewish Messianic ideal is the common source of the three temptations.

[1] *Cf.* the interesting essay of W. Hönig on the story of the Temptation in *Prot. Monatshefte*, iv. Heft 9 and 10.

Interesting parallels to this narrative are found in the Iranian and Indian legends. Ahriman, the evil spirit, proffered to Zarathustra, after vainly threatening him with death, the impious suggestion, " Renounce the good law of the worshippers of Mazda, and thou shalt attain strength like to that of Zohak, the ruler of the nations." To this Zarathustra answered, " No, I will never renounce the good law of the Mazda-worshippers, though my body and life and soul should be broken in sunder; the word which Mazda has taught is my weapon, my best weapon." Ahriman, smitten with this weapon, was obliged to retire. The Buddhistic legend narrates that Buddha began his life of holiness with severe self-discipline and fasting, according to the Brahminical rule; then there came to him, when completely exhausted, Mara, the Prince of Evil Pleasure, in order to tempt him away from his ascetic life: " One must live, my child; only as a living man will it be possible for you to teach the law." Buddha, however, repulsed him, being determined to remain faithful to his vow. Later, however, Buddha became convinced of the worthlessness of such asceticism, and discovered the four saving truths. Then, in the night in which he attained his highest illumination, the hostile hosts of Mara assailed him with all the terrors of hell, but he victoriously opposed them with the shield of virtue. Then Mara essayed to tempt him with the allurements of fleshly lust, and caused his daughters, the Apsaras, to display all their charms before him. He, however, fought them with the words of the sacred book Dhammapadam, so that they withdrew in shame, recognising that he could not be overcome.

Mara, however, did not yet leave him, but demanded that Buddha should recognise him as the ruler of the whole world; whereupon Buddha answered, "Even if thou art the Lord of Pleasure, thou art not the Lord of Light. Look at me, I am the Lord of the Law; Powerless One, before thine eyes I shall attain full enlightenment." Mara, in despair, acknowledges, "My sovereignty is gone." Then all the animals, and the hosts of heavenly spirits, offer Buddha their homage (*cf.* Mark i. 13, "He was with the wild beasts, and the angels ministered to him"). In another version of the Buddha-legend the temptation connected with hunger is wanting; on the other hand, Mara at once met the resolution of Buddha to renounce the world with the offer of world-sovereignty, on condition that he shall relinquish his plan of salvation. To this Buddha answered, "I well know that a kingdom is destined for me, but it is not worldly rulership that I desire. I will be a Buddha, and will make the world leap for joy." Thereafter the tempter followed him like a shadow, always watching for some false step. So, too, Luke says that the devil left Jesus "for a season," implying that later on he resumed his attacks. All these legends of temptation, between which we need not necessarily suppose a direct historical connection, have as their common basis the thought that the deliverer and bringer of saving truth must first have overcome in his own person the forces of evil before he could become the saviour of others.

Luke makes the public activity of Jesus begin with a sermon in the synagogue at Nazareth (iv. 16–30). That the introduction at this early point of this incident, which is in its right place in Mark (vi. 1–6) is unhistorical, Luke himself betrays by making the Nazarenes appeal to the rumour of the great deeds of Jesus at Capernaum, which, of course, manifestly implies a preceding activity of some length on the part of Jesus. Luke certainly intended, here too, to report more exactly "in order" than his predecessors; but it is easy to recognise that, for his view of the more correct order, it is not new and more accurate study of the sources, but a specific literary purpose, which is the determining factor. What this purpose was he reveals unmistakably by the discourse which he puts into the mouth of Jesus. First the Isaian promise of salvation is declared to be fulfilled in the work of Jesus, the Saviour (iv. 21; *cf.* Mark i. 15). Then, while Mark tells us that the Nazarenes were offended at the greatness of their fellow-townsman, Luke does not say this, but speaks only of the surprise at His gracious words; at the same time, however, he retains the saying, for which only Mark supplies the explanation, about the prophet's not being honoured in his own country; and indeed he goes very much farther. While the original report only spoke of a want of respect for Jesus and belief in Him on the part of the Nazarenes, Luke, on the other hand, records, immediately on this first appearance of Jesus, an outbreak of deadly hatred on the part of His countrymen, called forth by His pointing to the instances in the Old Testament in which Gentiles were preferred to Israelites. It must be admitted that this discourse, so deliberately offensive to Jewish self-respect, would have been so little in accordance with Jesus' wisdom as a teacher—even supposing that the Nazarenes had given more cause for it than, in Luke's account especially, they appear to have done—that we can hardly suppose it to be historical. Luke was manifestly led to this transformation of the historical account by the intention of illustrating at the beginning of Jesus' ministry, in the conduct of His countrymen in the narrower sense, the attitude which was taken up later by His countrymen in the wider sense, the Jews in general, towards Christ and the Christian community in general. It is the bitterness—which at the time of the author was constantly finding more and more violent expression—of Judaism, jealous of its national privileges, against the Christ who, according to the Pauline preaching and the belief of the Gentile Churches, was turning to the Gentiles, which the Evangelist here represents in a symbolical story. It is for this reason, too, that he places this narrative at the very beginning; it is intended to symbolise in advance the fate of Christianity as rejected by the Jews and transferred to the Gentiles as determined from the first by fixed necessity (in the sense of Rom. ix.–xi.).

Of the call of the first pairs of disciples, which Luke, departing from Mark's order, places immediately after the beginning of Jesus' activity, on the first Sabbath at Capernaum (v. 1 ff.), he gives an expanded account, illustrating the phrase "fishers of men" by the allegorical narrative of Peter's miraculous draught of fishes. Then he closely follows the order of Mark in all the narratives up to the choice of the Twelve. After this he brings in his "first interpolated section"

(vi. 20–viii. 3). Just as Mark introduces the greater parables of Jesus immediately after the choice of the Twelve, so Luke now proceeds to give a specimen of Jesus' manner of teaching in the discourse to the disciples corresponding to the Sermon on the Mount in Matthew, which, however, according to Luke, was spoken, not on the mountain, but after His descent from the mountain, upon the plain.[1]

It begins with the benediction upon the poor, upon those who now hunger and weep, and those who are persecuted for bearing Christ's name; and a corresponding fourfold woe upon the rich, the full, those that laugh now, and those whom everyone praises. There is here no reason to understand these "poor" and "hungry" in a spiritual sense (as in Matthew); the thought of this beatitude and its reverse is exactly the same as that which Luke has already expressed in the song of Mary (i. 51–53), and corresponds to the description which Jesus gives in His sermon at Nazareth, and in His message to the Baptist of the aim of His mission, namely, to preach glad tidings to the poor (iv. 18, vii. 22). It is not to be overlooked, however, that these poor and distressed are at the same time thought of as disciples of Jesus, for the beatitudes were spoken "as he looked upon his disciples," and were addressed to them: "Blessed are ye poor, for yours is the

[1] According to vi. 20 it was spoken "as he looked upon the disciples," but as, at the time, according to what precedes (vi. 17 ff.), Jesus was in the midst of a great multitude, we must, of course, assume for this sermon also a wider circle of hearers beyond the disciples, and, moreover, this is distinctly stated in vii. 1.

kingdom of God."[1] We are to understand by these "poor" real poor men, but at the same time pious humble men, longing for salvation, friends of Jesus and members of His community, in the same sense, therefore, as the "pious sufferers" of the Psalms (*anavim*); and similarly the rich are to be understood as the proud, arrogant betrayers and oppressors of the pious sufferers (*cf.* i. 51 and 53). Light is thrown on both sides of this contrast by the Lucan parable of Dives and Lazarus. We may recall, too, the contrast between the simple, to whom salvation is revealed, and the (worldly) wise and prudent, from whom it is hidden (x. 21). At the basis of all these sayings there lies undoubtedly the real experience of daily life, according to which the needs and sufferings of earth create a longing and a receptivity for the consolations of the gospel, whereas pleasure and comfort easily make us dull and indifferent towards the higher life. As Jesus Himself had doubtless had occasion to observe this (*cf.* Mark x. 23 f.), we have every reason to hold the Lucan form of the beatitudes to be, not merely the original, but also the historically correct version.[2]

[1] *Cf.* Joh. Weiss, *Predigt Jesu vom Reich Gottes,* p. 182: "It is quite beyond doubt that Luke here desires sharply to emphasise social contrasts. That the beatitudes do not receive a special ethical or religious imprint is due to the fact that this can be dispensed with because it is necessarily implied." The pertinent remark of Jülicher regarding the parable of the Great Supper applies here too: "In Luke it is rather a social, in Matthew rather an ethical, revolution which forms the last epoch in the history of the Kingdom of God" (*Gleichnisse Jesu*, ii. 430).

[2] That the Matthæan form is secondary will be shown below. Here it may be provisionally observed that no reason whatever can

This applies at least to the first three beatitudes, which promise to those who now hunger and mourn, satisfaction and joy in the Kingdom of God, whereas to the rich, who are now sated and happy, the prospect of hunger and trouble is held out. In both cases this is not to be understood of circumstances of the world to come, but of a transformation of the earthly order of society, in accordance with the prophetic ideal of the people of God enjoying happiness as a consequence of righteousness (*cf.* the similar promises to the disciples that they shall reign with Messiah, and eat and drink at His table (xii. 32, xxii. 29 f.) — sayings which there is no warrant in the text for interpreting as a reference to spiritual or heavenly things).

On the other hand, verse 22 f. is an addition of the author, who, on the ground of the experiences of a later time, makes Jesus say in advance that even the name of Christian should be held a crime, on account of which those who confessed allegiance to the Son of Man, and who hope for the renewing of the world at His Parousia, shall be despised and cast out, viz. from civil and religious society (*i.e.* the synagogue); that, however, should only be a cause of lively joy to them, since they may remember that the prophets of old fared no better, and console themselves with the prospect of the rich reward which was laid up for them in heaven, until it should

be discovered why Luke should have omitted the sayings regarding the merciful, meek, etc., which would undoubtedly have been sympathetic to him, if he had found them in his source. On the other hand, Matthew's reason for altering the Lucan form of the beatitudes and woes is easy to understand, and will be shown later.

come to manifestation and realisation at the appearing of the "Son of Man" (according to Apoc. xxii. 12). After the woe upon the rich and the men of the world who were praised by all, the discourse turns again to the present hearers with an exhortation to love their enemies, to bear patiently even gross injustice, and to show kindness to all men (verses 27–30). Not violent self-assertion, but, on the contrary, the most complete selflessness, is the condition of obtaining the Messianic salvation—this is the essential ethical distinction between the religious-social ideal of Jesus and the efforts, based upon self-seeking and violence, of the irreligious socialists of ancient and modern times. Whereas the latter have always made shipwreck upon the eternal laws of the world-order, the ideal of Jesus has had the power to overcome and to renew the world, even though in another fashion and by a slower process than was at first supposed by its adherents. The social attitude proper to the disciples of Jesus is summed up in the "golden rule" (which had also been described by Jewish teachers like Hillel as the quintessence of the law), "As ye would that men should do unto you, do ye also to them likewise" (vi. 31). This principle of mutual obligation includes, of course, by a logical necessity, its converse of mutual rights, and serves in this respect as a corrective to what precedes. Whereas the natural inclination of men is in the direction of thinking only of their rights, without thinking of the corresponding duties, the ethic of the Gospels sets up from the outset the opposite principle, and leaves the inference of the recognition of universal human rights to be drawn in the natural course from the recognition of mutual obligations. As the pattern and motive of unselfish benevolence towards all, Jesus holds up the goodness and mercy of God, even to the unthankful and the evil; by imitating this unbounded Father-love of God, Jesus' disciples are to show themselves to be the sons of God. Here, therefore, it is quite definitely implied that, in the usage of Jesus, sonship to God is quite simply an ethico-religious conception. The inculcation of a God-like mercifulness is appropriately followed by a warning against arrogant and hypocritical censoriousness. The image of the beam and the splinter in the eye seems to have suggested to the Evangelist the other image of the blind leading the blind; the association of ideas between this and the eye-doctor with sore eyes (vi. 42) is very natural, but the connection of thought between the warning against censorious judgments and of the uselessness of the spiritually blind as a teacher of others is not entirely obvious. The rebuke of hypocrisy in verse 42 leads to a reference to the fruits by which the kind and value of the man, as of the tree, is to be recognised; the test of a man being, moreover, not so much words as actions (verses 43–46). To this is appropriately attached, by way of conclusion, the parable of the prudent man who built his house upon the rock, and the foolish man who built his house upon the sand (verses 47–49). The whole discourse is so well arranged and rounded off, and corresponds so well to the situation, as an example of the public teaching of Jesus, that a comparison with the much more diffuse Sermon on the Mount in Matthew, which is an amalgam of various elements, is entirely to the advantage of the Lucan form. And this discourse certainly contains not merely genuine thoughts of Jesus, but also, for the most part, an essentially true reflection of the original words of Jesus, though, of course, the translation of these from Aramaic into Greek is not to be overlooked.

Having now begun interpolating, Luke adds some further narrative material; in the first place, the story of the healing of the servant of the centurion of Capernaum, and of the raising of the son of the widow of Nain (vii. 1–10, 11–17). In both these narratives the legends of the miracles of the prophets Elijah and Elisha, to which Luke has already alluded in the discourse at Nazareth, supply the pattern. The centurion of Capernaum, with his humble and trustful faith, is the antithesis to the Syrian captain, Naaman, who was unwilling to believe in a healing at a distance, and held it to be due to his dignity that the prophet Elisha should come to him in person, in order to heal him with a touch (2 Kings v. 11). The comparison of the miracle-working word of Jesus with the military word of command (verse 8) is a characteristically Lucan touch; for this Evangelist shows elsewhere a great interest in the Roman military system, whereas this is quite foreign to Matthew. The expression of surprise, "I have not found such faith, no, not in Israel" (verse 9), only exalts the faith of this Gentile as, in comparison, the stronger, without necessarily including any reproach against Israel as unbelieving, for which the circumstances gave no occasion. It is possible, therefore, that the words of Matt. viii. 11 were not omitted by Luke, but inserted here by Matthew (they stand in a more appropriate connection in Luke xiii. 28 f.) Only Luke gives, in addition to the companion picture to Naaman the Syrian, a companion picture to that of the widow of Sarepta, or of the Shunamite woman; as the son of the one was raised by Elijah (1 Kings xvii. 17–24) and the son of the other by Elisha (2 Kings iv. 33–37), so, Luke narrates, the son of a widow at Nain was raised by Jesus. The imitation of the story of Elijah is here obvious: Elijah, like Jesus, met the woman at the door, spoke comforting words to her ("fear not," as in this case "weep not"), gave the son, when raised up, to his mother, and was recognised by her as a man of God, *i.e.* a prophet, just as here the people praised God that a great prophet was risen up among them (vii. 16).

It may have been the fact that he had been imitating the story of Elijah which suggested to the Evangelist the idea of inserting here (vii. 18–35) an episode concerning John the Baptist, whom he had described at the outset as the second Elijah or Fore-runner of the Lord, whose coming was predicted by Malachi. John sent, the Evangelist tells us, on hearing the report of the works of Jesus, two of his disciples to Him, bidding them ask Him, "Art thou he that should come, or look we for another?" Whereupon Jesus pointed to the bodily and spiritual results of His work as Saviour in words taken from the prophet Isaiah (lxi. 1 ff., xxxv. 5 f.); but the healing of the leprous and the raising of the dead are added by the Evangelist to the works of healing enumerated there (which, moreover, are in the original passage intended metaphorically), the raising of the dead being obviously added with reference to the immediately preceding narrative (verses 11–17). To this incident the Evangelist attaches a discourse referring to John the Baptist, in which his historical significance, and his relation to Jesus and the Christian community, are defined by Jesus Himself. He is declared to be the Fore-runner predicted by Malachi (iii. 1) whom Jahweh was to send before the Messiah (properly, in the original passage, before Himself) to prepare his way for him. He is therefore the greatest of the prophets, but yet less than the least in the Kingdom of God—how much more was he inferior to the Lord Himself, Jesus, the Christ! This mission of John as the Fore-runner of the Messiah had been practically recognised by the common people and the publicans, who accepted his baptism; only the Pharisees and legalists made the Divine plan of salvation which was revealed in the mission of the Baptist ineffectual, so far as they themselves were concerned, by refusing his baptism. These words were in any case not originally spoken here, but have been adapted by the Evangelist from a saying preserved by the tradition in another connection (Matt. xxi. 32), and put in here by the Evangelist under the heading "John the Baptist" (Holtzmann, *Kommentar*). The discourse, which in Matthew also is similarly compounded out of various elements, closes with the picture of the children quarrelling at their play, which is interpreted with reference to the attitude of the people towards John and towards Jesus. It is not elsewhere the custom of Jesus Himself to interpret His simple figures—is it likely that He made an exception in this case? The image in verse 32 expresses the experience of finding it impossible to please people, whether one speaks to them cheerfully or gravely—an experience which Jesus, in the course of His own work, quite apart from John, had often enough occasion to encounter, and may have expressed in some figurative saying of this kind, which in itself needed no special interpretation. The special interpretation, however, which is given to this figure in verse 33 f. as a reference to John and Jesus, is not so simple, and leads, so soon as one endeavours to carry through the comparison, to insoluble difficulties. That is proved by the standing controversy among exegetes over the question whether John and Jesus are compared with the children who called to the others, and wished to set the tune, or with those who were called to and did not wish to follow, or partly with the one and partly with the other, all the solutions being equally difficult and unsatisfactory. Is not that a proof that this is one of those instances where, as is notoriously the case with many of the Gospel parables, figurative expressions which were originally meant in a quite general sense have been given a special application and interpretation by the Evangelists, or in some cases perhaps by their sources? Whatever opinion may be held on this point, I hold it to be in any case certain that the closing saying in verse 35, "And wisdom has been justified by (all) her children," did not belong originally to the discourse of Jesus, but came from the same hand as verse 29, to which the term justify clearly points back; being added as an expression of the Christian conviction that the wisdom of God, which was manifested in Jesus (*cf.* Sirach

iv. 11) finds in the faith of the Church the seal of its truth.

On the suggestion, perhaps, of the contrast between the Publicans and Pharisees (vii. 29 f.), Luke now brings in (verses 36–50), at the close of his first interpolated section, the narrative, peculiar to his gospel, of the penitent woman, who, at a feast in the house of Simon the Pharisee, washed the feet of Jesus with her tears and kissed and anointed them. At this the Pharisee was offended, whereupon Jesus showed him that this woman who had displayed towards Him a so much more intense and humble love than the cold and haughty Pharisee, had thereby proved how deeply grateful she was for the forgiveness of her many sins. While the narrative in this form is peculiar to Luke, it shows striking resemblances to the other story of anointing, the scene of which is placed by the original account (Mark xiv. 3 ff.) at a feast in the house of a certain Simon, not, however, in this case a man proud of his legal purity (a Pharisee), but a man who had been healed of uncleanness (leprosy), and not in Galilee, but in Bethany of Judæa, two days before the final Passover; in this case, moreover, the woman who anointed Jesus was not a penitent sinner, but a pious disciple and friend of Jesus. Her action, it is true, offends the spectators and is justified by Jesus, but the ground of blame lies not in herself but in the uselessly extravagant mark of reverence shown to Jesus; and Jesus' defence of her against those who blamed her involved a rebuke, not of the Pharisee, but of Jesus' own disciples for not recognising the worth of this act of love by the nameless disciple. It is evident that both narratives are, point for point, parallel, but also, point for point, different. How is this relationship to be explained? That the Lucan story is a free adaptation of the anointing at Bethany is not probable: it has too much that is peculiar to itself for that; its leading thought—especially the illustration, in a particular case, of Jesus' mercy and love towards sinners—is quite foreign to the other story; and the parable of the Two Debtors (41 f.), as well as the beautiful saying of Jesus in verse 47, "Her sins, which were many, are forgiven, because she loved much," make a strong impression of genuineness. Moreover, Eusebius states (*H.E.*, iii. 39. 17) that the "Gospel according to the Hebrews" contained a story of a woman who was accused to Jesus on account of her many sins, which was perhaps the common source of the Johannine story of the woman taken in adultery (John vii. 53–viii. 11) and of the present narrative in Luke. We may perhaps suppose that in the tradition there were originally two independent stories side by side: one of a penitent sinner who washed Jesus' feet with her tears, and one of the disciple at Bethany who anointed Jesus' head. The Lucan story of the anointing may then have arisen out of a combination of the two.[1] Whether this combination had already taken place in the tradition through the insensible fusion of the respective characteristics of the two stories, or was first effected by Luke with the intention of substituting another anointing for that at Bethany, may remain an open question. It is, however, to be remarked that the identification—which has established its place in

[1] *Cf.* Holtzmann, *Kommentar zu den Synoptikern*, 3rd ed., p. 347.

Church tradition—of the "woman who was a sinner" with Mary of Magdala "out of whom went seven devils" who is mentioned in viii. 2 as a disciple of Jesus, has no foundation either in Luke or elsewhere in the Gospels. The mistake is doubtless to be explained from the fact that the notice of the ministering women who followed Jesus (Luke viii. 1–3) comes immediately after the story of the anointing, and that the Fourth Evangelist calls the woman who anointed Jesus (who elsewhere in the Gospels remains nameless) Mary, though identifying her with Mary of Bethany, and not with Mary of Magdala.

From viii. 4 to ix. 50 Luke again follows, in general, the order of Mark's Gospel. Of the three parables taken from the processes of the sowing and growth of seed (Mark iv.), Luke here (viii. 4–18) gives only the first, along with the explanation of it; the second he omits. The third (the grain of mustard-seed) he brings in later, as a companion parable to that of the leaven (xiii. 18 ff.). Then he inserts the narrative of the visit of Jesus' relatives in a very much abbreviated version (viii. 19–21). He suppresses Mark's reference (iii. 21) to the special purpose of the visit, and suppresses in the answer of Jesus the sharp rebuff in the question, "Who is my mother, or my brethren?" retaining only the positive statement, "My mother and my brethren are they that hear the word of God and do it." We have already spoken of the reason for this omission in discussing the narrative as it appears in Mark's Gospel (*sup.*, p. 14); we have also found it to be probable in discussing the section ii. 41–52 (p. 112 f.)

that the point of the original narrative which is here suppressed has been preserved by Luke in a different form and setting.

In the story of the storm, which in Mark succeeds these parables, and in those of the Gerasene demoniac, of the healing of the woman with an issue of blood, and the raising of the daughter of Jairus, Luke follows him step for step. The sermon at Nazareth he has inserted at an earlier point, and therefore passes over it here and proceeds at once to the sending out of the Twelve, the directions for their journey being almost identical with those in Mark. Then the supposition of Herod with regard to Jesus is mentioned, but the episode of the death of John the Baptist is omitted. The return of the Twelve is followed in Luke, as in Mark, by the feeding of the five thousand; but Luke entirely omits Mark vi. 45–viii. 36, only returning to his order at Peter's confession (Luke ix. 18), which is followed by the prediction of Jesus' sufferings and the exhortation to follow Him in the path of suffering, the Transfiguration, and the healing of the lunatic boy. Further predictions of the Passion, and the strife for precedence among the disciples, follow, all in the order of the Marcan narrative.

CHAPTER VI

THE LUCAN JOURNEY-NARRATIVE

(Luke ix. 51–xviii. 14)

AT ix. 51 begins the section known as Luke's "great interpolation," which extends to xviii. 14. The setting which Luke has chosen for this is the journey of Jesus from Galilee to Jerusalem, which Mark handles very briefly. In the first place, the route demands notice, since Luke does not, like Matthew and Mark, represent it as lying through Peræa, but through Samaria, in order thereby to indicate that Jesus did not share the usual Jewish horror of contact with heathenism (whether complete, or, as in the case of the Samaritans, partial). The fiery zeal, too, similar to that of Elijah, which James and John displayed towards a village of the Samaritans, was not according to the mind of Jesus. When they proposed to Him to call down fire from heaven upon the impious village, He rebuked them with the significant words, "Know ye not what spirit ye are of?"—a genuine saying of the Saviour, which is not derived from Marcionite antinomianism, but which, from fear of its being used in favour of Marcionism, was omitted from the Eastern manuscripts and only preserved by Cod. D and the Latin versions.[1]

Before coming to his typical and significant story of the sending forth of the seventy disciples, he gives three stories of disciples in which the qualities necessary to efficient discipleship are illustrated (ix. 57–62). A disciple of Jesus must, following the example of his Master, (1) renounce earthly pleasure and comfort, and (2) must place all ordinary duties, even the highest obligations of natural piety, on a lower level than the duty to which he is called of preaching the Kingdom of God; (3) he must with unwavering determination give himself completely to the higher calling which he has once embraced, not letting his heart grow heavy through yearning affection for the friends who surrounded him in his old life. That this three-fold mirror for disciples in Luke is independent of the parallels in Matthew (viii. 18–22) and is the more original of the two, is clear for several reasons: (1) this narrative stands in Luke, but not in Matthew, in close connection of subject with the story which follows of the sending out of the seventy—it shows the presuppositions of a personal nature which are necessary for the efficient discharge of the duty of the missionary; (2) it is in Luke only that the narrative stands at the right point in the chronological order, since it is not appropriate for Jesus to speak at the outset of His work in Galilee (as in Matthew) of the homelessness of the Son of Man (ix. 58) while He still had His dwelling in Capernaum—it only becomes appropriate during the journey to Jerusalem, when He had, so to speak, broken down the bridges behind Him;

[1] *Cf.* Zahn, *Einleitung*, ii. 357.

(3) the words in Matt. viii. 21, "Suffer me first to go and bury my father," are quite unintelligible apart from the presupposition of a previous demand that the disciple should follow, which is found in Luke ix. 59, but which Matthew, with his usual habit of abbreviating, has omitted; finally, (4) Luke gives (verse 61 f.) the third example, which essentially belongs to the completeness of the picture of the conditions of discipleship, whereas Matthew has omitted it, because, in failing to recognise the unity of idea which runs through the three stories, he has also overlooked their connection.

Whether the narrative, peculiar to Luke, of the mission and work of the seventy "other" disciples (x. 1–24) has any basis of historical tradition, or whether it was freely invented by him, cannot be discovered, but it may be said with great probability that, for the author, its significance essentially consisted in the fact that it represents the typical example of a universal mission to the Gentiles as planned and sanctioned by the Lord Himself. The number seventy, indeed, may have been suggested by the seventy elders whom Moses gathered about him (Num. xi. 16, 24 f.), but that alone hardly explains the great significance which Luke attributed to this second mission. The explanation doubtless is that in Jewish theology the number seventy was held (on the ground of Gen. x.) to be the number of the heathen nations; and legend made the Divine voice at the giving of the Law audible in seventy voices or languages; and, according to legend also, the Greek version of the Old Testament, which was intended for the Gentile world, was prepared by seventy inspired men. Accordingly, the seventy "other" disciples of Luke are simply representatives of evangelistic preaching among the heathen—the type and pattern of the Pauline mission to the Gentiles. All that is said with regard to their mission and its consequences harmonises with this explanation. It is to be noted, first, that Jesus sends these disciples before Him into every town and village where He himself intended to come —namely, on His journey through half-Gentile Samaria; that is almost as much as to say that He sent them among the Gentiles. But could the historical Jesus really have done this? We should have reason to doubt it, even if we did not hold Matt. x. 5 to be an authentic saying of Jesus. It is to be added, moreover, that, assuming that there was such a mission by the historical Jesus, the Lucan representation would involve the contradiction, in that the disciples first appear as preparing the way for Jesus' own activity in the Samaritan towns, but later appear as completely independent workers—not as fore-runners of a Jesus who is to follow them in person, but rather as the representatives of the Christ who works through them and not after them, and "comes" only in a spiritual sense. This contradiction is to be solved, however, very simply from the historical standpoint of the Evangelist, according to which the Apostles of the Gentiles were certainly sent by the Lord in order to prepare the way for His victorious advance through the Gentile world; only it was not the earthly Jesus by whom they were sent, and for whom, as about to follow them in person, they were to prepare the way, but the exalted Christ, the heavenly Lord of the Church, who sent forth Paul and the other Apostles to the Gentiles in order that, in and through their activity, He might effect His spiritual entrance into the heathen world. The command which follows, too, to pray to the Lord of the harvest that He would send forth more labourers into His harvest, since the labourers are too few for the greatness of the harvest, is more suitable to the great harvest-field of the heathen world than to the narrowly bounded mission in Palestine. Especially the saying, "I send you forth as lambs in the midst of wolves," is obviously to be most naturally understood of the sending forth of the innocent, harmless, unarmed, and peaceable preachers of the gospel amid the savage, heartless, and ruthless violence of the heathen world. On the other hand, in the case of the first sending forth of the first disciples there was no reason to think of Jewish hostility, for neither Mark nor Luke mention anything of the kind in regard to the historical mission of the Twelve. Finally, verses 7 and 8 contain distinctively Pauline sayings (1 Cor. ix. 14, x. 27), and imply the circumstances of Gentile Christianity—for to what else could the direction refer, "Eat what is set before you," if not to the Pauline principle of eating what was set before one in the Gentile houses, unembarrassed by Jewish scruples of conscience about unclean meats? In the face of so many concurrent proofs, scarcely any doubt can remain as to the correctness of the explanation of the Lucan mission of the seventy as a type and symbol of the Pauline mission to the Gentiles.

Further confirmation of this conjecture is furnished by the description of the great success of the seventy (x. 17 ff.). When the returned disciples reported that even the devils were subject unto them, that is, yielded to their command, spoken in the name of Jesus, Jesus answered, "I beheld Satan as lightning fall from heaven." That is the victory which is also represented in the Apocalypse (xii. 9) under the same figure—the victory over the demonic power of heathenism, which the Evangelist represents Jesus as anticipating in vision as the glorious result of the preaching of the gospel among the heathen. Then the emissaries of the gospel are promised a decisive victory over the whole hostile world-power of Satan, with the assurance, also, that their names are written in heaven; both in the spirit of the Pauline hymn of victory in Rom. viii. 35–39. And a similar hymn of victory is here placed by the Evangelist in the mouth of Jesus. Filled with the spirit of the seer, which enables him intuitively to perceive the victory of the simple word of the gospel over the proud heathen world, He praises the Father that it has been His good pleasure to reveal the truth of the gospel to babes, and to hide it from the wise and prudent. Similarly, Paul had said in 1 Cor. i. 19–25[1] that it was the will of God to bring to nought the wisdom of the wise and prudent, and by "the foolishness of preaching" to save them that believe, and that the wisdom of God was hidden in a mystery from the great ones of this world, but revealed to us by God through His Spirit, who alone is capable of knowing the mind of God, and who also makes

[1] The affinity of our passage with the thoughts and words of 1 Cor. i. 19–iii. 1 is so striking (*σοφοί, συνετοί, μωρόν, νήπιοι, σοφίαν ἐν μυστηρίῳ ἀποκεκρυμμένην, ἀπεκάλυψεν, εὐδόκησεν, οὐκ ἔγνω, οὐδεὶς ἔγνωκεν*) that its dependence on Paul is very probable.

known to us, who have not the spirit of this world but the mind of Christ, the riches bestowed upon us by God (ii. 7–16). It is just this last specifically Pauline thought—that the true knowledge of Christ and of God is hidden from the natural man and only revealed to the mind of man by the Spirit of God, who is also the Spirit of the Son of God —which the Evangelist now (verse 22) makes Jesus Himself express in words which are so strongly distinguished by their dogmatic character from Jesus' usual manner of speaking in the Synoptic Gospels, and have such a remarkable affinity with the Pauline and Johannine theology (*cf.* John i. 18, x. 15, xiii. 3, xvii. 10), that one can hardly avoid the impression that we have here, not so much a saying of Jesus Himself, as a Christological confession of the Apostolic community in the form of a solemn liturgical hymn: "All things are delivered unto me of my Father (*cf.* 1 Cor. xv. 27, and Matt. xxviii. 18), and no one knoweth who the Son is but the Father, and who the Father is but the Son, and he to whom the Son wills to reveal Him."[1] The

[1] Or, according to another reading, which has equally good patristic attestation: "No man hath known the Father except the Son, or the Son except the Father and he to whom the Son reveals" —whom, or what, remains uncertain, since the natural reference to the Father is rendered difficult by this transposition of the clauses. This difficulty is, in the opinion of Bernard Weiss, a proof that this reading is not original. On the other hand, it has lately been preferred by many critics, because it seems to favour an interpretation of the saying which would fit into the frame of the Synoptic picture of Christ, viz.: All truths of the gospel have been "delivered" to me (*i.e.* revealed, although elsewhere an ἀποκάλυψις of God is the antithesis of παράδοσις) by my Father; and no man hath (hitherto) known God as Father except Him (Jesus) who by this very

Evangelist seems, moreover, himself to indicate that these words were not spoken for the narrower circle of disciples, but for the whole community of those who through the revelation of God have recognised in Christ the Son of God; for in what follows (verse 23) he expressly distinguishes the disciples in the special or narrower sense (κατ' ἰδίαν), *i.e.* the original Apostles, and calls them blessed because of what their eyes are permitted to see and their ears to hear, for which prophets and kings might envy them—as much as to say, even if the knowledge of who the Son is and who the Father is belongs to the things which no eye hath seen and no ear heard, but which the Spirit of God hath revealed to spiritual men according to His purpose and will (1 Cor. ii. 9 ff.), yet the first disciples are nevertheless to be counted blessed above others because of the special advantage which they enjoyed in seeing Jesus with their eyes during His personal manifestation upon earth, and in hearing His teaching with their ears.

After this hymn embodying the confession of Christ by the community—which forms the climax of this Gospel in the same way as the prophetic saying about the Church founded upon the rock, Peter, against which the gates of hell shall not prevail, forms the

knowledge has become "the Son," and that he is the Son has not as yet been recognised by anyone except God, and those to whom He Himself reveals Himself as the Son (of God). So Schmiedel (in *Prot. Monatshefte*, iv. 1), with whom also Brückner and H. Holtzmann are in agreement. I will not dispute the possibility of this interpretation, but cannot, for my own part, hold it to be probable. We shall recur to this point below, when treating of the prophetic-messianic self-consciousness of Jesus.

climax in Matthew — the Evangelist proceeds to illustrate some main points of Christian ethics. First (x. 25–37) comes the question regarding the greatest commandment (Mark xii. 28), to which Luke, however, gives a turn taken from the story of the rich young man (Mark x. 17). "What must I do to obtain eternal life?" In answer, Jesus directs the questioner to the Law, and the latter immediately selects the two chief commandments of love to God and love to one's neighbour, which Jesus accepts as correct. Obviously, Luke has here reversed the rôles of Jesus and the lawyer, which the original report gives correctly—the recognition that the love of God and man is the essence of the Law was not, after all, so self-evident, or so universally familiar, that the lawyer was likely immediately to give this answer. What Jesus actually said, and what He alone could say, is put by Luke into the mouth of the lawyer in order to gain in this way a suitable introduction to His parable of the Good Samaritan. To the question, "Who is my neighbour?" Jesus does not answer with a theoretic exposition of the conception of neighbourship in general, but shows by a parable, in a concrete case, that the good man makes himself neighbour to anyone who needs his help, without stopping to ask in what national or social relation he would stand to him at ordinary times, but simply on the ground that he is a fellow-man who needs help. Jesus thus makes out of the theoretical scholastic question regarding the content and scope of the term neighbour, a lesson of practical duty: "Do likewise"—be, to everyone who needs you, a helpful neighbour.

It is not without reason that the Evangelist immediately (x. 38–42) follows this parable of active love with the beautiful story of the two sisters Martha and Mary, which forms, in a sense, its complement and counterpart. For, while active love is the fulfilling of the whole Law, it has the roots of its strength in the religious belief in Jesus' person and work which is shown by Mary, and therefore it is, in this respect, the one thing needful, and the better part in comparison with the anxiety and trouble of the actively serving Martha. The pair of sisters represent the two types described by Paul in 1 Cor. vii. 34 f.—the pious virgin who, constantly cleaving to the Lord, cares for the things of the Lord, and the diligent housewife who cares for the things of the world. If, moreover, the reading in verse 42, which has good patristic attestation, "only a few things, or one, are necessary," is correct, it would leave the hospitable cares of Martha their relative justification, without calling in question the superior advantage of Mary's choice.

With contemplative adoration which hangs on the words of Jesus prayer stands in the closest relation, and Luke immediately adds here Jesus' lesson to His disciples on the right way of praying (xi. 1–13). The occasion of this he makes the request of a disciple for teaching on this point such as John had given to his disciples. The prayer which Jesus taught is simpler in the Lucan than in the Matthæan version. The introduction is formed by the simple address to God, "Father," which Jesus Himself doubtless used in His own prayers. Then follow the five petitions "Hallowed be Thy name; Thy kingdom come; give us daily our sufficient bread;[1] and forgive us our sins, as we ourselves forgive everyone that trespasses against us; and lead us not into temptation." Matthew has extended the invocation by adding to "Father" his customary description of God as He who is in heaven; to the second petition he adds the explanatory interpolation, "Thy will be done, as in heaven, so on earth," which does not really contain anything which is not already stated in the preceding petition; finally, the last petition, for preservation from temptation, is also reinforced by a formula which is, strictly speaking, only a paraphrase of it, "but deliver us from the evil one," *i.e.* from the devil, who is thought of as the immediate agent in temptation. The conclusion, too, in Matthew is not genuine, but interpolated from the Church liturgy into the later manuscripts. That the simpler Lucan form is also the more original is not open to doubt, but it cannot be quite so certainly determined whether it consists of the accurate tradition of a prayer taught by Jesus just in this form and with this definite object, or only of a collection of forms of petition which the disciples had often heard Jesus use and therefore adopted in imitation of His example, and which only gradually attained fixity in the usage of the community. The absence of this prayer, or of any allusion to it, in Mark, Paul, or the Apocalypse makes it very doubtful whether it can

[1] *Cf.* Prov. xxx. 8, לֶחֶם חֻקִּי; LXX, τὰ δέοντα καὶ τὰ αὐτάρκη = what is needful and sufficient. Reuss (*Das Alter Testament übersetzt und erklärt,* vol. vi. p. 186) translates the Hebrew text "my sufficient bread," and explains (note 3) that this is also the correct rendering of ἐπιούσιος in the Lord's Prayer. So, too, A. Meyer, *Die Muttersprache Jesu,* p. 108.

have been the standing formula of prayer in the Apostolic community. The difference, too, between Matthew and Luke points back to an uncertain and fluctuating tradition which could hardly be explained if the prayer had been taught as a whole by Jesus Himself. If we further take into account the fact that various similar formulæ (especially in the case of the first and second petition) occur also in the prayers of the Synagogue, the possibility cannot be denied that this prayer, based upon reminiscences of the communion of the disciples with Jesus, gradually attained in the usage of the community a more or less fixed form, and then in this form, which had gathered sacred associations about it, had been attributed to Jesus. To this lesson on how to pray Luke attaches, in the form of a parable peculiar to himself, an exhortation to earnest and persistent prayer, to which an answer is assured; for if even earthly parents, sinful as they are, yet know how to give good gifts to their children, how much more shall the Father in heaven give the Holy Spirit to those who ask Him. Apart from this last Pauline-sounding expression (πνεῦμα ἅγιον), this and similar discourses about prayer, to which Mark also has parallels, certainly belong to the oldest and most faithful memories of the community.

After the discourses, so full of significance for the inner life of the community, Luke gives a series of anti-Pharisaic polemics, including, in the first place, the discourses, which he passed over at an earlier point, in answer to the charge of being in alliance with Beelzebub (xi. 14–26) and that repudiating the demand for a sign (verses 29–32). Between the two is wedged in the mention of a woman who cried out in blessing upon the mother of Jesus—a vindication of Mary by which Luke desires to weaken or remove the impression of the story of the rebuff to Jesus' mother and brethren which occurs in the same context as the Beelzebub-accusation in Mark (iii. 31). After the discourse relating to the sign of Jonah follow short parables about the lamp on the lamp-stand and the light of the body (xi. 33 ff.). The connection between these and what precedes is not obvious; and they are connected with one another rather by the similarity of the figure than of the subject, for in one the reference is to the vocation of the disciples to proclaim the truth of the gospel, in the other, to the soundness of the inner sense, upon which depends receptivity for truth. There follows a discourse against the Pharisees (xi. 37–54) which begins with reference to the reproach brought against the disciples of eating with unwashen hands (Mark vii. 2), and is therefore represented as spoken at a social meal, the scene of which the Evangelist places —not very appropriately, it must be admitted—in the house of a Pharisee who had invited Jesus to his table. After dealing with the Pharisees, the discourse also turns to the lawyers, against whom the reproach is brought that they themselves are not willing to touch the heavy burdens of the law which they lay upon others, and that they raise handsome monuments to the prophets whom their fathers put to death, while really they are not merely the bodily, but also the spiritual descendants of the murderers. Therefore to them applies that utterance of the " Wisdom of God " according to which God shall visit (*i.e.* avenge) upon this generation the blood of all the martyrs which had been shed from the beginning of the world down to the death of Zacharias, who was slain between the altar and the temple. This is an allusion to the death, recounted by Josephus (*B.J.*, iv. 5. 4), of a Zacharias the son of Baruch, as he is also called in the Matthæan parallel, who was murdered by the Zealots, during the siege of Jerusalem, in the forecourt of the Temple. From this we may conclude that the writing which is here cited under the title the "Wisdom of God" was an apocalypse dating from that period, from which also verses xiii. 34 f. were probably taken. Finally, the lawyers are rebuked for taking away the key of religious truth, and so, by their presumptious affectation of wisdom, barring, for themselves and others, the approach to true knowledge.

The warning, borrowed from Mark viii. 15, regarding the leaven (*i.e.* the hypocrisy) of the Pharisees serves as a link of transition from the anti-Pharisaic polemic to the addresses of exhortation to the disciples urging them to courageous confession of their faith, to exaltation above earthly cares, and to loyal watchfulness. The discourse concerning confession begins, strictly speaking, with xii. 4 ("But I say unto you, my friends," etc.), while the two preceding verses, which speak of what was hid becoming known, no doubt originally (Mark iv. 22 = Luke viii. 17) also referred to open confession on the part of disciples, but are here perhaps understood by Luke in the sense that the hypocritical character of the Pharisees (xii. 1) must necessarily come to light. As motives for fearless loyalty in confessing faith in the gospel are mentioned confidence in the Divine protection of the godly, and the hope that the Son of Man will acknowledge His confessors at the judgment before the angels of God, while He will deny those who deny Him. This last thought gives Luke occasion to bring in here the warning against blaspheming the Holy Spirit which originally and more correctly has its place in Jesus' defence against the accusation of complicity with Beelzebub (Mark iii. 29). The discourse about confession closes with the promise, taken from the eschatological discourse of Mark (xiii. 11), of the help of the Holy Spirit when the disciples are called upon to appear before earthly judges (xii. 11 ff.). The request to Jesus to settle a dispute between two brothers regarding an inheritance gives the occasion for a discourse about earthly cares, introduced by the parable of the rich man who was surprised by death in the midst of his schemes (xii. 16–21). In the following illustration of the ravens, who have neither barn nor storehouse, but are fed by God, and in the question, "Who can add a span to the length of his life?" the thoughts of the parable are so clearly echoed that we can hardly doubt that this connection, and consequently the report of Luke as compared with that of Matthew, is original. Then, as the positive side of this warning against caring for the things which the heathen seek, we have the exhortation to seek the Kingdom of God as the highest good, to which the minor good of the supply of earthly needs will be added by God. This seeking of the highest things is secure of its result, for it is the good pleasure of the Father to give to the little flock of believers "the kingship."[1] Therefore the disciples, instead of seeking earthly treasures, should rather sell what they have and give alms, in order thus to lay up for themselves an imperishable treasure in heaven, and at the same time secure their citizenship in the coming Kingdom of God. Matthew has this saying about laying up treasure in heaven (vi. 20) without the explanatory addition about selling one's possessions and giving alms, because this command, addressed thus to the disciples in general, appeared to the ecclesiastical consciousness of his time no longer opportune (the case of the "counsel of evangelical perfection" in xviii. 22 is rather different); we have the less reason, therefore, to doubt the high antiquity of the version of the saying preserved by Luke, with which, also, the parables of chapter xvi. may be compared. To the exhortation to set the affections upon heavenly things the exhortation to loyal watchfulness (xii. 35) naturally attaches itself, this, too, introduced by a parable—that of the servants whom their lord, returning late from a wedding, shall find watching (the germ of the Matthæan parable of the wise and foolish

[1] On this Dalman (*Worte Jesu*, p. 101, E.T. 123) makes the noteworthy remark, "There can be no doubt that Luke in placing this saying (xii. 32) just after the command to seek first the Kingdom of the Father (verse 31) meant to use 'kingdom' in both cases in the same sense. As, however, verse 32 must from its form and content originally have stood in a different connection, the 'kingdom' here in the mouth of Jesus is doubtless used of actual rule, which is to be given in the future to His, at present, powerless disciples." And the same applies to the related passage in Luke xxii. 29, where *βασιλείαν*, in view of the absence of the article, can only be understood in the sense of "lordship, rule, kingly power."

virgins). Faithful watchfulness is the more necessary since, through the gospel, a firebrand has been introduced into the world—its coming must inevitably give rise to a fearful and painful excitement and division among men (xii. 49 ff.). Therefore men are not to allow themselves to be led astray, but rather to recognise from these signs the nearness of the crisis, just as men can foretell what the weather is going to be from the wind and the clouds (xii. 54 ff.). This saying about the signs in heaven, which is appropriate here, is less appropriately brought by Matthew (xvi. 2 f.) into connection with the demand of the Pharisees for a sign. But, even apart from the general signs of the times, each man individually must show the right, the genuine, prudence, and make his peace with the heavenly ruler while time is still granted him to do so (this is the original sense of the parable in xii. 58; it is different in Matt. v. 25 f.). The fate of those whom Pilate slew while they were sacrificing should be an example to each of what may befall himself. God still exercises patience with the Jewish people, as a gardener with an unfruitful fig-tree, but the time is already fixed at which the judgment shall inevitably be executed (xiii. 6–9).

After these discourses, the inner connection of which is easily recognisable, there follows (xiii. 10 f.) a series of sections which are but loosely connected. The two cures upon the Sabbath (Luke xiii. 10–17, and xiv. 1–6) are companion pictures to that of Mark iii. 1–6. The pair of parables about the mustard-seed and the leaven (xiii. 18–21) form an expansion of the third parable in the discourse of Mark iv. The question whether many shall be saved gives rise to the exhortation: Strive to enter in through the narrow gate, for the time is coming when it shall be shut, and then the appeal of those who are excluded to their connection with the Master of the House, the Messiah, as His compatriots, will be of no avail; they shall be excluded, as workers of unrighteousness, from the Messianic feast, while countless numbers from all quarters of the earth shall have a part therein with the patriarchs and prophets (xiii. 23–30). Matthew has used different portions of this discourse, freely adapted, in various places (vii. 22, viii. 11 f., xxv. 11 f.). The warning that Herod was seeking to put him to death (xiii. 32 f.) Jesus answers by pointing to the fate of the prophets, who never met with martyrdom anywhere else than in Jerusalem, and to this the Evangelist attaches a lamentation over Jerusalem (34 f.) which betrays itself as a quotation from an apocalyptic writing by the closing words, which are without meaning on the lips of Jesus when He is actually travelling up to Jerusalem: "Ye [people of Jerusalem] shall see me no more until the time cometh when ye shall say, Blessed be he that cometh in the name of the Lord." It is doubtless from the same writing as that from which the quotation xi. 49–51 is derived (in Matthew they stand side by side, xxiii. 34–39).

As above, in xi. 38, the scene of the polemic against the Pharisees is placed by Luke, somewhat inappropriately, at the table of a Pharisee, so here, in chapter xiv., several sayings, not closely interconnected, upon modesty, and generosity to the poor, together with the parable of the Great Supper, are combined to form a discourse spoken at the table of one of the chief men among the Pharisees (xiv. 1, 7–24). The occasion of the parable the Evangelist represents to have been the exclamation of one of the guests (verse 15), "Blessed is he who shall eat bread in the kingdom of God!" *i.e.* shall have a part in the Messianic feast; this is an example of Luke's favourite way of introducing a discourse of Jesus as spontaneously suggested by the situation. The story of the parable is here simpler than in the parallel Matt. xxii. 1–14, the striking allegorical traits of which are wanting in Luke; but even his version of it shows a tendency to add a slight colouring of allegory to the original. The main thought of the parable is that the indifference of the guests who were first invited, namely the upper classes of the Jewish people, who, preoccupied with worldly interests, ignored the invitation to the Messianic kingdom, becomes to the servant of God (Jesus) the reason for turning to the poor and miserable of the town, who respond eagerly to His invitation. To this the Evangelist adds yet a third invitation, addressed to the homeless upon the highway, through whose coming the house is at length filled—these are the heathen, who showed themselves as receptive towards the Apostolic preaching as the publicans and sinners of Israel did towards the gospel of Jesus. There are excluded, however, as verse 24 emphatically asserts, those who were first invited, *i.e.* the upper classes in Israel, who are hardened in their pride—the well-off and outwardly respectable people like the Pharisees.

The multitude of doubtful followers gives Jesus occasion to emphasise (xiv. 25 ff.) the seriousness of the sacrifices and renunciation which His service demanded. He warns them, by the two parables of the building of the tower and the king entering on a campaign, against over-hasty resolves, for the carrying out of which their strength would be insufficient. For no one could be His disciple who did not renounce all his possessions, who did not hate father and mother, wife and children, brothers and sisters, yea, and his own soul also (his life), who did not take up his cross and follow Him—sayings which in this severe, and therefore doubtless original, form are only preserved by Luke, but to which similar sayings are found in Matthew and Mark, and which certainly belong to the most genuine tradition. According to this, we have in Jesus not so much the apostle of peace as the man of heroic resolution, the vehement reformer, who, in His resolve to combat the worldly powers which stood in His way (xii. 49 ff.), and confident in the victory of His cause (xii. 32), demands from His followers the same radical breach with all social bonds which He Himself has effected in His own case (Mark iii. 31; Luke ix. 58 ff.). The figure of the salt which has lost its savour, which each of the Evangelists brings in at a different point—doubtless because it was afloat on the stream of tradition without any exact point of attachment as regards its original occasion and connection—is inserted here by Luke (xiv. 34), perhaps with the meaning that without the needful resolution and endurance the disciples will be as useless as spoiled salt. In chapter xv. Luke collects three parables of the love of God to sinners, of which Matthew only gives the first (xviii. 22 ff.). They are introduced by the remark that the Pharisees and Scribes murmured because Jesus received sinners and ate with them. To this Jesus answers first with the two parables of the Lost Sheep and the Lost Piece of Silver, which illustrate the love and faithfulness of God in seeking, in whose eyes each individual soul is of such value that He will not let it be lost, and that the winning of it, the saving of the lost, arouses greater joy in heaven among the angels of God than the safety of the others which has never been endangered. It is the same thought as in Mark ii. 17, "They that are whole need not a physician, but they that are sick; I am come not to call the righteous, but sinners." The gospel of Jesus is addressed, in contradistinction to the national legal religion, and also to John the Baptist's preaching of repentance, to individuals, and His saving love is most eager about those who most need deliverance. In the third of these parables, the Prodigal Son, which is peculiar to Luke, the seeking of the lost is less emphasised, and loving mercy towards those who repent and return becomes the main point. The full treatment of the details of the story is due to Luke's effort after vividness of narration. It is possible, perhaps, to find an allegorical elaboration of the main idea, in the shape of a reference to the heathen, in the fact that the younger son goes away into a far country, and, during the famine, takes service with a citizen of that country, herding swine for him (a Jewish symbol for the heathen life); but this interpretation is not necessarily implied. That the son in his wretchedness comes to a better mind and resolves to return to his father, but yet, in the consciousness of his guilt, does not feel himself worthy to be received as a son, and is prepared to be content with the condition of a hired servant; but that the father, full of compassion, receives him again, and holds a feast in celebration of his return; that, finally, the elder son is jealous at this, and that his vexation is gently soothed by the father, who assures him of his inalienable right of sonship, yet with the mild reproach that he also ought to share in the general joy at the coming to life again of his brother who was spiritually dead—these are traits of abiding truth, which find their application not merely in the relation of Jewish sinners to the Pharisaic righteous, or of the Gentiles to the Jews, but in human society at all times. In the attitude of the earthly father to the two sons, which is explained with such accurate psychology, there is reflected the main thought of the gospel, that God, without detriment to His righteousness, will have mercy upon repentant sinners, and that He expects, from those who have not gone astray, sympathy with His own attitude of love towards those who have gone astray, but have returned. Thus this parable is "the loftiest apology for the religion of Jesus," as Jülicher[1] well says. But his further remark also deserves notice, that the God of Luke xv. does not receive sinners on the ground of the death of Christ, but because He cannot do otherwise than forgive; Jesus did not first by His death make possible the Divine forgiveness, but by revealing the Divine attitude of mercy He called forth belief in it on the part of men. It is further to be remarked that this parable has a certain affinity with that of the two sons in Matt. xxi. 28, which is

[1] *Gleichnisreden Jesu,* vol. ii. p. 365.

not, however, so close that the latter must necessarily be assumed to be the basis of the former (the main point of the Lucan parable, the fatherly forgiveness of the son who is first disobedient and then goes, is absent in Matthew). The affinity is almost closer in the case of the following Buddhist parable: A son who has long lived in a far country in poor circumstances comes to the mansion of his father, who in the meantime has become rich, and fails to recognise him; but the father recognises him, and, in order to test him, engages him as a servant. After the son has proved himself by long service, he offers him the position of a son of the house; but the son, feeling his unworthiness, refuses the offer. Then the father makes himself known to him, and delivers over to him, in the presence of all his servants and friends, his whole possessions as his inheritance. Here, indeed, the main point of the Lucan parable is wanting—guilt, repentance, and forgiveness, but it is a noticeable coincidence that in both cases the returned son feels himself worthy only of the position of servant in the father's house; but whereas in the Christian parable the exaltation to the dignity of sonship follows immediately, in the Buddhist parable it is only attained by a long period of service. Whether the resemblance is due to mere chance, or whether similar folk-tales influenced both, may be left an open question.[1]

In chapter xvi. there follow the two parables, peculiar to Luke, of the Unjust Steward and of the Rich Man and Lazarus. The difficulty which

[1] Foucaux, *Le Lotus de la bonne loi,* chap. iv., Parabole de l'enfant égaré, Paris, 1854.

exegetes have found in both, and especially in the former, is due to the fact that they think themselves bound to interpret the individual traits allegorically, a method of interpetration in which, indeed, the Evangelist himself made a beginning, and for which he gave the suggestion, by the additions which he has made to the groundwork of the parables.

In the allegorical interpretation of the unjust steward and his master, who commends him for his astuteness, in spite of his dishonesty, the most curious suggestions have been made, which only serve to betray the perplexity of the interpreters. If the master represents God, there result the amazing consequences that the steward by his dishonesty in the administration of the property of God can hope to gain for himself a place in the everlasting habitations, that is, in heaven (verses 4 and 9), and that God not merely does not censure this dishonest conduct but actually praises it (verse 8). To avoid these difficulties, others have thought of the master of the house, on the contrary, as the devil, or personified Mammon, so that the stealing of his property would be a use of earthly goods which contravened the interests of the devil, and which was therefore a pious and praiseworthy act. But unfaithfulness is always unrighteousness, even when the object of it is a bad master; and who, on this interpretation, are the devil's debtors, what the remission of their debts, what the dismissal threatened by the devil to his servant, and what is the meaning of the devil's praise? This interpretation, as every one feels, cannot be carried through. Other artificial schemes, such as, for example, the interpretation of the householder as the Romans, and his steward as the publicans, may be set aside without hesitation. No satisfactory treatment of this parable is possible on the customary assumption that every individual feature in the parable must have an allegorical interpretation. If, however, this erroneous assumption is dropped, and it is remembered that a parable only aims at illustrating a single thought, and, in order to represent this vividly, uses pictures from daily life, without taking into account the significance of the actions from other points of view—their moral value or otherwise—then everything becomes simple. The point of this parable is that true wisdom in the use of earthly goods consists in applying them to benevolence in order thereby to gain an entrance into the Kingdom of God—a thought which we frequently meet elsewhere in the Gospels (*cf.* Luke xi. 41, xii. 33; Matt. xix. 21, xxv. 40), and which is well known to have been current in Jewish thinking (*cf.* Prov. xix. 17). This true wisdom is in this case illustrated by the vulgar prudence which the children of this world, within their own sphere and from their own standpoint, exercise with marvellous astuteness, so that in this point, in the skill and precision with which they choose the right means to attain their ends, they may serve as a pattern to the children of light. It is only from this one point of view, *i.e.* as regards its prudence—the moral aspect of the action being left out of account—that the conduct of the steward is held up as a model, to stimulate the children of light in the exercise of the highest wisdom. Beyond this, the steward and the master and the debtors have no further significance, but are simply familiar figures from daily life. Although, however, in the parable itself the steward is only praised in respect of his cleverness and is looked at without reference to his moral character, the Evangelist could not refrain from a reflection on this side of the matter, although it tends to obscure the point of the parable, and so came, by an obvious association of ideas, to add to the parable some sayings which assuredly did not originally belong to it—that about faithfulness in little things, especially in the use of the earthly goods which so easily lead to unrighteousness, and of the reward of faithfulness in this, namely, the being entrusted with the true riches of the Kingdom of God (verses 10–13). As this thought is further developed in the parable of faithful stewardship, the parable of the Talents (xix. 12–27), the counterpart of this parable of the prudent but unfaithful steward, the conjecture naturally suggests itself that these verses, which are joined by Luke to the latter, originally stood in connection with the former.

In the case of the other of these two parables also, which are connected in their fundamental thought, we have to distinguish between their original sense and the additions of the Evangelist. Fundamentally, it is an illustration of the Lucan beatitudes (vi. 20 f.) upon the pious sufferers, who are to receive their consolation in the future, and of the woes pronounced upon the godless and loveless rich, who have received their good things in this life, and therefore must expect evil in the other world (xvi. 25). Even this groundwork of the parable differs so strikingly from the usual parables of Jesus that there are grounds for suspecting that it is not properly to be reckoned as one of them; and indeed the Evangelist has not, as he usually does, expressly introduced it as a parable. It is rather a typical *example*, which gives a concrete representation of the general thought in an individual instance taken from the same sphere, than a *parable*, which symbolises and makes vivid a truth belonging to the higher, ethico-religious sphere by analogous events or circumstances of common everyday life. In a regular parable the agents, who only represent general types, never have individual names affixed to them, and the action never goes beyond the sphere of present experience into transcendental regions, as is the case in the instance before us. For these reasons we may doubt whether this irregular parable originally belonged to the parables of Jesus. But that does not mean that the Evangelist has invented the groundwork of the parable, but that he has taken over and used material from some other source, probably from Jewish legend, in order thereby to introduce a further thought which was important to him, but is quite foreign to the original material. The concluding portion of the parable, in fact (verses 27–31), is an allegory composed by the Evangelist himself. The rich man with his five brothers now becomes a type of the Jews, whose ancestor Judah had, according to Gen. xxix f., five brothers; and when Abraham says that they will not believe, even though one rose from the dead, this is an unmistakable allusion to the unbelief of the Jewish people in Jesus the Messiah, even in spite of His resurrection. The Fourth Evangelist wished to insist on this obstinate Jewish unbelief, even in face of a return of

Lazarus from the dead, and therefore represented the return of Lazarus from the dead, which is here only suggested, as actually taking place (John xi.). This is a good example of the way in which what is originally a legend becomes a parable, the parable is expanded into an allegory, and the allegory is finally transformed into a miracle-story.

Between these two parables Luke has inserted some sayings which certainly did not originally belong to this context (verses 14–18). With the remark that the avaricious Pharisees mocked at the sayings directed against the worship of Mammon, the author seeks, in his favourite fashion, to create a situation appropriate to the ensuing discourse, which deals first with the pretended piety of the Pharisees, who only gain the applause of men, while their pride is an offence to the Searcher of Hearts. The connection of what follows with this is not, however, quite clear. Perhaps the Evangelist desired to indicate that the self-righteousness of the Pharisees, even if they could appeal under the old covenant to the Law and the Prophets, now, at any rate, had no further justification, because the old covenant of the Law had come to an end with John the Baptist, and since then the good tidings of the Kingdom of God held the field, and to that Kingdom all, without distinction, sinners and righteous, Gentiles as well as Jews, may, if their zeal be sufficient, press in and find entrance. In verse 16, therefore, there is contrasted with the Jewish exclusive principle of legal righteousness the new principle which the preaching of the Kingdom of God has brought into force, of the universality of the Kingdom of God, which stands open to all, and into which all may press. The similar saying in Matthew (xi. 12 f.) is to be understood somewhat differently, as we shall see later. But having now paraphrased the Pauline thought, " Christ is the end of the law for everyone that believeth," he desires at the same time to avoid, in the interests of Church apologetic, the misunderstanding and misuse of this bold thought in an extreme antinomian sense, and sets side by side with this Pauline statement its antithesis, the inexpugnable validity of the Law, to the last jot and tittle (verse 17). In order, however, to blunt the dangerous point of this watchword of Jewish conservatism, and to confine it to its proper measure of validity in the Church, he immediately proceeds to give (verse 18), in the definite instance of the Christian law of marriage, an example of the extent to which the Law maintains its validity unimpaired. Its ethical demand, protecting and consecrating social life, is not merely to retain its significance in Christianity, but is to be accepted and followed as having an even stricter sense, going beyond that of the Mosaic Law. In this way Luke seeks to reconcile, upon a basis of ecclesiastical morality, the antithetic religious principles of universalism apart from the Law and of legal conservatism.

In chapter xvii. there follow some short discourses upon offences, readiness to forgive, the power of faith to remove mountains, or properly sycomores, as Luke says instead of mountains, probably because in Mark he found this saying connected with the incident of the barren fig-tree. Then follows, in xvii. 7–10, a genuinely Pauline saying about the absence of "merit" in the doing of duty, which is peculiar to

Luke. Peculiar to him also is the section about the grateful Samaritan (xvii. 11–19) who is distinguished from the nine ungrateful (Jews) in the same way as the good Samaritan is distinguished from the priest and Levite. In xvii. 20–37, Luke gives an eschatological discourse additional to those in Mark, which he introduces by the question of the Pharisees regarding the time of the coming of the Kingdom of God. On this there follows, in the first place, the answer, "The kingdom of God cometh not with observation [*i.e.* in a striking way which arrests observation]; they shall not say, Lo, here! or, Lo, there [it is coming]!' for, behold, the kingdom of God is within you." This is a very strange answer—how can it be said to the Pharisees that the Kingdom of God is within them, in their hearts?—and that is the only possible meaning of ἐντὸς ὑμῶν; "in your midst," "in your neighbourhood," would be expressed by ἐν μέσῳ ὑμῶν. And how can the presence of the Kingdom of God be asserted, and its catastrophic coming denied, when everywhere else in the Synoptic Gospels the latter is expected, and is so clearly implied in the very discourse which follows immediately upon the above answer? In verse 22 we have the words, "And he said unto the disciples, The days shall come when ye shall desire to see one of the days of the Son of Man [of the Messianic time of salvation], and shall not see it [because its coming is delayed]. And they shall say unto you, See here! or, See there! Go not thither, and seek it not. For as the lightning lightens from one quarter of the heavens to another, so shall the [coming of the]

Son of Man be in his day." This discourse to the disciples stands in such complete contradiction with the preceding answer to the Pharisees that here no exegetical art will avail,[1] and the only hypothesis that remains open is that verses 20 ff. were composed by the Evangelist himself (in the sense of Rom. xiv. 17) and prefixed to the following discourse (verses 22 ff.) with the aim of restraining the impatience of those whose thought was set upon apocalypses. It seemed only possible completely to avert the dangers of eschatological enthusiasm, against which the warning of verse 23 is also directed, by making the capital change of substituting for the apocalyptic catastrophe the inward presence of the Kingdom of God (verses 20 f.)—a turning to the Johannine idea of immanence similar to that which is found also in Matt. xxviii. 20 and xviii. 20.

At the close of his long interpolation Luke has placed two parables peculiar to himself. The first, that of the Unjust Judge and the importunate widow (xviii. 1–8), expresses exactly the same thought as the parable, which is also peculiar to Luke, in xi. 5–13: exhortation to earnest and persistent prayer, which cannot fail to be answered. Here again, as in the parable of the Unjust Steward, we have a case where the allegorical interpretation of the details which make up the picture is excluded by the absurdities to which it would lead; for it is self-evident that it cannot here be intended to describe God as an "unjust judge," any more than,

[1] The suggestions in this connection of A. Meyer (*Jesu Muttersprache*, p. 87 f.) are rejected by Dalman (*Worte Jesu*, p. 116 f., E.T. p. 143).

in the other parable, it is intended to assert of Him that He takes pleasure in the unrighteousness of men. At the close, the parable connects itself with the expectation of the future of the previous chapter, and gives the reason why the appearance of the Son of Man is not to take place so soon as impatient hope desires—namely, because there is still too little faith on earth; and in saying this the Evangelist is probably not thinking merely of the still unconverted world of Jews and heathen, but of the absence, in many quarters, of true faith, even within the Church. The second parable, that of the Pharisee and the Publican (xviii. 9–14), expresses once more the favourite thought of the Evangelist—the penitent sinner is justified (note the Pauline phrase), and is therefore worth more in the sight of God than the Pharisee who is counted righteous in the sight of men; as, in general, he who exalts himself is abased, and he who humbles himself is exalted (verse 14). The last, very instructive, addition shows us how in Luke the central religious thought of the Pauline theology receives a generalised application in which it is transferred from the dogmatic sphere to the ethical, and indeed—if the expression may be permitted—to the Christian-social sphere. The often-expressed sympathy of our author for the world of sinners is not merely an expression of his dogmatic conviction with which certain Ebionite or Judaising traits are brought into a quite external connection, the purpose of this binding together of heterogeneous elements being to smooth the way for an external compromise between the various parties in the Early Church; that is a fundamental error which wholly misrepresents what is most essential in Luke's way of thought, and certainly also misrepresents the great majority of the Christian churches of his time. Luke's love for sinners arises at least as much, if not more, from his ethico-social views in general as from his Paulinism; it is to a great extent the religious expression of a human sympathy with the poor and lowly, who are despised by those who are of better social station and legally "righteous" (the respectables), but are highly esteemed by God on account of their humility and longing for salvation. And as Luke certainly did not stand alone in this, but represented the prevailing temper of the whole of early Christianity, we may here recognise what the really comprehensible and attractive side of Pauline doctrine was for the majority of the Christian communities—not, by any means, the doctrine of justification, not his Rabbinical dialectic or transcendental speculations, but his truly humane and all-embracing love, wholly opposed to both Gentile and Jewish aristocratic intolerance or exclusiveness towards those who in the eyes of the world are despised as of no account, but who have been chosen by God (1 Cor. i. 20–29; *cf.* Luke x. 21, vi. 20 ff., i. 51 ff., xiv. 21–24).

CHAPTER VII

The Final Conflict, Defeat and Victory

(Luke xviii. 15–xxiv. 53)

In xviii. 15, Luke returns again, after the conclusion of his long interpolation, to the text of the foundation narrative (Mark x. 13), and follows its order, in essentials, up to the story of the Passion. Only the discourse suggested by the ambitious request of the sons of Zebedee (Mark x. 35–45) is passed over by Luke, because he intends to give his substitute for it in the story of the Last Supper. After the cure of the blind man at Jericho he inserts the story of the chief of the publicans, Zacchæus, and the parable of the Pounds. The former (xix. 1–10) is peculiar to Luke. As a companion picture to that of the blind beggar Bartimæus ("son of the unclean") he gives us that of the publican Zacchæus (meaning "pure") as the representative of men who were despised by the Jews and placed by them on the same level with the heathen, but who by reason of their penitence and faith in Jesus were purified from their guilt and made worthy to have Jesus come to them, and thus were taken up among the sons of Abraham's faith and into the true Israel of God. The saying of Jesus to Zacchæus, "To-day is salvation come unto this house, forasmuch as he also is a son of Abraham," reminds us of the Pauline description of the spiritual sons of Abraham (Gal. iii. 9, 29; Rom. iv. 11 ff.).

The parable of the Pounds (xix. 11–27) has a double application, which is always a certain proof that a simple groundwork has undergone expansion and elaboration. The original groundwork consisted only of the picture of the faithful and unfaithful servant, and served to emphasise the duty of the faithful use of earthly riches. The lesson of the parable is declared in xvi. 10–12, verses which originally belonged, doubtless, not to the parable of the Unjust Steward, but to that of the Pounds. With this is interwoven, however, the quite disparate picture of the prince who went into a far country to receive for himself a kingdom, and whose subjects meanwhile revolted against him; for which reason they were put to death by him on his return (verses 12, 14, 27). This second story serves, indeed, as a frame for the first about the servants, but it has no inner connection with it. How have the two parts come into their present combination? Were they originally two separate parables, which had already been fused together in the oral tradition, or were welded together by the Evangelist? Neither of these alternatives is probable. For the story of the prince going into a far country and of his rebellious subjects is no proper parable, it does not set forth a general truth of the higher life by means of events taken from ordinary experience; it is rather an allegory, every feature of which had an allegorical significance. The prince who goes into a far country in order to receive for himself a kingdom signifies Christ, who has left the scene of His earthly work in order to be exalted to be King of the Kingdom of God, to be heavenly Lord of the Messianic community. The rebellious citizens who will not have Him to be King over them are the Jews, who refused, after Jesus' departure from the earth, to acknowledge Him as their lawful sovereign. His return after receiving a kingdom signifies the Parousia of Christ, and the suppression of the rebellion stands for the judgment on unbelieving Judaism. It is clear that an elaborate allegory of this kind is quite different from the simple parables of Jesus; it cannot, therefore, have been handed down as such, but was doubtless composed by the Evangelist, influenced probably by a reminiscence of the account given by Josephus (*Ant.*, xvii. 11. 1–4) of the journey of Archelaus to Rome to obtain the kingship (instead of which, however, he only obtained an ethnarchy), and the arrival there at the same time of a Jewish embassy, to protest against his rule. These incidents have been applied by the Evangelist to give to the parable of the Pounds a secondary, eschatological significance. To this purpose, too, must be referred what he says in verse 11 about the occasion of the whole parable, that the people thought the Kingdom of God would immediately appear. He desires to restrain this impatient expectation of the Parousia by the reminder that Christ Himself must first receive a kingdom before He returned from the far country to which He had departed; but, the Evangelist reminds men, retribution will not on that account fail—neither the reward of the true servants, nor the punishment of the unfaithful and rebellious.

In his account of the triumphal entry, in which he in other respects follows Mark, Luke makes (xix. 38) the crowd of enthusiastic disciples hail Jesus definitely as the king that cometh in the name of the Lord (whereas Mark speaks less definitely of the coming kingdom of our father David), and adds words which recall the hymn of the angels in the birth-story, "Peace in heaven, and glory in the highest"—the earthly echo, as it were, of the heavenly greeting with which the first entry of the Heavenly King into His earthly Kingdom was hailed. The narrative which follows in Mark's Gospel, of the cursing of the barren fig-tree, symbolising the unfruitful Jewish nation, is omitted by Luke, because he has already given the parable which lies at the basis of the miracle-story (xiii. 6–9); in place of it he gives, perhaps as a substitute for this curse, which seems to him too severe—a touching picture of Jesus, at the approach to the city, weeping tears of pity over it, because it had been blind to the salvation which had come near unto it, and was now irrevocably condemned to the judgment of destruction (xix. 41–44). The cleansing of the Temple which, according to Mark, plays so important a part in the course of events during the Passover week in Jerusalem, is reported by Luke in such an abbreviated form that he seems to have wished to make it an episode of small importance, and he does not make this the cause, as Mark does—and doubtless with historical justification—of the murderous plans of the chief priests and rulers against Jesus, but finds the cause in His daily teaching in the Temple; referring, for example, the official question as to His authority for "doing these things" to the previously mentioned teaching (xx. 2; *cf.* xx. 1 and xix. 47), not to the cleansing of the Temple, as in Mark. What moved the Evangelist to this obviously intentional departure from the narrative which he is in the main following, was without doubt his dislike, evident elsewhere in his writings (especially in Acts), of anything which looks like violence, like a revolt against established custom and order. Just as he gives, for this reason, a very much softened picture of the anti-legalistic reforming action of the Apostle Paul, and almost reduces the point at issue to a less dangerous question of teaching, so in the same way he has suppressed the decisive consequences of Jesus' reforming act, and has instead made Jesus' harmless teaching, which won the approval of "all the people," the occasion of the enmity of the rulers of the people (verse 47). In this way the antithesis of religious principle between the legal positivism of the Jewish hierarchy, as the representative of Judaism in general, and the moral and spiritual idealism of the prophet and reformer of Nazareth is practically lost sight of, and in its stead there appears only the social antithesis between the jealousy of the upper classes about the privileges of their position and the favourite teacher of the populace, who, moreover, in confining Himself to harmless teaching, gives no occasion to the civil authority (Rome) to harbour any suspicion against Him. This instance is thoroughly characteristic of the whole mode of thought and literary method of the author, who has written the history of the beginnings of Christianity from the point of view of the apologist.

The polemical discourses at Jerusalem are reported by Luke in the same order as by his source, and in general agreement with it, the sole exception being the dialogue with the Scribe regarding the greatest commandment, for which he has already given a substitute in x. 25 ff. That he had the story before him at this point is proved by the fact that he preserves the beginning and end of this story as told in Mark (xii. 28 and 34), and has attached it to the polemical discourse about the resurrection (Luke xx. 39, 40). In the great eschatological discourse, he gives to the apocalyptic enigmas of a time of sore distress a quite definite and plain reference to the destruction of Jerusalem and the dispersal of the captive Jews among all nations, and represents Jerusalem as trodden under foot by the Gentiles "until the times of the Gentiles shall be fulfilled" (xxi. 24), by which is meant the restoration of Israel, after the conversion of the Gentiles, to which Paul looked forward. The saying in Mark xiii. 32, that the day and the hour of the end were known to none but God, has been omitted by Luke here, perhaps because he intended to bring it in later, in Acts i. 7.

In the story of the Passion, Luke departs in many respects from his source, whereas Matthew holds more closely to it and takes no notice of Luke's divergences. The anointing in the house of Simon at Bethany is passed over by Luke, because he has, in place of it, the earlier anointing in the house of Simon the Pharisee (vii. 36 ff.; *cf.* above, p. 134).

The betrayal by Judas, Luke endeavours to make more intelligible by saying (xxii. 3) that Satan entered into him, a statement which is further elaborated in the Fourth Gospel. The discourses of Jesus at the Last Supper are reported by Luke in a form which is for the most part peculiar to himself. From the first the note of farewell is struck by Jesus' declaration that He had desired with longing to eat this Passover with His disciples before He suffered, for He will not eat it again until it be fulfilled (or, according to Cod. D, eaten new) in the Kingdom of God (xxii. 16)—an anticipation of the thought of verse 18, which belongs to the common tradition, "I will drink no more of the fruit of the vine until the Kingdom of God has come," which no doubt bears the same meaning as the more definite phrase in Mark, "until the day when I drink it new in the Kingdom of God." But whereas in the parallel passages this saying is only loosely connected with the distribution of the symbolic cup at the Last Supper, in Luke (verse 17) it forms the essential explanation of the fact that Jesus handed the cup to His disciples immediately after the prayer of thanksgiving which He offered over it, with the command to divide it among themselves (alone); it is intended, that is, to declare that He Himself for the present, until the coming of the new order of things which is to be introduced by the Divine Kingship, will abstain from the use of wine. That this is the sense of verses 17 f. can scarcely be doubted,[1] however obscure may be the motive of this abstinence, which at a Paschal meal (if such it really was) is doubly surprising. Perhaps it may be explained as a kind of vow, in which the confident belief in the near approach of the hoped-for end was expressed (*cf.* Acts xxiii. 12). A trait so peculiar has

[1] *Cf.* B. Weiss-Meyer, *Komm.*, pp. 527 f.

certainly not been invented by the Evangelist, but taken from the earliest tradition. Not until after this distribution and explanation of the first cup does Luke proceed to tell of the distribution of the symbolic bread and cup of the Supper; and it is only in the first half (down to the words, "This is my body") that his account runs parallel to that of the other Evangelists. Peculiar to him is the addition "which is given for you: this do in remembrance of me," and also the formula used in the distribution of the second cup (20), "and the cup also [*sc.* he took and gave to them] after the supper, saying, 'This cup is the new covenant in my blood, which is shed for you.'" This Lucan version of the words of Jesus at the Supper (19b, 20) is evidently derived from 1 Cor. xi. 24 f., with which it is almost verbally identical; only the latter part of verse 20, "which is shed for you," is adopted from Mark xiv. 24 and added to the Pauline words in a grammatically awkward way. The question arises whether the Evangelist himself interpolated into his narrative these sayings derived from 1 Cor., thus displacing another form of the tradition, or whether the interpolation is due to a later hand, the original Lucan narrative having in that case closed with "This is my body." In favour of the latter is the fact that verses 19b and 20 are wanting in important Western manuscripts (Cod. D), and the omission of these important words is as difficult to explain as the insertion of them is easy to account for. The omission of the distribution of the symbolic cup was unwelcome, and it was therefore added to the Lucan account, which originally contained only one giving of the cup, without any reference to the ritual of the Supper (verse 17) in the form of a second giving of the cup (verse 20), by means of an interpolation derived from 1 Cor.[1] We shall have more to say on this point in a later context.

The prediction of the betrayal, which the parallel narratives place at the beginning of the meal, is only inserted by Luke at this point (verses 21–23), and in a simpler form, without special reference to Judas; only in verse 22, where the "going" of the Son of Man is referred to the fore-ordination of God, which nevertheless does not exclude the accursed guilt of the betrayer, does he follow the lines of the Marcan apologetic (xiv. 21); except for this, he seems here, as also in what precedes and follows, to use a special, and as it seems, indeed, an older form of the tradition. To the question of the disciples, which of them was meant by the betrayer (verse 23), he subjoins the strife about precedence which Mark narrates earlier, in connection with the ambitious request of the sons of Zebedee (x. 41 ff.). Jesus calms the dispute with the striking saying, "It shall not be so among you as it is among worldly rulers and wielders of power, but the greatest among you shall be as the youngest, and the leader as he that serves"; and He pointed to His own example, for He did not play the part of the master among them, who makes others serve him (at table), but rather of the servant (verse 27). Here we have the original form of the saying which in Mark and Matthew has been elaborated in a dogmatic

[1] *Cf.* Westcott and Hort, *Select Readings*, p. 64: "These difficulties . . . leave no moral doubt that the words in question were absent from the original text of Luke." So, too, Zahn, *Einleitung*, ii. 358 f.; Brandt., *Ev. Gesch.*, p. 301.

sense and applied to the atoning death of the Son of Man, and in John has been illustrated by the symbolic act of the feet-washing. After this rebuke of the ambition of the disciples, they are, however, promised that those who remain faithful to their Master amid all attacks on the part of the hostile world shall share the position of authority which is destined for Him by His Father, shall eat and drink at His table in His Kingdom, and shall sit on thrones judging (that is, ruling) the twelve tribes of Israel (verses 29 ff.)—a saying, the realistic stamp of which should not be obliterated by allegorising, but recognised as a mark of the completest genuineness (*cf.* xii. 32 and the note thereon, p. 153). To the promise of lordship given to all the disciples Luke immediately attaches, in intentional contrast, the prediction of Peter's denial (verses 31–34), which the parallel narratives represent as given later, on the way to the Mount of Olives, and in connection with that of the flight of the Apostles in general. To this last there is found in Luke only the slight allusion in verse 31, "Satan hath desired to have you (pl.) that he may sift you as wheat." The more definite saying in Mark xiv. 27 f., that the disciples shall all be offended, and be scattered like the sheep of a shepherdless flock, has been suppressed by Luke, because it was not appropriate to his representation of the ensuing history and was opposed to his feeling of respect for the original Apostles; the same feeling is expressed in the saying in verse 32, which is intended to make Peter's fall more forgivable by recalling his subsequent conversion and position of influence as a pillar of the Church. These discourses at the Last Supper close with the command, peculiar to Luke, to buy a sword. That is now the most necessary thing: so much so, that purse and scrip, and even cloak, should be given in exchange for one (verse 36). According to the usual interpretation, these words were only meant in the sense that the disciples must henceforth reckon on the enmity of the world. But the disciples themselves certainly did not understand them in this sense, for they answered, "Lord, here are two swords" (verse 38), to which Jesus answered, "It is enough." That this was irony directed against the disciples' misunderstanding of His allegorically meant command is not suggested by the text. As Jesus' words run, they could scarcely be understood otherwise than in the literal sense; if this was not Jesus' meaning, a clear correction of the misunderstanding might have been expected, not an ironic saying which was itself open to misunderstanding. If the text, then, imposes upon us a literal interpretation of the words, they imply, since the only reason for procuring swords is to use them as weapons, that Jesus intended to defend Himself against an attempted assassination, and such an attack, therefore, must have been what He expected from the enmity, which was well known to Him, of the hierarchs, not an official arrest by the servants of the Government. Therefore, as soon as He recognised that it was the latter with which He had to deal, He immediately restrained the attempt at resistance on the part of His disciples (verse 51, "Hold, no more!"). But however well this decision of Jesus to defend Himself with arms against hireling assassins suits the historical situation, it by no means suits the dogmatic theory, which arose subsequently from the apologetic reflection of the community, of the divinely ordained necessity of the atoning death of Christ, which He Himself had known of long beforehand and predicted. It is therefore quite intelligible that, later, people did not know what to make of the sword-buying, and it is therefore omitted in the other Gospels. Luke, however, has here, as in the account of the Supper (p. 177 f.), preserved a fragment of the oldest tradition, from which he attempted to remove the strangeness and difficulty by making Jesus at the same time refer to the necessity which was laid on Him, according to the Scriptures, of meeting the death of a criminal (verse 37), which is difficult to reconcile with the intention to defend Himself. It is just because this appeared from the later standpoint unthinkable, that the saying about buying a sword (verses 36, 38) cannot be held to be a later legend, but must belong to very early, historically valuable, tradition.

In the scene in Gethsemane Luke has added the appearance of the angel to Jesus to strengthen Him, and the question of the disciples at the arrest, whether they should smite with the sword, which implies that several of them were armed, and thus confirms verse 38. Jesus forbids them to fight (verse 51, "Hold, no more!"), and heals the ear of the apparitor—one of the legends which can be explained from the motives which are peculiar to Luke. Then Luke strangely represents the words of Mark xiv. 48 f. as being addressed to the chief priests and elders, as though these had come out in person along with the soldiers, and adds, "This is your hour (ordained by God) and the power of darkness" (verse 53). Of the flight of the disciples, however (Mark xiv. 50), he says nothing, doubtless from delicacy.

The denial of Peter, and the mocking of Jesus by the soldiers, are represented by Luke as preceding the trial before the Sanhedrin, which only began at daybreak. According to this (though not according to Mark's account), it becomes possible for Jesus to be present at the time of the denial, and by His reproachful look to move Peter to repentance—the depth and bitterness of which is evidenced by his bitter weeping (xxii. 61 f.). The trial is related by Luke more briefly than by Mark; in particular, he passes over the accusation about the saying attributed to Jesus to the effect that He would break down the material Temple and build up a supersensible temple (Mark xiv. 58), doubtless from the same motives which led him to reduce the cleansing of the Temple—the practical illustration of this saying—to a mere episode of no special significance; our prudent and universally conciliatory historian naturally likes to soften down anything that could make his heroes appear bold innovators and reckless opponents of established usages, even if these were only the Jewish customs of worship. The same purpose of showing that the complete loyalty and unimpeachable good-citizenship of Jesus (and consequently of the Christian community) was testified to by all the authorities concerned, rules and directs his further account of the judicial proceedings. For this reason Luke cannot allow that Jesus, as Mark reported, made no answer whatever to Pilate, His legally constituted judge; instead, according to Luke, to the first question, whether He was the king of the Jews, He promptly replied in the affirmative, whereupon Pilate—frankly, one does not see why—recognised and declared Jesus' innocence (xxiii. 3 f.). Then, hearing that He belonged to Herod's jurisdiction, he sent Him to Herod, who, after mocking Him in frivolous fashion, sent Him back to Pilate. He thereupon twice repeated before the chief priests the solemn declaration (verses 14 f., 22) that neither he nor Herod, the Roman and the Jewish authorities, found any fault in Jesus; finally, however, overcome by the fury of the mob, which was stirred up by the chief priests, he delivered Jesus over to their will. Now, we cannot exactly say that this representation of the trial is wholly unhistorical; that it has a certain kernel of genuine history is confirmed by the trustworthy account in Mark. But it must, on the other hand, be clearly recognised that a repeated declaration of innocence in the case of one who was subsequently condemned, such as Luke, and similarly John, has put into the mouth of Pilate, the procurator, passes the bounds of probability in the case of a Roman official; and also that the attempt to hand over the trial to the Jewish authorities is too little in accordance with the methods of Roman policy and administration to allow us to hold these things to be historical, even apart from the fact that the silence of the other Evangelists would in itself throw doubt on the Lucan additions to the narrative.

When Jesus is led away to the place of execution at Golgotha, Luke represents that He was not merely, as Mark tells us, followed afar off by a number of women-disciples from Galilee, but accompanied by an imposing procession of mourners, consisting of a great multitude of the people, and of sympathising women from Jerusalem, whom Jesus addressed in moving words of prophecy, predicting the future destruction of the blind city (xxiii. 27–31), thus reiterating, at His departure, the thought which had moved His compassionate soul to painful emotion at His entry into the city (xix. 41 f.). And while Mark speaks of only one cry of lamentation uttered by the Crucified, in the words of Ps. xxii., immediately before His death, it is in harmony with Luke's sympathetic nature to lighten the grim silence of those fateful hours when Jesus hung upon the cross by some tender utterances of mercy and consolation. First the prayer for His enemies, who "know not what they do"—which Luke similarly records in the case of the dying Stephen—then the promise of mercy to the penitent thief (verses 40–43), an episode peculiar to Luke, which stands in contradiction, it is true, with the earliest tradition, according to which both of those who were crucified with Him reviled Him (Mark xv. 32), but is admirably adapted to exhibit the merciful tenderness of the Saviour to the lost who long for salvation. Finally, Luke has substituted for the cry of lamentation from Ps. xxii., and the loud death-cry, the consolatory saying from Ps. xxxi. 5, "Father, into thy hands I commit my spirit" (xxiii. 46). To the rending of the veil of the Temple, which Mark records, Luke adds the darkening of the sun; the heaven shrouds itself in darkness at midday for the passing of the Lord, just as His birth was celebrated by a miraculous brightness in the heavens by night. While, according to Mark, the centurion at the cross, as the representative of heathendom, recognised the Crucified as the "Son of God," Luke has "transferred to the ethical plane" (Brandt) this dogmatic confession: the centurion declares Jesus to be "a righteous man," *i.e.* an innocent person, the blamelessness of Christianity as exemplified in the person of its Founder being thus once more solemnly attested from the lips of a Roman official—quite in harmony with the apologetic tendency which runs throughout this Gospel. The statement, too, that all the people remorsefully beat their breasts, is less in accordance with the historical situation (as pictured by Mark) than with the anxiety of Luke to remove the guilt of the rejection of Jesus from the lower classes and ascribe it only to the upper classes of the Jews.

The last chapter of the Gospel narrates the events of the Easter Sunday. As in Mark, three women-disciples (the two Maries, with Joanna in Luke, and Salome in Mark) go in the early morning to the sepulchre, with the intention of embalming the body of Jesus. They find the stone rolled away, and beside it two men in shining raiment (Mark: a youth in a white garment), by which are meant angels. These give to the frightened women the comforting assurance that the Crucified, whom they sought, is not in the grave, but is risen. So far Luke follows the ground-document. At this point, however, he makes a significant departure from it. Whereas in Mark the women were charged to tell His disciples that the risen Master was going before them into Galilee, and that they should see Him there, Luke omits the command to go to Galilee. As he does not, however, like to pass over without any reference the mention of Galilee which he found in the document before him, he gives it a different turn, viz. that the women were reminded by the angels of what Jesus had said to them while He was still in Galilee regarding His approaching death and resurrection (xxiv. 6); thus, instead of a reference forward to the seeing of Jesus again in Galilee in the near future, we have a reference back to their former intercourse with Jesus in Galilee. The reason for this alteration is that Luke wished to make the scene of the appearance of the risen Lord, not Galilee, but Jerusalem; the subsequent centre of the Early Church, and the seat of Apostolic authority, was also to be the birthplace of the Church; therefore, even those first experiences of the disciples, from which, in a miraculous fashion, their conviction that the Crucified was alive grew up and became the standard to which the scattered disciples rallied again and united to form a community, were not to take place in distant Galilee, but in Jerusalem itself, on the consecrated ground upon which the disciples had lost their Master, and where the disciples had gathered together again and closed their ranks about their unseen Head. It was these motives, which so naturally suggested themselves to later apologetic reflection, which led Luke (and subsequently John) to place the appearances of the risen Jesus, not in distant Galilee, but in Jerusalem, and immediately upon the Easter day itself. That was, however, a bold alteration of the earliest tradition; for that this placed at least the first appearances of the risen Jesus in Galilee, and therefore some little time after the day of His death, is to be taken as beyond doubt, on the ground of the genuine conclusion of Mark (xvi. 7 f.), with which agrees also the fragment of the Gospel of Peter (*sup.*, p. 84 f.). Confirmation of this may be found in the Gospel of Matthew, which, no doubt following its usual method of combination, tells of two appearances, one in Jerusalem, to the women as they returned from the sepulchre, and one in Galilee, to the assembled disciples; but the first of these, in which Jesus only repeats the charge which had just before been given to the women by the angel, is so obviously void and aimless, that it is impossible to see in it anything else than an artificial attempt to harmonise the later legend of the appearances at Jerusalem with the earlier tradition, attested by Mark, which knew only of Galilæan appearances.

From this follows the further conclusion that all that Luke xxiv. tells us of the appearances of Jesus on the Easter day in and about Jerusalem does not rest upon the earliest tradition, but is intended to supplant it. It is not necessarily on that account freely invented by the Evangelist; from analogies elsewhere, it is possible that he had before him legends of appearances of Christ in Judæa, which were probably current in the primitive community alongside of the Galilæan tradition, and which he then, with his usual freedom, worked up and put in the place of the older tradition. So, in particular, the story of the appearance to the disciples on the way to Emmaus may be a no longer recognisable legend of the Jerusalem tradition; but the moulding of the legend into this beautiful and artistic story we owe to the skill of the epic poet whom we have recognised in Luke from the stories of the Childhood at the outset of his Gospel. This idyll of the Easter joy overcoming the Good Friday mourning is worthy to take its place beside those exquisite pictures which adorn the fore-court of the sacred history. It combines dogmatic reflection and poetic intuition into such an admirable harmony that, at first sight, it appears to have the naturalness of actual truth, and is only recognised as allegory upon a closer examination. To two disciples not belonging to the Twelve, of whom one was called Cleopas ("the famous"), the Lord appears upon the road, while their eyes, at first, are holden that they should not know Him. The necessity of the sufferings of Christ as a means to His exaltation is explained to them out of the Scriptures. Finally, in the breaking of bread at the evening meal they suddenly recognise the Lord; they are convinced that He is alive, even though He withdraws Himself again from their bodily eyes; and, returning home, they tell the disciples what has happened to them on their journey. What else is this than an allegory of the manifestation of Christ as it happened to the most famous of the Apostles, Paul, on the way from Jerusalem to Damascus, but which also elsewhere, whenever two or three, or a company of disciples, are gathered together in His name, constantly repeats itself anew, in particular in every celebration of the Lord's Supper, that sacramental union with the Crucified and Risen One? In striking contrast with this ideal narrative stands the harsh realism of the following narrative of the appearance of Jesus at Jerusalem to the Eleven, who were convinced of His corporeity by feeling His hands and feet, and seeing Him eat some fish (xxiv. 39–48).

That the material corporeity here implied can hardly be reconciled with His sudden appearances and disappearances and with His subsequent ascension, and that we have here not history but legend, is clear; moreover, it is not to be overlooked that this materialistic representation of the resurrection-body stands in contradiction with the genuine Pauline view of the spirituality of the risen Lord and of the character of His body of "glory" (δόξα). Then the Scriptures are opened up to the Eleven, as previously to the disciples on the way to Emmaus, in order that they may recognise the fore-ordained necessity of the suffering and resurrection of Christ, and, as a consequence, their own vocation to proclaim, in the name of Christ, repentance and forgiveness of sin among all peoples, beginning at Jerusalem.

The Evangelist closes his Gospel with the brief statement that Jesus, after this farewell discourse, went out with His disciples to Bethany, and, as He blessed them, was parted from them; whereupon they returned to Jerusalem and praised God in the Temple. How this "departure" of Jesus is to be conceived, the Evangelist seems originally to have left vague, since the genuineness of the phrase "and he was taken up into heaven" is open to suspicion. Yet, even if they were originally wanting, the "departure" can scarcely mean anything else than His Ascension, which the author, in the second part of his historical work, describes more fully (Acts i. 2–11); and it is doubtless only for this reason that he has not definitely mentioned it at the end of his Gospel.

THE ACTS OF THE APOSTLES

CHAPTER VIII

The Beginnings of the Church

(Acts i. 1–xii. 25)

The author of this work is the same who wrote the third Gospel (and provisionally, therefore, we may simply call him Luke). Since in i. 1 he refers to the Gospel as the first division of his historical work, he gives us the right to assume that the point of view which is announced at the outset of the Gospel also governs his presentation of the Acts of the Apostles. His object therefore, here as there (Luke i. 4), in writing his history was to supply his reader with the basis of a firm religious conviction (ἀσφάλειαν). The reader Theophilus was doubtless, to judge from his name, of Greek origin, and therefore a Gentile Christian. To confirm him, and so the Gentile Christians of his time in general, in the conviction of the truth of his Christian belief by showing the strength of its historic foundation, was, according to the author's own statement, the primary aim of his work, with which was very naturally connected the wider aim of defending this faith in the eyes of the Gentile world, and especially in the eyes of the Roman civil authorities, by proving its complete political innocence, and the frequently attested loyalty of its first preachers. But a proof of the inner religious and outward political justification of the Gentile-Christian Church could not be given without at the same time putting Judaism in the wrong, since it had in irreligious blindness rejected this belief, and in disloyal factiousness was everywhere arousing riots and persecution against the innocent Christians. Thus, with the twofold apologetic aim is quite naturally combined a polemic against the Jews. The more distinctly the Jews could be shown to be in the wrong, from the religious point of view, in their enmity against Christ, the more clearly was it evident that the Gentile-Christian Church was in the right in regarding itself as the true people of God, as the legitimate heir of the Old Testament promises. And the more definitely all the previous persecutions of the Christians were referred to the instigation of jealous Jews, the more clear became the political innocence of the Christian Church, and its claim to toleration from the Romans. But it corresponded not merely with the apologetic aim of the writer, but also with the conviction and tone of feeling of the Gentile Church of the time, to emphasise, on the one hand, the antithesis between Christianity and Judaism, in view of the hostility of the Jews as a nation towards Christ, and, on the other hand, the agreement, the essential unity, of Christianity with Judaism as a divinely revealed and legally acknowledged religion. But at the same time it was inevitable that in proportion as the religious distinction between Christianity and Judaism became of less significance in the consciousness of the increasingly universal

Church, that, also, between Gentile and Jewish Christians should become of less importance. This latter distinction did not in the time of the writer by any means retain its original sharpness; on both sides the opposition had been softened, obscured, almost obliterated. The victorious Gentile Christianity had no longer anything to fear from the insignificant Jewish-Christian minority as regards its right to exist and its freedom from the Law, and had, moreover, never properly understood the specifically Pauline explanation of the abrogation of the Law, and was the less inclined to see a point of controversy in it the more this question lost its practical importance. The Jewish-Christian minority, on their part, had accepted the position as regards the unalterable fact of the predominance of Gentile Christianity, and in the authority of the Old Testament as a revelation of God they brought with them into the young Church a gift of inestimable value, which naturally wound an ever closer bond of union about the two parties the more the Gentile Christians familiarised themselves with this Word of God, the authority of which they reverently acknowledged. This process has so much antecedent probability in its favour, and is so strongly confirmed by the evidence of the literature of the second century, that it can hardly be doubted that we are justified in assuming it. If this opposition within Christianity had at the time when Acts was written so greatly diminished in intensity and had so far disappeared that it was of very little importance in comparison with the outward opposition, it is quite intelligible that the author of this apologetic history could not, or would not, see that opposition at the beginning of Christianity; it would have disturbed his purpose. He understood, that is, primitive Christianity and the origin of the Gentile-Christian Church in the light of his own present, both in regard to its actual circumstances and as regards its apologetic interests; and both the interests and the circumstances of his own time influenced his conception of the history of the past in the same direction. It was natural, therefore, that the history should be seen from a point of view which rendered a right representation, in some essential points, difficult almost to impossibility. To this extent it is undeniably true that the author of Acts was ruled by practical interests in his treatment of his material. In a greater or less degree this is always the case in regard to every record of religious history: it has always practical ends, aiming at edification, at strengthening, confirming, justifying, and defending faith; in the figures of the past it seeks to find lofty ideals, in its events warning and instructive examples and patterns for the present. By these practical aims its objectivity is always more or less disturbed. That this is true in the case of Acts, every unprejudiced reader must admit. But it was a mistake to assume that its aim was to win from Jewish Christianity recognition for Gentile Christianity by means of concessions to the former, and, in the interest of an agreement between them, to draw an artificial imaginary picture of both tendencies, especially of the Pauline. This hypothesis cannot be accepted, if only because the strongly anti-Jewish attitude and the strong Gentile-Christian sympathies which Acts everywhere displays are obviously a most inappropriate means of gaining the assumed end of winning and reconciling Jewish Christianity. Moreover the presuppositions of that hypothesis—that in the second century Gentile Christianity had still to buy and beg from Jewish Christianity, at the price of half its content, the right to exist, is not in accordance with the historical circumstances. Nay, half a century earlier, when Paul wrote the Epistle to the Romans, the position of things was that, on the contrary, it seemed necessary to explain the inferior position of the Jews in the Christian Church, and to maintain before the Gentile Christians, who were already certain of victory, the ultimate justification of their national hopes (Rom. ix.–xi.).

So much may be said provisionally in regard to the purpose of Acts; we shall frequently have to recur to the point in our detailed treatment of the book. With regard to his methods also the author gives us some information in the preface to the Gospel, of which we found numerous confirmations in the course of the book. He had carefully investigated all the old traditions, had therefore used whatever he could discover in either written or verbal sources, and moreover desired to present this material exactly in proper order. What this means is shown at large in the Gospel. The author everywhere endeavoured to bring individual traditions into their ideally appropriate connection, and thus place them in what is, in his opinion, the proper light. With this object he has not only permitted himself the greatest freedom in the arrangement of his material, but has also in some cases freely moulded his material, as in the case of the sermon at Nazareth or the visit of the mother and brethren of Jesus, and has added, when he thought fit, new, freely composed pictures, as the expression of his Christian ideas (*e.g.* the stories of the Childhood, the mission of the seventy disciples, Peter's draught of fishes, the appearance to the disciples on the road to Emmaus). In all this he shows a creative freedom which it would be impossible to reconcile with our conceptions of writing history. But the fact is that the ancient conceptions of history were very different, and Luke might well be of opinion that he was exhibiting history in the true light by this very process of filling in the gaps in the tradition, restoring the colour where it had become faint, erasing what was disturbing or unedifying, or clothing it in another and less dangerous form. In Acts he has followed the same procedure. Here, too, he wished to write a history, and, to that end, he has used sources and traditions so far as he had access to them. But he gives the history in the way in which it appeared to his own mind and that of his contemporaries, and which seemed to answer to the purpose of edifying his Gentile-Christian readers and the defence of Christianity. Therefore each of his narratives must be examined with care; but even when they do not give strictly accurate accounts of events, they are not without historical value, for, in any case, they at least show us the form which the history of primitive Christianity took in the consciousness of later times, and starting from that we can indirectly infer the actual course of events.

The Acts of the Apostles attaches itself immediately to the end of the Gospel, taking for its impressive opening picture the scene with which the Gospel closes. It is true there are some discrepancies in the two narratives, which are deserving of notice, in so far as they show how little account Luke made of such discrepancies when repeating one and the same story (*cf.* Acts, ix., xxii., xxvi.), and therefore how little importance he can have attached to exactitude of detail.[1] Whereas the Gospel makes the Ascension take place on the evening of the Easter day, it is now postponed till the fortieth day after Easter: for exactly as long a period as Moses had intercourse with God upon Mount Sinai and received His commandments for the people of Israel, do the disciples have intercourse with their glorified Lord and receive His instructions concerning the Kingdom of God (i. 3). When Jesus bids them remain in Jerusalem and there wait for the promise of the Father (the mission of the Spirit), they ask Him whether He will at this time restore the Kingdom to Israel (verse 6). They expected, therefore, from Jesus the realisation of the theocracy promised by the prophets in a politico-religious ideal condition of Israel, which is quite in conformity with the hope of the Kingdom as proclaimed in the Gospels. Even in the answer to this question there is no indication that its presupposition regarding the character of the expected Kingdom of God was mistaken, and needed correction: it is here, as in the earlier answer to the sons of Zebedee (Mark

[1] The close affinity of this story of the Ascension with the account given by Josephus of the translation of Moses (*Ant.*, iv. 8. 48) has been pointed out by Holtzmann and Krenkel (*Josephus und Lukas*, pp. 148 ff.), and they have justly inferred therefrom that the passage in Josephus influenced Luke's narrative.

x. 39 f.), tacitly accepted; it is only the desire to know the exact point of time which is rebuked, on the ground that the Father has reserved this to His own power, and the disciples are then told what they are immediately to experience, and what they are afterwards to do, when they have received the Holy Spirit as the equipment for their vocation to be witnesses. The latter is now more exactly defined as regards its principal stages than in Luke xxiv. 47, "Ye shall be my witnesses in Jerusalem, and in all Judæa and Samaria, and to the ends of the earth" (verse 8). From the later attitude of the disciples towards the mission to the Gentiles when begun by Paul, it is to be concluded that they did not remember any such command of Jesus; and that we, therefore, should see in verse 8 a programme for the development of Christianity attributed to Jesus, which the historian has set forth as the thesis of his book, and on which he has moulded his work. According to this scheme, it may be simply divided as follows: In the first part (chaps. i.–xii.) the beginnings of the community at Jerusalem are first portrayed (i.–v.), then the extension of Christianity to Judæa and Samaria, in consequence of the first persecutions (vi.–xii.); with chapter xiii. begins the second main division, which describes the extension of the Gospel beyond Palestine by Paul. This again falls into two sections: in the first, the three missionary journeys of the Apostle (xiii.–xx.) are described; in the second (xxi.–xxviii.), his arrest and trial, the story being continued up to his arrival at Rome, as the point at which the mission acquired a firm foothold in the western part of the Roman Empire and ensured its extension to the farthest bounds of the West.

After the return of the disciples from the Mount of Olives, the scene of the Ascension, the number of "The Twelve" was, on the proposal of Peter, completed by the choice of Matthew in place of the traitor Judas. In the speech delivered by Peter upon this occasion, the traitor's end is described otherwise than in Matthew (xxvii. 5): evidently, several versions of the story were current. Moreover, this first speech in Acts shows at once with what freedom the author has acted in the composition of the speeches which he puts into the mouth of his characters: not only does he make Peter relate in detail an event which had occurred only a short time before, and which is expressly said to have been generally known, but he also makes him speak of the Jewish language, which he was of course himself speaking, as "their [*i.e.* the Jews'] own dialect" (verse 19). These words cannot be separated from the rest of the speech as an addition of the narrator; they form part of it, and unmistakably betray that it cannot really have been spoken by Peter in this form, but is a composition of the author, who, by an oversight, has here fallen a little out of character. As similar phenomena will meet us later on more frequently, and in more important cases, it may be well to note here that a change of rôle such as this is not to be explained as a "tendency" fiction, but as an accidental literary blemish.

The fulfilment of the promise given by Jesus at His departure took place, according to chapter ii., under miraculous circumstances, in which we can without difficulty recognise the symbolical allegory of the narrator. As we speak of the "afflatus" or the "glow" of inspiration, it seems natural to bring the Spirit with which holy men of God are filled into close connection with wind (in Hebrew and Greek the affinity of the word itself suggests this) and with fire. This affinity took shape for the poetic imagination of our author in outward miraculous events: he represents the communication of the Spirit as accompanied by the sound of a mighty wind, which, coming down from heaven, filled the whole house where the disciples were assembled, and by the appearance of tongues, dividing like tongues of flame, which rested on the disciples. So had God revealed Himself in the wilderness, and at Sinai; so did the Jewish Rabbis believe that when they were engaged in pious meditation there often streamed down about them a miraculous fire or light; so should the "Greater than John the Baptist" baptize with the Holy Spirit and with fire. That the fire here takes the form of tongues, points to the ensuing narrative: the disciples, filled with the Holy Spirit, began to speak in foreign languages, and the members of different peoples who were assembled for the feast heard the disciples speak, each in his own language. Whether the miracle which is here narrated took place in the hearers or the speakers; whether, in other words, the disciples themselves, in consequence of being endowed with the Spirit, were enabled to speak in foreign languages which they had not known before, or whether their speech was only the "speaking with tongues" which occurs elsewhere in early Christianity, which was, by a miracle, heard by the listeners in their own different languages, must remain an open question. This only is certain, that here the intention is to describe an actual miracle, which is distinguished from the usual speaking with tongues, which is not precisely miraculous, by its peculiarly miraculous character. That the author was acquainted with the latter, in the form described by Paul in 1 Cor. xiv., is not only probable in itself, but is confirmed by the cases mentioned later (x. 46, xix. 6), in which the reception of the Spirit manifests itself in a "speaking with tongues" (γλώσσαις λαλεῖν); here the expression used scarcely justifies us in thinking of a speaking in foreign languages, for it is the same expression, and has doubtless the same significance, as that which Paul uses for the ecstatic manifestations in the Corinthian church, and in that case we have certainly not to think of a speaking in foreign languages (*i.e.* languages not learned before), but of ecstatic utterances of feeling in unintelligible sounds, with which neither the speaker nor the hearers was able to associate clear conceptions, unless someone present was able to understand and to interpret this wordless hymn in intelligible language (*cf.* vol. i. p. 168 f.). Utterances of pious inspiration of this kind were held in high esteem in the first Christian communities as a specific sign of being endowed with the Spirit, and Paul himself reckoned them among the "charisms," even if he rated their value for purposes of edification rather low; but for us there is no reason to regard them as a supernatural miracle, since we can quite well understand them from a psychological point of view, and find numerous analogies to them in the experience of all times. But from this "speaking with tongues," as found elsewhere, the occurrences at Pentecost are, according to the Lucan representation, essentially distinguished by the fact that here the listeners are said to have heard their own languages spoken. This does not at all agree with the Pauline description of the "speaking with tongues," which was without power to edify just because the hearers could not understand anything definite from it, and had consequently no definite thoughts brought to their minds; and for this reason a stranger who was not familiar with the phenomenon might form the impression that such "speakers with tongues" were mad (1 Cor. xiv. 23).

A trace of the true Pauline representation of the "speaking with tongues" has been preserved even in the Lucan narrative, though, it must be admitted, not in agreement with what is said just before about the hearers understanding what was said; I mean the statement that some mocked, and said that the disciples were filled with new wine (verse 13). This is precisely what we have to imagine in the case of the Corinthian "speaking with tongues," according to Paul—an ecstatic, inarticulate speech, similar to the babbling of drunkards or madmen. But excellently as this trait agrees with all that we learn elsewhere about the early Christian "speaking with tongues," it makes it the more inconceivable how this same "speaking with tongues," which made upon some hearers the impression of drunken babbling, could have been understood by others, and in fact the majority, as the speaking of their own languages. That this was impossible, except by an absolute miracle, is clear.

The question therefore takes this shape for us: How did the author come to compose such an account, which on the one side allows us to recognise the "speaking with tongues" of early Christian enthusiasm which is well known from other sources, and in no way supernatural, but, on the other, implies an unheard of and absolutely supernatural speaking in foreign languages? The explanation is simply that there lies at the basis of our narrative the tradition of an important event, in which, in a large gathering, the "speaking with tongues" of the young community of disciples made a deep impression on those present, and was recognised as the effect of high inspiration; but this tradition has been remoulded by the author with the greatest freedom, and embellished with an addition of an allegorical character. The miracle of the "gift of languages" is therefore to be ascribed exclusively to the narrator, who has here imitated the Jewish legend according to which the Voice which gave the Law at Sinai divides itself into the seventy languages of the peoples of the world. Just as this legend signified the destination of Law to all nations, so by this analogous miracle of speech at the Christian Pentecost the historian desires to express the thought that the Spirit of the gospel was destined from the first for all nations, and not simply for Israel: the universality of the Christian salvation, which has already been expressed in the successively wider spheres to which the Apostles were commissioned to witness, in i. 8, is illustrated in the miracle at Pentecost in an allegorical scene. But this allegorical colouring is painted upon a background of historical tradition still clearly visible through the miracle-picture which has been superimposed upon it, and allows us to recognise the familiar features of the early Christian "speaking with tongues." What was the character of the event which lies at the basis of this tradition we cannot indeed certainly determine, but at the same time the conjecture is a natural one that it may have been the same event which is alluded to by Paul in 1 Cor. xv. 6, when a gathering of more than five hundred brethren was seized with that kind of enthusiasm which took the form of visions of Christ. That occurrences of this kind should have played an important part in the beginnings of Christianity is, according to all the analogies of history, extremely probable.

The charge of drunkenness brought against the disciples furnishes the occasion for a discourse of Peter (ii. 14–36). In this the remarkable phenomenon of the speaking with tongues (there is no further reference to the "gift of languages," which confirms the view given above) is first explained as the fulfilment of the prophecy of Joel about the outpouring of the Spirit and the general gift of prophecy in the last (Messianic) times; then the exaltation of Jesus to be Lord and Messiah is proved from passages in the Psalms (Ps. xvi., cxxxii., cx.), the reference of which to the resurrection and ascension of Jesus is indirectly inferred from the fact that David himself was not preserved either from death or corruption, nor had he ascended to heaven, therefore the hope expressed in those Psalms cannot refer to himself, but only to Jesus, the Messiah—a method of proof which was without doubt frequently used in early Christian apologetic, and also in the later polemics of the Christians against the Jews. Out of this material of early Christian apologetic, with which he was familiar, our historian may well have composed this speech without needing to use any special tradition. That we have not here the real speech of Peter, but the thoughts of the narrator put into his mouth, is proved by the repetition of the same arguments in the mouth of Paul in xiii. 35 ff.; and also by the close of this speech of Peter (verse 38), in which is mentioned already a calling of "those who are afar off," *i.e.* the heathen—a thought which was still far from the minds of the original Apostles, as the later negotiations with Paul allow us clearly to recognise. It is therefore quite vain to seek a source for this speech, while as for thinking of an Aramaic original, that is forbidden by the citation of the Old Testament according to the Greek version of the LXX.

When the effect of this first Christian missionary discourse in producing a great increase in the number of believers has been recorded, there follows a description of the earliest circumstances and experiences of the primitive community, in two symmetrical groupings (ii. 42–iv. 31 and iv. 32–v. 42), each of which first paints the inner life of the community in ideal traits, then the outward success produced by miraculous acts, and finally records the persecutions, the narrative of the second group containing, however, an enhancement of the events of the first. The inner life of the primitive Christian community is described by Luke as a religious-socialistic brotherhood, bound together partly by the common dependence for edification upon the preaching of the Apostles and prayer, partly by a common brotherhood-meal and an almost complete community of goods. The latter is doubtless exaggerated by Acts when it says that all who possessed houses or lands sold them and laid the proceeds at the Apostles' feet, to be distributed among all as each had need (ii. 44, iv. 34 f.). With this complete community of goods there could not have been any poor left in the community to need a special organisation to look after them, such as is mentioned later on in Acts itself (vi.). And if the selling of houses had been a universal custom, how could Mary the mother of Mark still have possessed a house in Jerusalem (xii. 12)? And if *all* owners of lands had sold them for the benefit of the common purse, why is this act specially mentioned in the case of Barnabas (iv. 36 f.) and of Ananias (v. 1)? Yet these very statements, which evidently rest upon a definite tradition, show us, on the other hand, that the picture given in Acts, even if it is over-idealised, has nevertheless an historical basis, and is no mere legendary illustration of the "world-renouncing" spirit of the early Christians. We ought to keep in view, much more than German criticism has hitherto done, the indisputable fact that the primitive Christian community was not a school united by idealistic theories, nor a church united by spiritual doctrines, but simply a religious brotherhood which expected from the coming in the near future of the heavenly Messiah, Jesus, a new organisation of things on earth which would bring happiness to men; but how could such a hope have maintained itself if it had remained a mere empty hope, and had not translated itself into practice, and anticipated the expected condition of happiness at least in the form of a life of brotherly union and mutual succour? No one who knows men can have any doubt that in the earliest communities of Christians, in addition to faith and hope in Jesus the Messiah, the social expression of brotherly love in the form of a community of goods—carried to a considerable extent—and in common meals, formed the most essential bond of union. How important in those times was the practical question how and whence the satisfaction of the material needs of the community could be obtained can be seen, not only in the account in Acts of the first disputes within the Christian body—which, most significantly, were not concerned with points of doctrine, but about the care of the poor—but also in the Gospel stories of the feeding of the multitudes by Jesus, in which just these anxieties of the primitive community have found an allegorical expression (p. 26 f.).

That in a community founded upon the belief in the miracle of the resurrection of Jesus and upon the hope of the miracle of His return to establish His Kingdom, there were not wanting events of a more or less miraculous character, will appear entirely natural. There is therefore no objection to supposing that the miracles of the Apostles which are recorded in Acts rest upon some basis of historical tradition, though they doubtless assumed their present form under the moulding hand of the author. How much in the stories of the healing of the lame man, or the punishment of Ananias and Sapphira, is to be put down to the account of the narrator, how much to tradition, can no longer be discovered. The significance of these stories in their present position in a didactic history consists in the fact that they are intended to explain either the growing successes of the community or the beginnings of persecution; and at the same time they serve the author as appropriate occasions for the introduction of missionary or apologetic discourses by the Apostles. The missionary discourse of Peter introduced by the healing of the lame man (iii. 12–26) explains, in the first place, that this miracle is not performed by the strength of man but in the power of faith in the name of Jesus, and is therefore a mighty work of God, intended to honour His Servant Jesus, the consecrated and sinless Prince of Life, whom they (the Jews) had rejected and slain, but whom God had raised from the dead. This guilt of theirs they had, indeed, incurred in ignorance, not recognising the Messianic dignity of Jesus, and thereby had been fulfilled the decree made known by the prophets, that Messiah must suffer. Therefore they must repent, in order to obtain forgiveness and to share in the blessings which the restoration of all things by Christ on His return from heaven would bring to all nations, but which were primarily designed for them as the sons of the Covenant People. Here again, as in ii. 33, the reference to the destination of the Kingdom of Messiah for all nations betrays the Pauline standpoint (Rom. i. 16) of the historian, who has composed this speech from the same point of view as the former ones. The defence before the Council (iv. 8–12) is, according to Luke's favourite habit of adapting the situation to the speech which he has to report, introduced by the somewhat improbable question of the judge, by what power, or in what name, they had done this (miracle of healing the lame man); whereupon Peter points to the name of the crucified and risen Jesus, in whom was fulfilled the prophecy about the stone which the builders rejected which had become the head of the corner, and in whom alone salvation, the Messianic deliverance, was vouchsafed (Ps. cxviii. 22; *cf.* Mark xii. 10). "This representation aims equally at the exaltation of the original Apostles and the shaming of their incapable opponents, in whose very presence they urge, uncontradicted, all the arguments that formed the apologetic and polemic armoury of the Christian community" (Holtzmann). But when the narrator proceeds to relate that the joyfulness with which the disciples met the charge, and the indisputable fact of their having performed the miracle, made so powerful an impression on the Sanhedrin that they let them go with a simple warning, this can hardly be considered probable in the case of a body which only a short time before had procured the execution of Jesus. This impression is strengthened by the proceedings which are reported in connection with the second arrest of the disciples (v. 17–42). On that occasion the imprisoned Apostles are first released from prison by an angel, the doors meanwhile remaining shut, the guards standing without and seeing nothing (verses 19 and 23). Then the captain of the Temple-guard betakes himself with his men to the Temple, where the disciples are teaching, and courteously urges them (for he is prevented from using force by the fear of the people, who seem to take the side of the Apostles) to accompany him to the presence of the Council, which calls them to account for the excitement aroused by their teaching. Peter declares this teaching to be a duty laid upon them by obedience to the God who had raised up Jesus to be a Prince and a Saviour, to which facts they were witnesses together with the Holy Spirit which God had given to those who obey Jesus. Thereupon, the highly respected Pharisee Gamaliel puts in a plea on behalf of the Apostles, and advises prudent tolerance, since it is not certain whether, after all, this work of the Apostles may not be from God. In conformity with this advice, the Apostles are released after chastisement, with the renewed command to refrain from preaching Christ; but nevertheless preach undisturbed the whole day long in the Temple and in private houses. This narrative is, from beginning to end, so full of improbabilities and impossibilities of every kind that there can be no question of its having any historical foundation; the question can only be whether it reached Luke as a legendary tradition, or whether it was freely invented by him. So much is in any case certain, that this second story of arrest is related to the first (chap. iv.) as an imitation raised into the sphere of the miraculous, and that the summary account of the miracles of Peter in v. 15 makes the impression of a deliberate attempt to outbid other miracle-stories found elsewhere. In particular, the miraculous "judgment" upon Ananias and Sapphira (v. 1–11) proves itself by its physical and moral impossibility to be a legend, the historical background of which — perhaps the sudden death, attributed to a Divine visitation, of a married couple who had offended in some way—is unknown, but of which the "tendency" embellishment serves the end partly of an exaltation of Peter as the head of the Apostles, partly of the edification and warning of readers. All this suggests that in these chapters we have before us, for the most part, freely invented pictures, in which the inventive genius of the narrator has set forth his representation of the ideal circumstances of the primitive community. This impression of their unhistorical character is strengthened by the surprising historical errors in Gamaliel's speech (v. 36 f.). The rising of Theudas took place, according to Josephus (*Ant.* xx., 5. 1), in the reign of the Emperor Claudius, and in the administration of the Procurator Cuspius Fadus, about the years 44–46 of our era, therefore not "before these days," but about a decade later. And it was not "after this" that Judas of Galilee arose; it was a full generation before Theudas that the rising of Judas took place. This anachronism can only be explained as due to an inaccurate recollection of the passage in Josephus in which the account of Theudas is immediately followed by a mention of the ill fate of two sons of Judas of Galilee. The author of the speech of Gamaliel, therefore, presumably had that passage in the History of Josephus in his recollection, but confused the obscure sons with the well-known father, Judas, and thus came to make the appearance of the latter subsequent to that of Theudas.[1] Incidentally, this is one of the most decisive proofs of the dependance of the author of the Lucan writings upon the works of Josephus.

In chapter vi. is introduced the story of Stephen,

[1] *Cf.* Krenkel, *Josephus und Lukas,* pp. 163–173; and see also Holtzmann, *Kommentar.*

with which begins the expansion of Christianity beyond the narrow borders of its quiet life in Jerusalem. The discontent of the Hellenists at the neglect of their widows in the daily distribution of alms gave the occasion, according to the narrative in Acts, for the appointment of seven deacons, who, to judge from their names, were all Hellenists; the first and most important among them being Stephen, who signalised himself not only by working miracles but by disputing with the Jewish Schools, and thereby laid himself open to accusation, the statement being attributed to him that Jesus would destroy "this place" (the Temple) and change the customs of Moses. This narrative is noteworthy in many respects. In the first place, it was a question of the care of the poor about which the first dissension arose in the community, and for the regulation of which the first officials of the community were appointed. The care of the poor was not, therefore, a matter of subsidiary importance, but an essential keystone of the primitive community; and this was naturally the case, for in the mutual helpfulness of the members in respect to their material needs was found a provisional commencement and foretaste of those "times of refreshing" which were to be expected as a consequence of the "restoration of all things" by the return of the Lord Jesus Christ. Secondly, the contending parties were Hellenists and Hebrews, *i.e.* Greek-speaking Jews or proselytes from the Greek "Diaspora," and Aramaic-speaking Jews from Palestine. The latter regarded themselves as the pure and full-blooded Jews, alongside of whom the Hellenistic Jews did not rank as of equal birth and standing. These higher claims of the "Hebrews" were therefore already making themselves felt in the early Christian care of the poor to the disadvantage of the Hellenists — thus prefiguring the later opposition between Jewish and Gentile Christians. Thirdly, the Hellenists were the first who, in their controversies with the Jewish Schools, were able to defend the Christian faith with success; and this was naturally the case, for they had the advantage, as compared with the Palestinian Messianic community, of possessing a familiarity with the Greek language and culture which put them in a position to make their belief the object of theological reflection and to champion it with arguments drawn from the arsenal of the Jewish scholastic wisdom. Fourthly, it was from this coming-forward of the Hellenists that there arose the first serious conflict between the Christian community and Judaism, because Christianity now began to be charged with an anti-Judaic bias, of which there had been no trace in the earlier attitude of the community. This also is quite intelligible. The Hellenists were, in consequence of their constant intercourse with the world of Greek culture, never so strictly Jewish and so narrowly legal-minded as the Palestinian Jews; many elements of Greek thought had found an entrance to their minds, and had so modified the simplicity of their Jewish faith that it was only by means of allegorising exegesis that they could reconcile themselves to many doctrines and usages of the Law. For that reason it was natural that they, much more than the Palestinian members of the Christian community, should be disposed and enabled to perceive the necessity for a reform of Judaism involved in faith in the crucified Messiah, Jesus. In this connection it is also a significant circumstance that the accusation brought against Stephen (vi. 14) is very like that brought against Jesus (Mark xiv. 57 f.); in both cases, no doubt the accusation is declared by the narrator to be the statement of a false witness, but the following speech of Stephen, and—if we may lay no stress on the historicity of that—in any case the result of the trial, indicate that here, as in the case of Jesus, there was some foundation for the charge. From this it follows that the Hellenist Stephen grasped more fully than the Apostles, Jesus' purpose of reform, and made no concealment of his perception of it, but by that very means gave occasion for the breach between the Christian community and Judaism which was a necessary condition of the growth of an independent Christian religion and Church.

Stephen's speech (vii. 2–53) aims at proving from the history of Israel that this people had always resisted with ingratitude and slowness of heart God's purpose of salvation, revealed to them by many tokens of mercy. In particular, after a somewhat prolix introduction, this thought is illustrated from three epochs of Israel's history. (1) From the story of Moses, whom God sent to be the ruler and deliverer of his people, in order to give salvation through him, to reveal words of life, and by type and prophecy to point onward to Christ, and whom, nevertheless, the Israelites did not understand, but denied and rejected (25, 35–39); in punishment for which God turned away from them, and gave them over to the worship of heathen idols (verse 42 f.). (2) From the story of David and Solomon, of whom the former found acceptance with God, making request (only) that he might build Him a tabernacle, while the latter (presumptuously) built Him a house, whereas the Most High, who has made all things, dwelleth not in houses made by men's hands (verses 46-50). (3) From the whole history of the prophets, since the fathers had, from of old, persecuted and slain all the fore-runners of Christ, even as their children had now become the betrayers and murderers of the Righteous One (Christ). Thus they had always shown themselves stiff-necked and uncircumcised in heart and ears, men who kept not the law which they had received by the ministration of angels (verses 51–53). It is plain that this speech has very little relation to the immediate occasion of the charge in vi. 14; only the few verses 47-50, in which unmistakably the building of the Temple is repudiated as an undertaking which was displeasing to God, have direct reference to the charge of his accusers, which, it must be admitted, they do not refute, but confirm. The remainder has nothing whatever to do with his defence, but is a harsh indictment of the Jewish people, as having always shown itself unworthy of the revelation given to it by God, and having thereby incurred the loss of His blessing. This speech has its nearest analogue in the Nazareth sermon of Jesus in Luke iv. In both cases the rejection of Israel is inferred from historical examples, the passionate wrath of the listeners is evoked, and their murderous thoughts express themselves in tumultuous violence, but in the former case they are not actually carried into effect. In both cases the contents and aim of the speech is remarkably unsuitable to the situation to which the narrator has referred it—a situation which seems to demand a discourse calculated to conciliate rather than to exasperate the audience. Accordingly, the similar problem of the two speeches is to be explained in a similar way: neither was really delivered as it is given, but both were composed by the narrator, and placed in a prominent position at the outset as a kind of programme to indicate the subsequent course of the history. Neither speech implies the use of any historical source, but both are free variations of the thoughts of Rom. xi. 7–10, 19–22, though without the consoling prospects which Paul still holds out to fallen Israel; the relative anti-Judaism of Paul (Rom. xi. 28) has become absolute in this member of the Pauline School. The conjecture deserves notice also, that the author had in mind, when composing Stephen's defence, the speech of Josephus to his countrymen (***B.J.***, v. 9. 4), in which, just as here, the reproach of stiff-neckedness and blood-thirstiness is justified out of the history of Israel, from Abraham down to the speaker's own day.[1] Moreover, the numerous divergences from the Old Testament narrative which are found here (verses 2–4, 22, 38, 53) have their nearest parallels in the writings of Josephus.

The death of Stephen, which Luke describes in a way which recalls his narrative, in the Gospel, of the death of Jesus (*cf.* vii. 56, 59, 60, with Luke xxii. 69, xxiii. 34, 46), was the beginning of a persecution of

[1] Krenkel, *Josephus und Lukas*, p. 176 f.

some severity, which had as its consequence the dispersion of the members of the Jerusalem community over Judæa and Samaria (viii. 1). The first steps towards that extension of Christianity which was indicated in advance in Christ's saying in i. 8, were made in the course of this dispersion. It is especially the activity of Philip the deacon which is described, as being a preparation and prototype of the great mission to the Gentiles of Saul-Paul, who has already been mentioned incidentally in connection with the tragedy of Stephen's death (viii. 5–13, 26–40).

At this point Acts introduces the peculiar episode of the conversion of a magician named Simon, who gave himself out to be something great, and in consequence of his enchantments was held by his fellow-countrymen to be "the Great Power of God." When this man saw that by laying on of the Apostles' hands the Holy Spirit was given, he offered them money, desiring to buy this power of communicating the Holy Spirit by the laying on of hands; whereupon Peter rebuked him sharply, and commanded him to repent of his unworthy thought. This narrative is instructive in many respects. It translates us to a time at which the magical conception of the communication of the Spirit by the sacramental act of the laying on of hands, and of the specific supernatural endowment of the Apostles for the performance of this act, had grown up in the Christian churches, and when these had thus come into rivalry with the Gnostic sects, such as the Simonians, who boasted of their mystical knowledge and their magical powers. It is just this rivalry between the Christian communities, which were themselves infected with Gnostic-magic conceptions, and the older Gnostic sects, which had built up their syncretistic religion out of heathenism and Judaism, and now began to come into hostile contact with Christianity—it is this rivalry which lies at the heart of our narrative, and this narrative therefore carries back the circumstances of its own time (second century) into the Apostolic period and gives a typical illustration of them in an imaginary incident. In view of these important points, the questions are of subordinate importance whether there was an historical Simon Magus; and if this question can be answered in the affirmative with some probability, in what relation he stood to the Gnostic sect of Simonians; was he actually their founder, or only their deified hero, to whom heathen myths concerning the gods were referred? We shall recur to this in a later context. The question, too, can only be suggested here, whether the author was aware of the identification which occurs in the Jewish-Christian literature of the second century of Simon the magician and arch-heretic with the Apostle Paul, and of Paul's collection (2 Cor. viii.) with Simon's offer of money to the Apostles, and whether, perhaps, he intended to cut the ground from beneath this anti-Pauline legend by placing the story of Simon before the conversion of Saul, and thus excluding the identification of Simon with Paul.

The following narrative of the conversion of the Ethiopian by Philip (viii. 26–40) forms a further preparation for the Pauline mission to the Gentiles. The miraculous interposition of the angel at the beginning (26 and 29), and the miraculous translation of Philip at the close (39), may be put down to legend; but it serves also to show that the first instance of the conversion of a Gentile took place under the direct ordering and guidance of God, which is repeated in the case of the conversion of Cornelius by Peter in chapter x.

When Saul has first been introduced at the death of Stephen as a sympathiser with the persecution, and when a preparation has been made for his later missionary activity in that of Philip, the event is narrated which was decisive for the future progress of the diffusion of Christianity: the conversion of the enemy of Christ into the leading Apostle of Christ (ix. 1–19). The kernel of this narrative—that Paul had earlier been a violent persecutor of the Christian community, had been suddenly converted by a miraculous revelation of Christ, and at the same time called to be an Apostle—is proved by the witness of Paul himself to be an historical fact. How, exactly, we are to conceive the decisive event was discussed above upon the ground of direct and indirect indications in the Pauline letters (vol. i. p. 85 ff.). As regards the details of the event recorded in Acts, the author himself seems to have laid no special weight upon them, since in repeating the story upon two occasions, he tells it in each case somewhat differently—incidentally a remarkable proof of the great freedom which the author allows himself in the treatment of the literal facts of his narrative. Since, according to Acts, the miraculous revelation of Christ was received not only by Paul himself but also, in part, by his companions, in so far that these are once said to have heard the voice without seeing anyone, the other time to have seen the light, but not to have heard the voice (xxii. 9), it is clear that the narrator thought of an objectively real appearance. But Paul himself did the same, and indeed the distinction between subjective and objective in visionary experiences was not understood in antiquity. In addition to this, we know from numerous analogies in the Gospel that it is one of the literary characteristics of Luke to depict miraculous events with the utmost realism (*cf.* the stories of the Baptism of Jesus, of the Transfiguration, and of the appearances to the disciples after the Resurrection). His description of what happened on the road to Damascus is to be explained in the same way, without our needing to suppose that he had some special object in view, *e.g.*, to establish the reality of the appearance of Christ to Paul, and his call to be an Apostle, against the doubts of the Judaisers. It would not, indeed, agree with a purpose of that kind that he nowhere speaks of a bodily visibility and manifestation of Jesus Himself, but always of the seeing of a light and the hearing of a voice. Doubtless he thinks of both as really emanating from Jesus, and assumes, therefore, His presence, but His person remains behind the scene, and is only mediately recognised, not beheld immediately, face to face. That this representation agrees with Paul's own conception of his vision of Christ (1 Cor. ix. 1, xv. 8) cannot be affirmed with certainty, but may be conjectured with probability. In any case, this narrative shows how the vision of Paul was conceived in the Pauline circles of that time, and for that very reason it is of historical value. As regards the further mention of Paul's being blinded for several days by the brightness of the light, we may, indeed, find therein an allegory of his former Jewish blindness and spiritual enlightenment by Christ; nevertheless, the possibility ought not to be dismissed that this blindness was not only meant in a literal sense but historically well-founded; it would be possible to combine with this the allusion to Paul's suffering from an affection of the eyes in Galatia (Gal. iv. 14 f.), and in this way secure a wider basis for the historical explanation of the event on the Damascus road. And so, too, it is not to be doubted that there is an historical kernel in the reference to Ananias, who visited the sick man in Damascus, and effected his bodily and spiritual cure, even if the vision of Ananias, on account of the close analogy with the story of Cornelius, is to be ascribed to the narrator, especially as the words of the Lord which are here spoken to Ananias with reference to Paul (verse 15) are in the later doublets addressed to Paul himself: in the one case as spoken by Jesus (xxvi. 16 f.), in the other as spoken by Ananias (xxii. 15).

After his conversion, Paul, as Acts proceeds to narrate, immediately began to preach Jesus as Messiah in the synagogues, until an attempted assassination by the Jews compelled him to escape by night over the town-wall of Damascus. Thereupon he came to Jerusalem, was made known to the Apostles by Barnabas, preached boldly in the name of Jesus, and disputed with the Hellenists, but in order to withdraw him from the persecution which these were preparing for him, the brethren brought him to Cæsarea and sent him forth to Tarsus (ix. 20–30).

This narrative disagrees in many respects with Paul's own version of the facts in Gal. i. 17 ff. The journey into Arabia mentioned there is here omitted. The interval before the journey to Jerusalem is there given as three years, here only as "many days"; the visit to Jerusalem lasts there only fourteen days, and brings Paul into contact only with Peter and James the Lord's brother; of his being made known to the Apostles in general, of public preaching and disputation, and persecution aroused in consequence, there is there no mention. These differences are too considerable for it to be possible to harmonise them or to regard them as accidental; and though it is a matter of controversy whether the author of Acts had the definite intention of correcting in his account of these events the description given by Paul in Galatians, it cannot in any case be overlooked that this description is determined by the presupposition that Paul, soon after his conversion, entered into relations with the original community of disciples and began under their sanction his public activity as a teacher in Jerusalem—a presupposition which does not correspond to the facts, but finds its explanation in the view regarding the Apostle Paul and his relation to the original Apostles which had grown up in ecclesiastical circles in the second century.

With the departure of Paul from Jerusalem, the author of Acts drops the thread of his history in order to recount, in the first place, some events of Peter's activity outside Jerusalem, which, as a prelude and counterpart to the activities of Paul, have here their appropriate place. The two miracle-stories of the cure of the lame man Æneas at Lydda, and the raising from the dead of Tabitha at Joppa (ix. 32–43), are variations of similar miracle-stories in the Gospel history; the story of the raising of the dead woman, especially, reminds us so exactly of the raising of the daughter of Jairus in Mark v. 22 ff. that it might be considered a doublet of this story. That traditional narratives of this kind are accustomed to attach themselves to various persons and places wherever anything in the circumstances offers a point of attachment, is a well-known phenomenon of all legendary history. Of greater importance is the narrative of the conversion of the Gentile centurion Cornelius through Peter (x. 1–xi. 18). The extreme importance which the author attached to it is shown by the detailed character of his narrative, and by the recapitulation of it in the discourse of Peter (xi. 1–17), and especially by its being led up to by no less than three visions: first that of Cornelius, which occasioned his sending to Peter; then the vision of Peter in which, by God-given signs and utterances, the abrogation of the Old Testament law of clean and unclean meats—that great hindrance to the meeting at table, and consequently to all intimate intercourse, of Jew and Gentile—was made clear to him; finally, the voice of the Spirit to Peter, which commanded him to accept without scruple the invitation to enter the house of this Gentile. He begins his speech by giving expression to the perception which has dawned on him that God is no respecter of persons, but in every nation he that feareth God and worketh righteousness is acceptable to Him, *i.e.* is welcomed as a partaker in the blessings of the Kingdom of Christ. Then he proclaims Jesus as the Saviour anointed with Spirit and with power, whom the Jews had crucified but whom God had raised up and appointed judge of living and dead, through whose name everyone who believes in Him shall receive forgiveness of sins, as the prophets have testified. While he was yet speaking the Holy Spirit fell upon all the hearers and manifested itself in "speaking with tongues," in which Peter recognised a Divine intimation that he was to proceed to baptize Cornelius and his household. After his return to Jerusalem, the Jews reproached him that he had gone in to men uncircumcised and had eaten with them. He, however, recounted to them, in justification of his conduct, the whole story, and thereby convinced even the Jerusalem community that "God had also granted to the heathen repentance unto life" (xi. 18). This conclusion of the narrative is evidently the significant point; it is intended to show that the beginning, in baptizing Gentiles, was made by Peter, by the direct ordering of God; and, after some hesitation, was approved by the original community. This is contradicted by the subsequent course of events, not only according to Gal. ii., but also according to Acts itself, for the proceedings of the Apostolic Council (chap. xv.) would be quite unintelligible if the questions which are there obviously dealt with for the first time, regarding the possibility of the Gentiles becoming Christians, had been already, in consequence of an impressive series of miracles, practically solved and decided for Peter and his fellow-members of the Jerusalem community. The events can therefore hardly have occurred as here narrated; both the anachronistic anticipation of the universal principle which Paul first brought into operation, and the preparation of multiplied miracle by which this insight is reached, show beyond doubt the ideal character of the narrative. The question nevertheless suggests itself whether there may not be some historical basis for the story. In favour of the supposition that there is, may be noted the circumstance that both the reproach brought against Peter in Jerusalem (xi. 3) and also the revelation by vision which forms the main point of his defence (xi. 5 f.) relate, not to the question of principle involved in the baptism of Gentiles, but to the ritual question whether a Jew might so far set aside the Mosaic law of clean and unclean as to live in the house with and sit at table with Gentiles, whether baptized or unbaptized. This question was not solved by the Apostolic Council—in fact, was not even touched by it. It was the question which gave rise to the strife between Peter and Paul at Antioch; and at a much later time, when the permissibility of baptizing Gentiles had long ceased to be contested, this practical question had not lost its significance, as the Clementine Homilies (i. 22 and ii. 19) show. On these grounds, it might perhaps be conjectured that the Cornelius story might be based on events in the later life of Peter, similar to those which led to the sending of "certain men from James" to Antioch, and to the contention between the Apostles there. It is true that at that time Peter actually adopted the narrower position of the original community, whereas, according to our narrative, on the contrary, the latter adopted his advance in enlightenment, of which, however, his conduct at Antioch shows no trace. Thus the historical "kernel" becomes very problematical. In any case, it has been freely transformed in the interests of the author's didactic purpose, according to which "the universalism of Christianity had been introduced by Peter, by word and act, long before Paul" (Holtzmann), with the approval of the whole of the original community of disciples. This does not correspond to actual history, but to the ecclesiastical postulate of a united authority of the whole body of the Apostles as the basis of the one universal Church.

In xi. 19 the author returns to the extension of the gospel in consequence of the persecution "which arose about Stephen," which he had mentioned in viii. 4, and narrates that it was through some Hellenists of Cyprus, who had come to Antioch, the Syrian capital, that the gospel was here first taught to the Greeks, and in this way an independent Christian community was founded, to which the name of "Christian" was applied for the first time. On hearing of this formation of a church at Antioch, the church in Jerusalem sent Barnabas thither; and he brought Saul from Tarsus and took him with him to Antioch. The two worked there successfully for a year. Then came prophets, *i.e.* men who had the gift of prediction and inspired speech, from the Jerusalem church to Antioch, and caused great joy to the church there. One of these, named Agabus, predicted a general famine, which came to pass (in Judæa) in the time of Claudius. In consequence of this prophecy, the Antiochian Christians resolved to make a collection for the brethren in Judæa, and this was sent, the author adds, by Barnabas and Saul (xi. 19–30). In this report an historical kernel is to be distinguished from some additions of the narrator. That through the activity of some scattered Hellenists, whose freer type of thought is already known to us from Stephen, the beginning of a mission to the Gentiles was made, appears to be quite in the natural order of things, and is the less to be doubted because Acts expressly distinguishes this Hellenistic mission to the Gentiles from the mission to the Jews only (*cf.* verses 19 and 20), and introduces it as something new, without any reference to the problematical story of Cornelius, which has just before been narrated. The origin of Gentile Christianity is thus admitted by Acts to have been independent of the original community, both in regard to the persons by whom it was founded and the place where it first arose. This is the historical kernel of the narrative, which is the less open to doubt because here, at the commencement of the story of the Antiochian church, begin the "we" sections of the eye-witness, that is of Luke the Antiochian.[1] The only question is how far this report guarantees the details of the narrative. It is obvious that the mention of the fulfilment of the prophecy regarding the famine in the time of Claudius is not derived from it (verse 28); that was added by the author from his knowledge of Josephus, who several times mentions a famine which prevailed in Judæa in the time of Claudius (*Ant.*, iii. 15. 3, xx. 2. 5 and 5. 2), during which the queen Helena of Adiabene sent munificent aid to the inhabitants

[1] According to the reading in verse 28 which has the support of the Western MSS. (Cod. D and its allies), *ἦν δὲ πολλὴ ἀγαλλίασις. συνεστραμμένων δὲ ἡμῶν ἔφη εἷς ἐξ αὐτῶν ὀνόματι Ἄγαβος σημαίνων, κ.τ.λ.* The originality of this reading cannot, in my opinion, be doubted.

of Jerusalem.[1] That this famine was confined to Judæa, naturally did not hinder the author from expanding it into a universal one, as he has done in the case of the census of Quirinius also (Luke ii.). It is possible that it was Josephus' mention of the munificence of Helena towards the people of Jerusalem which suggested the sending of the collection of the Antiochians to Jerusalem, which is at all events ante-dated. But even assuming that the Antiochian collection (verse 29) belongs to the report of the eye-witness (verse 28) and is guaranteed by it, it is at any rate certain that the sending of the collection by Paul and Barnabas mentioned in xi. 30 cannot be historical, since it stands in direct contradiction with the fact, solemnly attested by Paul, that in the fourteen years between the short visit (in Gal. i. 18 = Acts ix. 26) and the journey to the Apostolic Council (Gal. ii. 1 = Acts xv. 2) he had not been in Jerusalem. On the latter occasion Paul went as a delegate from Antioch together with Barnabas, but not to bring a collection; on the other hand, he travelled in Acts xxi. without Barnabas, but bringing a collection, as we know from Corinthians and from Rom. xv. 25 f., but not from Acts, which there says nothing about the collection, only giving an incidental hint of it in a later passage (xxiv. 17). From these considerations, the conjecture seems to me to suggest itself very naturally that the author has combined the bringing of the collection (on the last journey) with the mission from Antioch together with Barnabas (on the next-to-last journey), and has thus made a new journey, which he places in xi. 30 before these other

[1] Krenkel, *Josephus und Lukas*, p. 199 f.

two. And his motive in doing so may perhaps be guessed. The bringing of the collection on his last journey was interpreted by the Judaisers in a hostile sense, as if Paul had desired to buy with money a recognition of his Apostolic authority. Therefore it seemed advisable, in order to turn the point of this suspicion, to represent the collection as brought, not by Paul alone, but by him together with Barnabas, and, moreover, at an earlier time, when the relations of Paul with the original community were still untroubled. The author's reason for inserting the new journey just at this point may perhaps be most simply explained by supposing that he really found in his source here a journey of Paul and Barnabas from Antioch to Jerusalem, namely, to the Apostolic Council. For that this originally preceded the first missionary journey (chaps. xiii. and xiv.) is necessarily to be supposed, because Paul in Gal. i. 21 speaks only of a mission in Syria and Cilicia, and because it is only on this presupposition that the limitation of the address of the Apostolic decree to the Christians of Antioch, Syria, and Cilicia (xv. 23) becomes intelligible: there were, in fact, at that time no other Gentile Christians. If the journey to the Apostolic Council stood at the point where we have now the collection-journey invented by the author (xi. 30), the source would agree admirably with Gal. i. 21, according to which Paul had not, before the Apostolic Council, gone beyond Syria and Cilicia, and had only once been in Jerusalem. Our author has transferred this journey to the Apostolic Council from its original place because he wanted to make room here for a new collection-journey.

The first part of Acts closes with the story of the martyr-death of James the Apostle, and of the liberation of Peter from prison by the miraculous intervention of an angel (chap. xii.). The latter narrative is only an expanded repetition of the similar story in v. 19 ff., and a companion-picture to the miraculous liberation of Paul in xvi. 25–34. As there has been mention, immediately before, of the angel of death who caused the sudden death of the tyrant Herod, the conjecture lies near at hand that the angel of deliverance is identical with the angel of death, *i.e.* that the sudden death of Herod was the historical cause of the unexpected liberation of Peter from prison. The story of the death of Herod shows both a close affinity with, and at the same time numerous variations in detail from, the somewhat more realistic narrative in Josephus (*Ant.*, xix. 8. 2). Both are probably based on a popular legend which circulated in various forms; it is from such a source, rather than from a written one, that our author's narrative is taken. These finely-conceived pictures of delivering and destroying angelic powers, which hold sway over the Church and the world, form a fitting close to the first portion of the Acts, which contains as much poetic invention as truth. In the second part we begin to find ourselves on somewhat firmer historical ground.

THE ACTS OF THE APOSTLES

CHAPTER IX

The Expansion of the Church through the Work of Paul

(Acts xiii. 1–xxviii. 31)

The second part begins with the report of the sending forth of the missionaries Paul and Barnabas by the heads of the Antiochian church. This is prefaced by an enumeration of the prophets and teachers who belonged to the Antiochian church itself, in contradistinction to the prophets who came to it from Jerusalem as temporary guests (xi. 27). It is worthy of notice that Paul and Barnabas seem to be mentioned here as if they were introduced for the first time: probably in the source on which the narrative is based they were first mentioned here, which confirms our conjecture that the mention of their being sent to Jerusalem in xi. 30 has been antedated by the author. The statement that their being sent forth was due to a prophetic revelation of the Spirit may well be derived from the source, whereas the solemn preparation for their mission by fasting, prayer, and the laying-on of hands, is to be put down to the author's liking for ecclesiastical correctness.

As regards the missionary journey of Paul and

Barnabas which is described in the following chapters, the definite statements regarding their route doubtless rest upon some kind of tradition, whether a tradition of the Antiochian church, or a written source, in regard to which we cannot say whether, or if so, how, it is related to the "we-source," which first occurs in xi. 28.[1] That this included more than the few "we-sections" of Acts is certainly probable; on the other hand, we cannot fail to observe that the narrative in chapters xiii. and xiv. contains too many unhistorical traits to be referred back, in the same direct sense as the "we-sections," to the report of an eye-witness. At the outset, the narrative of the meeting which took place in Cyprus between the Apostle Paul and the Jewish magian and false prophet Bar-Jesus (son of Jesus) gives ground for doubt. The punitive miracle by means of which Paul is said to have brought about the blinding of the sorcerer is as little historical as the miraculous destruction of Ananias and Sapphira by Peter (chap. v.). The magian here overcome by Paul is the counterpoise to the magian Simon who was overthrown by Peter (Acts viii.), and both are perhaps to be referred back to the magian Simon, a native of Cyprus, who, according to Josephus, was attached to the suite of the procurator Felix, and played the part of pander in his wooing of Drusilla (*Ant.*, xx. 7. 2). This was the Simon who, as we learn from the Clementine writings, was made in Jewish anti-Pauline circles into a caricature of the Apostle Paul. If this was known to the author of Acts, as may quite well have been the case, he must

[1] According to the reading of Cod. D. See footnote, p. 227 *supra*. —TRANSLATOR.

have desired to dispose of this wicked calumny against his hero, and this could be effected partly by representing Simon Magus—Paul's double, according to the Judaisers—as having been defeated by Peter before Paul appeared on the scene (viii. 9 f.), partly by representing the same caricature of Paul as having been, under another form, visited with judgment by Paul himself (xiii. 9 ff.). These two narratives, therefore, are both apologetic fictions, called forth by the same Judaising travesty of Paul under the features of Simon Magus;[1] to this is due, in the former case, the offer of money (travesty of Paul's bringing of the collection), in the latter case the favour of the Roman procurator (travesty of Paul's relations with Felix) and the blinding of the magician (travesty of Paul's being blinded on the road to Damascus). In addition to this special anti-Judaising purpose, the general apologetic purpose is here in evidence "to show the Roman Government as favourable to the Apostle of the Gentiles from his first entry into the Gentile world, and to show at the same time that the disturbing influence of Judaism must be got rid of" (Weizsäcker and Holtzmann).

The story that in consequence of the healing of a lame man at Lystra the Apostles were taken for Zeus and Hermes, and could only with difficulty prevent the people from worshipping them with sacrifice (xiv. 11–18), must also be considered an unhistorical legend. The enthusiastic reception which the Apostles met

[1] This hypothesis has the support of Lipsius (*Quellen der röm. Petrussage und apokryphe Apostelgeshichten*, vol. ii. p. 2), Hilgenfeld (*Zeitschr. f. wissenschaftl. Theol.*, 1868, "Magier Simon"), and Krenkel (*Josephus und Lukas*, pp. 178–189).

with in this district may have been embellished by the author or by tradition with traits taken from myths of which the scene was laid in that very region, regarding the visits of gods to men (Baucis and Philemon). On the other hand we have no reason to doubt the historicity of the stoning, due to the enmity of the Jews, by which Paul's life was endangered at Lystra (xiv. 19), since an experience of this kind is mentioned by Paul himself (2 Cor. xi. 15).

The culminating point of the first missionary journey was, according to the description given in Acts, the discourse which Paul is represented as delivering in Antioch, the capital of Pisidia (xiii. 14–41). After an historical introduction similar in character to that in Stephen's speech (chap. vii), but not so detailed, Paul proclaims Jesus as the Saviour, sprung, according to the promise, from David's seed, whom the Jewish authorities in ignorance had delivered to death, in fulfilment of the sayings of the prophets, but whom God had raised up, and thus fulfilled the promises given to the fathers, as is shown from passages in the Psalms; therefore the forgiveness of sins mediated through Christ is now to be made known to all; that, namely, every one that believeth in Him shall be justified from all things from which they could not be justified by the law of Moses; those who despised this message, however, are reminded of the threatenings of the prophets. To argue about the historicity of this and other speeches in Acts is really absurd. One need only consider all the conditions which would need to be fulfilled in order to render possible a verbally accurate, or even a generally correct, record of such a speech. It would need to have been immediately written down by someone who was present (indeed, to secure an exact record, it would need to have been taken down in shorthand), and these notes of the various speeches would need to have been preserved by the hearers, who were for the most part Jews or heathen, and were either hostile or indifferent towards what was said, for more than half a century, and finally collected by the historian from the most diverse localities! Anyone who has once made clear to himself all these impossibilities, will realise once for all how he is to look upon all these speeches—that, in fact, in Acts, just as in all secular historians of antiquity, the speeches are free compositions, in which the author makes his heroes speak as he thinks that they might have spoken in the circumstances of the moment. That explains in a natural way why the fundamental thoughts, and the order in which they are presented, are almost the same in most of these Apostolic speeches; they are the thoughts of the author himself, who was not able, and indeed did not wish, to hide himself, even though he had literary skill enough to adapt the speeches in some measure to the different persons and situations. Thus, in this first discourse of Paul, which is in general very closely parallel to the earlier discourse of Peter, he has not neglected to weave in a reference (verse 39) to the Pauline doctrine of justification. It is true that it is rather doubtful whether he thought of it exactly as Paul did. The formula "in Christ everyone that believeth shall be justified [acquitted] of all things from which it was impossible to be justified in the law of Moses" is not exactly Pauline, and does not exclude the possibility that the justification by faith in Christ is a mere supplement to the partial or imperfect justification by the Law, and is thus materially different from the Pauline conception. But even supposing that this were so (and the indefiniteness of the expression hardly admits of certainty upon the point), it would obviously be a very rash conclusion that because the author has not made Paul speak exactly in character, he must have deliberately misrepresented his teaching, in order to adapt it to that of Peter. Of a deliberate falsification of Paulinism it would only be possible to speak if we could assume an exact acquaintance on the author's part with genuine Paulinism; but what justification have we for making this assumption? Anyone who is convinced, as the writer is, that the author of Acts was not a hearer and disciple of Paul, but a "deutero-Pauline" of the second century, must also admit that, with the best will in the world, he could not make Paul speak otherwise than just as he himself understood him, *i.e.* in the sense of the transformed Paulinism of his own time.

The return from the first missionary journey was followed, according to Acts, by the journey of Paul and Barnabas to Jerusalem to attend the Apostolic Council (xv.). We have already seen that this journey must have preceded the first missionary journey (xiii., xiv.), and had its original place at the point where our author has substituted the collection-journey of xi. 30. As to the occasion of this journey and the negotiations at Jerusalem, our author gives a report which diverges in several respects from that in Gal. ii. The connection of the two reports has been, as is well known, the subject of much theological controversy, in which the zeal of the combatants on both sides has not exactly contributed to the elucidation of the matter. Anyone who examines the two passages calmly, quietly, and without prepossession will come, as I have done, to the conclusion that the only serious material difference is in the outcome of the discussions, the decree of the Church which Acts reports; the other differences are rather of a formal character, and are easily to be explained by our author's habit of giving to important events their appropriate setting of graphic detail.

That applies even to the reason for the journey. Paul speaks of a revelation which was given to him; Acts speaks of his being sent by the Antiochian Church. The one does not exclude the other, and some kind of concurrence of the Church in Paul's resolution is the more probable because the ultimate reason of it was the agitation set up by the Jewish legal zealots. This statement of Acts contains, indeed, a welcome expansion and explanation of the enigmatic word "revelation" (Gal. ii. 1), since this, according to all analogy, cannot have occurred to Paul unmediated and without cause, but points to a painful situation demanding a decision, such as was naturally brought about by the Judaising agitation in the Church.[1] Next, Acts tells of negotiations of

[1] The explanation of this journey to Jerusalem, and the situation which the Antiochian delegates found there, is, especially in the longer reading of the Western texts (D and allies), so clearly and graphically presented that the conjecture of Hilgenfeld (*Akta Apost.*, p. 284), that the description in verses 1–6 is based on the Lucan "we-source," does not appear impossible. But one may also think of oral tradition, which would leave more room for the free invention and elaboration of the author.

the Antiochian deputies with the Apostles and presbyters, in which, owing to the legalistic demands of the Pharisees, keen contention arose, until Peter and James, by their speeches in Paul's favour, brought about a pacification and understanding. This is not only probable in itself, but is in agreement with Gal. ii.; for though it has been maintained that there the reference is to private negotiations with the leading Apostles, that is certainly a mistake, for in verse 2 "those who were of reputation" are distinguished clearly, as a smaller circle, from a wider one, and the presence of the latter is clearly implied by the sharp contention indicated in verses 3 ff. It is true that nothing is said there of the speeches of Peter and James; but that after hot debates an agreement was not reached without some calming words from the authorities is surely a self-evident assumption. As regards the content of these speeches, we expect here, not historical protocols, but compositions of the historian, in regard to which the only question which can arise is whether he has put into the mouths of his heroes words in harmony with their individuality and the situation. That this is, generally at least, the case cannot be contested. For that the leading Apostles spoke in a sense favourable to Paul is evidenced by the actual result—namely, that they gave him the right hand of fellowship and recognised his Gentile-Christians as Christian brethren. How could this have been possible, if they had taken the side of his opponents, the legal zealots of the Pharisaic party? Even though Paul speaks in Gal. ii. 6 with some asperity and no great reverence of "those who were reputed to be somewhat," in spite of the fact that they had then just recently given him the right hand of fellowship, still we must not forget that Paul wrote the letter to the Galatians under the stress of his violent struggle with Judaising agitation in Galatia and Corinth, and that he, as all men of strong feeling are wont to do, allowed his mood of the moment to influence the tone of his narrative of things which had happened in the past. This tone of the narrative certainly forms a contrast to the peaceful tone which prevails in the speeches in Acts; but the fact of the "right hand of fellowship" which Paul records forms no contrast to these speeches, but is in harmony with them. The author of Acts shows a right instinct also in making Peter support the cause of Gentile liberty with very much greater heartiness and less reserve than James: exactly the same relative attitudes of the two men will meet us in a later connection. The details of the two speeches, however, give rise to various difficulties. The thoughts are rather those which the author might naturally ascribe to an ecclesiastically-minded Jewish Christian of his own time than those which the Apostles are likely to have expressed at the Apostolic Council. When, in xv. 7, Peter appears as an instrument of God chosen from of old for the mission to the Gentiles, that agrees no doubt with that view of the later Church regarding the attitude of the Apostles towards the mission to the Gentiles which lies at the basis of the Cornelius story (Acts x.), but it does not agree with historical reality, according to which Peter was commissioned and endowed with strength to preach to the Jews, Paul to preach to the Gentiles (Gal. ii. 7). Moreover, the grounds on which Peter urges that the Gentile Christians should be spared the burdens of the Law are not, indeed, as has often been said, genuinely Pauline, but they are certainly quite in the spirit of that ecclesiastical universalism in which the moderate Jewish Christian of the second century reconciled himself with the deutero-Pauline, but which, on the other hand, we have no right to assume in the case of the original Apostles. If these had really recognised the Law as a yoke which neither they nor their fathers were able to bear (verse 10), it would be inconceivable that after this realisation no less than before it they felt themselves conscientiously bound to this very Law, as Acts itself proves by many instances. And if they had really believed that they were to be saved only through the grace of Jesus in the same way as the heathen (verse 11), it would be impossible to understand why they attached such high value to the Jewish Law that they continued to maintain it as a wall of partition between themselves and their Gentile brethren, and even shrank from and avoided the brotherly intercourse of meeting at the same table as an injury to their Jewish conscience, as was seen at Antioch. To this extent it is true to say that the speech of Peter has a Pauline colouring, and gives no true picture of the historical Peter's way of thinking; but this must not be understood in the sense that the historian has invented a false picture of Peter, and has really made him exchange rôles with Paul. There is no question of that; the real state of the case is that he makes Peter speak like an ecclesiastical Jewish Christian and Paul like a deutero-Pauline of his own day; but, as these two tendencies had by that time approached each other so nearly as to become almost indistinguishable, it comes to pass quite naturally that their typical representatives in Acts seem to have occupied much more nearly the same position that they did in reality.

Finally, as regards the speech of James and the decision of the Church which was brought about by it, we have here three things to distinguish: (1) The permission to the heathen of freedom from the Law, (2) the assumption of the continued obligation of the Law for the Jewish Christians, and (3) the command to abstain from certain heathen offences, which, in spite of their general freedom from the Law, was laid upon the Gentiles. In regard to the first point, the agreement with Paul's account is obvious, and is not contested; the motive assigned for this concession, the sayings of the prophets which pointed to the conversion of the heathen (verses 15 ff.), is significant of the process of thought by which Jewish Christianity succeeded in reconciling itself with Pauline universalism, when once this had to be recognised as an accomplished fact. As regards the second point, the continued obligation of the Law for Jewish Christians, that is not expressly mentioned, but obviously it forms the tacit presupposition, in regard to which nothing is said expressly because no one attacked or denied it; on this point also there is now general agreement. It is only the third point of the decree proposed by James (verse 20) which gives occasion to critical difficulties: the Gentiles are to be required to abstain from pollution of idols (that means, according to verse 29, from eating the flesh of idol sacrifices), from unchastity, from things strangled, and from blood.[1] The last two points find their explanation in Levit. xvii. 10 ff., where the use of blood, and of flesh from which the blood has not been drained (which is not "kosher"), is forbidden to the Israelites and to those who dwelt among them, because the blood contained the life,

[1] In Cod. D and its allies "things strangled" is wanting, and at the end is added the "golden rule," "Whatsoever ye would not that men should do unto you, do ye not to others." In spite of the good patristic evidence (Irenæus, Tertullian, Cyprian; Clement of Alexandria, however, supports the received text), this can scarcely be held to be the original text of the decree of James. For in this, instead of a provision specially intended for the regulation of the Gentile Christian life in such a way as to facilitate intercourse with Jewish Christians, it gives an "elementary moral code" which has its parallels in the "Teaching of the Twelve Apostles," i.–vi., and in apologists like Aristides (xv. 4) and Theophilus (xxi.). The ritual prohibition of eating flesh with the blood is transformed into a moral prohibition of bloodshed ("homicidium," Tertullian, though with some uncertainty), and the prohibition of meats offered to idols is expanded to include idolatry in general ("idololatria," Tert., Cypr.). To this moral version the "golden rule" is quite appropriate as a summary of the individual commands, whereas there was in this connection no place for "things strangled." Now it is intelligible, and is indeed of frequent occurrence, that a special and partly ritual provision should be transformed into a general moral code, whereas the reverse process is unintelligible and unheard of. On this ground, Zahn (*Einleitung*, vol. ii. pp. 344 f.), Harnack (*Sitzungsbericht der pr. Akad. der Wiss.*, 1899, xi.), Holtzmann (*Komm.*), and others who reject the D text are doubtless right. Yet the possibility should be borne in mind that perhaps the transformation of the decree may be due to the author of Acts himself, and the Western text may have therefore faithfully preserved the author's version, whereas the Eastern has corrected it on the basis of an accurate remembrance, which was retained in the East, of the original form of the decree. In that case the D text, which has such good Western support, would be correct from the point of view of textual criticism, whereas historical accuracy would be on the side of the Eastern (the received) text.

and served as a means of expiation, *i.e.* because it was something holy, a taboo, which must not be profaned. The second point, too (πορνεία), recalls Levit. xviii. 6–27, where the Israelites and the strangers in their midst are forbidden the sexual "abominations of the heathen," namely, sexual intercourse within the proscribed degrees, with the wife of another man, with a man's own wife during her period of menstruation, finally "paiderastia" and unnatural lust. The limitation of the enigmatic prohibition in the Apostolic decree to marriage of near relatives is therefore unjustifiable and unsupported by analogy; on the contrary, the word is here, as always (especially Apoc. ii. 20 ff.), to be understood in the widest sense, of unchastity in general. As this was regarded among the heathen as something morally indifferent, a prohibition of this kind was, for Gentile Christians, by no means superfluous. The four abstinences therefore all relate to heathen customs or immoralities which were especially offensive to the Jews on account of their habits of legal and moral purity, the abandonment of which on the part of the Gentile Christians appeared indispensable as a condition of brotherly intercourse, especially of fellowship at table in mixed congregations. This is pointed to also in the explanation of these demands in verse 21, which is to be understood in the sense that since there has long been a Jewish community in every heathen town, at least that minimum of accommodation to the Jewish Law is to be required of the Gentiles which even the Law-giver Moses required of the strangers who dwelt among the Jews. It cannot be denied that a demand of that kind is quite in keeping with the situation of that time—much more so, at any rate, than with the time of the author, a half century or so later, when it would no longer have been possible to think of imposing on the Gentile Christians, now become the majority, an obligation which went so deep into daily life as abstinence from things strangled, *i.e.* from meat which was not "kosher." Yet, though such a demand laid by the original body of disciples at Jerusalem upon the Gentile Christians is perfectly intelligible, it cannot be held to be historical, because it stands in open contradiction with the express declaration of Paul (Gal. ii. 6, 10): "They of reputation laid nothing further upon me, ... except that we should remember the poor." In his contention with Peter at Antioch, when the question at issue was the legitimacy of table-fellowship between Gentile and Jewish Christians, a question closely connected with the contents of the Apostolic decree, Paul, according to Gal. ii. 11 ff., did not refer to it by a single syllable. Further, in 1 Cor. viii. and x., Paul, in discussing the question of the eating of meats offered to idols, not only makes no reference to the Apostolic decree, but decides the question in a liberal sense which is at variance both with the letter and spirit of the Apostolic decree, declaring the eating of meats offered to idols to be in itself a thing indifferent, and entrusting the decision in particular cases to the conscience of the individual (x. 23–33). How could that have been possible if this decision had been taken at Jerusalem in his presence and he had been commissioned to communicate it to the churches? The conclusion to be drawn from this, that Paul during his missionary activity knew nothing of any such decree, finds a final confirmation in Acts xxi. 25, where, at the last meeting of Paul with the "elders" (not the Apostles) of the Jerusalem church, James says: "In regard to the Gentiles which believe, we have decided that they must abstain from things offered to idols, from blood, from things strangled, and from fornication." That does not read like a reminder of a decree of the Apostles which has long been known to Paul, in the drawing up of which he had himself had a part, but like the communication of an arrangement hitherto unknown to Paul, which had been adopted by James and the Jerusalem presbyters to regulate the relations of the Gentile to the Jewish Christians. "It is therefore natural to conjecture that a written edict of this tenor had *only recently* been issued from Jerusalem, that Luke mistakenly referred it to the Apostolic Council, and gave it the embodiment which we find in Acts xv. What had occasioned the issuing of this decree we are not told; and whether it was issued in the fifties or the sixties is a question of little moment when once it is admitted that it was not issued by the Council."[1]

While Paul reports, as a sequel to the treaty of peace at Jerusalem, the contention between Peter and himself at Antioch (Gal. ii. 11 f.; *cf.* vol. i. p. 120 f.), Acts has also to tell of a contention, not, however, between Paul and Peter, but between Paul and Barnabas, and not in regard to the question of principle, but owing

[1] Harnack, *Sitzungsbericht der pr. Akad. der Wiss.*, 1899, vol. xi. p. 20. According to Weizsäcker also (*Ap. Zeitalter*, p. 187), the decree was not issued by the church in Jerusalem until after the Antiochian dissension.

to a less important difference of opinion regarding John Mark (xv. 37–39). Without doubt we have here a softened reminiscence of the more serious strife between the Apostles, which cannot, moreover, have been unknown to the author of Acts. We must therefore suppose that he wished to cast the mantle of love over this, for the Church-consciousness of his time, unedifying scene, just as in his Gospel he has suppressed Jesus' sharp rebuke of Peter which he found in Mark viii. 33, and has given a milder tone to the words about the mother and brethren of Jesus (Mark iii. 33). He is everywhere a peace-maker, and, in particular, desires to remove from the revered figures of the primitive Church every possible shadow.

After the departure of Barnabas and Mark, Paul entered on his second missionary journey with Silas for companion, to whom, from Lycaonia onward, Timothy was added as a new helper in the mission (xvi. 1 ff.). Him, Acts records, Paul circumcised because of the Jews of the district, who knew him as the son of a Jewish mother and a Greek father. This deference to Jewish feeling on the part of Paul forms such a striking contrast to his unyielding firmness a short time before at Jerusalem in the similar case of Titus, that doubt as to the correctness of this statement seems to be justified. Especially the circumstance that Acts makes no reference at all to Titus, whose uncircumcision offended the Judaisers at Jerusalem (Gal. ii. 3 f.), makes the mention of the circumcising of Timothy doubly suspicious; one can hardly avoid the impression that Acts aims at softening the unpleasant memory of Paul's successful resistance to the demand for the circumcising of Titus by the conciliatory assurance of the circumcision of Timothy, just as, a little before, it endeavoured to soften the memory of the contention between Paul and Peter by recording the less significant contention with Barnabas.

This time Paul found no rest in Asia Minor; he was urged onwards towards the West. The decisive resolution to carry the gospel into Europe clothed itself for him in the form of a dream in which he saw a Macedonian standing and beseeching him, "Come over and help us." He recognised in this the Divine guidance in regard to his further missionary progress, and crossed over from Troas to Macedonia. Here (xvi. 10) the narrative again begins to use the "we," from the report of an eye-witness (the Luke-source), which first occurred at the beginnings of the Antiochian church (xi. 28). The route from Troas to Philippi is accurately described. Then follows a very vivid description of how the missionaries spoke to the women who assembled at the place of prayer of the Jews and proselytes, how a proselyte named Lydia was converted and offered them hospitality at her house, how then a woman who practised divination, a ventriloquist or hypnotic medium, who had annoyed the Apostle by crying after him, had her trade stopped by the Apostle, and how this led to an accusation against him, and judicial chastisement, on the ground of introducing illicit religious customs. At this point, however, the hitherto quite natural story suddenly takes a very unnatural turn—an earthquake during the night opened the doors of the prison and broke the chains of the prisoners; in consequence of this the jailer at once believed, took Paul and Silas to his house and cared for them. In the morning the chief magistrates of the town commanded them to be set at liberty, but Paul, appealing to his Roman citizenship, demanded satisfaction for the ill-treatment that he had received, and obtained it, in so far that the chief magistrates themselves appeared in person and escorted the Apostle out of the town. All this is too improbable to allow us to hold it to be historical. It is not confirmed, either, by Paul himself, for while he speaks of the ill-treatment and contumely which he had suffered at Philippi (1 Thess. ii. 1), he says not a word of his miraculous deliverance and the splendid satisfaction which he had received. Moreover, this miraculous deliverance by means of an earthquake has its exact counterpart in the two miraculous deliverances of Peter (chaps. v. and xii.), so that obviously all three are variations of the same legend. And as regards the satisfaction, amounting to an apology, which the authorities of Philippi were compelled to render to the Apostle, the author doubtless intended to give the Roman officials of his own period (the time of Trajan) a warning example that they should not allow their official authority to be compromised in trials of Christians by careless procedure or complaisance towards mob-violence.

From Philippi Paul and Silas made their way through Thessalonica and began there to preach in the synagogue, and while few Jews were converted by this preaching there was a large number of converts among the proselytes, both men and women, some of them people of distinction. This roused the jealousy of the Jews, who were able to procure the expulsion of the Apostles by the magistrates of the town (xvii. 1–9). In Berœa their preaching met with a better reception from the Jewish colony of that place, but the Jews from Thessalonica stirred up the populace against Paul, so that he was obliged to depart from the town, leaving the prosecution of the work which he had begun there to his helpers Silas and Timothy (verses 10–15). This report is confirmed by the First Epistle to the Thessalonians. On the other hand, the account which follows in Acts of the appearance of Paul in Athens gives rise to some difficulties. Even the circumstance that Paul fell into discussion in the market-place with Epicurean and Stoic philosophers (xvii. 17 f.) is little in accordance with his practice elsewhere of beginning his preaching in the narrow circles of those who were religiously receptive and desirous of salvation. It is still more improbable that he delivered an apologetic discourse upon the Areopagus, which was no place for popular speeches, but the highest court of justice in the city. It is possible that the narrator wished this discourse to be regarded as a legal defence, after the analogy of the speeches delivered by Peter and by Stephen before the Sanhedrin, and therefore laid the scene of it on the Areopagus; but as nothing is said of a regular legal process with accusation, examination, and reply, the whole situation has obviously been freely invented in order to give the speech which was to be introduced here a dignified setting. As regards the contents of the speech, it is certainly to be recognised that it does much credit to the literary skill of the author, as an able and well-conceived defence of Christianity before the world of heathen culture, and to this extent, as the first example of Christian apologetic in the face of heathenism, it has undeniable historical value;[1] but we must not seek in it documentary evidence of the character of Apostolic preaching—still less than in the Petrine speeches of the early chapters. The speech begins by a laudatory reference to the God-fearing character of the Greeks, which was shown in the fact that the Athenians had dedicated an altar to an unknown god. (This is an allusion to the actual occurrence of altars dedicated "to unknown gods"; the plural has been changed into the singular by the author to serve his oratorical purpose.) This God, whom they worshipped though they knew Him not, the speaker desires to set forth to them. He is the Creator, and the Lord of heaven and earth, who dwells not in temples made with hands, nor needs anything from man, for He Himself is the source of all life. He has caused the whole race of man to spring from a single ancestor, and has given to individual peoples their dwelling-places and their historical vocation, that they may seek God, if haply they may find Him, for He is not far from every one of us, since in Him we live and move and have our being; as even the Greek poets (the Stoic Cleanthes, who taught in Athens, and the Cilician Aratus) had said, "We are the offspring of God." Man ought

[1] Norden, *Antike Kūnstprosa,* ii. 475, well remarks: "If ever a scientific book is written on the relations of Christianity to Greek philosophy, the speech at Athens must stand as the earliest catholic attempt at compromise between Christianity and the pure Hellenic Stoicism, just as the prologue to the Johannine Gospel fulfils a similar function in regard to Christianity and the Jewish-Hellenic Stoicism."

not, therefore, since he is thus related to God, to worship material images. Hitherto, it is true, God has in His longsuffering overlooked this ignorance, but now He commands men everywhere to repent, since He has appointed a day in which He will judge the world by a man whom He has authenticated before all by raising him from the dead, as the future ruler of the world. This speech revolves round the two poles of the Gentile-Christian consciousness: the monotheistic belief in God, and the expectation of the return of the risen Jesus as ruler of the world. Though it may doubtless be assumed to be certain that both points played a prominent part in the speeches of the Apostle of the Gentiles, yet it is not to be overlooked that the Pauline Christ is not primarily the Judge of the world, but the Saviour of the world, and that the purpose of His resurrection is not to mark Him out as the appointed Judge of the world, but as the Son of God, in whom we are to find justification (Rom. i. 4, iv. 25). Similarly, the mild censure of idolatry as "ignorance" which God has overlooked is difficult to reconcile with Rom. i. 19 ff., where the worship of images appears rather as the reason for the revelation of God's wrath against the heathen world. Whether, too, Paul would have adopted the saying of the Greek poet regarding the kinship of men with God is open to doubt, when we remember that Paul thought of man under the categories flesh, soul, earthly being, which stand in direct contrast to the heavenly, spiritual being of God (1 Cor. xv. 45, ii. 15 f.). In all this is betrayed the point of view of the author of the speech, who stands incomparably nearer to the apologists of the second century than to genuine Paulinism. We notice, too, the interesting fact that the historical Paul has here, at a stroke, been given by his biographer a Gentile aspect, as elsewhere he gives him a Jewish aspect. If the former is not to be explained by any party tendency, then the latter cannot logically be explained in that way; both alike find their most natural explanation in the mode of thought of the Gentile-Christian church in the second century, which the author has assumed to be also the mode of thought of his hero. Another argument in favour of the free composition of the speech on the Areopagus is its affinity in part with the speech of Stephen (vii.), in part with several passages of Josephus. As the former was an apology for Christianity before the Jewish authorities, so the present speech is an apology before the heathen authorities; the occasion in both cases being the charge of making innovations in religion, culminating in both cases in the rejection of the service of the visible temple, as being in contradiction with the spiritual idea of God. This pure monotheism, forming the common pole of Jewish and Christian Hellenism, is precisely what we find in many passages in Josephus (*Ant.*, viii. 4. 2; *Adv. Apion.*, ii. 16. 22), described in phrases which have such close verbal affinity with that of the speech on the Areopagus that the dependence of the author of that speech upon Josephus is very probable.[1]

The stay of the Apostle in Athens seems to have been brief and to have had very little result, for we never hear anything in his letters of the existence of a Christian community there. On the other hand,

[1] Krenkel, *Josephus und Lukas*, pp. 224–228.

Corinth offered him a rich field of work, in which he laboured for a year and a half (xviii. 10 f.). Apart from the ever-recurring conflict with the Jews, whose machinations were in this instance frustrated by the correct attitude of the Roman proconsul Gallio, Acts unfortunately gives us no detailed account of the history of the foundation of the Corinthian church—passes over, in fact, in complete silence all the inner difficulties with which Paul was so much occupied, both personally when on the spot, and in his correspondence. Whether the author did this because his source here failed him (the eye-witness of the "we-source" first met Paul again upon his return to Philippi, xx. 5), or because these stories seemed to be neither interesting nor edifying for later readers, is a question which, in our ignorance of the sources of Acts, we must be content to leave open.

There are difficulties, too, in the report of the journey which, according to xviii. 21 f., Paul made from Ephesus—before returning there for his longer stay—to Antioch and, as used to be supposed, to Jerusalem. It is not in itself very probable that Paul, after what had happened at Antioch and the dispute with Peter and the James party from Jerusalem, would now have gone up to Jerusalem in order to keep a feast. Moreover, the reception which Paul later (chap. xxi.) finds in Jerusalem decidedly makes the impression that this is the first meeting (since the Council) of the Apostle of the Gentiles, who preached freedom from the Law, with the legalist primitive Church. On the other hand, it is not easy to see any reason why the author should have invented this whole journey without any historical basis, and then have given only so cursory an account of it. Besides, it is natural to suppose that Paul, when he returned from Corinth to Asia Minor, was anxious to visit first his churches in Antioch and in Galatia. We find confirmation of this conjecture, and a simple solution of the whole difficulty, in the explicit and certainly original reading of the Western text (D), in which the purpose of the journey is, indeed, first explained in xviii. 21 with the words, "I must by all means keep the feast in Jerusalem," but continues (xix. 1), "When Paul was intending of his own motion to go to Jerusalem, the the Spirit bade him return to Asia; and when he had passed through the upper regions he came to Ephesus," etc. The author who wrote this cannot possibly have meant in xviii. 22 that Paul travelled up to Jerusalem, but only that he went to Cæsarea and Antioch to greet the churches there.[1] Only when a later hand had omitted the two corresponding statements of the intention to travel up to Jerusalem and of the non-fulfilment of it on account of the (supposed) contradiction between them, could xviii. 22 be misunderstood as referring to a completed journey to Jerusalem.

The account which Acts gives of Paul's work in Ephesus is prefaced by an interesting episode relating

[1] It may, moreover, be conjectured that in the source used here xix. 1 followed immediately upon xviii. 22, and that verse 23 as well as the passage about Apollos was added by the author; for in D, xix. 1 does not contain any reference to Apollos nor to the travel notices of xviii. 23, which the author probably inserted because the slight reference of the source to his having travelled through the "upper regions" seemed to him to need some further explanation.

to disciples there who had been baptized with John's baptism, and to the Alexandrian scholar Apollos, whose faith was in some respects similar to theirs (xviii. 24–xix. 7). It is true that the picture of this man which is given in xviii. 25 ff. is as obscure as his relation to the disciples of John who are spoken of in xix. 2–7. He has this in common with them, that he is only baptized with John's baptism; but while they first heard from Paul of Jesus as the fulfiller of John's message, and then, believing, were baptized in the name of Jesus, and received the Spirit by the laying-on of the hands of Paul, the Spirit manifesting His presence by their "speaking with tongues" and "prophesying," it is on the contrary said of Apollos that he (according to D) had already in his home (Alexandria) been instructed in the word, or way, of the Lord, *i.e.* in regard to Christianity, and that he spoke fervently in the Spirit and taught accurately the things of the Lord, knowing only the baptism of John. Then, in Ephesus, he was taught more fully the way of God, and thereafter went with letters of recommendation from Ephesus to Corinth, and there disputed powerfully with the Jews and convinced them from the Holy Scriptures of the Messiahship of Jesus. How are we to reconcile the statements that Apollos, while he only knew the baptism of John—therefore had not been baptized in the name of Jesus—was filled with the fervency of the (Christian ?) Spirit, and taught accurately concerning Jesus? And, since Apollos is said in that passage to have belonged to the disciples of John, how came it that the other disciples of John remained so entirely unaffected by his knowledge of Christianity and his relations with

Aquila and Priscilla as, according to xix. 2, they evidently did? This want of connection between the two, the accounts of Apollos and of the disciples of John, might perhaps be most simply explained by supposing that the former has been inserted by the author (which is in conformity with what has been remarked on xix. 1), while the latter is derived from his source. While the sketch of Apollos is obscure and self-contradictory, representing him as a Christian before he was baptized in the name of Jesus, the picture of the disciples of John, on the other hand, who knew nothing either of the (Christian) Spirit or of Jesus, and first became Christians through Paul's preaching, is quite clear and simple. Here there is, at any rate, an historical basis. That there was really a school of disciples of John the Baptist at Ephesus, and that it was not uncommon to pass over from it to the Christian Church, may be inferred with much probability from the Gospel of John also. For this reason it would be difficult to raise any valid objection against the record that such conversions did actually take place through Paul's preaching. There is therefore no ground for the conjecture that the story of the Ephesian disciples of John in xix. 2–7 was freely invented by the author in imitation of viii. 14 ff.; the not very probable narrative there is much more likely to be an imitation of xix. 2 ff.

Of the two years' work of Paul at Ephesus, Acts gives (xix. 8–40) only a fragmentary picture. It mentions miraculous cures wrought by means of handkerchiefs of Paul, a legendary trait, which is, however, quite explicable in view of the keen appetite for miracle which usually prevails in the lower strata of society when under the influence of religious excitement. Then follows a story of Jewish exorcists who got into trouble through misusing the name of Jesus; then the incident of the burning of valuable books of sorcery; finally, a popular tumult is described which was stirred up against Paul by a silversmith named Demetrius because he found himself injured in his trade, which depended on the worship of Diana, by the success of the mission. This narrative seems, indeed, from the mention by name of some of the persons who are prominent in it, to rest upon a definite basis of tradition (perhaps the "we-source"); yet this cannot have been very definite, or else was not followed with much accuracy by the narrator, for it is difficult to make out the rôle which was played by the Jew Alexander (verses 33 f.) in the tumult. Moreover, Paul's escape in complete safety from the tumult does not agree with Paul's own reference to a mortal danger in which he found himself at this time, in which he even despaired of deliverance (2 Cor. i. 8). Perhaps the author has, in conformity with his apologetic aim, represented the attitude of the Roman authorities as more favourable than it actually was; or perhaps, by narrating a (politically) innocent occurrence, he has sought to soften the impression of a more serious collision with the Roman authorities—much as he did in xv. 37 ff.

The journey of Paul through Macedonia to Greece, of which there is confirmation in the Corinthian letters, is only mentioned incidentally in xx. 1 f.; but, to make up for this, the return journey through Macedonia and Troas to Jerusalem is reported very fully.[1] At Philippi the writer of the travel-diary, whom we lost sight of at Paul's first visit to Philippi, seems to have rejoined his company; for, from verse 25 on, the "we" appears again. The authority of this source attests the story in xx. 7–12 of how Eutychus fell from the window and was taken up as dead, but was brought to life again by Paul; and in the story itself there is nothing impossible, for though the narrator may of course have thought of a real raising from the dead, this opinion of his need not hinder us from explaining the occurrence as natural, since there is nothing in the wording of the narrative to contradict this impression. By this strict reserve the narrative is distinguished, much to its advantage, from the raising from the dead which is narrated of Peter in ix. 36 ff. If, therefore, the parallelism of the narratives is intentional, it would in any case be the Peter story which was the imitation.

While the exact statements regarding the route of travel are derived from the travel-diary, the speech which Acts makes Paul deliver to the Ephesian elders at Miletus (xx. 18–35) is to be considered in the same light as all the speeches in this history; it is a composition of the narrator's, who has inserted it here in order, at the close of Paul's missionary activity, to cast a glance back along its course, to

[1] It is worth noticing that in verse 3 according to D, the reason for the land journey, instead of the sea journey which was at first intended, is explained as being a warning oracle of the Spirit, which here, as in xix. 1, is omitted in the received text; in both cases D has obviously the original reading, while the redactor of the received text omits these oracles of the Spirit as savouring too much of enthusiasm.

testify to its leading principles, and at the same time, looking forward to the future of the Church, to put various exhortations into the mouth of the Apostle as he takes his leave. That this is done in an attractive and sympathetic fashion may well be admitted, without overlooking the fact that the speech is in many respects less adapted to the situation of Paul than to that of his pious biographer. Even the definite prediction, going far beyond anxious presentiment, that they will henceforth see him no more, could scarcely have been spoken by Paul; this must be due to the author, with his knowledge of the course of the history. Moreover, while the attacks and plots are mentioned which the Apostle encountered from enemies without, namely, the Jews, the fightings and cares which assailed him from the side of factions and opponents within the churches themselves, and which at that time gave him as much or more concern than the persecutions from without (2 Cor. vii. 5), are passed over in complete silence. This would be as unintelligible in a real speech of Paul as it is completely intelligible from the standpoint of the deutero-Pauline author, who really—as his whole history shows—knew little of the controversies within the Christian church of Apostolic times, and was not anxious to tell what he knew. With this is connected the further circumstance that the exhortations addressed by the speaker to the leaders of the Ephesian church are couched in such general language that absolutely no picture of the real condition and circumstances of that church can be gathered from them, whereas Paul always in his letters (think of the Corinthian letters, for instance) discusses in such detail the circumstances and needs of the church to which he is writing that we can make for ourselves a vivid picture of it. Instead of going into the actual circumstances of the present, the speaker dwells rather on future dangers which after the departure of the Apostle will threaten the church owing to the efforts of seductive teachers of error. That is exactly the way in which the "Pastoral Epistles" also put into the mouth of the Apostle, as a *vaticinium post eventum*, a warning against the heretical teachers of the second century. The true Paul was kept so busy by the opponents of his own time that he had no leisure to think of the heretics of the future. Another thing that reminds us strongly of the Pastoral Epistles is that the leaders of the church are treated as the responsible representatives of the church and the guardians of the purity of its faith in the struggle against heresy—a view of which we find no trace in the genuine Pauline epistles; indeed, we may find in this discourse the whole "scheme of the Pastoral Epistles": "diminution of the rights of the members of the church, close association of the ideas of official status and endowment with Spirit, prescription of hierarchic organisation of the church as a defence against error, and the still-subsisting identification of the presbyterate with the office of bishop" (Holtzmann). From the point of view of later circumstances, what is said regarding the principles of Apostolic teaching acquires a special significance. When the speaker repeatedly (verses 20, 27) emphasises the fact that he had held nothing back, but communicated to his hearers the whole counsel of God, that serves not merely as a defence of Paul against the charge of misrepresenting and keeping back the truth of the gospel, which was brought against him by the Judaisers, but also as a repudiation of those unorthodox doctrines which were put forth by gnosticising and libertine professed followers of Paul as the true core and the completion of Pauline teaching. And when the speaker dwells on the unselfishness of his missionary activity, and expressly holds it up as a pattern for his disciples (verses 34 f.), there is obviously in this a warning against covetousness—a vice with which the teachers of the second century, especially the heretical teachers, are repeatedly reproached in the Pastoral Epistles and elsewhere (*e.g.*, 1 Pet. v. 2 f. ; Matt. x. 9). Thus, this whole discourse appears to presuppose the circumstances of the second century, and to be a defence not merely of Paul, but of ecclesiastical Paulinism, represented in his person.[1]

Throughout the rest of Paul's journey to Jerusalem the source is closely followed, and the repeated warnings of the imminent danger and suffering are thus confirmed as historical. Especially as regards the prediction of Agabus in xxi. 10 f., the way in which the prophet is here introduced without reference to the previous mention of him (xi. 28) must be derived from the source which the author is using. Whether the earlier mention is to be referred to the same source or was freely invented by the writer, who knew the name from this passage (Hilgenfeld), remains an open question.

In the last section of Acts, which begins with the

[1] The parallels cited by Krenkel (*ut sup.*, pp. 236–240) from Josephus' account of the farewell discourses of Moses, Samuel, and King Agrippa (*Ant.*, iv. 8. 2, 3, 48 ; vi. 5. 5 ; *B.J.*, ii. 16. 4 f.) are worthy of notice.

arrival of Paul in Jerusalem, we notice with especial clearness the carrying out of the ideas which were indicated at the outset (see p. 191 f., *sup.*) as fundamental in this work: defence of Christianity before the Roman civil authority; its agreement with the Jewish religion, alongside of the sharp opposition between the Church and the Jewish people; finally, the minimising of dissensions within Christianity in comparison with this outward opposition. This applies especially to the speeches which the author has interwoven into this last section, as to the historicity of which the analogy of all the other speeches which we have considered thus far leaves us in no doubt. The case is less certain in regard to the proceedings here reported which led to Paul's imprisonment. Though the connection of these narratives is in many respects obscure, they contain, on the other hand, such definite statements and such vivid descriptions that we cannot help seeing in them traces of the "we-source," though perhaps used only in extracts and partially worked over by the author.

A much debated point of controversy is furnished by the very first of the scenes which take place in Jerusalem (xxi. 17–26). After mention of the friendly reception of the Apostle and his travelling companions in Jerusalem, it is next narrated that the presbyters assembled about James informed Paul that it was currently reported among the thousands of Jewish Christians who were zealous for the Law that he taught the Jews of the Diaspora to abandon it; they therefore counselled him to associate himself with some men who had taken upon them the Nazirite vow, letting himself be purified along with them and bearing the costs of discharging their vow; thus it would be seen that there was no truth in this report, and that he too continued to observe the Law. Then, too, as regards the Gentiles who believed, his adversaries were not in a position to find fault with him (verse 25, acc. Cod. D[1]), as, by their (the Jerusalem presbyters') decree, the Gentiles had been set free from any further obligations beyond those of abstinence from idolatry, from blood (things strangled), and from unchastity. This counsel Paul followed, and it was precisely his presence in the Temple, in order to fulfil the vow, which gave occasion for the tumult raised by the Jews which ended in Paul's arrest by the Roman garrison. Not without reason have difficulties been found in this narrative. Was, then, we must ask, the rumour of Paul's rejection of the Law a groundless calumny? Had he not really taught that Christ was the end of the Law for everyone who believes, for the Jew as well as for the Gentile? That circumcision was of no more religious value than uncircumcision? That everyone who caused himself to be circumcised had fallen from Christ and from grace? (Rom. x. 4; Gal. v. 2–6). And even if he could, on occasion, become a Jew to a Jew in order to win him for Christ, could he, in view of his indifference in principle towards the Mosaic Law, wish to maintain that he always walked according to it? Indeed, it seems clear that the historical Paul could not, without insincerity, have adopted the proof of his continued observance of the Law which was here demanded of him. Which is the more probable? the critics ask:

[1] After "as touching the Gentiles which believe," D adds οὐδὲν ἔχουσι λέγειν πρὸς σέ, and proceeds ἡμεῖς γὰρ κ.τ.λ.—TRANSLATOR.

that Paul should really have thus denied his principles, or that the author of Acts (not the "we-source") should have attributed to him here, as in xvi. 3 and the speeches of xxiii., xxiv., xxvi., the rôle of a law-abiding Jew? To this it is replied by the other side that it is still a question whether Paul was not really justified in denying the reproach that he taught the Jews to reject the Law; he had, on the other hand taught that every Christian should remain as he was when he was called, the Jew in his circumcision and the Gentile in uncircumcision (1 Cor. vii. 17 f.; *cf.* Acts xv. 2, acc. D[1]). If, then, in order to conciliate those who were unjustly opposing him, he took part in a Jewish ceremony, that was no denial of his conviction of the religious worthlessness of the legal forms, but an application of his principle of Christian freedom, viz. that in things indifferent each one should act as his conscience and the needs of the weaker brother dictate (1 Cor. ix. 19 ff., x. 23; Rom. xiv.) Moreover, it is not strictly implied in the wording of the narrative that Paul had taken a vow upon himself, but only that he had undergone a purification, and had assisted others in the discharge of their vow by a contribution of money, a thing which was frequently done, *e.g.* by King Agrippa, according to Josephus, *Ant.*, xix. 6. 1. Finally, it is asked whether it is probable that a story so detailed, and involving such fine points of Jewish ritual, as that which is told in xxi. 20–26, could have been freely invented by the Gentile-Christian author of Acts without any dependence on the source which he

[1] After "Paul and Barnabas had no small dissension and disputation with them," D has ἔλεγεν γὰρ ὁ Π. μένειν οὕτως καθὼς ἐπίστευσαν διισχυριζόμενος.—TRANSLATOR.

follows both before and after? I admit that these difficulties appear to me too serious to permit me to deny that the story has any historical basis. How far accommodation is rightly possible in things which one holds to be indifferent is a question to which such different answers would be given by different persons that it seems useless to make any *a priori* assertions in regard to it. That Paul held compromise for the sake of peace to be admissible in principle is certain (*cf.* 1 Cor. viii. 1 f., x. 23; Rom. xiv.). We should not be justified in giving a definite opinion as to whether he ought to have practised it in the present case unless we were exactly acquainted with all the circumstances. Perhaps we come nearest to the truth if we suppose that the narrative has a foundation of fact, but that the motive assigned for Paul's action (in verse 24), to which objection is taken, is to be attributed to the author, in regard to whom we have long recognised that, in the light of the ecclesiastical circumstances of his own time, he thought of his hero as more conservative than he really was.[1]

Immediately after Paul had been torn from the hands of the Jewish mob by the intervention of the Roman soldiers and led away to the castle, Acts represents him as delivering his first defence before the assembled people (chap. xxii.). He recounts how he had at first been a Jew zealous for the Law and a bitter persecutor of the Christians, then by the miraculous vision on the road to Damascus had been

[1] This is the opinion of Wendt, *Komm. z. Ap. G.*, pp. 346 ff., and Joh. Weiss, *Über Absicht und literar. Charakter der Apostelgeschichte*, pp. 36 ff., where the question is discussed with much discrimination.

converted to Christianity and, by a second vision in the Temple, had been sent forth as an apostle to the heathen, because his testimony to Christ would not be received in Jerusalem. At this significant statement, which forms the main point of the speech —that the unbelief of the Jews was the cause of the mission to the Gentiles—the popular excitement broke out afresh, whereupon Paul was led away to be examined by scourging, which he prevented, however, by appealing to his right as a Roman citizen. On the following day he is brought before the Jewish Sanhedrin. The proceedings here begin in a very dramatic fashion. When Paul appeals to the good conscience in which he has always lived, the High Priest commands him to be smitten on the mouth; whereupon Paul allows himself to be carried away by indignation, and calls him a "whited wall," for lowering his judicial dignity by an illegal act of violence. When he is told that it is the High Priest whom he is abusing, he excuses himself by saying that he did not know it. If this beginning arouses some surprise, this is increased by the astute stroke of Paul in declaring, in order to win the support of the Pharisees among his judges, that he is a Pharisee and is being accused because of his belief in the resurrection (xxiii. 6). The strangest thing of all, however, is that the Sanhedrin not only allowed this assertion to pass unchallenged, but immediately began to quarrel over this article of belief in regard to which Pharisees and Sadducees were opposed, while the Pharisees even testified to Paul's innocence (verse 9). The improbability of these proceedings is so obvious, that we may spare ourselves the trouble of justifying Paul in regard to the moral difficulties which are involved. But at the same time we must not understand the author too pedantically, as if he intended to imply that the belief of the Apostle was exactly identical with that of the Pharisees. We must make allowance for the taste of the author for dramatically painted scenes, and also for his antipathy to the Jewish hierarchy. There is more historical probability in the following account of the plot of the Jews against Paul, who was informed by his sister's son of the intended attempt at assassination, and was thereupon sent, for safety, under a strong military escort, to Cæsarea, to Felix, the procurator of Judæa (xxiii. 12–35).

In regard to the two years' imprisonment of Paul at Cæsarea, Acts seems to have little in the way of fact to narrate; it therefore inserts here several apologetic discourses. The first, that delivered before the tribunal of Felix (xxiv. 10–21), seeks to rebut the accusation of the Jews which charged him with stirring up sedition among the people and desecrating the Temple, by proving both that his faith was one with the faith of the Jews in regard to the Law and the Prophets, and that his conduct had been blameless before God and man. Towards his own people, moreover, he had been so far from feeling any enmity that he had come to Jerusalem for the very purpose of bringing alms and offerings, and while he was discharging this duty with all quietness he was encountered by his accusers in the Temple. These could themselves testify whether they or the Council could find any fault in him, except that he acknowledged his belief in the resurrection of the dead. Criticism of this speech must not, naturally, start from the point of view that Paul really delivered it (could anyone suppose it possible that the historian found the report of the trial in the judicial archives of Cæsarea, and copied it out!); the only question is whether it serves the apologetic purpose of Acts. In this respect it is very characteristic. It is, we must especially notice, *an apology for Christianity before the Roman Government.* In relation to the Roman authority, the point was to defend it against the charge of being a *religio illicita*, and of a revolutionary character which caused popular outbreaks, by showing that it stood on the basis of historic Judaism and was constituted a special sect by mere doctrinal differences from the latter, and by emphasising its innocence in regard to civil affairs, and representing the hatred of the Jews as caused by no provocation on the part of the Christians, but as due solely to dogmatic fanaticism. That was exactly the standpoint of Christian apologetic in the second century. In its dealings with the heathen State, Christianity took up its position on the basis of Judaism as a religion, sharing its belief in a revelation and its ancient records, and therefore claiming the toleration which was accorded to it by the State; at the same time, however, it placed itself in the sharpest opposition to the Jewish people, whose hatred was derived from causeless fanaticism. This apologetic aim is admirably attained by the speech before Felix: to find in it a dogmatic confession of faith, or even a Judaising attitude fictitiously attributed to Paul to conciliate Jewish Christians, is wholly to misunderstand its meaning; the author has not thought at all of tendencies adapted to party relationships of that kind within Christianity, at any rate here, where he is wholly and solely concerned with the position of Christianity in the Roman State. The under-estimation or neglect of this feature of Acts, and the over-estimation of its relationship to the parties within the Church, have done much to hinder an unprejudiced understanding of the book.

The speech before the Jewish King Agrippa and the Roman Festus (xxvi. 1–23) is slightly different in aim and content. As the last of the apologetic discourses, it very appropriately unites the aims of the earlier one before the Jews (chap. xxii.) and that before the Roman Governor (chap. xxiv.). Paul declares that he is being accused on account of his faith in the fulfilment of the Messianic prophecies of Israel. Formerly he had lived as a strict Pharisee and persecuted the Church of Christ, but had been converted by a heavenly vision to belief in Jesus and called to witness for Him among the Gentiles. Obeying this heavenly vision, he had since then fulfilled his calling, proclaiming in Damascus, in Jerusalem, throughout the whole of Judæa, and among the Gentiles, that men should turn from darkness to light, and from the power of Satan to God, and do works meet for repentance, in order through faith in Jesus to obtain forgiveness of sins and a share in the inheritance of the saints. Such was the testimony that he had borne hitherto before small and great, and in doing so he was saying nothing else than what Moses and the Prophets had foretold, namely, that Messiah should suffer, and, as the first-born from the dead, should bring light both to Israel and the Gentiles. This speech before

Agrippa, who was well acquainted with the Jewish religion, makes more prominent than that before Felix the new and distinctive element in the faith and preaching of Paul: the proclamation of a suffering and risen Messiah, whose salvation is destined for the Gentiles also (verse 23). The defence, however, rests upon two grounds, of which one or other had been prominent in each of the two preceding longer speeches: (1) that Paul had not come to his Christian faith and Apostolic calling by his own will, but by the overmastering power of a revelation from heaven, which he, as a pious and believing Pharisee, could not resist; (2) that the preaching which had this supernatural beginning did not contain any arbitrary innovation, but was in complete harmony with the Old Testament revelation, especially with the (Messianic) hopes of the fathers. Here we have, in fact, something like a short summary of the faith, not indeed of Paul himself, but of his biographer and the Gentile-Christian Church of his time, namely, that Christianity is the religion of faith in the God of Israel and in the promises to the fathers, which has been opened up to the Gentiles also by the death and resurrection of Jesus the Messiah. It is therefore in essentials nothing else than what Moses and the Prophets have already announced; but this old revelation has now become, through the new revelation of God in Jesus the Messiah, a universal light, for Gentile as well as Jew, to all whom the preaching of the gospel turns from Satan (false gods) to God, and so becomes to them the means of the forgiveness of sins, and the hope of salvation. That these thoughts do not exactly coincide with the theology of Paul himself is, of course, indisputable, but it would be quite mistaken to suppose that it is an intentional misrepresentation of it in the direction, and in the interest, of Petrinism; rather, it is the simplified precipitate of Paulinism in the consciousness of the Gentile-Christian Church, which could not grasp the subtleties of the Pauline dialectic, and, it must be admitted, had little understanding of the deeper mysticism of the Apostle.

The effect of these defences was, according to Luke's account, increasingly favourable to Paul. Of Felix, it is said that he made a pretext to adjourn the trial, and so dismissed Paul's Jewish accusers, being well acquainted with the character of this teaching (xxiv. 22 f.). This means, without doubt, that he knew enough of Christianity to be aware that the Jewish complaints against it were groundless, and accordingly he made Paul's confinement as little irksome as possible. It is no doubt difficult to say why, on this assumption, he kept him imprisoned at all, and did not simply set him at liberty. As this fact of the long imprisonment by the Roman authorities could not be very easily explained from the presuppositions of Acts, the author has sought a reason for it in the well-known greed and venality of the Roman Governors of the Provinces; in the hope of receiving money, as he says in xxiv. 26, Felix kept Paul in bonds for two years, and then, on his departure, did not set him free, in order thereby to show the Jews a favour—neither of them very probable reasons, for how could Felix hope to obtain any considerable ransom from a poor tentmaker and missionary; and if he desired to please the Jews, why did he not simply deliver his prisoner over to them? In the case of Festus, who followed Felix as Governor, the same reasons are repeated; he, too, wished to show the Jews a favour, and therefore proposed the resumption of the trial in Jerusalem, although he, as Paul told him to his face, knew quite well that Paul had done the Jews no wrong. Thereupon Paul appealed to Cæsar, in order to withdraw himself from Jewish jurisdiction. The defence before Festus and Agrippa made, according to Acts, so powerful an impression upon the latter that he himself showed signs of a disposition to become a Christian, and if he did not quite go so far, both he and Festus were so fully convinced of Paul's complete innocence, that nothing stood in the way of his liberation except the appeal which he had previously made to the Emperor (xxvi. 31 f.) This whole account decidedly makes the impression that the author's fragmentary knowledge of this period was supplemented by edifying material of an apologetic character. He has told the story of the trial of Paul from exactly the same point of view as he told, in the Gospel, the story of the trial of Jesus. In both cases it is only the Jewish hierarchs who appear as fanatical persecutors, whilst the Roman judges, in harmony with the Jewish kings (Antipas, Agrippa), are convinced of the innocence of the accused, and give unambiguous expression to that conviction, but allow themselves to be prevented by worldly motives from resolving, in accordance with that conviction, to set the prisoner free. This representation is, however, too closely suggested by the interest of the Church in relation to the Roman Government to be considered as historically true.

"When the proof of the innocence of Paul, not merely in relation to the Roman administration, but even as regards the Jewish hierarchy, is constantly given with such completeness that even the Jew Agrippa is forced to acknowledge it, it finally comes to be incredible that he should be kept so long in prison and ultimately deported to Rome" (Holtzmann). Another argument in favour of the free composition of this section are the numerous parallels with Josephus, some of which are so striking as to suggest direct imitation.[1]

With the departure of Paul from Cæsarea the report of the eye-witness begins again (xxvii. 1). He proves himself to be so by the exact description of the route of travel and the very graphic picture of the storm and the shipwreck. It is noteworthy, too, that in this section there are no miracle stories, properly so called; for what is said of the reassuring dream of Paul during the storm (xxvii. 23), of his escape from a danger which threatened his life in Malta, of the cures wrought by him there (xxviii. 3–6, 8 f.), in no way goes beyond what is naturally possible and probable. The hypothesis that the report of the eye-witness originally gave fuller information regarding the three months' stay in Malta, which has been abbreviated by the redactor, is possible, but not exactly probable, and in any case is not susceptible of proof. The statement in xxviii. 15, that the Christian brethren from the church at Rome came to meet the Apostle as far as Appii (Forum) and Tres

[1] Krenkel, *ut sup.*, pp. 255–280. *Cf.*, *e.g.*, Acts xxiii. 22 f. with Jos., *Vit.*, 17, 24; Acts xxiv. 25, 26 with Jos., *Ant.*, xx. 8. 5 and ix. 5.; Acts xxv. 11 with Jos., *Vit.*, 29.

Tabernae is covered by the report of the eye-witness and is quite in harmony with what we should infer from the Epistle to the Romans regarding the attitude of that predominantly Gentile-Christian church; from the members of such a church it was only to be expected that they would accord a warm welcome to the Apostle, whom they did not as yet know personally, but who had introduced himself to them in so impressive a fashion by his letter.

The close of Acts is formed by the address of Paul to the heads of the Jewish colony in Rome (xxviii. 17–28). In view of all that we have observed hitherto regarding the speeches in this book, we shall not expect exact historical reminiscence in this address. Just in the manner with which we have become familiar in the other apologetic discourses, Paul assures his hearers that he has come to be imprisoned by the Romans through no fault of his own, owing to the machinations of the Jews. The Romans had desired to set him at liberty when they had convinced themselves of his innocence, but the opposition of the Jews had obliged him to appeal to the Emperor; but in doing so it was not his intention to accuse his own nation, nay, it was for the hope of Israel that he bore this chain, and for that reason he had sought to come to a friendly understanding with them. The Jews replied that they had heard nothing against him, and would be glad to hear his views, as they knew, concerning this sect, that it was everywhere spoken against. (This sounds as if they had previously had no accurate knowledge, not only of Paul, but of the Christian communities in general, which would be very improbable in view of the existence of one at

Rome. Perhaps the author only intended to make them say that they were ready to listen, in an unprejudiced spirit, to the preaching of Paul.) When, on a later day, Paul preached to them of the Kingdom of God and sought to convince them from the Scriptures of the Messiahship of Jesus, only a part of them believed, and the assembly broke up in dissension, whereupon Paul applied to them a saying from Isa. iv. 9 f., in which the hardening of Israel is declared by the prophet to be their inevitable punishment. This saying he now saw finally fulfilled, and therefore he concluded by declaring to the Jews, "Be it known unto you that this salvation of God is offered unto the Gentiles, and that they will hear it." So separating himself from the Jews, the imprisoned Apostle worked two years without hindrance as a witness for Christ in the capital of the heathen world (xxviii. 30 f.).

Thus was repeated once again, in Rome, what Paul, according to the representation of Acts, had often experienced in the course of his missionary journeys: that his attempt to find a point of attachment in the Jews of the Diaspora was frustrated by their repugnance to the crucified Messiah Jesus, and he was obliged to confine his work entirely to the heathen. This representation of Acts has been held by some to be a "tendency" fiction, intended to justify Paul's mission to the Gentiles in the eyes of the Jewish Christians as not originally intended, but brought about against the will of the Apostle by the actual resistance of the Jews. But this is, in several respects, mistaken. It is especially to be observed that the commencing of the missionary preaching with the Jews of the Diaspora was so inevitable that we should be obliged to assume it even if Acts said nothing about it.[1] Naturally, it was not Paul's intention to confine his work to the Jews ; but neither does Acts say that, but repeatedly indicates that in these discourses in the synagogues he addressed himself to the pious Gentiles who took part therein (the σεβόμενοι), and found in these his most receptive hearers. Where else than in the synagogue could he have found these Gentiles who were interested in the Jewish faith in God? And if in thus making the synagogue the starting-point of his missionary activity his experience was that it was precisely the Jews who showed least receptivity for his preaching and offered most resistance to it, must not this experience have seemed to him a divine judgment? And must not this judgment appear, from his teleological standpoint, as an appointed means to the conversion of the Gentiles? That Paul really looked at the matter in this light is shown beyond question by his authentic declaration in Rom. x. 16–xi. 31, where he again and again expresses the thought, in many different forms, that Israel must, according to the divine appointment, be hardened in unbelief, in order that its fall and deprivation of privilege might be the cause of blessing and salvation to the Gentiles. Certainly, therefore, not only according to Acts, but equally in Paul's own

[1] According to Hausrath's convincing argument, even the choice of the route of travel in Paul's missionary journeys was determined with reference to the Jewish synagogues to be found in the various towns. It is, moreover, to be noticed that Paul himself, in Rom. x. 18 f., emphasises it as a consequence of his missionary preaching that thereby a knowledge of Christ had been extended to the Jews throughout the whole world, so that their unbelief could not be excused as due to ignorance (*cf.* vol i. p. 240).

teaching, the believing Gentiles take the place of the unbelieving Jews; but that does not mean that the mission to the Gentiles arose only incidentally and accidentally owing to the caprice of the Jews; the unbelief of the Jews and the faith of the Gentiles alike have their cause in the eternal counsel of God, and therefore each is a divine necessity, raised far above all chance and human caprice. It is indeed impossible to see that there is anything un-Pauline in these thoughts. I hold, on the contrary, that they are derived from nowhere else than from Paul himself —to be accurate, from Rom. ix.–xi.[1] It is true that in one point the thought of Acts differs from that which is set forth there, but the divergence is so far from indicating a Judaising tendency that it is due rather to the exaggeration of Paul's love of the Gentiles into absolute anti-Judaism. The difference is, that while Paul thought of the unbelief of the Jews as divinely determined, with a view to the salvation of the Gentiles, but, after all, as only a temporary judgment which will be in the future removed, and replaced by the conversion of the Jews, only after, instead of before, the Gentiles, Acts has abandoned this reconciling view of the Apostle of the Gentiles, and describes the Jews as unconditionally and hopelessly rejected. It is precisely this extreme anti-Judaism which is the most characteristic motive of Acts, and which underlies its many and carefully painted pictures of the Jewish unbelief. That is not, however, to be explained on the hypothesis of a conciliatory tendency towards the Jewish Christians,

[1] The quotation from Isaiah which forms the point of Acts xxviii. is also the main point of the Pauline argument in Rom. xi. 8.

but on the ground of the strong self-regard of Gentile Christianity and its deep-rooted antipathy to the Jewish people in general. And this brings us to the last reason which obliges us to hold the above-named hypothesis to be unsatisfactory. It presupposes a relation between Gentile and Jewish Christians which had either never existed, or at least existed no longer in the second century. At no time after the Apostolic Council, and therefore at no time after he began to found churches, had Gentile Christianity been in a position in which it was obliged to bargain with the Jewish Christians for the right to exist and only secure it by compromises. Its existence was already, when Paul wrote Romans, so firmly assured, its self-confidence was so strong, its certainty of victory so proud, that Paul found it actually necessary to damp this self-confidence, which was already tending in the direction of arrogance and contempt for the Jews (Rom. xi. 17–25). How is it conceivable that in the next half-century things could alter so much to the detriment of the Gentile Christians that they were compelled to justify their existence in the eyes of the Jewish Christians by skilful historical fictions? The contrary, however, is quite conceivable, namely, that the attitude of the Gentile Christians to the Jewish Christians which betrays itself even in the Epistle to the Romans had developed in the course of the next half-century into the uncompromising anti-Judaism which Acts everywhere displays. As regards the Jewish Christians, on the other hand, it is no doubt the case that in the time of Paul they found an offence in the character and success of his mission to the Gentiles and in the growing preponderance of Gentile Christianity—an offence which Paul sets himself to mitigate in Rom. ix.–xi. But that the Judaic Christianity of the second century, so far as it maintained connection with the universal Church (and there was no need for the author to take account of any which did not), disputed the right of Gentile Christianity to exist, is a wholly groundless and impossible hypothesis. Indeed, Acts itself gives evidence against it, inasmuch as, in conformity, evidently, with the general view of the Church of the time, it ascribes to the original Jewish-Christian community and its Apostles the merit of taking part in—nay, more, of initiating—the mission to the Gentiles; which implies that the latter can no longer have been a point of controversy between different ecclesiastical parties. With this, however, falls to the ground the presupposition on which alone the special purpose of justifying the Pauline mission to the Gentiles in Acts could be thought probable, and this hypothesis must therefore be considered untenable.

As to the reason why Acts tells us nothing further of what befell Paul at Rome and of the result of his trial, we can only suggest hypotheses, of which the most probable are:—(1) The tragic turn taken by the trial was so much opposed to the apologetic interest which rules throughout the whole description of the trial in Acts, that such a conclusion would have sounded a harshly discordant note, and it therefore seemed better to suppress it. (2) It may have seemed to the author less needful to retell this tragic story because it was well known to his hearers by a living tradition.

THE LUCAN WRITINGS

CHAPTER X

Origin and Characteristics

In order to reach a decision in regard to the historical value of the Lucan writings, we must first inquire into the sources used by the author, and then into the way in which they were worked up as regards the selection, arrangement, moulding, and expansion of the material. When that has been done, we may be able to form a conclusion regarding the literary and religious characteristics of the author.

In Acts we found evidence of the use of a document written by a pupil and occasional travelling-companion of Paul, which, on account of the narratives being frequently couched in the first person plural, we designated the "we-source." It occurred first in xi. 28, when the origin of the church at Antioch was narrated, from which we concluded that the author was the Luke who came from Antioch,[1] and who is mentioned also in Philem. 24, Col. iv. 14, and 2 Tim. iv. 11 among the companions of Paul. But this source can hardly be thought of as confined to the few and unconnected passages which are introduced by the "we"; it

[1] Eusebius, *H.E.*, iii. 4: Λουκᾶς τὸ μὲν γένος ὢν τῶν ἀπ' Αντιοχείας.

must have contained a continuous narrative of the missionary journeys and imprisonment of Paul, and therefore must be considered to have formed the basis of the second part of Acts, from chapter xiii. onward, to which xi. 19–30 is related as a preparation and introduction. The sources of the first part of Acts, too (chaps. i.–xii., with the exception of the section xi. 19–30), have lately been the subject of very diligent inquiry, but the result has not been in proportion to the diligence displayed. I will not assert that documentary sources may not have been used even here, but I do not believe that their use can be convincingly shown, or that we need to assume them in order to explain the facts as we find them. It seems to me that the hypothesis of an oral tradition consisting of reminiscences and legend current in the Palestinian and Syrian churches, to which the literary art of the narrator gave for the first time a more definite form, completely suffices to explain the facts of the first half of Acts, and is, indeed, better adapted to explain them than the assumption of any sort of fixed documentary source. The question seems to me, moreover, to be of no very great significance.

The Gospel of Luke has at least two written sources: the Gospel of Mark, and the primitive Aramaic Gospel, which was probably used by Mark also, in one or several of the Greek versions of it. The Gospel of Mark, with the exception of the omitted section vi. 45–viii. 26, can be rediscovered in Luke in a generally similar order, and often with an almost verbally identical text. But Luke, in conformity with his desire for completeness (i. 1–4), has enriched

Mark's account with much new material. He has added the birth-stories of the Baptist and of Jesus, the story of the childhood of Jesus and His genealogy, a full description of the Baptist's preaching, of the Temptation, of the sermon at Nazareth, and of the miraculous draught of fishes at the call of the first disciples. In vi. 20–viii. 3 he has inserted his first long interpolation into the text of his Marcan source: it contains the "Sermon on the Plain" (= Matthew's "Sermon on the Mount"), the healing of the Centurion's servant at Capernaum, the raising of the young man at Nain, the question of John's disciples and Jesus' discourse upon John, the anointing of Jesus by the penitent sinner in the house of the Pharisee, and the brief reference to the women who ministered to Jesus. The second long interpolation (ix. 51–xviii. 4) is of still greater extent. It consists of the narrative of Jesus' journey from Galilee through Samaria to Jerusalem, forming the second division of the work; the first consisting of the Galilæan days, and the third of the events at Jerusalem. Into the framework of this journey through Samaria, which is peculiar to him, Luke has inserted most of his non-Marcan material, in particular many discourses of Jesus, which he has for the most part in common with Matthew, but in a quite different order from his, and with many divergences in his version of the words of Jesus. The most significant narrative in this portion is the sending of the seventy disciples into the villages of Samaria into which Jesus intended to come: a narrative which stands in direct antithesis to the words to the Twelve which Matthew records, "Go not into any town of the Samaritans." With the third portion of the Gospel, the scene of which is laid in Judæa, the author returns (xviii. 15) to the Marcan text and follows it for a long time fairly closely. He interpolates, however, the incident of Zacchæus, the chief of the publicans at Jericho, and the weeping of Jesus over the blindness of Jerusalem at His entry into the city. He has omitted the cursing of the barren fig-tree, having anticipated it in another form in the parable of xiii. 6 f. The cleansing of the Temple he reports in a much less striking form as compared with Mark; the polemical discourses, however, in fairly close conformity with Mark. In the eschatological discourse he departs from him by referring more definitely to the destruction of Jerusalem. He omits the anointing at Bethany, having anticipated it by the narrative in vii. 36 ff. The discourses at the Last Supper are fuller than in Mark, and have certain traits of high antiquity (the original account of the Supper, according to D, and the command to buy swords). To the description of the agony of prayer in Gethsemane is added the appearance of the angel; and, at the arrest of Jesus, the blow struck by the disciple is set in striking contrast with the healing touch of the Saviour. In the account of the trial before Caiaphas, the two examinations which Mark describes (at night, and in the morning) are combined into one (in the morning), and the charge referring to the saying about breaking down the Temple is omitted. Pilate is made to bear witness to the innocence of Jesus repeatedly, and still more decisively than in Mark. The trial before Herod is peculiar to Luke. On the way to the Crucifixion he represents Jesus as followed by wailing women, and as addressing to them a solemn warning of future calamities. Instead of the lamentation from Ps. xxii., he puts into the mouth of Jesus three other sayings from the cross, which give a last beautiful expression to His mercy and love towards sinners, and His filial submission to the will of God. The burial, and the discovery of the empty grave by the women, are narrated by him in close conformity with Mark's account, omitting only the declaration that they should see the risen Jesus again in Galilee. Peculiar to him, however, are the stories of the appearances of the risen Christ upon the Easter day to the disciples at Emmaus and to the eleven disciples at Jerusalem, and of His departure (Ascension) at Bethany.

If we inquire whence all this material is derived, there can be no question of its all being drawn from documentary sources. Both in the prologue of the first two chapters, in the genealogy, and also in the epilogue of the closing chapter, Luke goes his own independent way. No doubt he has here used legendary material derived from many different quarters—Christian, Jewish, and even heathen—but the form into which he has cast it is exclusively the work of his poetic intuition and literary art. It would be doing a grave injustice to the high artistic talent of the author to leave him no original creative ability and to make him everywhere only a copyist from his sources. It is otherwise, no doubt, in the case of those narratives and discourses which Luke has in common with Matthew; for these a second source must be assumed, which cannot be our Gospel of Matthew; for the form and arrangement there given to the common material is everywhere divergent from the Lucan, and for the most part secondary, as we shall see later. It can therefore only be a case of a source common to Matthew and Luke. As we have already found it probable that an Aramaic primitive Gospel is to be assumed as the source of the Gospel of Mark, I do not see what is to hinder us from seeing in this primitive Gospel, upon the basis of which Mark has composed his Greek Gospel, the common source of the further material which Luke and Matthew have added to the Marcan narrative. This hypothesis seems to me much simpler and more natural than the now widely received hypothesis of the "collection of discourses." For the existence of such a source, consisting solely of discourses without any narrative, is, in my opinion, highly improbable in itself, and is not supported by a single patristic testimony (for the notice in Papias, which we shall have to discuss later, proves nothing in favour of it), while, on the contrary, the Fathers, as is well known, often speak of a Hebrew Gospel, or Gospel according to the Hebrews, thereby testifying to the existence of an Aramaic Gospel (for that is doubtless what is really meant), which naturally did not arise out of the Greek, but preceded it. In that case, however, this must be regarded as the common source from which our canonical Evangelists have derived their material, whether immediately, like Mark, or mediately, through a Greek translation of the primitive Gospel, like Luke and Matthew. Such translations, which were at the same time revisions and expansions of the original source, arose in large numbers, in imitation of Mark's Gospel, in the last decades of the first century, and those of them which best answered to the needs of the Church won for themselves a more or less wide acceptance. That is clearly implied by the introduction to Luke's Gospel (i. 1). And there is nothing more natural than that the author of a new Greek Gospel should take the work of the first or best of his predecessors (Mark) as the ground-plan of his own, while filling in the gaps in it from the common source, and at times from other fuller sources. We shall see later that this simple hypothesis offers the simplest explanation of the origin even of Matthew's Gospel, the most problematical of all.

Almost more important than the question regarding the sources is the question regarding the way in which the author has worked up his material—regarding, that is, his special point of view and literary methods. Here the twofold character of Luke's work—Gospel and Acts—comes to our aid. In both cases we can to some extent check his account by parallel testimony—in the one case by Mark and Matthew, in the other by the Pauline Epistles—and if in both works the same peculiarities of treatment can be perceived, we can deduce with some certainty the peculiarities of the author and the historical value of his work.

Luke's freedom, and at the same time his purposefulness, in the way he handles his material, are shown, in the first place, by his arrangement of it. The twofold division of Mark's Gospel is extended by him into a threefold division by the insertion of the journey through Samaria, so that his material is divided into three fairly equal parts, according to the geographical theatres of the action—Galilee, Samaria, and Judæa.

Similarly, the material of Acts arranges itself geographically according to the scheme set forth in i. 8: beginnings in Jerusalem; extension to Judæa and Samaria; expansion throughout the whole heathen world as far as its centre, Rome. With this geographical arrangement there coincides a second division according to the principal heroes of the action: the first half has for its centre Peter, the leader of the mission to the Jews; the second half, Paul, the missionary to the Gentiles. Luke pursues the parallel between these two with remarkable diligence through all the details of their actions and sufferings, as if he wanted by this symmetry of treatment to suggest to the reader that neither of the two was before or behind the other. The counterpart of this parallel between Peter and Paul which prevails in Acts is formed by the parallel in the Gospel between the sending forth of the Twelve to a mission in Galilee and of the Seventy to a mission in Samaria. Not seldom, too, Luke allows himself to alter the traditional arrangement in order to serve his literary purpose. Thus he has transferred the sermon at Nazareth from its original place and inserted it at the beginning of Jesus' public ministry, in order to typify in advance the unbelief of the Jews and their rejection; and this is confirmed once again by the discourse of Paul in Rome. Similarly, in Acts he has anticipated the beginning of Paul's missionary activity by the story of the conversion of Cornelius through Peter; whereas, according to Gal. ii., Peter appears at the Apostolic Council as exclusively a worker among the Jews, and the ground would have been cut from beneath the whole controversy at the Council had the incident of the conversion of Cornelius preceded it. Similarly, he has antedated Paul's collection-journey, placing it before the beginning of his missionary journeys (xi. 30), whereas it ought really to fall at the end of the missionary journeys (chap. xxi.); and in order to make room for the collection-journey at this earlier date, which seemed to him desirable, he has postponed the journey of the Antiochian delegates to the Apostolic Council to a date after the first missionary journey (chap. xv.)—two interdependent transpositions, which our author held to be advisable in the interest of the purpose of his history.

After these deliberate transpositions, we have to notice the alterations and retouchings of the traditional material, by which sometimes hardnesses are softened, sometimes high lights are touched in, and thus a harmonious colouring is given to the whole, calculated to make an edifying impression on those within and an impression of innocence on those without. The austerely heroic features of Mark's picture of Christ are toned down, omitted, painted over into something more edifying, or simply suppressed. So, above all, in the case of Jesus' breach with His family (Mark iii. 31), the sharpness of which is toned down in the corresponding passage (Luke viii. 19 ff.), while its significance is shown by means of a skilful transformation at another place (ii. 48 f.); the polemic against human ordinances is omitted (Mark vii. 1 ff.); the saying about breaking down the Temple is suppressed (Mark xiv. 58); the importance of the cleansing of the Temple is minimised; the anointing at Bethany, which caused difficulties on account of its Messianic background, was replaced by the touching incident of the anointing in the house of Simon the Pharisee; the tragic and awful cry of despair from the cross is replaced by three touching and edifying farewell sayings. Similarly, in Acts the inner life of the community is painted in the rosiest colours as an untroubled idyll of peace and joy; and if at any time a faint shadow of difference of opinion occurs, harmony is at once restored by the combined effort of all parties; of the serious dissonances and hard struggles of the Apostolic times as we learn to know them from Paul's letters there are only faint traces in the Lucan narrative. The contention at the Apostolic Council about the circumcision of the Gentile Christians is, indeed, mentioned, but it is confined to the outer circles of the community—it does not penetrate into the Apostolic body; Peter speaks of the Law in as liberal a fashion as if he were a disciple of Paul; the contention between Paul and Peter at Antioch (Gal. ii. 11) is quite suppressed, and replaced by a comparatively unimportant dissension between Paul and Barnabas with reference to Mark; then, again, Titus, about whom the strife of parties had raged at the Apostolic Council, is completely ignored throughout the whole of Acts; and, on the other hand, it is expressly told of Timothy that he had undergone circumcision, and similarly that Paul himself, in order to placate Jewish-Christian fanaticism, had accepted the requirement that he should take part in a Jewish ceremony (xxi. 26). Everywhere there is manifest the same effort to remove from the hard realities of history that which is unedifying, to tone down the oppositions within

Christianity, to reduce conflicts of principle to insignificant differences of opinion—in short, to draw an ideal picture of peace and innocence, from which the Christian could gain edification while the non-Christian could convince himself of the inoffensiveness of the Christian cause.

The same purpose of idealising history in the interest of the edification of the reader is served by Luke's independent expansions of his material. That the opening and closing stories of the Gospel belong to this category has been remarked above. To it belong also the allegorical narratives of Peter's miraculous draught of fishes, of the mission of the seventy disciples, of the appearance of the angel in Gethsemane, of the healing of the High Priest's servant's ear; the miracles of Pentecost, which are obviously symbolic; the judgment upon Ananias and Sapphira, and upon the sorcerer Elymas or Bar-Jesus; the miraculous deliverances of Peter and Paul from prison by angels and earthquakes. Yet it must be admitted that in these and similar cases it cannot be determined with certainty how far a traditional story has been remoulded by the narrator, and how far the narrative has been freely invented by him. But the latter is to be maintained with certainty in regard to the whole of the speeches in Acts; they are as certainly free compositions of the narrator as the speeches are known to have been in the case of his favourite model Josephus and of all the other historians of antiquity. They are not therefore "fictitious" in our sense, since the custom was then generally prevalent; it was, in fact, expected of a skilful writer that he should adorn his narrative with cleverly composed speeches, and it did not occur to anyone to ask from what source or by what line of tradition he had received information regarding the actual delivery of such speeches. The fact is that antiquity did not distinguish between historical reality and poetic truth quite in the same way that we do; therefore we are not justified, when studying ancient historians, in applying to them the standard of our present-day demand for realistic exactness. If that be admitted as generally true, we should draw the inference in matters of detail and not continually renew the foolish strife as to how much in this or that speech in Acts is drawn from a "source," or from tradition.[1] In so doing we are wronging the author as much as if we were to ask for the source of his beautiful opening and closing stories. Just as he shows himself in these a simple poet of sensitive feeling and fine tact, so in the composition of his speeches he shows himself a thoughtful writer of high literary culture, according to the standards of his age. If we compare the Apostolic discourses of Acts with the discourses of Jesus in the Gospel of Luke, the essential distinction is obvious at the first glance. The former are reflective products of literary art; the latter (with the exception of the discourse at Nazareth in iv. 17 f.) are simple reproductions of the sayings of Christ as preserved by tradition, in which reverence forbade the making of essential alterations.

[1] The traditional apologetic argument from the skilful and often impressive composition of these speeches to their historical reality is of so touching a *naïveté* that it is hardly possible to treat it seriously.

Here we have, in the main, genuine "source" material, which the author has only here and there smoothed down from a stylistic point of view, explained, and—in the parables—once or twice expanded.

Luke, therefore, as is obvious from all these considerations, certainly desired to write true history, and to this end used the best sources diligently; but he understood the historian's task in the sense of his own time, and not of ours. What he aimed at was not so much the objective presentation of what had really happened, as the production of a beautiful and edifying picture, pleasing and impressive to the taste of the reader, of *ideal truth*, which, to him, as to the whole of antiquity, seemed infinitely higher than objective reality. Accordingly, he used, in the handling of his material, a measure of subjective freedom which we should never allow to an historian. Any special tendency in favour of one party or another, as for example the promotion of a reconciliation between Jewish and Gentile Christians, by means of historical fictions, was far from his mind. He was much too naïve for that. He narrated things according to his *bona fide* conception of them, but that means as best commended itself to his æsthetic taste and his religious temperament. His tender, sensitive, and sympathetic nature had little taste for sharp antitheses and heroic struggles, but delighted in pictures of peace and traits of compassionate love. With this corresponds especially his portrait of Christ: it is not the heroic reformer and assailant of an ossified Judaism whom Mark has drawn, but the merciful Saviour of the sinner and the poor, whom Luke again and again sets before us in glowing colours. That is not, of course, the whole of the historical Jesus, of whose character the strenuous hero of Mark shows another aspect; but it is an essential, and perhaps for the history of Christianity the most important, side of the historical Jesus, which Luke, by reason of his personal affinity of mind with it, was enabled to apprehend and to preserve with special skill. With the religious love of the Saviour which lays hold on repentant sinners forgivingly and with saving power there is most closely connected in Luke's picture of Christ an ethico-social love to the poor and lowly and disinclination towards the proud and sated rich. At His first appearance in Galilee, Jesus declares it to be His task to preach good tidings to the poor. In the "Sermon on the Plain" it is the (literally, not spiritually) poor who are called blessed, as those to whom the coming Kingdom of God will bring consolation and satisfaction. Poor shepherds are the first to whom the birth of the Saviour is made known. He praises the Father because He has hidden the secret of the gospel from the wise and prudent and revealed it unto babes. Lazarus the beggar goes to Abraham's bosom, and Dives to hell. None of the first-invited wealthy and worldly guests partake of God's feast, but the humble people who are gathered from the streets. At the very beginning, in the song of Mary, there stands, as a kind of social programme, the declaration, "God scattereth the proud, He putteth down the mighty from their seats and exalteth the humble, He filleth the hungry with good things, and the rich He sendeth empty away" (i. 51). In harmony with this, there is demanded from the followers of Jesus above all active benevolence and renunciation of their own possessions for the benefit of the poor (xii. 33, xiv. 33, xviii. 22). Wealth, as such, even appears as "the unrighteous Mammon," or idol, which can only be rendered innocuous by using it in the form of alms to purchase friends for the eternal habitations (xvi. 9). Alms have power to purify, and to cancel sin (xi. 41, xix. 9). In general, turning from the world, renunciation of earthly goods, the severing of all earthly ties, even that of the family, are the duty of the disciples, who are to look forward to and announce the coming of the Kingdom of God (ix. 57–62, xiv. 26–33). In this, as in the description of the community of goods of the primitive Church, some have found traces of the influence of a special "Ebionitic source" upon the Lucan writings. That is wholly mistaken. There never was such a source. What Luke here records belongs to the most authentic stratum of the gospel tradition. The preference of Jesus for the poor as compared with the rich is as certainly historical as His mercifulness towards sinners and His sternness towards the proud and self-righteous. The former is as little derived from Ebionism as the latter from Paulinism; both alike are inseparably connected traits of the religious socialism of the historical Jesus, which Luke did not invent, but only grasped and described with special emphasis, precisely because they were particularly sympathetic to his own temper and tone of mind.

A further trait, closely related to the last, which runs through Luke's writings from beginning to end, is his enmity towards the Jews and friendliness towards the heathen. It is unreservedly expressed in Jesus' first sermon at Nazareth. It underlies the mission of the Seventy Disciples—peculiar to Luke—as the representatives of the mission to the heathen, and he celebrates their success much more highly than that of the Twelve. So, too, the Samaritans, who were counted heretics and heathen by the Jews, are conspicuously preferred in the parable of the Good Samaritan and in the story of the ten lepers. It is in harmony with this that Luke has omitted the command not to preach the gospel to the heathen, and the saying about the mission of Christ being exclusively to the lost sheep of the house of Israel, both of which Matthew has retained from the oldest tradition, and which Luke must therefore have known. It is the more remarkable and the more significant in regard to Luke and the Gentile Christianity of his time in general, that he has not based the Pauline thought of the universal destination of the Christian salvation upon the Pauline teaching regarding the end of the Law. He takes up, on the contrary, a remarkably conservative attitude towards the Jewish Law, as towards all existing ordinances; for that we have the testimony, apart from the saying about the imperishable validity of the Law (xvi. 17), of a number of traits which are undoubtedly to be put down to Luke himself. Even in the story of the Childhood, the submission of Jesus to the usages of the Jewish Law is intentionally emphasised. The strong sayings against Jewish legalism which Mark reports are partly omitted, partly softened, and the cleansing of the Temple is reduced to insignificance. Of the first disciples it is said in Acts that they continued daily in the holy place (the Temple), and were in favour with all the people (the Jews). Paul is repeatedly made to testify, both in word and act,[1] his loyalty towards the Law and the faith of the fathers; nay, even to testify to the teaching of the Pharisees, in a way that appears to us very curious in the author of the letters to the Galatians and Romans. In short, while the historical Paul was anti-legalistic but not anti-Judaic, his biographer, on the contrary, was anti-Judaic but not anti-legalistic. That is not to be explained by some special "tendency" in Luke's writings designed to promote union; it corresponds to the general habit of thought of the ecclesiastical deutero-Paulinism of his time, in which the breach with Judaism had been completed and the dissensions of the Apostolic time left behind, while the ordering of church-life by means of a new law, freely modelled on that of the Old Testament, had become a pressing need.

But this conservative attitude towards the Law is connected with a further point of view which is of paramount importance in reference to Luke's work as an historian, namely, its apologetic aim. He wished to write the history of early Christianity in such a way that it should not only be edifying to his Christian readers, but also adapted not to offend those without, and calculated to give them the impression of the political innocence and loyalty of Christianity. To this end he has suppressed anything in his heroes which could in any way be interpreted as contrary to

[1] Word—xxiii. 6; xxiv. 14 ff.; xxvi. 4 ff., 22. Act—xvi. 3; xxi. 24 ff.

established order and custom, while he emphasises their conservative attitude towards the usages and beliefs of the fathers, especially their good repute with the authorities, Roman as well as Jewish.[1] Just as Jesus falls a victim to the hatred of the Jewish hierarchs only, and is repeatedly and formally acquitted by His civil rulers, Pilate and Herod, so it was constantly with Paul; whenever Jewish fanaticism hounded on the mob to persecute the Apostle, in Philippi, in Corinth, in Ephesus, and in Jerusalem, the civil authorities, in some way or other, either first or last, acted in his favour. In Philippi the rulers of the city make a formal apology for their over-hasty proceedings against Paul; in Corinth the proconsul Gallio curtly dismisses his Jewish accusers, on the ground that he had nothing to do with these theological questions; in Ephesus the Asiarchs, who are friendly to Paul, send him warning not to expose himself to danger by appearing in the theatre; in Jerusalem Paul is rescued from the hands of the raging mob by the intervention of the Roman soldiers, and it is under their strong escort, to protect him against a murderous attack by his fellow-countrymen, that he is conveyed to Cæsarea. Finally, in the repeated trials here, before the Romans Felix and Festus, and the Jewish King Agrippa (who here plays a rôle of assessor similar to that which Herod played to Pilate in the trial of Jesus), the in-

[1] The question, which naturally suggests itself, whether this insistence on the respect of Christianity for law and order was consistent with Luke's pronounced socialism, is, from an objective point of view, doubtless to be answered in the negative, but it does not appear probable that Luke was conscious of the inconsistency.

nocence of Paul is so clearly recognised and acknowledged that the only thing which is unintelligible to the reader is how it was possible that Paul was not set at liberty, instead of the trial and imprisonment proceeding until Paul finally appeared before the judgment-seat of the Roman Emperor. Obviously Luke, whether he knew the actual history of these proceedings or not, has in any case very decidedly adapted his account of them to his apologetic aim; in particular, the speeches delivered by Paul on these occasions are composed so exclusively from this point of view that they might be described as pattern speeches for the defence by a Christian advocate on behalf of fellow-believers when accused before the Roman authorities.

We have thus seen that Luke, in both his historical works, has adapted his representation of the history to his practical aims, and sought to serve the ends of religious edification on the one hand, and of the defence of Christianity at the bar of the Roman world-power on the other. As the occasion for the latter did not arise until the second century, when, under Trajan, official trials of Christians first occurred in Asia Minor, we have here a definite point of departure for the determination of the time of composition of the writings of Luke which suggests a date in the first decades of the second century. There is a second argument confirmatory of this in the relation of the Lucan writings to the works of Josephus. The dependence of the former on the latter, previously suggested by other scholars, has lately been proved by Max Krenkel in the work which we have so often had occasion to cite, *Josephus und Lukas*, by so comprehensive and thorough a comparison of the two, that while some details of his argument may be questioned, the general impression made by it cannot be resisted, and compels the recognition of the dependence of the Lucan writings on Josephus as a fact. Now as Josephus' literary activity falls in the last two decades of the first century and extends into the beginning of the second, *it necessarily follows that the composition of the Lucan writings cannot fall earlier than the beginning of the second century.* Here we have a sure landmark for early Christian chronology which rises above the fogs of patristic tradition, and of which the significance for other questions must not be underestimated. In the first place, as regards the author of the two writings: if they were written as late as this, it is very improbable that they are directly derived from Luke, the travelling companion of Paul, since he must at this time have been an old man of nearly a hundred. From this Antiochian Luke is derived, it may be conjectured with great probability, at least the "we-source" which is used in Acts; but we have seen that this source is used by the author of Acts with just the same freedom with which he has handled the Gospel sources—with rearrangements, omissions, additions, of so far-reaching a character that the general impression of the Apostle Paul and of his relation to the primitive community becomes considerably altered from that which meets us in the authentic witness of the Pauline letters. Would so free a handling of the "we-source" on the part of the author of Acts be psychologically possible if he himself were the author of that source and the immediate disciple and travelling-companion of Paul? I think that, for every unprejudiced person, this question answers itself. The author of the Gospel and Acts, which have been attributed by tradition to Luke, on account of the Lucan source which was worked up in the latter, was therefore in reality a Gentile Christian of post-apostolic times, and probably a member of the Roman church, among whose archives he may have found the Lucan travel memoirs. He was, moreover, a man of literary culture, well acquainted with the writings of Josephus, and of remarkable literary talent, who understood admirably how to present, in accordance with the taste of his time—which delighted in idealised biographies and descriptions of travel—the beginnings of Christianity in a form which would not only appeal to Christians but was calculated also to attract and convince the Græco-Roman world. His work does not, indeed, consist of history in the modern sense of the term, but of "truth and poetic imagination" (*Wahrheit und Dichtung*—in allusion to Goethe's *Dichtung und Wahrheit*), in accordance with the tastes and ideas of his time and with the way in which history was generally written at that period. And it is precisely this mixture of truth and imagination, this adaptation of the history to the needs of pious feeling, this sublimation of the reality into the ideal world of faith, that gives the Lucan writings the incomparable value which they have had for the Christianity of all ages, and which they still retain; for we must not forget what Aristotle said long ago, that poetry is truer than history.

THE GOSPEL OF MATTHEW

CHAPTER XI

The Stories of the Birth and Infancy
(Matt. i. and ii.)

Matthew—so, for the sake of brevity, we may call the author of the first canonical Gospel, without thereby intending to prejudge the question of its relation to the Apostle—prefaces, like Luke, his account of the public ministry of Jesus with a proem on His birth and childhood which, however, is completely different in every respect from the Lucan story. That the latter cannot have had any historical foundation we have already seen; we have now to inquire whether Matthew's narrative had any such basis, or, if not, how otherwise his divergence from Luke is to be explained. The genealogy with which he begins carries the descent of Jesus back through three times fourteen generations, through Zerubbabel and David to Abraham. But the well-articulated symmetry of this genealogical tree is purchased at the cost of numerous offences against historical accuracy. In order to make fourteen generations between David and the Babylonian exile, four generations of the Davidic line are simply left out. Moreover, the full number of fourteen can only be made up by counting either David at the beginning or Jeconiah at the end twice over; in the third series, which covers the six hundred years from the beginning of the exile to the birth of Jesus, forty-six years must be allotted to each generation, which, according to the elsewhere universally current reckoning of the average length of a generation (*i.e.* the age of the father at the birth of the son), is much too long. Moreover, the Matthæan genealogy from David to Zerubbabel, and again from the latter to Joseph's father, contains quite different names from the Lucan genealogy—in the one, Joseph's father is called Heti, in the other Jacob; even if these were brothers, one of whom, according to the custom of Levirate marriage, might represent the other in a Hebrew genealogy, they must have had the same father, but instead of that the difference of the names goes back to Zerubbabel, and begins again with his ancestors. A reconciliation of these differences is impossible; it is also unnecessary, since the Matthæan genealogy shows itself by its other defects to be a free compilation with as little claim to historicity as Luke's. Both genealogies are alike free inventions, guided by different motives, the influence of which explains their differences. Luke, with his popular sympathies, preferred not to derive the descent of Jesus from the ruling dynasty, but from an obscure collateral branch; Matthew, on the other hand, held the royal line to be the only one worthy of the Messianic King. Again, the Jewish-Christian circles in which this genealogy originated—for it was not constructed by the author[1]—attached importance only to the

[1] As the genealogy is designed to prove the Davidic sonship of

Davidic and Abrahamic sonship of Jesus the Messiah, whereas the Gentile-Christian Luke had an interest in tracing Him, as the second Adam, back to the primal man.

The birth-story is told by Matthew very much more briefly than by Luke. It would, however, be a mistake to see in this brevity a proof of the greater antiquity of his narrative. We have seen above in regard to the miraculous birth (p. 117) that it was originally foreign to the Lucan writings, and was only interpolated into his story of the childhood by a later hand. The Gospel of Matthew is therefore the first and, indeed, the only canonical writing of which this narrative forms an integral part, a circumstance which is in itself a sufficient proof of the late redaction of the Gospel. Of course the redactor did not invent it himself, but found it as a legend which was already current in his time in certain quarters; to that is due the abrupt fashion in which he introduces it, saying nothing of the events which concerned Mary, and representing the super-

Jesus, it presupposes the natural fatherhood of Joseph, the descendant of David, and cannot therefore have been composed by the Evangelist, who goes on to tell of the supernatural conception of Jesus, but must be derived from a circle and a period in which nothing was known of the miraculous birth of Jesus. Therefore verse 16 must originally have run "and Joseph begat Jesus." This original version is still traceable in the reading preserved by the Syriac translation of the Gospels lately discovered at Sinai, with which also one of the Latin versions agrees: "Joseph, to whom was betrothed the Virgin Mary, begat Jesus." (*Cf.* Merx, *Die vier Kanonischen Evangelien nach ihrem ältesten bekannten Text*, and P. Rorbach, *Geboren von der Jungfrau.*) The present canonical wording of verse 16 is therefore a correction, similar to the ὡς ἐνομίζετο of Luke iii. 33.

natural facts as only subsequently made known to Joseph in a dream. That he knew the Lucan birth-story according to our canonical text is not probable; in any case he has not taken it into account; he presupposes on the part of his readers, belief in the miraculous birth of the Messiah, and only seeks to confirm it by representing it as the fulfilment of the Isaian prophecy of the birth of Immanuel. It is true that in this passage (vii. 14) Isaiah was not thinking of the future birth of Jesus the Messiah, nor of a supernatural birth at all, but of the natural birth, within a year's time, of a child within whose lifetime the Divine help should be so signally given to His people Israel that the child should justly bear the name "God with us"; but for Christian readers it was natural to interpret this passage as a reference to Jesus the Messiah, in whom the promise "God with us" had first been fulfilled; and as the word which the prophet here uses of the mother of the child (*almah*) might mean either virgin or young woman (the sense in which Isaiah used it), it was possible to look upon this passage as a prophecy of the virgin-birth or supernatural conception of Jesus. Of course only such readers of Isaiah as already had reason on other grounds to think of Jesus as more than a natural man could have any occasion to interpret the passage in this way. The prophecy is not, therefore, to be regarded as the actual source of the legend of the miraculous birth; its source is rather to be sought in the motives and analogies of non-Jewish religious history, of which we shall have more to say later.

In its later course, also, the childhood-story of

Matthew diverges completely from that of Luke. If Luke found it necessary to account for the birth of Jesus, the Nazarene, in the Judæan town of Bethlehem by an elaborate contrivance (p. 105 f.), Matthew, on the other hand, simply assumes the birth at Bethlehem as something self-evident (ii. 1), and confirms it by a saying from the prophets (ii. 6 = Micah v. 1). In this Gospel both parents of Jesus are residing from the first at Bethlehem in the land of Judæa, and are only later led to settle in Nazareth by an oracle. This is obviously a correction of historical reality in accordance with ideal postulates, which goes far beyond Luke; the point being that it seemed in accordance with theocratic decorum that the Messiah should belong, even as regards the home of His family, to the purely Jewish Judæa, and not to "Galilee of the Gentiles." Luke had represented the new-born Saviour as proclaimed by companies of angels who appeared with a heavenly radiance, and as first greeted by poor shepherds. This heavenly radiance is derived from Isaiah, who prophesied under this figure the future glory of the people of God (lx. 1 ff.): "Arise, shine, for thy day is breaking and the glory (splendour) of Jahweh beams upon thee! Behold, darkness covers the earth, and gross darkness the peoples, but upon thee doth Jahweh shine, and his glory is visible upon thee! The nations draw near to thy light, and kings to the brightness of thy dawn . . . . the riches of the sea are given unto thee, and the treasures of the people flow in upon thee . . . . the Sabæans throng to thee; they bring unto thee gold and incense, and they sing hymns of praise to Jahweh." The latter part of the prophecy was not applied by

Luke, because poor shepherds seemed to him the most fitting representatives of "the poor, to whom the gospel is preached." It could not, however, fail to be the case that once legend had taken possession of that passage and had begun to interpret it Messianically, it should seek to represent the coming of the peoples and their great ones to pay homage and bring offerings as fulfilled in the life of Jesus the Messiah. Again, the prophecy of Isaiah recalled a similar oracle which the seer and magician Balaam, who came from the Euphrates, had proclaimed in old times concerning the future glory of Israel. "A star cometh forth from Jacob; from Israel there ariseth a ruler's sceptre" (Num. xxiv. 17). This pictorial expression had already suggested to Jewish theology the expectation of a Messianic Star or "sign in (or from) heaven," as the signal for the coming of the Messiah (*cf.* Apoc. xii. 1 with Matt. xvi. 1). How natural it was for Christian legend to represent the birth of Jesus the Messiah as proclaimed by the appearance of a wonderful star! And as of old Balaam, a Magian from the East, had seen that star arise out of Jacob, so now it must be Magians from the East who perceived the miraculous Messianic star. Further, as Balaam came from afar, in order to bless Israel, and as, in Isaiah, nations and kings were to come to pay homage to the God of Israel with hymns and offerings; so now the Magians from the East must be drawn and guided to Bethlehem by the miraculous star which announced the Messiah, in order to offer to the new-born King of the Jews their homage, and their tribute of gold, frankincense and myrrh (Isa. lx. 6 with Ps. xlv. 9). Thus out of prophetic word-pictures which had already received a Messianic interpretation among the Jews was formed the Christian legend of the coming of the "Wise Men" from the East, which our Evangelist thought the more worthy of insertion in his book, since he saw in these Magians the representatives of the heathen who were turning to Christ, among whom there were in his time many wise and influential men—otherwise than in the time of Paul (1 Cor. ii.).

This narrative further suggested to him the addition of another legend which was originally unconnected with it—that of the persecution and flight of the Messianic Child. This story, too, had its prototypes and roots in the Jewish apocalyptic writings, and beyond that in the common stock of universal folk-lore. According to Apoc. xii. 1 f., the demonic dragon seeks to devour the new-born child of the woman with the crown of twelve stars (Israel's son, the Messiah), but the child is caught away to God, and the woman flees into the desert. The dragon, which is derived from the Babylonian mythology, is interpreted in the Christian legend as the false Jewish King, who, as the rival of the true King of the Jews, Jesus, endeavours to destroy Him; just as, in fact, the last "King of the Jews," the pseudo-Messiah Barcochba, as the rival of Jesus, the Christ, endeavoured to destroy the Christian Church. And as, according to Apoc. xii. 17, the dragon, in his wrath at the escape of the woman and her son, "made war with the remnant of her seed," so in Matthew, King Herod, in wrath at the frustration of his designs, causes the children of Bethlehem to be slain. Instead of the undefined place in the wilderness where the woman of the Apocalypse hid herself, the Evangelist has chosen Egypt, which lay beyond the wilderness, as the refuge of the persecuted Messiah, Jesus, because the young Messiah was to be brought from the same country from which of old the young Israel had come out. This motive he himself indicates by representing the saying of the prophet, "Out of Egypt have I called my son"—which in Hosea xi. 1 means the people of Israel—as fulfilled in Jesus.

The quotation by which Matthew finally seeks to sanction the removal of the family of Jesus to Nazareth (ii. 23), which he represents as caused by a revelation in a dream, is less felicitous.

Parallels to this narrative of the persecution and deliverance of the Messianic Child are found in great numbers throughout all folk-lore. In the first place we may recall the myth of the birth of Apollo. When Leto had conceived by Zeus, it was prophesied to the dragon Python that her son would slay him; therefore he pursued Leto, in order to destroy her and her son, but Boreas delivered the persecuted goddess to the care of Poseidon, who brought her to an island and concealed her, by the billows of the sea, from the pursuing dragon. The popularity of this myth is proved by pictures of Leto fleeing with her children from the dragon which have been found upon coins in Asia Minor[1]; probably the same story is the basis of the apocalyptic vision of the persecution of the Messianic Child by the dragon in Apoc. xii. Further, we may recall the deliverance of the child

[1] Dietrich, *Abraxas*, p. 117 ff.

Moses by Pharaoh's daughter (Ex. ii.); in the Rabbinic legend, the exposure of the child took place at the command of Pharaoh, because he had been warned by a scribe of the danger which threatened him.[1] There is a similar story in the Assyrian legend of the deliverance of the young Sargon, whom his mother, in order to save him from the enmity of his uncle, exposed in an ark of reeds in the Euphrates, and whom a water-bearer drew out of the water and brought up.[2] An Indian legend related of the god-man Krishna that King Kansa, in consequence of a warning oracle, plotted against the life of the new-born Krishna, who was a prince of his own house, and when he escaped, caused all the boys of like age in his country to be put to death; Krishna, however, grew up in the house of poor shepherds with whom his father had concealed him.[3] Cyrus the young King of Persia was ordered to be put to death by his grandfather Astyages, in consequence of a threatening vision which he had seen in a dream, but the shepherd who had been charged to slay him brought him up as his own child.[4] Before the birth of Augustus, the senate, in consequence of an oracle which announced that the birth of a Roman king was about to take place, issued an order that all the children born in that year were to be put to death, but the parents of Augustus did not obey the order.[5] The common motive of all these legends,

[1] Josephus, *Ant.*, ii. 9. 2.

[2] Smith, *Early History of Babylonia*, p. 46.

[3] Wheeler, *History of India*, London, 1807, i. 462 f.

[4] Herodotus, i. 108–113.

[5] Suetonius, *Octavianus*, 94.

the ultimate roots of which are perhaps to be sought in sun-myths, is to enhance the dignity of the life of a great man by representing him as from the first the centre of a struggle between the powers of good and evil.

THE GOSPEL OF MATTHEW

CHAPTER XII

From the Baptism of John to the Departure of Jesus from Galilee

(Matt. iii. 1–xviii. 35)

While Matthew's proem is not dependent on any gospel source, his dependence on Mark immediately shows itself in the first of the narratives which are common to the Synoptists. "In those days came John the Baptist, preaching in the wilderness of Judea." Of what days is Matthew speaking (iii. 1)? From what immediately precedes, we should have to think of the time when the "young child" Jesus was brought back from Egypt by His parents and taken to Nazareth, and the appearance of John the Baptist would therefore take place in the earliest youth of Jesus. That is historically impossible, and is in contradiction with the note of time in Luke, who can have had no reason for contradicting Matthew. Accordingly, the Evangelist in saying "in those days" cannot have meant the time which the context would seem necessarily to imply. How came he, then, to use this expression? The explanation is that he had it before him in Mark i. 9, where it is said of Jesus that "He came in those days (namely, when John was baptizing) to Jordan." The resemblance to Elijah in the outward appearance and manner of life of the Baptist is pictured by Matthew (iii. 4) in close conformity with Mark (i. 6), whereas Luke has here passed over this, because he had already indicated it in a general way in his birth-story (i. 15). The preaching of the Baptist, however, runs in Matthew exactly as in Luke, with the exception of the special exhortations in the latter to the various classes among John's hearers; in this, therefore, he follows a source which is fuller than Mark, and which he uses in common with Luke. It is peculiar to him that he does not, like Luke, represent the preaching of repentance as directed to the multitudes, but specially to the Pharisees and Sadducees, making it a prelude to the great polemic of Jesus against the Pharisees (Matt. xxiii.); in contradiction, it must be admitted, to the historical fact that the Pharisees and Sadducees held aloof from the baptism of John, as Luke distinctly says in vii. 30, and Matthew himself admits in xxi. 26 and 32. The desire to find in the work of John the exact prototype of that of Jesus moved him also to put into the mouth of the Baptist the same preaching of the Kingdom as into that of Jesus Himself (iii. 2), for which there is no confirmation in any of the parallel narratives.

Matthew's story of the Baptism of Jesus is extremely instructive in its divergence from, as well as in its agreement with, the common text. In iii. 14 f. he narrates that John desired to prevent Jesus from being baptized by him, because he, John, needed rather to be baptized by Jesus, to which Jesus answered that it befitted him to fulfil all righteousness, *i.e.* to conform to all that belonged to the righteousness of a true Israelite. According to this, John recognised Jesus from the first as his superior, nay, actually recognised Him as Messiah, which would not have been possible without supernatural knowledge. Besides, the other Evangelists know nothing of it, and Matthew himself at a later point (xi. 3) tells of the question addressed by the Baptist to Jesus, which implies the contrary of such a confession. Obviously we have here an addition made by Matthew to the older text, the object of which is easy to perceive. To later Christological views it was offensive that the Son of God should have submitted, like anyone else, to the baptism of John, but the well-known story could not be suppressed, and therefore it must at least be modified in a way which would remove the difficulty. This was done by making the Baptist himself recognise the higher rank of Jesus, and explaining the Baptism of Jesus as a mere accommodation to a good practice. A similar thought is expressed in the story of the Baptism in the Gospel according to the Hebrews, which was used by the Jewish-Christian party of the Nazarenes. Jesus is invited by His mother and His brethren to go with them to John and be baptized by him for the forgiveness of sins. He replies: "What sin have I committed, that I should go and be baptized by him—unless this very word of mine is a sin of ignorance?" And, accordingly, He goes to baptism against His will, compelled by His relatives, but Himself not needing it. After the baptism Matthew, like Luke, reports the opening of the heavens as an objective occurrence; like Mark, the descent of the

Spirit as subjectively perceived by Jesus; and, lastly, the voice from heaven as an objective utterance in the third person ("This is my beloved Son"), intended, therefore, not so much for Jesus Himself as for the other hearers. Thus the Baptism is here no longer the moment of the real exaltation of Jesus to be the Messianic Son of God, for in this Gospel He is so from the supernatural birth, but only the solemn attestation of His Sonship.

The story of the Temptation is told by Matthew just in the same way as by Luke, only that the second and third temptations are reversed, the resultant order leading up to a more natural climax than that of Luke; after the temptation to worship the devil, the vehement "Get thee behind me, Satan!" is appropriate as the close of the whole. Whether this version is the more original is, nevertheless, questionable[1]; if it is, why should Luke have altered it? The introduction to the narrative reads, indeed, more smoothly in Matthew than in Luke, since the inconsistency between the statements that the temptation occurred *after*, and also *during*, the forty days (*sup.* p. 118) is removed, but this advantage is, perhaps, too dearly purchased by the curious represenation that Jesus was led by the Spirit into the wilderness for the very purpose of being tempted by the devil. At the close Matthew says, "Then the devil left him" (not, as Luke says, "for a season"), "and behold, angels came and ministered to him" (as in Mark).

After the temptation, Matthew makes Jesus re-

[1] It is, however, to be remarked that Justin Martyr (*Dial.*, 103 and 125) cites the story of the Temptation, which he found in the "Memoirs of the Apostles" according to Matthew's version.

move immediately from Nazareth to Capernaum in order to take up His abode there permanently, and by this the promise of Isaiah of a dawning of the light in dark Galilee of the Gentiles is fulfilled (iv. 13 ff.). According to Mark, it was not until after the call of the first two disciples that Jesus went with these to their home in Capernaum, and not then with the intention of settling there (Mark i. 21). The change was doubtless made by Matthew for the sake of the fulfilment of the prophetic saying. The call of the first two disciples is next narrated, the account in Mark being followed. But whereas Mark depicts the first public appearance of Jesus on the Sabbath at Capernaum, the first works of healing, and the growing multitudes, in very graphic fashion, Matthew gives, in the first instance, a mere summary notice of the general teaching and healing ministry of Jesus (iv. 23 f.), which betrays its dependence on Mark i. 32 ff. by the fact that it is again brought in by Matthew at the point where Mark has it (viii. 16 f.). He postpones the narrative of individual acts of healing in order, in the first place, to give a full specimen of Jesus' teaching. This seemed fitting, if only for the reason that Mark (i. 22) had spoken of the great impression made by the first appearance of Jesus as a teacher in the synagogue at Capernaum; this result should in Matthew's view be explained by a more detailed representation of the mighty work of Jesus as a teacher. Luke, too, opens the work of Jesus with an introductory sermon, and uses for this purpose the sermon at Nazareth, which he ante-dates and expands, but which is inappropriate, partly because it makes reference to His previous work in Capernaum, and partly because its effect was by no means favourable. Very much better adapted to serve the purpose of a typical example of Jesus' teaching is the next discourse, which, according to Luke, Jesus delivered soon after the choice of the Twelve, and to the circle of the disciples (Luke vi. 20–49). Even if this was not, in the simpler form in which Luke had taken it from his source, sufficient for Matthew's purpose, it could be used as an appropriate framework in which to insert further material of the same kind. Thus it was that Matthew, before following Mark in his further account of the activity of Jesus, placed at the commencement the great "Sermon on the Mount," the counterpart, expanded by numerous interpolations, of the Lucan "Sermon on the Plain." This seems to have been delivered on the plain at the foot of the mountain upon which, just before, the twelve disciples had been chosen (Luke vi. 12 f., 17 ff.); Matthew, however, who here passes over the choice of the disciples, transfers the scene of it to the mountain itself, which he makes Jesus ascend for the special purpose of delivering His great opening discourse from it, as from a pulpit (v. 1). For this deliberate alteration he had, doubtless, a deeper reason. This mountain recalls at once Mount Sinai, from which, in the times of old, Moses had proclaimed to the people the Law of God. Thus the Sermon on the Mount is marked out by its very scene as the antithesis of the Old Testament giving of the Law, as the giving of the true Law of the New Covenant.[1] And He who here

[1] *Cf.* Brandt, *Die evang. Gesch.* 354. The representation of the mountain is connected with the fact that Matthew thought of this sermon as a solemn declaration of the principles and precepts

speaks is no longer the teacher who instructs His disciples in parables concerning the nature and growth of the Kingdom of God, but the Lord of the new People of God, who with the God-given authority of a second Moses prescribes to His people the fundamental laws of their Christian life. Accordingly the "disciples" who form the audience are not only the Twelve—who, in Matthew, are not even chosen at this time—but the company of disciples in general, the "People of God" of the New Covenant. It is in this sense that the discourse is to be understood. The historical discourse of Jesus to the first disciples, which Luke has preserved, is transformed by Matthew into a counterpart of the giving of the Law at Sinai, the establishment of the New Law for the People of the New Covenant, and in the process the original thoughts and motives of the Galilæan work of Jesus have been largely reminted to suit the ideas and needs of later generations.

The discourse begins, as in Luke, with beatitudes (v. 3 ff.). But while in Luke the four beatitudes are followed by four "woes," the latter are here omitted and replaced by an equal number of new beatitudes, which give a further development to the

of the new religious relation, as the giving of the Law of the Kingdom of Heaven, analogous to the giving of the Old Testament Law, and therefore, like it, given forth from the top of a mountain. As on Sinai God spake with Moses while the people stood afar off, and only looked on, so the Evangelist makes the great multitudes, drawn from all parts of the land, stand in sight of Jesus, lower down the mountain, while on the top only the disciples approach close to Him and hear what the Master says. Only this parallel with Exod. xx. 18–22 explains the otherwise very peculiar representation of Matt. iv. 25–v. 2.

thoughts of the first series. But there are changes also in the original form of the beatitudes. In Luke the poor and the hungry were blessed, whom we are to think of, no doubt, as pious men, but also as actually poor and needy (p. 125); here, on the other hand, the actual poor are made into the "poor in spirit," and the hungry into those who "hunger and thirst after righteousness," which implies a corresponding change in the meaning of the satisfaction which is promised to them. The conception "poor in spirit" is not very easy to define, as the constant hesitation of the exegetes shows; and the reason that it is not so, is that it was not the original thought; the addition of the determination "in spirit" suffices to obscure the original literal sense of the term "poor," but it fails to express any other definite sense, so that now the meaning of the saying is rather to be vaguely apprehended than distinctly defined. The meaning which perhaps most naturally commends itself is "those who feel themselves to be poor, without means, strength, or help, whether in a moral or in a natural sense, or both, and therefore long for help from above." That a chameleon-hued conception of this kind, which cannot be fixed down either to a literal or metaphorical, natural or moral significance, is less original than the simpler one, is immediately obvious, and is confirmed, moreover, by the fact that both in the Clementine Homilies (xv. 10) and in the Epistle of Polycarp (ii. 3) this beatitude is cited in the simple form, without the addition of "in spirit."[1] There is,

[1] Otto Holtzmann, *Leben Jesu*, p. 187, rightly remarks that Matthew in verse 4, where the beatitude is pronounced simply upon "those who mourn" without any reference to mourning for sin,

therefore, no room for doubt that the original beatitude upon the poor, which did not cause the slightest difficulty to the primitive community, was no longer in accordance with the later ecclesiastical ideas which Matthew represents—a notable indication of the transformation of the social attitude and position of the Church in its growing catholicity during the second century. A Church to which there already belonged numerous members of the propertied classes, and which was inevitably only too much disposed to give these men of wealth and standing a position of honour and influence corresponding to their social position in the world—a condition of things against which the Epistle of James, indeed, vigorously protests (ii. 1–7), but in doing so clearly testifies to its existence—such a Church could only find a difficulty in the Lucan beatitude upon the poor, in contrast with the rich, which it seemed advisable, indeed necessary, to remove by a spiritual interpretation.[1] This applies, not only to the "poor in spirit," but also to those who hunger and thirst after righteousness. The beatitude upon the meek who shall "inherit the land" is verbally from Ps. xxxvii. 11, and (as it is quoted according to the LXX) is pro-

or other ethical qualification, "has left a clear indication that he has altered the original wording" (of the other beatitudes). *Cf.* also H. Holtzmann in the 3rd edition of his *Konmentar zu den Synopt. Ev.* p. 201 f. The dative τῷ πνεύματι is certainly an explanatory addition which has grown up with the Greek version of the words of Jesus, as is also τὴν δικαιοσύνην in verse 6 and ἕνεκεν δικαιοσύνης in verse 10, and probably also τῇ καρδίᾳ in verse 8.

[1] *Cf.* Brandt, *Ev. Gesch.*, p. 358 f.: "Matthew obviously was in closer relations than Mark with the leaders of church politics, who already knew how to value worldly means."

bably an addition of the Evangelist. The beatitudes upon the merciful, the pure in heart, and the peacemakers, are so much in accordance with other utterances of Jesus, that they, whether they rest upon an older tradition or not,[1] are certainly spoken in the spirit of Jesus; and indeed there can be no doubt that the beatitudes of the Matthæan Sermon on the Mount are an inestimable enrichment of the Gospel tradition and a splendid revelation of the genuine Spirit of Christ which was present in His Church.

The sayings with reference to the duties of the disciples which follow the beatitudes (verses 13–16), comparing them to the salt of the earth and the light of the world, are gathered together by our Evangelist on account of their connection of subject. The parallels in the other Gospels stand in a different context, but are also connected with the duties of disciples (Luke xiv. 34 f.; Mark iv. 21). In verse 16, however, the interpretation of "letting one's light shine" as a reference to the practice of good works instead of to diligence in teaching is peculiar to Matthew, and is certainly far from the original sense of this saying. It shows that in the author's time the interest in the special missionary duty of the disciples in the narrower sense, *i.e.* the original apostles, had waned in comparison with the general ecclesiastical interest, that the members of the Church in general should do honour to the Christian name by a blameless walk and the diligent practice of good works in brotherly love (*cf.* 1 Pet. ii. 12).

[1] The beatitude upon the merciful rests upon the often quoted saying of the Lord, ἐλεᾶτε ἵνα ἐλεηθῆτε (Clem. R., i. 13. 2; Clem. Al., *Strom.*, ii. 18. 91; *Acta Johannis*, ed Zahn, 73).

In verse 17 Jesus begins to speak of His attitude towards the law, and speaks in a peculiar fashion, reported only here, which makes the impression of deciding an ecclesiastical controversy by giving each side its due. In the first place, the general principle is laid down, "Think not that I am come to destroy the law or the prophets" (*i.e.* the word of God in the Old Testament); "I am not come to destroy but to fulfil." Next, the negative side of this statement is emphasised: so far from the law's being destroyed, not the smallest letter of it shall perish (verse 18 f.); then the positive side: Christ brings about, and teaches, the true fufilling of the law (verses 20–48). That is, Jesus will give the law its full validity according to its true divine intention, for He demands from His disciples a better righteousness than that of the Scribes and Pharisees, a righteousness which is not confined to mere outward legality, but consists in the pure motive which is well-pleasing to God. That is illustrated by six examples. (1) Not merely murder, but anger against one's neighbour and bitter speech to him is before God a sin deserving of punishment. (2) To lust after the wife of another is to commit adultery in one's heart. (3) Divorce, which was permitted by the law, and about which there was in practice a good deal of laxity among the Jews, is contrary to the Divine will, except for the cause of unfaithfulness, as Matthew adds, thus modifying the absoluteness of the statement, as he does also where this saying is repeated (xix. 3 ff.). (4) Swearing is unconditionally forbidden. (5) In place of the legal principle of compensation the disciples are to adopt the principle of the patient bearing of wrong.

(6) In place of loving only one's neighbour (fellow-countryman, Lev. xix. 18) and hating one's enemy, to love one's enemy is to be the rule. At this point Matthew returns to the Lucan framework and sums up this exposition of the "better righteousness" in the saying, "Be ye therefore perfect, as your Father in heaven is perfect"; corresponding to the Lucan saying, "Be merciful, as your Father is merciful," a difference which is perhaps due merely to different translations of the same word in the Aramaic.[1] The only difficulty in this passage is the introductory declaration of the unalterable validity of the law (verse 18 f.). How does that agree, we must ask, with the prohibition of divorce and of oaths, both of which were provided for by the Mosaic law? And what of the command to interrupt the making of an offering (verse 23 f.)—which is forbidden in the law—in order to discharge an obligation imposed by love? And are not the ceremonial laws, *e.g.*, regarding unclean meats, invalidated by the statement that only that which goes out of the heart, not that which enters into a man from without, can make him unclean? (Mark vii. 17 ff. = Matt. xv. 17 ff.). In view of these criticisms of the law we may conjecture that verses 17–19 were not spoken by Jesus, but put into His mouth by the Evangelist or his source. In support of this conjecture the following arguments may be adduced: (1) The expressions to fulfil (πληρῶσαι), and to abolish (καταλῦσαι), the law, are specifically Pauline formulæ, the latter only occurring

[1] שְׁלָמִין, which, according to Nestle (*Philologia Sacra*) may mean either "blameless" or "kind." *Cf.* also Deut. xviii. 13, "Thou shalt be perfect (τέλειος) before the Lord thy God."

again in Gal. ii. 18. (2) Verse 17 contains a defence against a charge which could not have been brought against Jesus prior to the saying mentioned in Mark xiv. 58, since, for all His freedom in dealing with the tradition of the schools, His manner of life was not contrary to the Mosaic law. (3) The phrase "Think not that I am come" (verse 17), is found again in Matt. x. 34 in a saying peculiar to Matthew. (4) In verse 19 the estimate of the teacher who teaches against the law as "the least in the kingdom of heaven" seems to contain an allusion to Paul, who had described himself in 1 Cor. xiv. 19 as the least (ἐλάχιστος) of the apostles. (5) Verses 18 and 19 do not seem appropriate in this connection as an introduction to the exposition of the "better righteousness," for such an exposition "could not possibly have been founded by Jesus upon the basis of the absolute authority of the letter, for in this respect the Pharisees could not be surpassed" (Holtzmann). On the other side, it is to be noted that verse 18 has a parallel in Luke xvi. 17, where the same thought of the permanent validity of every letter of the law is expressed in a slightly simpler form; there must therefore have been a saying of this kind in the common source of Matthew and Luke, and it must accordingly belong to the oldest tradition. Further, the Talmud has preserved a parallel to verse 17 in the Aramaic saying of Jesus, "I am not come to take away from the law of Moses, but to add to it."[1] Finally, it is not to be overlooked that the attitude of the primitive community was quite in harmony with a principle of this kind, for in its belief and practice the law retained,

[1] A. Meyer, *Die Muttersprache Jesu*, p. 80.

up to the time of Paul, an unquestioned authority. In view of all these considerations the preponderant probability is in favour of tracing back at least the contents of verse 17 f. to a saying of Jesus, while verse 19, on the other hand, might well be a later addition. Only the form and position of verses 17 and 18 are to be ascribed to the Evangelist, who intended to give in verse 17 a formal statement of the mean[1] which was to be maintained between antinomianism, on the one hand, and legalism on the other, and then brought in verse 18 in order to tone down this Judaising conservative saying by suggesting that the following examples of the deeper meaning of the law will show in what sense the permanent validity of the law is to be understood, not with reference to the letter, but to its moral essence. Luke followed exactly the same procedure in regard to the saying in xvi. 17, placing it between two sayings of which the one (verse 16) puts the Gospel in the place of the law, while the other (18) increases the stringency of the law of marriage; by these surroundings he sought to guard against any Judaising application of the saying in verse 17. To this extent it must be admitted that those exegetes who propose to understand Matt. v. 18 = Luke xvi. 17 of the permanent validity of the ethical spirit of the law, only, are right *as regards the meaning of the Evangelists*, but the question remains whether

[1] The same end is served by the addition of the "prophets" to the law, which is not found either in the Talmudic parable nor in the quotation in the Clementine Homilies, iii. 51, and which, in the mind of the Evangelist, widened the meaning of "the law" to include the Old Testament revelation as a whole.

that is also the meaning of the saying in the mouth of Jesus? That is another question which could only be answered in the affirmative if it could be supposed that this saying was originally spoken in the same connection in which it now occurs in our texts. That, however, is undoubtedly not the case, as the different connections in which it occurs in the two Gospels would alone suffice to prove, so we must understand the original sense of the saying according to its clear and unambiguous wording; as a declaration, that is, of the permanent validity of the letter of the Mosaic law. How it is related in that case to other sayings of Jesus of a different purport is a further question to which we shall return in a later connection. Here, we have only to add that just as the beginning of the section dealing with the giving of the law (verses 17–20) is to be referred to reminiscences of sayings of Jesus, so it is also with the remainder of it as regards its contents, but the form of the sayings and their combination is due to the Evangelist; that is proved by the fact that some of these sayings occur in Luke—and are even in some cases repeated in Matthew—in quite a different connection and, to some extent, in a different form. For instance, the six-times repeated formula which occurs only in this Matthæan version of the giving of the law, "Ye have heard that it was said to them of old time, but I say unto you," can hardly be derived from Jesus Himself, since He ascribed to the law of the fathers, even in its letter, an unalterable validity, and therefore could hardly have thus decisively set Himself as the *new* law-giver over against the old. It is therefore rather to be regarded as the expression of the Church's consciousness, which saw in Christianity the "new law" and in Christ the perfect Lawgiver, who had not, indeed, done away with the old, but by supplementing it and giving it a deeper interpretation, had, in truth, fulfilled it.

The saying about love to enemies concluded in Luke (vi. 36) with the exhortation to be merciful, as our Father is merciful, to which was appropriately attached the warning against censorious judgments. In Matthew (v. 48) this saying receives a wider scope, "Ye shall be perfect, as your heavenly Father is perfect," and thus forms the transition to the mirror of all the Christian virtues in chap. vi. It is only in chap. vii. that the thread of the Lucan discourse is taken up again with the warning against judging others. Obviously, therefore, Matt. vi. is an interpolation into the framework of the original discourse as preserved by Luke. The keynote is given by the exhortation in verse 1 not to practise piety in order to be seen of men, for those who do so will receive no reward from God. And this is illustrated by the three examples of almsgiving, prayer, and fasting. Prayer, therefore, appears here under the aspect of a good work, for which we may expect a reward from God (verse 6), whereas in Mark (xi. 22 ff.) and Luke it is an utterance of confident faith springing from the natural human sense of need of help, the result of which depends upon this power of faith. The question which of these two ways of regarding it is the more primitive and the more in accordance with the mind of Jesus, answers itself. We have seen above (p. 147 f.) that the Matthæan form of the Lord's Prayer is also secondary as compared with that given in Luke. In the warning against hypocritical ulterior motives in the practices of piety there is attached, further, a warning against worldly-mindedness (vi. 19–34). Here Matthew has for the most part made use of the sayings which in Luke are attached to the parable of the rich fool (xii. 22–40), and occasioned by the request made to Jesus to settle a dispute between two brothers regarding an inheritance; we have seen above (p. 152) that this was probably the original connection. Only verses 22–24 are found in Luke in two different passages (xi. 44 ff. and xvi. 13), and contexts which are less appropriate to them than that in Matthew. In vi. 22 the eye as the light of the body is compared with the inner light (the ethico-religious sense of truth); what the normal or abnormal condition of the eye signifies for the bodily life, the soundness or darkening of the inner light signifies for the spiritual life. This thought is clearer in the simpler version of Matthew than in that of Luke, who has also attached this figure inappropriately, so far as its meaning is concerned, under the influence of a mere association of ideas, to the other figure of the lamp on the lamp-stand (xi. 33 f.). The saying, too, that a man cannot serve two masters—cannot, that is, serve God and mammon at the same time—which Luke (xvi. 13) has attached to the parable of the dishonest steward, is found in Matthew in a more appropriate setting under the warning against worldliness (vi. 24). The exhortation to pious trust in God, who feeds the birds of the air and clothes the lilies of the field without their taking any care or trouble, and who, much more, shall give His children what they need, leads up in all the

Evangelists to the command to strive for (Matthew adds: before all else) the Kingdom of God, *i.e.*, to establish the sovereignty of God upon earth, since with the fulfilment of this highest aim all lesser needs will find their appropriate satisfaction. To the sovereignty of God Matthew adds, as an object to be striven after, the righteousness of God, *i.e.* a condition of righteousness which the judicial verdict of God can approve, which is the qualification for partaking in the blessedness which is to be brought about by the reign of God.

With the prohibition of censorious judgments (vii. 1) Matthew returns to the order of the Lucan discourse to the disciples (vi. 37), but interweaves with it many sayings which are found also in Luke, but in a different connection. Peculiar to Matthew is the warning (vii. 6) against profaning that which is holy (the gospel) by giving it to the unworthy. The exhortation to confident supplication which is assured of an answer (vii. 7–11) is, in Luke, introduced by the parable of the importunate friend whose request is granted because of his persistence (xi. 5–13). The golden rule of mutual obligation which is found in Luke vi. 31 in a very appropriate setting, is brought in here by Matthew (vii. 12) without any connection, and amplified by the additional saying that this is the essence of the Law and the Prophets. The saying (vii. 13 f.) about the strait gate and the narrow way to life, which but few find, which in Luke (xiii. 23 f.) forms the answer to the question whether but few are saved, and introduces the warning to the Galilæan fellow-countrymen of Jesus against a false confidence based on their outward relations with Him, serves in

Matthew to introduce a warning against false prophets (vii. 15), who in their outward bearing appear harmless as sheep, but in their intentions are as dangerous as ravening wolves. As the tree is known by its fruits, so men may be known by their fruits (vii. 16–20), *i.e.* by their moral conduct; in a later repetition of this figure (xii. 33 ff.) the fruits are to be understood as their utterances, in which the fulness (the contents) of the heart is made known. The same double interpretation is given in Luke, who in vi. 45 makes the fruits the utterances of the lips, but in vi. 46 directly opposes the unprofitable repetition of "Lord! Lord!" to the doing of the will of Jesus. It is very probable that Jesus frequently used this figure of the fruits, and, according to the circumstances, may have referred it on one occasion to words and on another to actions. While in Luke the figure of the tree and its fruits is very appropriately followed by the concluding parable, in which the right hearing and doing of the words of Jesus is compared with the solid and well-built house, the superficial and unfruitful hearing with the house on insecure foundations which tumbles down, Matthew, on the other hand, has here added a prediction—which connects itself rather with the warning against false prophets in verse 15—of the coming of false disciples, who shall, indeed, prophesy in Jesus' name, cast out devils, and perform many mighty deeds, but in spite of that shall be denied and rejected by Him (at the day of judgment) because they did not do the will of His Heavenly Father but "worked iniquity" (lawlessness) (vii. 21 ff.). This is a transformation, very characteristic of Matthew, of a saying of which Luke has preserved the original form (xiii. 25 ff.), in which the

Jewish fellow-countrymen of Jesus were warned against a false confidence in their outward relations with the Messiah, and which similarly closes with the quotation from Ps. vi. 8. Matthew makes these Jewish contemporaries of Jesus into future heretical teachers, who in spite of their emphatic profession of Christianity ("Lord! Lord!") and their capacity as prophets and wonder-workers, are nevertheless to be excluded from the Church on account of their lawless conduct. This is clearly a reference to antinomian and enthusiastic teachers who, in the second century, arose among the Gnostics, or in close relations with them, and opposed the beginning of the ecclesiastical ordering of faith and life. Thus we have at the close of the Matthæan Sermon on the Mount a confirmation of the conclusion which we had drawn from its transformation of the Lucan beatitudes and from the section giving the (new) law (v. 17 ff.), namely, that it is a compilation of the Evangelist, from the point of view of his own time, which handles in a somewhat free fashion the discourses of Jesus as they were preserved by tradition.

In chapter viii. the narrative of the healing of the leper is first (verses 1–4) repeated in the same form as in Mark i. 40 ff. Then follows, in verses 5–13, the healing of the centurion's servant at Capernaum, which Luke also places immediately after the Sermon on the Plain (vii. 2–10), and which was therefore probably found at this point in the common source. Peculiar to Matthew is the concluding saying (11 ff.) about the coming of men from the East and from the West to eat bread in the Kingdom of Heaven, while the children of the Kingdom (the Jews) are cast out—a saying which is appropriate in Luke xiii. 28 f. in connection with the warning to Jesus' fellow-countrymen which we have just discussed, but is quite inappropriate in Matthew as an addition to the story of healing in viii. 1–10, since here, at the first beginning of Jesus' public ministry, there was no reason to pronounce such a sentence of rejection upon the Jewish people. The Evangelist has probably inserted it here only because he misunderstood the saying in verse 10, "I have not found so great faith, no, not in Israel," in a condemnatory sense, as a complaint of the unbelief of Israel. The incidents of the two disciples in viii. 19–22 have their parallels in Luke ix. 57–62, where they are told more fully; Matthew has obviously abbreviated them, and the position of the narrative is more appropriate in Luke, since Jesus is there on His journey to Jerusalem, and therefore actually homeless, while at the beginning of His Galilæan ministry (Matt. ix.) that can hardly have been the case. The following narratives of the stilling of the storm on the lake and the healing of the Gaderene (Gerasene) demoniacs are similarly connected with one another in Mark and Luke, but in a later context, after the parabolic discourse, which is doubtless their original position, since the discourse was delivered from the ship and the crossing would therefore naturally follow immediately after it (*cf.* Mark iv. 1 and 36). That Matthew has put them at an earlier point is doubtless to be explained from the fact that the general order of the source has been disturbed by his Sermon on the Mount. The story of the demoniac is much abbreviated in Matthew, and he has made the one demoniac into two, probably because he wanted to bring in here, by combining the two related stories of healing, the healing of the demoniac in the synagogue at Capernaum, which he had previously passed over without mention. In doing so he has dropped the characteristic point in the source that the madman supposed himself to be possessed by a whole legion of devils. And yet this multitude of devils is the presupposition for the further story of the destruction of the herd of swine, caused by the entering into them of the whole legion of devils. By omitting the "legion," Matthew has left it uncertain how we are to imagine this comprehensive action of the two demons upon the whole herd. It is therefore not at all a case of Matthew's giving the simpler, Mark the fantastically elaborated, narrative. The conception which forms the basis of the story is very fantastic in both cases; but in Mark there is at least a certain connection to be imagined between cause and effect, with which, as is well known, even fairy-tales cannot dispense, whereas Matthew, by his abbreviation of the story, has lost this. There is a similar abbreviation in the story which follows in Matthew of the healing of the paralytic (ix. 1–8). Whereas Mark and Luke narrate that the bearers of the sick man, prevented from approaching by the press, brought their sick friend before Jesus by the remarkable method of lowering him from the roof (we must think, of course, of the flat Oriental roof, to which there was an external staircase), whereupon Jesus recognised their faith, Matthew omits the extraordinary method of approach, and yet records that Jesus recognised their faith. How He did so is left quite unexplained, and here again the abbreviated secondary account betrays itself by failing to indicate the causal connection. The disciple who was called from the tax-gatherer's office is named Levi by both the other Synoptic writers; the Gospel of Matthew, however, names him Matthew (ix. 9), which is probably the surname which Levi received as an Apostle. The use of it here, at the time of his call, is an inaccuracy of the narrator similar to the mention of the surname Peter at the call of Simon (Matt. iv. 18). In the defence of Jesus against the charge of consorting with sinners which arose from His sitting at meat with tax-gatherers (in the house of Levi) there occurs the quotation, only found in Matthew, "Go and learn what this meaneth, I will have mercy and not sacrifice" (ix. 13), which was probably interpolated into the discourse by the Evangelist; for (1) it is not appropriate to the context, where there is certainly no reference to sacrifice or any other part of the ceremonial system, and (2) the following "for I am not come to call the righteous, but sinners," can only refer back to verse 12 and not to verse 13. The question about fasting is doubtless wrongly ascribed by Matthew to the disciples of John themselves (ix. 14), for in Mark they are only mentioned by those who put the question in order to contrast them with the disciples of Jesus. In the stories of Jairus' daughter and the woman with the issue, Matthew has again abbreviated at the expense of vividness and probability. Whereas in Mark and Luke Jairus at first only asks for aid for his daughter, who is grievously ill, and it is only in the course of the narrative that the news of her death is brought,

Matthew, on the other hand, makes him beg from the first for the raising to life of his daughter, who has just died. Later on, Matthew omits the question of Jesus, "Who touched me?" and the fear of the woman at finding herself detected; but he betrays that he had both before him in his source by the remark that Jesus turned Himself about (στραφείς, verse 22 = Mark v. 30), and by the words "Be of good cheer, daughter," which imply that she had previously been afraid. In the house of Jairus, Jesus found not only a tumult of weeping and wailing, which was natural, but also players of instruments, which is very unlikely, since the maiden was only just dead. The conclusion in Matthew (ix. 26), that the fame thereof went abroad through the whole land, is in contradiction with the command in Mark not to make it known, and is probably taken from Luke vii. 17, where the story of the raising of the son of the widow of Nain ends in the same way. The stories which follow, of the healing of two blind men and a dumb man (ix. 27–34), are imitations of the story in Mark of the blind man at Bethsaida (Matthew is fond of double miracles) and of the deaf-mute (Mark vii. 32 f., viii. 22 f.).

The chapter about the sending forth of the Twelve begins in Matthew, as in Mark and Luke, "And he called to him his twelve disciples, and gave them power over unclean spirits," etc., although nothing has been said previously of the twelve disciples, since Matthew, in his preoccupation with the great Sermon on the Mount, has omitted their call (Mark iii. 14 = Luke vi. 13). He now gives their names (x. 2–4) parenthetically, and then proceeds to give the discourse which Jesus addressed to them before sending them out. This he begins (x. 5 f.) with the peculiar command not to go into the way of the Gentiles, nor to enter into any town of the Samaritans, but only to go to the lost sheep of the house of Israel; similarly, Jesus says in His conversation with the Canaanitish woman that He is only sent to the lost sheep of the house of Israel (xv. 24). This parallel favours the originality of the saying, which the Evangelist, who at the close of his work so strongly emphasises the universality of the gospel, would certainly not have put into the mouth of Jesus if he had not found it in his source. The exhortation in Jesus' charge to the disciples, which in the older account takes the form that they should not "take with them" any baggage or any money (Mark, "copper"; Luke, "silver"), is understood, or altered, by Matthew (x. 9) to mean that they should not "gain" any money (gold or copper), that is, by their missionary work; rather, they are to give their work freely, as they have also received their Apostolic gift freely (x. 8). That this warning not to make their evangelical preaching a means of gain would have been quite superfluous at the time when Jesus sent out the first disciples is certain; it is equally certain that the ecclesiastical Evangelist in the second century might feel moved to give such an exhortation by experiences such as are referred to in the Pastoral Epistles (1 Tim. vi. 5 ff.) and in 1 Pet. v. 2. That Matthew has altered the original form of the saying is also evident from the fact that it does not harmonise at all with the words of the source which he has retained. The warning not to make missionary preaching a means of gain has a sense in relation to the gaining of money, of greater or less value, but what is the meaning of saying that they are not to gain (by their missionary preaching) a wallet, or two coats, or shoes, or a staff (x. 10)? The attentive reader can hardly fail to observe that Matthew, by this new application of the saying (warning against superfluous baggage) as a warning against making their preaching a means of gain, has altered the sense of the passage in the source in a way which leads to a quite contradictory combination of incompatible ideas. In the following verses (11–16) the two sources are combined which Luke used separately in his accounts of the mission of the Twelve (Luke ix. 1–5 = Mark vi. 7–13) and the mission of the Seventy (Luke x. 1–16). The saying in Matt. x. 10 comes from the latter—"the workman is worthy of his meat" (Luke x. 7, "his hire")—so do the comparison of the inhospitable town with Sodom and Gomorrha (x. 15 = Luke x. 12), and the comparison of the disciples with sheep in the midst of wolves (x. 16 = Luke x. 3), to which Matthew adds the exhortation to be wise as serpents and harmless as doves. This forms the transition to the second part of the discourse, in which Matthew, turning aside from the historical situation implied in the ground-document, makes Jesus Himself predict the later persecutions of the Christians, and encourage the disciples to confess their faith boldly. Here various sayings are gathered together, most of which are also found in Luke, but in another connection, and at a later point in the narrative, at the close of Jesus' Galilæan ministry, where they are more appropriate (Luke xii. 2–9, 51–53; xiv. 25–27). Peculiar to

Matthew (x. 23) is the direction that when persecuted in one city they were to flee to another, since they would not have gone over the cities of Israel before the coming of the Son of Man—a saying which expresses the apocalyptic expectations of the primitive community, and its narrow limitation of the Messianic salvation to Israel, in so uncompromising a fashion that its inconsistency with the Evangelist's idea of a universal mission (xxiv. 14, xxviii. 19 f.) has always been found surprising. That, however, is a proof that the saying was not invented by the Evangelist, but taken from his source, as in the case of x. 5 f. Sayings of that kind, which reflect the narrow Jewish-Christian outlook of the source, have been omitted by the other Evangelists, but have been preserved by Matthew, not because he himself still shared this narrow view, but simply because they belonged to the oldest tradition, and their preservation no longer seemed to the latest Evangelist, in the circumstances of the Church in his time, likely to give rise to practical difficulties.

In chapter xi., Matthew first tells of the question addressed to Jesus by John the Baptist, "through his disciples" (as he says, more vaguely than Luke, who mentions two disciples), whether Jesus was the expected Messiah. The answer of Jesus is given in the same form as in Luke, and so, in the main, is the eulogy upon John the Baptist which follows. The two verses, however (Luke vii. 29 f.), which speak of the results of John's preaching and its reception on the part of the people and on the part of the Pharisees, are wanting in Matthew, who substitutes some other sayings about John, which are more or less closely paralleled in Luke xvi. 16 and Mark ix. 13. In Luke we find, "The law and the prophets were until John: thenceforward the gospel of the kingdom of God is preached, and every man presseth into it"; in Matthew (xi. 12 ff.), "From the days of John the Baptist even until now the kingdom of heaven suffereth violence, and the violent take it by force. For all the prophets and the law prophesied until John, and, if ye will receive it, this is Elias who was to come" (*cf.* Mark ix. 13). These last two verses (13 f.) are appropriate in the discourse upon John the Baptist, and attach themselves so naturally to verse 11 as the explanation of the remarkable significance of John that it is very probable that this is their original position. On the other hand, this can hardly be supposed in regard to verse 12: it makes the impression of being an interpolation; its Lucan parallel, also, stands in no connection with its setting (xvi. 16). Nor can we be certain of the original form of this saying, any more than of its original position. Are we to take the Lucan form as the more original because it is the simpler? If so, how does Matthew come to say that the Kingdom of Heaven is stormed, and the stormers have snatched it? Is that blame or praise? Does it refer to the zeal of the good, or the violence of zealots? Or is it simply due to a misunderstanding of the Aramaic word in the source?[1] No certainty can be arrived at in regard to it, and all that can be asserted with probability is that this saying, which distinguishes so clearly between the days of John and the present in which the gospel is preached, cannot

[1] Meyer, *Die Muttersprache Jesu*, pp. 88 f., suggests a confusion between חֲסִידִים (pious) and חֲסִינִים (violent).

have been spoken at a time when John had hardly left the scene, and the preaching of the gospel had hardly begun. It probably comes, like Luke vii. 29 f. (*sup.*, pp. 132 f.), from the apologetic reflection of the community. To the parable of the capricious children (xi. 20 ff.) Matthew attaches, not inappropriately as regards subject matter, though somewhat too early as regards time, the woes upon the impenitent towns of Chorazin, Bethsaida, and Capernaum which Luke (x. 13 ff.) inserts in the discourse at the sending forth of the Seventy, therefore at the end of the Galilæan ministry. This threatening of judgment against these cities is immediately followed in Matthew by its counterpart, the offering of praise to God for having given His revelation to babes (xi. 25 ff.). In Luke (x. 17, 21) this thanksgiving is appropriately occasioned by the joyful report brought by the returning Seventy of the success of their mission; in Matthew, who makes no mention of this mission, there is no historical occasion for it. To the thanksgiving is attached in both Gospels the liturgical Christological confession (*sup.*, p. 144). But the special benediction which in Luke is pronounced, immediately afterwards, upon the disciples is here omitted and left over for the parable-chapter (xiii. 16). Instead, Matthew gives to the hymn of Jesus a beautiful conclusion in the Saviour's invitation (xi. 28 f.), "Come unto me, all ye that labour and are heavy laden, and I will give you rest. Take my yoke upon you, and learn of me, for I am meek and lowly of heart, and ye shall find rest to your souls. For my yoke is easy, and my burden is light." These words are near akin to those in which, according to Sirach, li. 23 ff., the Divine Wisdom calls men to herself: "Come unto me, ye who are without knowledge; abide in the house of instruction. Because ye have need of instruction, and your soul thirsteth after it, I have opened my mouth. Come! Buy for naught! Bow your neck to the yoke and receive instruction; it is easy to find. Behold how I have laboured but little, and yet I have found rest and happiness." We shall not go far astray in seeing, in this saying from the Jewish Teacher of Wisdom, the germ of the sublime evangelical saying which Matthew has preserved in the Saviour's invitation.[1]

In chapter xii. Matthew brings in some narratives of cures which occurred at an earlier point in the source. As regards divergences of detail, I refer to what was said incidentally when discussing the account of them in Mark's Gospel. In connection with the general statement about the many cures wrought by Jesus, Matthew adds a quotation from Isaiah (xlii. 1–4) which he finds to be fulfilled in this saving work of the mild and patient teacher (xii. 15–21). The occasion of the Pharisees' charge against Jesus of being in league with Beelzebub is, in Matthew as in Luke, the cure of one possessed of a deaf and dumb devil, which made such an impression on the multitudes that they asked, "Is not this David's Son" (*i.e.* the Messiah)? (xii. 22 ff.). This probable explanation of the Pharisees' charge, which Matthew has already suggested once before (ix. 34), is not found in Mark, and therefore points to another source—that which is common to Matthew and Luke. From this is derived also Jesus' defence of Himself, which

[1] *Cf.* Spitta, *Zur Gesch. und Literatur des Urchristentums*, ii. 180. We shall return to the passage (Matt. xi. 25–30) at a later point.

resembles that in Luke more closely than that in Mark. The latter is expanded in both cases by the allusion, recognisable as an interpolation, to the Jewish exorcists, who were logically open to the same accusation (verse 27), from which, then, the conclusion is drawn (verse 28 = Luke xi. 20), "but if I by the Spirit [Luke, "finger"] of God cast out devils, then is the kingdom of God come nigh unto you"—a conclusion which is anything but a clear consequence of what immediately precedes, since there the work of the Jewish exorcists is put upon the same footing as that of Jesus, and therefore the epoch-making significance of the latter is obscured. Probably this saying (verse 28) was first brought into this connection by the Evangelists. In itself it contains the clear thought that in the victorious power of Jesus over the demons the beginning of the reign of God upon earth was made known, while its full realisation in the reorganisation of social conditions still remained an object of hope and endeavour. In xii. 31, Matthew returns to the Marcan source in order to bring in his saying about the unforgivable sin of blasphemy against the Holy Spirit. To strengthen the statement he makes the addition (parallel with Luke xii. 10) that even blasphemy against the Son of Man might be forgiven, but not that against the Spirit. This certainly is not specially appropriate in this connection, as, according to the Marcan account, the blasphemy against the Holy Spirit consisted precisely in the accusation against Jesus of being in league with the devil (Mark iii. 30), and is therefore not to be distinguished from blasphemy against the Son of Man. Perhaps the explanation of this difficulty is to be found in the phrase "the sons of men" (Mark iii. 28). In xii. 33–37 the image of the tree and its fruit, from the Sermon on the Mount, is repeated. There follows, in conformity with Luke's order, the demand of the Pharisees for a sign, and Jesus' answer to it, in which the "sign of Jonah" (verse 40) (by which, according to the correct interpretation in Luke (xi. 32), the prophet's preaching of repentance at Nineveh is to be understood) is referred to the deliverance of the prophet from the fish's belly as a type of the resurrection of Christ. The misunderstanding is very characteristic of the appetite for miracle, which, in spite of Jesus' reproof, could not be overcome, and of the whole body of apologetic of that time, which was closely connected with it, and which based itself by preference on bold typological interpretations of Old Testament prophecy. Of this, the literature of the second century offers numberless examples. In verses 43–45, without any real relation to what precedes, the saying is brought in, which in Luke forms the conclusion of Jesus' defence against the charge of complicity with Beelzebub, about the unclean spirit which, after being cast out, returns again with seven others (Luke xi. 24 ff.), and by a rather forced application to "this [the present] evil generation" is brought into some kind of connection with verse 39. The close of the chapter (xii. 46–50) is formed by the story of the visit of Jesus' relatives and His refusal to see them, which is placed by Mark immediately after the discourse about the Beelzebub charge, while Luke (who anticipates the main point of it in his story about the twelve-year-old Jesus) tells it in another place and in a form which softens the difficulties (viii. 19 f.). Matthew follows Mark more closely, but omits the motive which he assigns (Mark iii. 21) for the visit of the relatives, because it was not in harmony with his story of the virgin birth; consequently Jesus' treatment of His relatives here takes on the appearance of a harshness for which there is no motive.

Like Mark, Matthew next reports a discourse consisting of a series of parables (chap. xiii.). He follows the ground-document in its view of the purpose of the parables (p. 16 f.), but with the noteworthy alteration that he makes the failure of the multitude to understand, which, there, is only the intentional effect, the presupposition and reason of Jesus' choice of this method of teaching (verse 13): "Therefore speak I with them in parables: because seeing, they see not; and hearing, they hear not, neither do they understand." Then, however, he adds in full the quotation from Isaiah which is referred to in the parallel passages also, according to which the failure to understand is a Divine judgment. We cannot, therefore, say that Matthew did not share the predestinarian view of the earlier Evangelist as to the purpose in the parables of baffling the understanding and hardening the hearts of the hearers, but only that he sought to soften it by making this judgment the penal consequence of their already existing absence of understanding, for which they were themselves to blame. Historically regarded, this view that Jesus punished the people's want of understanding by speaking in parables, so that they might not be able to understand anything at all, has as little probability as the simple predestinarian view of

Mark, that the parables served the Divine purpose of hardening the hearts of those who heard them. In contrast to the people, who "see not," the disciples are then declared blessed, because they are allowed to see and hear what many prophets and righteous men have vainly desired to see and to bear (16 f.). This saying is found in Luke (x. 23 f.) in a more appropriate setting. There the disciples are declared blessed because they are allowed really to experience the victorious coming of Messiah's Kingdom, to which the prophets of old could only look forward with longing. Here, however, this is preceded by another contrast—that between the disciples, whose minds are opened to understand the secrets of the Kingdom of Heaven, and their blind and unreceptive contemporaries; and the saying thus acquires an uncertainty of meaning which it had not in Luke—but even there it is not in its original place, and we cannot therefore discover where this was.

While the first parable and its interpretation are given by Matthew in essential agreement with Mark, the following parable of the gradual growth and ripening of the seed is expanded into an allegory by the addition of the antithesis to the good seed—the bad, which is sown by an enemy amongst it, and grows up alongside of the good seed until the harvest, when the separation shall be made. In the interpretation it is allegorised point by point. The two kinds of seed are made to mean the children of the Kingdom and the children of the devil, the reapers are the angels of the Son of Man, who at the Judgment shall drive out of His Kingdom all who cause offence and work iniquity and cast them into the furnace (hell); until then, however, the tares are not to be violently rooted out, since the wheat would be uprooted with them. It is obvious that this allegory cannot be held to be a parable of Jesus, but is to be ascribed to the reflection of the Evangelist, and we have only to ask what he meant by it? The interpretation of the tares as the doers of iniquity and those who cause offence reminds us so exactly of the description in similar terms of those who are excluded from the Kingdom (vii. 23), that we are obliged to think of them as the same people, viz. antinomians and "false prophets" (heretical teachers), who, by claiming emancipation from the ethical usage of the community, gave rise to offences in it and caused the love of many to grow cold (xxiv. 12). Whether these children of the devil were to be at once excluded, or tolerated in the Church until Christ at His return should Himself purge the Church of these tares and deliver them over to the judgment which they deserved, was a question which greatly exercised the Church of the second century during its struggle with heresy. To this question the Evangelist has addressed himself in his parable of the tares, pleading for tolerance within the Church and against rigorism in Church-discipline. How important this question was to him he shows also by referring to it again in chapter xviii., and giving detailed instructions regarding the conduct of Church-discipline. But it can hardly be doubted that such questions of penitential discipline point to the second century.

In verses 31 ff., Matthew places Mark's third parable, that of the Mustard-seed, side by side with the related parable of the Leaven, which is found in the same connection in Luke xiii. 18–21, and seems to report both parables, now according to the former and now according to the latter (or, to the source which is common to him and to Luke). He begins like Luke, then weaves in a parenthetical reference from Mark to the smallness of the mustard-seed, and in doing so compares it, like Mark, with the herbs, and, like Luke, makes it grow into a tree; then he drops the narrative form of Luke and takes up the descriptive form of Mark, ending the parable as the latter does; then he jumps to Luke's second parable, and gives this word for word according to Luke, but in the closing observation in verse 34 he returns to Mark and takes verbally from him the statement that Jesus said nothing except in parables, which is appropriate in Mark, but in Matthew is contradicted by the long Sermon on the Mount. Then we have, within the space of a few verses, a characteristic example of Matthew's method of combining his sources into a kind of mosaic. In order to complete the favourite number seven, Matthew goes on to add (verses 44–50) to the previous four parables, which he has in common with his two predecessors, three more of his own—the connected pair of the Pearl of Great Price and the Hidden Treasure, which illustrate the supreme value of the possession of the Kingdom of God, and the parable of the Draw-net, which, like that of the Tares, typifies the future judgment. In conclusion, the Evangelist makes Jesus address to the disciples the question whether they have understood all these things. And when they answer that they have, he adds: "Therefore every scribe that is instructed unto the kingdom of heaven, is like a householder who brings forth out of his storehouse things new and old" (verse 52). If this is to be taken as a saying of Jesus, it seems to assert that every teacher who, like Himself, desired to serve the cause of the Kingdom of God, must not merely hold to the old traditions, but must also bring forward new truths when the time demands it. Though it cannot be doubted that the thought is worthy of Jesus, yet serious difficulties arise regarding the originality of the form and position of the saying as it is here found. What is the connection of thought to which the introductory "therefore" points? And is it probable that Jesus, who taught "not as the scribes" (Mark i. 22), would have classed Himself in the category of "well-schooled scribes"? It seems to me more probable that, *if* Matthew got it from his source, it springs from early Christian apologetic and contains a defence of the Christian teachers against the accusation brought by the Jews of innovation and heresy.

The narratives which in the source follow this series of parables—the Gerasene demoniac, Jairus' daughter, and the woman with an issue—have been already given by Matthew at an earlier point (viii. 23–ix. 26), so he now goes straight on to the narrative which follows these in the source, of the offence which was felt against Jesus by the Nazarenes, which he gives according to Mark's account, otherwise than in Luke (iv. 16–30), except that, on Christological grounds, he alters Mark's statement that, by reason of the unbelief of His townsmen, Jesus *could not* there do any miracle, into the simple statement that He *did not* there do any miracle (xiii. 38). In the ground-document there follows next the sending forth of the disciples, then the episode about Herod and the execution of the Baptist, then the return of the disciples from their missionary journey. As Matthew had already recounted the sending forth of the disciples in chapter x., he gives here only the episode of Herod and John the Baptist (xiv. 1–12). As a substitute, however, for the return of the disciples, which he has lost sight of owing to the distance of the narrative of their being sent forth, he makes (verse 12) the disciples of John come to Jesus with the report of his death, which, however, had taken place at a much earlier period (the episode of the death of the Baptist having only been brought in here in illustration of xiv. 2), and he makes Jesus, after receiving this report, withdraw to the eastern side of the lake (verse 13). The causal connection here suggested by Matthew, which makes the retirement of Jesus appear to be a flight from Herod, is inherently improbable, especially as Jesus returned again the following night, and rests only on the anachronistic combination of the coming of John's disciples (verse 12) with the return of the disciples of Jesus (Mark vi. 30 f.), to which there the crossing of the lake is attached, but for quite other reasons. The stories which here follow in Mark, of the miraculous feeding of the multitudes and the walking of Jesus on the sea, are told in a similar way by Matthew, only that in the latter case he makes the addition that Peter wished to imitate Jesus in walking on the water, but sank because he doubted, and was saved by the hand of Jesus (xiv. 28–32)—an enhancement of the miracle which also contains a transparent and impressive allegory of the fact that the Church would only be able to withstand the storms of the hostile world so long as she did not waver in her faith in her power to overcome the world.

In chapters xv.–xvii. Matthew follows Mark closely, and I may refer to what has been said above at the relevant passages. Only in Peter's confession are traits peculiar to Matthew to be noted (xvi. 13–19). Even the question of Jesus takes a different form, "Who do the people say that the Son of Man is?" (or, I, the Son of Man, am?). As the title has in this Evangelist a Messianic significance, the answer seems to be anticipated in the question. But this is not so, inasmuch as the answer here is not merely "Thou art the Christ" (Mark viii. 29), but has the addition "the Son of the Living God," which, in view of the Birth-story, is doubtless meant in a specifically supernatural sense; so that, according to the ecclesiastical Evangelist, it forms the counterpart, and higher complement, to the simple "Son of Man," as it does in xxii. 43 to the "Son of David." In this we may see an advance analogous with that in the Pauline antithesis between Christ "after the flesh" and "after the spirit," in the direction of the later Church dogma of the two natures. Still more significant, however, than the form of the confession of Peter is the *exaltation of Peter* which follows. Although earlier, at the miracle of the walking on the sea (Matt. xiv. 33), the disciples are represented to have as a body uttered the confession, "Truly, thou art the Son of God," Peter is, nevertheless, now pronounced blessed because flesh and blood have not revealed it unto him, but the Father in heaven. Here we can hardly fail to recognise an allusion to Gal. i. 12 and 16; as Paul there contrasts the revelation of Jesus Christ which, by the special favour of the Father, has been granted to him, with all mere human instruction and converse with flesh and blood; so here the same immediate Divine revelation is ascribed to Peter as *his* special privilege, and the basis of his pre-eminent position in the Church, to which he is entitled in virtue of his Divinely inspired confession of Christ. This benediction upon Peter was followed, according to the Evangelist, by his formal appointment as the bearer of supreme authority within the Church, the words being attributed to Jesus: "And I say unto thee, thou art Peter, and upon this rock will I build my church, and the gates of hell shall not prevail against it. And I will give unto thee the keys of the kingdom of heaven; and what thou shalt bind on earth shall be bound in heaven, and what thou shalt loose on earth shall be loosed in heaven." In spite of all attempts on the part of Protestants to weaken the force of these words, it cannot be doubted that this passage contains the solemn proclamation of the *primacy of Peter*. He is declared to be the foundation of the Church, the possessor of the keys; therefore the steward of the Kingdom of God (*cf.* Apoc. iii. 7), and the sovereign lawgiver, whose decision regarding what is permitted and what is forbidden (that is the meaning of "binding and loosing") has the authority of a Divinely sanctioned law. And though what is here said to Peter cannot be simply appropriated, without more ado, to the Roman successors of Peter, yet it is not to be denied that these words embody the fundamental thought upon which the system of the Catholic Church has been logically built up. It is, however, for that reason the more certain to everyone who is capable of forming an historical judgment that these words, so far from resting on ancient tradition, not to speak of being derived from Jesus' own mouth, are the Evangelist's expression of his own ecclesiastical view, and therefore a most important evidence of the character and origin of this Gospel. "The preaching of Jesus was concerned with the Kingdom of Heaven; the conception of the ἐκκλησία, on the other hand, was introduced by Paul (as, moreover, the ἐκκλησία of God, not yet of Christ), as also was the image of building, 1 Cor. iii. 10, Eph. ii. 19 ff." (Holtzmann, *Komm.*). But the conception of the Church as built on the foundation of Peter is absolutely unthinkable as occurring in the first century, for at that time Christ Himself was still always thought of as the *sole* foundation (1 Cor. iii. 9 ff.); and if in the deutero-Pauline letter to the Ephesians the apostles and prophets are named alongside of Christ, the Corner-stone, as the foundation of the holy temple of the Church, it is still a long step from that to the assertion of our Evangelist that Peter *alone* was the rock-foundation of the Church of Christ. Finally, the authority here given to him as administrator and lawgiver of the Kingdom of God stands in striking contradiction with the rebuke which is immediately afterwards addressed to Peter for not thinking the thoughts of God, but of men; in contradiction with the weak and hesitating conduct of Peter at Antioch, which led Paul to accuse him of hypocrisy; in contradiction with the conviction of Paul that he was of equal standing with the other Apostles, and that none of them were lords over the faith of the churches (2 Cor. i. 24);

in contradiction with the great saying of Jesus, that whosoever will be first, or a great one, among the disciples shall be the servant of all (Mark ix. 35, x. 44). Of the position of commanding authority such as is ascribed to Peter in this passage of Matthew there is no trace in early Christian literature up to the middle of the second century; but in the Clementine Homilies, which date from that period, Peter is exalted just in this fashion. Therefore, in Matt. xvi. 18 f., what we are to recognise is precisely the *first expression of the specifically Catholic self-consciousness of the Church*, which towards the middle of the second century began to consolidate itself under the watchwords "Peter" or—what comes practically to the same thing—of the "New Law."

At the close of chapter xvii. Matthew gives the story, peculiar to himself, of the stater in the fish's mouth, which, taken in its literal sense, is so extraordinary a miracle that even expositors who are in general prepared to believe in miracles have not found it easy to accept. Here, therefore, there is little difficulty about accepting the allegorical explanation which is naturally suggested by the preceding conversation regarding the paying of the di-drachma. The question was whether the Jewish poll-tax, which had to be paid to the Roman treasury instead of the former Temple-tax, ought to be paid by Christians or not. The Evangelist represents this question as decided by Jesus in the sense that, while Christians ought, properly speaking, to be free from the tax as sons of the house (of God), yet, nevertheless, in order to avoid giving offence, they must not claim exemption from this duty; the means for discharging it will be provided in the exercise of their calling. In connection with this it is possible to think either of the various earthly callings of individual Christians, in which case the stater in the fish's mouth would be an allegory of the profit made by each in the exercise of his calling; or the taking of the fish may be understood in the symbolical sense which is familiar from Jesus' saying about "fishers of men," in which case it would only apply to the special calling of the Christian missionaries, and the sense of it would be that if Christians diligently pursued their missionary work among the heathen, the common purse of the community would never lack the necessary means to defray, in case of need, all the demands of the State upon its individual members out of the common funds. Which of these is to be preferred, may be left to the taste of the reader.

In the discourse in chapter xviii., occasioned by the dispute about precedence among the disciples, different points of view are combined which have no clear connection with one another, but which can be all included under the general idea of rules for the inner social life of the Christian community. In the first place, an actual child is set in the midst as a type of the unassuming modesty which is the true qualification for the Kingdom of Heaven. But, farther on, the child is looked upon no longer as an example of this virtue, but a symbol of the humble members of the community, who are to be an object of loving, unselfish, sympathetic kindness and care, since to receive them is the same as to receive Christ Himself, while, on the other hand, to offend them by arrogant contempt involves terrible guilt. Then, by a loose association of ideas, the giving of offence suggests offence caused to oneself through the functions of the senses or the members (verses 8 f.). Thereafter the discourse recurs to the warning about despising "these little ones," whose guardian angels stand before God, but it remains doubtful whether the reference is to actual children, or to the humbler brethren in the Church (as in verse 6). In any case, the latter is necessarily the meaning in the further course of the sermon, where "these little ones" are synonymous with "those who go astray," whose being saved, or prevented from being lost, is the object of the Divine will (verses 12–14). Here the discourse connects with the Lucan parable of the Lost Sheep, the close of which, "There is joy in the presence of the angels over one sinner that repenteth" (Luke xv. 10), was obviously in Matthew's mind, and influenced the peculiar turn of expression, "It is not willed *in the presence of* (οὐκ ἔστι θέλημα ἔμπροσθεν τοῦ πατρὸς ὑμῶν) your Father in heaven that one of these little ones should be lost" (xviii. 14). After this saying about the Divine love to sinners there follow directions for the exercise of discipline within the Church towards sinful brethren, and for excluding them from fellowship in case of impenitent defiance; and there is ascribed to the decision of the Church—not here in the making of laws, but in judging offenders—validity before the judgment-seat of God, while to her united prayer the promise is given that it shall be answered by God, and the presence of Christ is assured to her when meeting in His name. To these rules for the public discipline of the Church there is attached, finally, an exhortation to placability on the part of individuals towards those who injure them; in connection with which the parable of the Unmerciful Servant is used to illustrate the thought that whosoever will not forgive his brother shall fail to obtain the forgiveness of God. Thus this discourse brings together various sayings regarding the moral relationship of the members of the Christian community towards one another, some of which rest upon very early tradition, while some presuppose the practical experience of an already developed Church-life, and lay down the lines for an organised system of penitential discipline.

THE GOSPEL OF MATTHEW

CHAPTER XIII

The Last Journey and Final Conflict

(Matt. xix.–xxviii.)

The events and discourses during the journey to Jerusalem, which in Luke form the contents of his long interpolation, are reported in Matthew in the same sequence as in Mark. In the story of the rich young man (xix. 16 ff.), Matthew's peculiar version of the answer of Jesus (verse 17) is noteworthy: "Why askest thou me about that which is good? There is One who is good." It is clear that this answer, which does not fit the young man's question, has arisen from a modification of the original form of the answer which is preserved in Mark: "Why callest thou me good? None is good save God." This humble refusal of the description "good" as appropriate only to God (in the absolute sense, it is to be understood, of perfect holiness) the later Evangelist could no longer reconcile with his exalted view of the Person of Christ as the supernaturally conceived Son of God, and he has therefore recast, in this somewhat artificial fashion, the saying of Jesus which was preserved by tradition. Even Luke had not thought this necessary, and Matthew therefore betrays himself here again as the latest, the "ecclesiastical" Evangelist. In the same way his version of the saying of Jesus in verse 21, "If thou wilt be perfect, go and sell," etc., already suggests the ecclesiastical doctrine of the two planes of morality—the higher perfection of the ascetic life in voluntary poverty and chastity (*cf.* xix. 12). In regard to Peter's question about reward which follows here (verses 27 ff.) and the promise of Jesus, we have already had something to say in our discussion of Mark's Gospel (p. 48 f.). Peculiar to Matthew is the parable of the Labourers in the Vineyard (xx. 1–16), which the Evangelist uses to illustrate the saying about the first and the last (xix. 30 = Mark x. 31), which he accordingly repeats at the close (xx. 16). The wording of the parable does not necessitate an allegorisation of the labourers who are called at different times of the day as representing various classes of men, grades of society, or nations. The point of the parable, if we consider the story alone, without taking the closing saying into account, is the simple thought[1] that those who are called early and those who are called late are equal in the Kingdom of God; God will display His free grace towards the latter in spite of their little service, while He gives the former their due according to their deserts. No one has the right on that account to find fault with the free goodness of God towards even the unworthy as unjust. Criticism of this kind, such as the Pharisees directed against the love of Jesus towards sinners, would only be a sign of miserable jealousy. That is

[1] *Cf.* Jülicher, *Die Gleichnisse Jesu*, ii. 459–471.

the same thought which is illustrated in the parable of the Prodigal Son by the attitude of the father towards his two sons—a defence of the Divine mercy against the charge of injustice which naturally suggested itself to legal-minded men. But by the connection of the parable—a connection perhaps due to the Evangelist himself—with the saying about the first being last, the further thought seems to be added that those who were first called and who in their self-righteousness bargained for a reward will for that very reason be set back, humiliated, and punished, while the humble shall receive the reward of grace before them—a reference to the rejection of the Pharisees and the gracious reception of sinners, as in xxi. 31 f.

In his account of the events of the first days at Jerusalem, Matthew has somewhat obscured the accurate order as given in Mark's account. In particular, he makes the cleansing of the Temple follow immediately after the entry into Jerusalem, upon the same day, whereas it did not take place until the following day; and the cursing of the fig-tree, which in Mark is separated from the perception of its withering, is brought by him into juxtaposition with it. In his account of the cleansing of the Temple he certainly follows the source more closely than Luke does, but he does not bring out its full significance so clearly as Mark does, since in xxi. 14 ff. he represents the anger of the hierarchs as caused by the cures wrought by Jesus in the Temple and by the acclamations of the children—an addition of the Evangelist which can hardly be historical, and which only serves to throw into the shade the decisive significance of the cleansing of the Temple.

Like Luke, too, Matthew diverges from Mark in referring the question of the hierarchs regarding Jesus' authority to His *teaching* in the Temple (xxi. 23), whereas according to Mark's account, which has historical probability on its side, it referred to His reforming *act* of cleansing the Temple.

The answering of this question is followed in Matthew (xxi. 28 ff.) by the parable, which is peculiar to him, of the Two Sons, of whom the one at first rejects in words his father's command to go and work in his vineyard, but obeys it in act, whereas the other does the reverse, professing obedience but not obeying in reality. The interpretation, which he adds, as a reference to the opposite conduct of the publicans and harlots on the one hand, and of the Pharisees and chief priests on the other, in regard to John the Baptist, the preacher of repentance (verses 31 f.), recalls Luke vii. 29 f., and is closely connected, as regards its substance, with the parable which there follows of the capricious children in the market-place (Luke vii. 31 ff.), which would therefore find a more appropriate place here than there, where it has less connection with the context (p. 132 f.). To the parable of the Husbandmen (*sup.*, p. 57) Matthew attaches, as a third in this series, that of the Royal Marriage-feast (xxii. 1–14), in which he has expanded the parable of the Great Supper, recorded by Luke in a simpler and more original form, into a Messianic allegory; for the marriage feast made by the king for his son is the regular image for the bliss which will attend the coming of the Messianic Kingdom. This is also suggested by certain other features added by Matthew, which betray themselves as an artificial allegory because they do not suit the natural course of the narrative. The first (verses 6 f.), about the invited guests who ill-treated and slew the messengers, in punishment for which the king sent and destroyed their city, has the fault, which is not unusual in allegories, of falling out of the figure into the reality (the destruction of Jerusalem), and thus robbing the allegory of all its force by loading it with improbable and not easily imaginable traits. This intrusion of reality has a parallel in the Lucan parable of the Pounds, where it breaks through in a way which is equally disturbing to the simple story of the parable (xix. 14 and 27). Equally inappropriate to the situation is the other addition about the guest who had come in without a wedding-garment (if he had just been brought straight in from the street, how could he possibly have brought a wedding-garment with him ?), and who, for this reason, was bound hand and foot and cast into outer darkness (xxii. 11 ff.). Enigmatic as this trait appears in the narrative, it can be simply enough explained if we look for the key to it in the Apocalypse, in the passage which tells of the marriage of the Lamb (xix. 7 ff.), where it is said that unto the Bride (the Church) it was granted to array herself in "fine linen clean and shining," and that "the fine linen is the righteous deeds (δικαιώματα) of the saints." It is from this apocalyptic figure that we must take the interpretation of that allegorical trait in the parable: he who desires to have a part in the blessedness of the Messianic Kingdom, access to which is open to all, must show himself worthy of it by good deeds answering to the Divine will; otherwise he will be turned out again as unworthy, even if he is already among the festal company of the Christian Church. "This is certainly an addition of Matthew, for the thought is in line with that of vii. 23, xiii. 41, xxiv. 12: love with its fruits must be added to faith" (Holtzmann, *Komm.*). It is *ethically* conditioned universalism—the ecclesiastical version of the Pauline universalism, which has a doctrinal basis—to which the Evangelist gives expression here, as in the eschatological parables of chapter xxv. It is this distinction between mere outward adherents and genuine, morally worthy members of the Christian community, that is referred to also in the antithesis of the many called and the few chosen in Matt. xxii. 14, which in this connection at any rate is not to be thought of as bearing a predestinarian sense.[1] In his account of the other sayings, in answer to the questions about the tribute-money, the resurrection, the greatest commandment, the Son of David, Matthew follows Mark (*cf. sup.*, pp. 58 ff.), except that in the question regarding the "great" commandment (as he calls it, instead of the "first") the "understanding" answer of the Scribe (Mark. xii. 33), that the love of God and of man was more than all burnt offering and sacrifice is omitted, perhaps because he was unwilling to attribute so much "understanding" to a Scribe. He has omitted, too, the beautiful story, told by both his predecessors, about the widow's mite which was

[1] The saying, which is not specially appropriate in this connection (for, after all, among all the guests, only one is cast out!), seems to have been inserted here by Matthew as a quotation from an unknown writing, which may be alluded to also in Barnabas, cap. v. (γέγραπται).

worth more than all the gifts which the rich made out of their superfluity (Mark xii. 41–44). The reason for this omission is easily understood in the case of the Evangelist of the catholic world-church, who also found it necessary to change the beatitude upon the poor and hungry to that upon the spiritually poor and hungry.

The brief remark in the source about the vanity and avarice of the Scribes (Matt. xii. 38–40) has been worked up by Matthew, along with other material from his sources—from which Luke also derived the polemic against the Pharisees (xi. 37–52) in his great interpolation—into a great polemical discourse against the Scribes and Pharisees (chap. xxiii.). Luke gives, first, three woes against the Pharisees, and then three against the lawyers, but Matthew combines both sets of adversaries from the beginning, and gives seven woes in all against them. Not all the sayings, however, apply equally well to both categories. It could only be said of the Scribes, not of the Pharisees, that they sat in Moses' seat and loved to be called Rabbi (teacher) by the people. What is meant by that is the well-known fact that the Jewish lawyers claimed for their traditional ordinances at least as great authority as for the law of Moses itself. Against the genuineness of the previously enunciated principle (verse 3) that men ought to do and observe what these teachers said, but not to imitate their works, since they themselves did not do what they said, objections have been raised on the ground that it does not seem to be in harmony with other utterances of Jesus regarding the "human ordinances" of the Jewish schools (xv. 3–14) and regarding the leaven of the Pharisees and Sadducees, which is explained in xvi. 12 to mean their doctrine. But according to the more original version of this saying in Luke (xii. 1), what is meant by the leaven of the Pharisees (Matthew alone adds the Sadducees) is their *hypocrisy*, therefore just the same discrepancy between their words and actions as is censured in this whole polemical discourse. In xv. 3 ff. the "ordinances of men" set up by the Jewish schools are contrasted with the Mosaic Law as an authoritative standard, so that neither is this passage in contradiction with xxiii. 3, since here authority is only ascribed to the words of the Scribes in so far as they "sit in Moses' seat," *i.e.* apply his law. That Jesus recognised the authority of the Mosaic Law cannot be doubted, in view of Matt. v. 17 f. = Luke xvi. 17 (*sup.*, p. 323 f.). And xxiii. 3 is in harmony not only with this but also with xxiii. 23 = Luke xi. 42; this saying, which is given by both Evangelists, "This ought ye to have done [the moral commandments of the Law] and not to have left the other undone," is a very significant expression of the conservative attitude of Jesus towards the Law, in which He certainly emphasised the ethical side as the main thing, but did not on that account wish to do away with the literal: xxiii. 3 and 23 may well be regarded as an authentic commentary upon v. 17 f. At the end of the polemical discourse (verse 33) Matthew makes Jesus repeat the invective which we have met with before in the preaching of John the Baptist (iii. 7), "Generation of vipers, how shall ye escape the condemnation of hell?" and the discourse closes with the prediction of the Divine judgment upon the prophet-slaying nation and city of the Jews (verses 34–39), which in the Lucan parallel (xi. 49 ff., xiii. 34 f.) is introduced as a word of the "Wisdom of God," *i.e.* a quotation from an apocalyptic "Book of Wisdom"[1] (p. 151). The woe pronounced against Jerusalem is given here by Matthew in its original connection, which in Luke has been disturbed.

The eschatological discourse in Matt. xxiv. is introduced, as in the other Gospels, by a prediction of the destruction of the Temple and the question of the disciples as to when this is to take place, to which Matthew, however, has added a further question which anticipates the content of the discourse—and alone retained an interest for his readers —regarding the sign of the Parousia of Christ and of the end of the world (xxiv. 3). Farther on, the eschatological discourse shows many divergences from Mark xiii., some of which point to later additions, and some to the earliest tradition. To the former belong certainly verses 10–12, where, among the signs of the end, are mentioned not only, as in Mark xiii. 9 ff., the persecution of the Christians by the hostile world, but also dissensions within the Christian community itself, mutual hatreds and offences, the appearance of many false prophets, who shall mislead many, widespread lawlessness, the love of many growing cold. The allusion here is, without doubt,

[1] The conjecture naturally suggests itself that this book of revelations is identical with the apocalypse which underlies Matt. xxiv. and its parallels in the other Evangelists (p. 68). The date would agree, as the martyrdom of Zachariah, the son of Baruch, mentioned in xxiii. 35 falls in the year 67 or 68, for the reference is probably to the same events as are mentioned by Josephus as occurring in the last years of the Jewish war (*B.J.*, iv. 5. 4).

to the same heretical teachers who are described at the close of the Sermon on the Mount (vii. 23), and in the parable of the Tares (xiii. 41), as workers of iniquity, namely, heretical antinomians and libertines, who gave so much trouble to the Church of the second century (*cf.* Apoc. ii. 2, 4). To the saying "He that endureth unto the end shall be saved" Matthew adds, "And this gospel of the kingdom [namely, that which lies before the reader] must first be made known throughout the whole world for a testimony to the heathen, and [only] then shall the end come"—an assertion of the Evangelist which stands in striking contrast with the rapid course of events described in the context, as also with x. 23 and xvi. 28. It serves the purpose, however, of postponing, in accordance with actual experience, the catastrophe which the apocalypses anticipate within so short a period. If these additions betray the correcting hand of the late, ecclesiastical Evangelist, he has, on the other hand, preserved in what follows, in its most original form, the early Christian apocalypse which was contained in the common source. In verse 15 the mysterious "abomination of desolation," which Luke had interpreted as a reference to the destruction of Jerusalem, is defined more exactly than in Mark by the words "which is spoken of by the prophet Daniel" and "standing in the holy place," which makes the indefinite "where it ought not" (Mark) into a direct reference to the Temple. By this the interpretation of the expected "abomination" as the setting up of a statue of the Emperor in the Temple, which had been in contemplation since Claudius and kept the imagination of the Jews in a constant state of excitement for decades, is placed beyond doubt. In verse 20 it is said, "Pray that your flight may not be in the winter *or on the Sabbath*"; the italicised words being peculiar to Matthew, though certainly not added by him but retained from the source as the original form of the saying. The same applies to verse 29, "Immediately after those days the sun shall be darkened," etc. By this "immediately," which is preserved only by Matthew, the appearance of the Son of Man described just afterwards is attached in immediate temporal sequence to the frightful affliction for which the "abomination of desolation" should give the signal. Naturally, this saying, which was contradicted by the course of events, could not have been added by the Evangelist, who has clearly implied his contrary experience in verse 14, but must have been taken over from the apocalypse which he had before him in his source, as unsuspectingly as the similar sayings in x. 23 and xvi. 28. But to argue from this to the early composition of our Gospel would be quite a mistake; the explanation rather is that the Evangelist here shows the characteristic ecclesiastical reverence for ancient oracular sayings, of which the disharmony with history is no longer noticed, and which, as mysterious, are verbally retained on the assumption that their enigmatic sense shall at some time be revealed and in some way fulfilled. To the early matter peculiar to our Gospel[1] belong, finally, the more detailed

[1] *Cf.* Wernle, *Die synoptische Frage*, p. 146. If, in the discourse about the Parousia, Matthew has preserved much that is ancient more faithfully than Mark, while, on the other hand, the influence of the catastrophe of A.D. 70 is hardly traceable, that does not

picture of the Parousia in verse 30 f.: the sign of the Son of Man in heaven (*cf.* Apoc. xxi. 7), the lamentation of the races of mankind when they see (Apoc. i. 7) the Son of Man coming on the clouds of heaven (Dan. vii. 13) with great power and glory, and sending His angels forth to summon the faithful with the loud trumpet-call (1 Thess. iv. 16, 1 Cor. xv. 52)—all features of the common material of the apocalypses.

To the eschatological discourse which is common to all the Synoptists, Matthew adds in chapter xxv. three eschatological parables. The first, that of the wise and foolish virgins, is an expansion and modification of the shorter parable in Luke xii. 35 ff. As there the master, returning from the marriage, is awaited by his servants, who open immediately to him when he knocks, and, as a reward, are made to sit at meat at his table, so here the bridegroom, coming *to* the marriage, is awaited by the bridesmaids, who on his arrival are allowed to go in with him to the marriage-feast, while those who were unprepared beg in vain for admission. Even the image of the lighted lamps is taken from the simpler parable (xii. 35): "Let your loins be girded about and your lamps burning." There is no indication of an allegorical meaning in the details; the point is the same in the simpler Lucan and in the fuller Matthæan form—a want of preparedness excludes from partaking in the Messianic Kingdom. The

necessarily prove the priority of Matthew, even in relation to Luke, but perhaps rather his reverence for authoritative documents; for Matthew himself the "immediately" and the "not on the Sabbath" have no longer any meaning, but he has not the courage to sacrifice these archaic touches.

parable of the Talents (verses 14–30) is a variation of the Lucan parable of the Pounds (xix. 12–27), and the suggestion for both is found in Mark (xiii. 34) in the brief simile of the master going away on a journey and entrusting to his servants the care of his property, while he "gives each of them his (special) work." This allotted task is more closely defined in the parable as the duty of trading with the capital entrusted to them, in order by investing it to increase it for the advantage of the owner. While Luke, however, speaks of ten servants, each of whom received the same capital (one "mina"), Matthew gives each of the three servants a different capital according to his ability, *i.e.* capacity for work—five talents to the first, two to the second, and one to the third. Each of the two faithful servants trades with his capital, and each doubles the amount entrusted to him; for this they are rewarded by the master on his return, by being made rulers over many things (their sphere of labour and their resources increased), and in addition they are bidden to enter into the joy of their lord, *i.e.* to the Messianic feast. The idle servant, however, who has buried his talent and excuses his idleness by his fear of the hardness of his avaricious master, not only has his talent taken from him and given to the possessor of the ten talents, but he himself is cast out into outer darkness, where there is weeping and gnashing of teeth—*i.e.*, he is excluded from the feast of the Messianic Kingdom. This eschatological reference to the reward of the faithful and punishment of the unfaithful betrays itself, even in the simpler Matthæan version, as an allegorising addition to the original parable, which was only intended to illustrate the simple thought that faithful work would be rewarded by growing success, while unfaithfulness would be punished by the loss even of what one had, by means of a story drawn from everyday circumstances.[1] That it was not originally intended as an allegory is shown by the unfavourable characterisation of the master in verse 24, which has its nearest analogues in the unjust judge and the unfaithful steward; in all these cases the un-ideal traits, which are taken from life, and merely serve to give vividness to the story, resist every attempt to allegorise them. This does not exclude the possibility that the Evangelists have embellished the original framework of the parable with allegorical traits; here Matthew has done this only to a small extent, Luke much more largely (p. 172 f.), while in the parable of the Supper the reverse is the case. At the close of the whole eschatological discourse Matthew has placed the dramatic picture, peculiar to him (it is not a parable), of the judgment of the nations which the Son of Man at His Parousia shall hold, amid His angels, determining the worth and fate of men by the standard of the works of love which they have done or not done towards His humblest brethren, *i.e.* the Christians (xxv. 31–46). That the Evangelist is here thinking of a judgment of the world, not however of Christians but of the heathen nations (ἔθνη) is clear; the Christians are the humble brethren of Christ, who are represented as deserving to receive kindness from the nations. That he can recognise among these heathen nations some who are blessed by God, and for whom the Kingdom is prepared, because they

[1] *Cf.* Jülicher, *Gleichnisse Jesu*, ii. 481 f.

have displayed the moral character which is appropriate to it, and therefore have unconsciously served Christ Himself, whom they never knew, is a beautiful evidence of the ethically humane temper of the author, who represents the want of Christian faith among the heathen as replaced by Christ-like love, and thus puts his ethically based universalism side by side with the dogmatically based universalism of Paul.

In the story of the Passion, Matthew keeps much more close than Luke does to the Marcan source: individual divergences from it have been pointed out in treating the earlier Gospels. Peculiar to him are only a few little episodes, such as the suicide of the traitor (xxvii. 3–10), in which he gives a rather different version of the legend from that which Luke gives in the Acts of the Apostles (i. 15–20). Whether he had access to another tradition or has freely moulded his version in accordance with the types and figurative language of the Old Testament (2 Sam. xvii. 23, Zech. xi. 12 f., Jer. xxxii. 6 ff.) may be left an open question. Further episodes introduced by him are the dream of Pilate's wife and Pilate's symbolical hand-washing (xxvii. 19 and 24), both highly improbable, and only serving the purpose of emphasising the innocence of Jesus by repeated solemn testimonies. An obviously legendary trait of late origin is the story that after the death of Jesus the rocks were split by an earthquake, the graves opened, and many bodies of the saints which slept arose, and, after Jesus' resurrection, came forth and appeared to many in the Holy City (xxvii. 51 ff.). It has, to begin with, the inherent difficulty that it is not easy to see any reason why the saints who arose immediately after Jesus' death should have only come out of their graves after the resurrection of Jesus, and how they kept alive in their graves in the meantime. The explanation of this difficulty is obviously to be found in the collision of two conflicting motives in the formation of the legend. On the one hand, the earthquake belonged to the moment of Jesus' death, which was thus solemnised by heaven and earth alike; and it was natural to imagine the opening of the graves and the rising of the dead as simultaneous with the earthquake. On the other hand, it seemed to offend the reverent sense of what was fitting that other saints should have left their graves before Christ; their coming forth ought rather to occur after His resurrection, and therefore the risen saints must wait in their graves until then before showing themselves in the city. Another thing which is peculiar to Matthew is the quite improbable story that the chief priests asked Pilate for a guard to protect the grave from the disciples, who, they feared, would otherwise steal the body; and that after the resurrection had taken place, the chief priests bribed the guards to say that the body had been stolen by the disciples of Jesus while they slept; so that this report was current among the Jews down to the writer's day (xxvii. 62–66 and xxviii. 11–15). The only historical fact in this narrative is, without doubt, the existence of a report of that kind among the Jews at the time of the writer, or, it may be, of his source (for that this and the preceding legend came into our Gospel from a Jewish-Christian source of some antiquity is the more probable since we find something similar in the Gospel of Peter); in order to discredit this report the Christian legend sought to explain its origin in the foregoing manner.

In the narrative of Jesus' resurrection and appearance to the disciples we can unfortunately only compare the Marcan parallel in the first part (xxviii. 1–10), since Mark xvi. 9–20 is not genuine. According to Mark, the two Maries and Salome (Luke, "Joanna") came on the Easter morning to the tomb, found it empty, and were told by a young man in white apparel of the resurrection of Jesus which had happened in the meantime, and sent to His disciples with the message that they were to await the appearance of Jesus in Galilee; whereupon they went away in terror, and said nothing to anyone. Matthew makes only the two Maries come to the grave; the third of the women he does not mention, perhaps from a harmonistic motive, because tradition was uncertain as to her name. Then he tells of the resurrection, or rather of the opening of the grave, as though it had occurred immediately under the eyes of the women, whereas in the source it is not the event itself, but only its result, which comes to the knowledge of the women. Moreover, Matthew's account of the course of events is not very clear. He tells of the earthquake, of the coming down of an angel from heaven who rolled away the stone from the door and seated himself upon it, of the alarm of the guards, of the cheering tidings given by the angel to the frightened women that Jesus had arisen; but, after all, the main thing, the actual resurrection of Jesus, is not related. We learn nothing definite either as to the when or the how of the decisive event; indeed, if we look at the matter closely, there is no room left in the chain of events in Matthew's narrative for the occurrence of the resurrection, for it naturally cannot have occurred *before* the opening of the grave, but if it happened *after* that, then it must have been witnessed by the women, as well as the coming down of the angel and the rolling away of the stone. But they would not have needed to be told by the angel about the resurrection of Jesus if they had themselves just witnessed it. No unprejudiced person who attempts to realise to himself Matthew's account of the events of the Easter morning will be able to get rid of this difficulty. The sole explanation of it lies in the fact that the Matthæan account is not original writing or original thinking, but is only a secondary elaboration of the Marcan source, in which the imported embellishments do not harmonise with the original. Whereas in the source the opening of the grave and the resurrection take place, so to speak, behind the scenes, and are only brought to the knowledge of the women, and of the reader, through the angel-messenger, Matthew, in order to make the Marcan narrative more lively and dramatic, has brought one half of the events (the opening of the grave) which Mark left in the obscurity of the background into the foreground of the picture while leaving the other half (the resurrection) still in the background; which naturally makes a serious breach in the unity and conceivability of the whole occurrence. It is the same with a second difficulty which presents itself in the further course of Matthew's narrative. Just as in Mark, the women are here charged to tell the disciples that Jesus has risen and has gone before them into Galilee, and that they shall see Him there; but whereas we should expect to be told only of the appearance of Jesus to the disciples in Galilee which is here announced, immediately after the departure of the women from the open grave an appearance of Jesus to them as they went is described, the only object of which appears to have been to repeat the direction to tell the disciples which had already been given by the angel. To what end, one involuntarily asks, is this aimless repetition? If Jesus could appear to the women as they returned from the grave, what need was there for the special revelation of the angel immediately before? Could not what the angel had to tell them have been communicated at once by the appearance of Jesus in person? But what, in any case, was the object of directing the disciples to expect His appearance in Galilee, and not immediately? If Jesus could now appear to the women, why could He not at once appear to the disciples in Jerusalem? This difficulty, which must strike every thoughtful reader of the Matthæan narrative, is to be explained, like the former one, by the fact that this narrative is a working over of a simpler source. In the latter, and therefore in the oldest tradition, there was no thought of an appearance of Jesus in Jerusalem (*cf. sup.*, p. 84 f.). Galilee was assumed to have been the sole scene of the appearances. Later, however, alongside of the Galilæan tradition, legends became current of appearances in and near Jerusalem to individual disciples, especially to Mary Magdalene. On the basis of this group of legends, Luke and John (xx.) had transferred the appearance to the eleven disciples to Jerusalem, thereby coming into conflict with the Galilæan tradition. Matthew, on the other hand, held to this as the oldest and best supported, but, after his conservative and harmonistic fashion, was unwilling to pass over the Judæan tradition of an appearance of the risen Christ to Mary Magdalene (*cf.* John xx. 14 ff.), and therefore narrated the appearance to the two Maries on their way back from the grave. The counterpart of this combination is found in the Gospel of John, which in chapter xx., following in Luke's track, holds to the Judæan tradition, but afterwards, in chapter xxi., brings in the Galilæan tradition.

The close of the Gospel (xxviii. 16–20) is formed by the very significant scene of the parting of the risen Christ from the eleven disciples upon the mountain in Galilee whither He had bidden them repair. The very scene of this event, "the mountain," gives us a hint that now again, at the close, we find ourselves upon the same *ideal* height as at the beginning of the Gospel, at the Sermon on the Mount, and again in the middle of the Gospel, at the Transfiguration. The mount of the Sermon and of the Transfiguration is the New Testament counterpart to Mount Sinai, where Moses gave the Law, and where the glory of God was reflected in his face. The mount of the leave-taking is the New Testament counterpart to Mount Nebo, whence Moses, when about to leave the earth, looked out upon the Land of Promise and beheld the glorious future of his people. So now the Evangelist represents Jesus here, now no longer belonging to the earth, as showing Himself once more to His disciples, in order to give them solemn assurance of the destiny which they shared with Him of exercising universal dominion, in order to send them forth as His messengers to the conversion of all nations, and to leave with them the promise of His abiding spiritual presence. These last words which the Evangelist here puts into the mouth of Christ at His departure contain, therefore, a brief summary of his Christian confession: Christ is the ruler of all things in heaven and earth; all nations are destined to become His disciples by means of baptism in the name of the Father, and of the Son, and of the Holy Spirit, and are to be taught and trained in the keeping of all the commandments of Christ; finally, Christ is present with His disciples to help them even in the present world "all the days" until the end. Here there is in the first place, at least, so much clear—that this parting discourse does not rest on any tradition with an historical basis or origin, but is only to be regarded as a confession of the faith of the Evangelist and the Church of his time. Of a command of Jesus to baptize, there is no trace in Paul's writings. Indeed, from 1 Cor. i. 17 it is to be concluded that in Apostolic times nothing was known of such a command, and it was only later that the custom of baptism, which had come into use, was sanctioned by being traced back to a command of Christ; but in this an historical reminiscence betrays itself in the fact that the baptismal command is, at least, not placed in the earthly lifetime of Jesus, but in the super-earthly life of the risen Christ the Lord. Finally, the baptismal formula—"in the name of the Father, and of the Son, and of the Holy Spirit"—would be absolutely unthinkable in the mouth of Jesus. It is nowhere found in the whole of the first century, or even in the beginning of the second century in the Acts of the Apostles; whenever there is mention of baptism, the standing formula is always the simple into the (or, in the) name of Jesus, into Jesus Christ. On the contrary, the Trinitarian formula is found first in Justin Martyr, about the middle of the second century, and even here not yet exactly in the same form as in Matthew (instead of "of the Son," it runs "of our Saviour Jesus Christ," *Apol.*, i. 61). Another thing which, not less than the Trinitarian formula, points to a riper stage of the Church's consciousness is that the promise of Christ, and the faith of the Church, are no longer primarily directed, as they still are in Acts (i. 11), to the visible return of Christ from heaven, but to an abiding, invisible presence with His Church on earth. Herein is manifested the change which was completed in the course of the second century from the apocalyptic and eschatological frame of mind to the expectation of an historical permanence of the Church—a change which did not, indeed, entirely do away with the hope of the Parousia, but greatly weakened the interest in it, and subordinated it to the more practical interests of the upbuilding of the Church to be a worthy abiding-place for the spiritual presence of Christ.[1] The parallel offered by the Johannine Gospel naturally suggests itself.

[1] According to Brandt, *Ev. Gesch.*, p. 358, we are to recognise in this whole scene of the appearance in Matthew "nothing else than an historical representation of the sanctioning of Church-organisation, as a foundation for the doctrine of the Divine authority of this organisation and of the Apostolic succession of its heads."

CHAPTER XIV

Origin and Characteristics

Critical opinion is still sharply divided in its estimate of this Gospel. And this is intelligible enough. It is not without reason that this Gospel has been described as the Gospel of contradictions. "Here are elements both of the earliest and the latest date; here are the narrow and the broad, the conservative and the reforming, the legal and the spiritual, the Judæan and the universalist."[1] The character of this Gospel used generally to be described as chiefly Jewish-Christian, because in the story of Jesus' life the fulfilment of Old Testament prophecies and types is everywhere pointed out. But to prove the truth of Christianity out of the Old Testament was the standing practice in the apologetic of the Church, without distinction of party—in the Gentile-Christian writings of Clement of Rome and Barnabas, of Justin, and of the other Apologists, not less than in the Gospel of Matthew. It is true that this Gospel contains some really Jewish-Christian elements, such as the sayings about the permanent validity of the Mosaic Law and the

[1] Carpenter, *The First Three Gospels, their Origin and Relationship*, 2nd ed., pp. 337 f.

authority of the Teachers of the Law (v. 17 f., xxiii. 3, 23), the limitation of missionary activity to the Jewish people in x. 5 f., xv. 24, xvi. 28; the assumption of the permanence of the Twelve Tribes in the new world of the Messianic Kingdom (xix. 28), and of the sacrificial system and Temple worship in v. 23 f. and xxiii. 18 f.; finally, the description of Jerusalem as "the holy city" and "the city of the great King" (God) (iv. 5, v. 35, xxvii. 53). On the other side we have the fact that it is precisely the Gospel of Matthew which has the most definite utterances regarding the rejection of Israel and the transference of salvation to the heathen (viii. 12, xxi. 43, xxiii. 28, xxiv. 14). The destination of Christianity for the whole world is manifested at the very beginning in the homage of the wise men from the East, and is solemnly sanctioned in the farewell command of Christ to baptise all nations (xxviii. 19). No doubt, this Christian universalism has a different basis from that which Paul gives it, a basis not doctrinal but ethical; it rests upon belief in the universal authority of the will of God which was made known by Christ, and upon the universal obligation, and enablement, of all men to fulfil it by doing good, by works of love in which we serve Christ Himself, as is shown in the impressive picture of the final Judgment (xxv. 34 ff.).

In its combination of the most heterogeneous elements, the Gospel of Matthew shows itself to be an ecclesiastical Gospel-harmony in which the consciousness of the Church, on its way to become the universal world-Church, has found its classical expression. The tendencies which were to culminate in the dogma, ethics, and organisation of the Church Catholic are all visible in this Gospel. It is ecclesiastical in its baptismal formula (xxviii. 19), the germ of the *regula fidei* and of the Apostles' Creed. It is ecclesiastical in its doctrine of Christ, in which the idea of the Son of David and of Abraham is harmoniously combined with that of the true, supernaturally born Son of God, to whom is given all power in heaven and in earth, who gives to His people who are gathered out of all nations a *New Law*, which, as the perfect fulfilment of the old imperfect Law, takes the place of the latter (*cf.* the antitheses of the Sermon on the Mount), who as Ruler of the world shall in the future judge not only Israel but all nations, and who must therefore be endowed with the Divine goodness and power without any limitation (xix. 17, xiii. 58; *cf.* Mark x. 18, vi. 5). It is ecclesiastical in its doctrine of salvation: all have access to the Christian community, but only those shall share in its salvation who adorn themselves with the wedding-garment of the good works of the saints, *i.e.* who keep the commandments of Christ; indeed, works of love stand so high in the estimation of the Judge of the world that He even allows them, in the case of the virtuous heathen, to take the place of faith as a ground of gracious recognition. Conversely, heretics are rejected by Him because they do not keep the law of Christ, but cause offences and division, in consequence of which the love of many grows cold. It is ecclesiastical in its ethics, according to which fasting and prayer and almsgiving, in so far as they are practised in the right spirit and not for display, are works well-pleasing to God, which may count on receiving a special reward from Him (vi. 1–6; *cf.*, on the other hand, Mark ii. 18–22), and according to which the ascetic life in voluntary poverty and celibacy is already counted a higher "perfection" (xix. 21, 12). It is ecclesiastical, finally, in the authority ascribed to Peter as the foundation of the universal "Church," the possessor of the power of the keys, whose binding and loosing is sanctioned beforehand in heaven. To these main points we may add some subsidiary features: the beginnings of the organisation of a penitential discipline (xviii. 15 ff.), the warning against making the preaching of the gospel a means of livelihood or source of gain (x. 9), the commendation of hospitality towards itinerant prophets (x. 41 f.), the rejection of the beatitude upon the poor and of the socialistic tendency of the primitive community;[1] finally, the notable cooling down of the eschatological expectations which is expressed especially in the closing saying about the unseen presence of Christ in His Church.[2] If we

1 Why, asks Brandt (*Ev. Gesch.*, p. 539), has Matthew omitted the passages about the widow's mite and the refusal of Jesus to arbitrate in the dispute about an inheritance (Luke xii. 13 ff.)? And he answers the question excellently: "Matthew obviously stood nearer than Luke to the leaders of ecclesiastical policy, who already knew how to value earthly property and did not despise the office of judge." This *ecclesiastical opportunism*, which makes compromises between the abstract ideal of the enthusiastic beginnings and the real conditions of life in human society, out of which grew the whole system of ecclesiastical morality, is the unmistakable sign of a period far removed from the Apostolic beginnings—of a date later still than Luke's.

2 *Cf.* Carpenter, *First Three Gospels*, p. 369: "But how long a time must have elapsed before such an interpretation of the Church's hope could have been possible, and still more before it could clothe itself in symbolic form."

combine all these features we have, trait for trait, the picture of the faith and life of the Church in the first half of the second century.

If, with the impression of the ecclesiastical character of Matthew's Gospel which we have gained from studying its peculiarities, we proceed to inquire into its origin, we shall be able, by the help of this Ariadne thread, to find our way more easily through the labyrinth of ecclesiastical tradition. In the early Church, Matthew's Gospel was held to be the work of the Apostle Matthew, who was supposed to have written it in Hebrew. This tradition rests partly on the statement which Eusebius records (*H.E.*, iii. 39) as having been made by Papias, Bishop of Hierapolis, about the middle of the second century, according to which Matthew wrote, in the Hebrew language, a collection of the Sayings (λόγια, *sc.* of Jesus), which each one then interpreted as best he could; partly on the fact that, among the Jewish Christians of the second century and later, an Aramaic Gospel was in use, which they ascribed to the Apostle Matthew and asserted to be the original of the Church's Gospel of Matthew, as Jerome reports, not without raising some objections on his own part. As regards the statement of Papias, it has been usual, since Schleiermacher, to understand it as referring to a mere "collection of sayings" in contradistinction to a Gospel such as our Matthew; but this is certainly a mistake. Neither Eusebius nor any other of the Fathers understood the statement of Papias in this sense—or indeed knew anything of the existence of such a collection of sayings. It is, moreover, obvious that in the passage in question Papias only intended to give his view regarding the origin of the then well-known Gospels; when he spoke of the λόγια he was referring to the Gospel *a parte potiori*, because to him—he had written an exposition of the sayings of the Lord—this part of its contents was the most important; in the immediately preceding statement regarding the Gospel of Mark, after first describing its contents more exactly as "that which was said or done by Christ," he subsequently refers to it under the inclusive term "the sayings of the Lord" (κυριακοὶ λόγοι). The early Fathers were certainly right in understanding the statement of Papias as meant to describe the original of the present Gospel of Matthew as written in Hebrew (Aramaic) by the Apostle Matthew. But this tradition is inherently untenable, since it is contradicted by the actual character of our Gospel of Matthew; for this is neither a unity nor a direct translation from the Aramaic, nor was it composed by an Apostle. It is worked up from a number of sources—in part, at least, from Greek sources—and by a redactor who was certainly not an Apostle, but was far removed both in date and sentiment from the Apostolic age, as the characteristics of the work which we have discussed above clearly indicate. If, therefore, we wish to form an historical view of the origin of the Gospel of Matthew, this can only be done—so far as, in the obscurity of literary matters in early Christianity, it can be done at all—by means of an investigation of its sources which, in the meantime, leaves that tradition out of account.

Of these sources, the most important was the Gospel of Mark, as the foregoing analyses of the contents of the two Gospels show. Matthew follows Mark's general order from beginning to end, and where he breaks through it in order to insert new material this is always evidenced by gaping seams, by inconcinnities and illogicalities which can only be explained on the hypothesis of the interruption of an underlying order, which can be no other than that of Mark. The narratives and the discourses of Mark have been reproduced by Matthew almost entire. The few exceptions can be explained, partly from their appearing to him too trivial (the young man who fled on the night of the arrest, Mark xiv. 51 f.; the parable of the Seed Growing Secretly, iv. 26 ff., for which he substitutes the parable of the Tares), partly from his having combined similar narratives into one for the sake of brevity (the two cures of demoniacs, Mark i. 21 ff. and v. 2 ff., are combined into the cure of two demoniacs on the same occasion, Matt. viii. 28 ff.; the cure of the blind man at Bethsaida and of the deaf-mute, Mark vii. 32 ff., viii. 22 ff., give place to the cures of two blind men and a dumb man, Matt. ix. 27–34); in some cases, from the point of a narrative not appealing to him (the healer who "followed not with us," Mark ix. 38 ff., where the lesson, verse 40, "He that is not against us is for us," seemed to conflict with the saying in Matt. xii. 30, "He who is not with me is against me"; the passage about the widow's mite, which raised difficulties from the practical point of view, *cf. sup.*, pp. 361 f., 381). The abbreviated form in which Matthew reproduces the narratives of Mark, omitting the graphic details, constantly betrays the secondary character of his description.

A similar impression as regards relative priority, though on different grounds, is made by a comparison between the records of discourses in the two Gospels. We may recall, for example, the defence against the accusation of being in league with Beelzebub (Mark iii. 23 ff. = Matt. xii. 25 ff.); the charge to the Twelve, which in Mark vi. 7 ff. is as brief and as appropriate to the occasion as in Matt. x. it is overladen with material not appropriate to the situation; in particular, the parable-discourse, in which Matthew first reproduces the three parables of Mark, expanding the second into the parable of the Tares, while after the third he adds the parable of the leaven and the reflection with which Mark closes the whole (Mark iv. 33 f. = Matt. xiii. 34), but then immediately proceeds to give, in addition to the interpretation of the parable of the Tares, the three further parables of the Hidden Treasure, the Pearl of Great Price, and the Draw-net, and finally concludes with a second closing reflection of his own minting (xiii. 51 ff.). For the rest, I may refer to the above analyses of the contents of the two Gospels, from which every unprejudiced reader must draw the general impression that the priority is on the side of Mark, the dependence on the side of Matthew. This general impression cannot be removed even by the individual exceptions in the case of a few sayings, which should not, however, be overlooked. Among these is perhaps to be reckoned (Mark vii. 27), "Let the children *first* be satisfied," which sounds like a softening of the harsher saying in Matt. xv. 24 and 26; and here belongs certainly Mark x. 12, where the prohibition of the divorce of the husband by the wife is not original, but is introduced by Mark in view of the circumstances of the Roman world, for the Jewish marriage-laws gave no occasion for such a prohibition. Further, we have seen above that in the apocalyptic discourse the version of Matt. xxiv. 15 ff. shows numerous traces of greater antiquity than the parallels in Mark xiii. 14 ff.; but, as we remarked above, no argument for the higher antiquity of the whole canonical Matthew can be drawn from these archaisms—the only conclusion which can be drawn from them is that even Mark has a pre-canonical Gospel-source, to which Matthew also had access, and which in certain cases the latter reproduced more exactly than the former.

Matthew therefore, like Luke, has used the Gospel of Mark as the ground-plan of his own work; but he has enriched it, as Luke has also done, by the addition of much new material, which is for the most part parallel to the new material in Luke, and has the closest affinity with it as regards subject-matter. But the material has been worked up in a different way in the two cases. While Luke has gathered together his additions—apart from his prologue and epilogue—chiefly into two great interpolations (vi. 20–viii. 3 and ix. 51–xviii. 4), within which he has placed the different sections in the loose connection in which he found them in his source, often inserting a particular occasion or situation as the frame for the individual sayings or discourses, Matthew, on the other hand, has distributed his new material over the whole extent of Mark's Gospel, and has gathered together the individual sayings, according to their connection of subject, into long discourses, which he inserts wherever there is an appropriate place in the Gospel history, namely, the Sermon on the Mount (v.–vii.), the charge to the Twelve (x.), the parable-discourse (xiii.), the discourse on the mutual relations of the members of the Christian community (xviii.), the polemic against the Pharisees (xxiii.), the apocalyptic discourse (xxiv.), and the eschatological exhortation in xxv. In almost every case he has marked the interpolation of these seven great discourses into the Marcan text by the closing words, "When Jesus had finished these sayings (vii. 28, xi. 1, xiii. 51, xix. 1, xxvi. 1). It is obviously very improbable that Luke, if he had had before him these long discourses of Matthew, would have broken them up into fragments and redistributed them—much more improbable than the converse, that Matthew has collected into his great groups of discourses, sayings of Jesus which in the tradition had no close connection. As regards their subject-matter, too, the shorter discourses and the sayings attached to definite occasions in Luke have been found in the foregoing analysis to be more original in form and arrangement than the elaborate discourses of Matthew—recall, for example, Luke's Sermon on the Plain (vi. 20 ff.), compared with the Sermon on the Mount of Matt. v.–vii., or the missionary discourse in Matt. x., where he represents as spoken at the sending forth of the Twelve all that Luke distributes between this and the sending forth of the Seventy, much of which is inappropriate to the occasion of the first mission in Galilee. There are comparatively few cases in which a saying or a parable appears to be in a more original form as compared with the Lucan parallel. Among these should perhaps be reckoned the saying about the inner light in Matt. vi. 22 = Luke xi. 34 f.; the lament over Jerusalem (Matt. xxiii. 37 f.) in a more appropriate context than Luke xiii. 34 f.; the discourse about the Parousia (Matt. xxiv. 15 ff.) compared with Luke's direct allusion to the destruction of Jerusalem in xxi. 20; the parable of the Talents (Matt. xxv. 14 ff.) compared with Luke xix. 12 ff., where the eschatological interpolation disturbs the story as much as the Matthæan extension of the parable of the Invited Guests.

Not all the additional material, however, which Matthew has as compared with Mark is found also in Luke, any more than all the additional material of Luke is found in Matthew. Each has a not inconsiderable number of narratives and discourses which are peculiar to him alone. We may briefly collect what is peculiar to each of the two Evangelists.

(1) Matthew:—

The earlier history, chapters i. and ii., which is parallel with Luke's but quite different from it. The justification of the baptism of Jesus by John, iii. 14 ff. The transformation and expansion of the Beatitudes, v. 3–9 (instead of the woes against the rich in Luke). The giving of the New Law, v. 17 ff. The warning against profaning that which is holy, vii. 6. The warning against false prophets and heretical teachers, vii. 15, 21 f. The prohibition of preaching to the Gentiles, x. 5 f. Prohibition of making gain by preaching, x. 8 f. The command, when persecuted in one city to flee unto another, and the promise that the Son of Man should come before the mission to the Jews was completed, x. 23. The Saviour's invitation, xi. 28 ff. The sign of Jonah interpreted as a reference to the resurrection, xii. 40. The peculiar saying regarding the Sabbath, and quotation from Hosea, in xii. 5 ff. The parables of the Tares, Hidden Treasure, Pearl, and Draw-net, xiii. The saying about the Scribe "instructed unto the kingdom of heaven," xiii. 51. The bringing of the news of John the Baptist's death by his disciples, xiv. 12. Peter's walking on the sea and sinking, xiv. 32; and, in the same passage, the first confession of Jesus as the Son of God by the disciples. The anti-Pharisaic saying about the plants that must be rooted out, xv. 13. The exaltation of Peter, xvi. 17 ff. The miracle of the stater in the fish's mouth, xvii. 24 ff. Rules for Church discipline, xxiii. 15 ff. Parable of the Unmerciful Servant, xviii. 23 ff. Saying about that which is good and Him who is good, xix. 17. Counsels of evangelical perfection, xix. 12, 21. Parable of the Labourers in the Vineyard, xx. 1 ff. Healings, and acclamations of the children, in the Temple, xxi. 14 ff. Parable of the Two Sons, xxi. 28 ff. Prediction of offences and apostasy caused by false prophets, xxiv. 10 ff. Parable of the Foolish Virgins, and picture of the Last Judgment, xxv. Suicide of Judas, xxvii. 3. Dream of Pilate's wife, and Pilate's hand-washing, xxvii. 19 f. Miracles at and after the death of Jesus, xxvii. 21 f. The guard set over the sepulchre, xxvii. 62 ff., xxviii. 11 ff. The opening of the grave by the angel, xxviii. 2 f. Appearance of Jesus to the two Maries, xxviii. 9 f. The parting command of Christ to the eleven, xxviii. 18 f.

(2) Matter peculiar to Luke:—

The stories of the Childhood, and the genealogy. The moral precepts of the Baptist, iii. 10 ff. Peculiar form of the Nazareth sermon, iv. 17 ff. Peter's draught of fishes, v. 4 ff. Woes against the rich, vi. 24 ff. Raising of the widow's son at Nain, vii. 11 ff. Anointing by the penitent woman, vii. 36 ff. Names of the women who ministered to Jesus, viii. 1 ff. Inhospitality of the Samaritan village and fiery zeal of the sons of Zebedee, ix. 51 ff. Mission of the Seventy, x. 1 ff. Report of their success, and Jesus' answer, x. 17 ff. Parable of the Good Samaritan, x. 30 ff. The incident of Martha and Mary, x. 38 ff. Parables inculcating persistent prayer, xi. 5 ff., xviii. 1 f. Pious enthusiasm and pious action, xi. 27 f. Refusal to arbitrate in a question of inheritance, and parable of the Rich Fool, xii. 13 ff. Parables of the reward of watchful and loyal servants, xii. 35 ff., 42 ff. Warning against self-satisfaction, and parable of the Barren Fig-tree, xiii. 1–9, 25 ff. Two cures upon the Sabbath, xiii. 10 ff. and xiv. 1 ff. Jesus warned against Herod, xiii. 31 ff. Discourse at the feast in the Pharisee's house, xiv. 7 ff. Parables about building a tower and commencing a campaign, xiv. 28 ff.; the Lost Piece of Silver and the Prodigal Son, xv. 8 ff., 12 ff.; the Unjust Steward, xvi. 1 ff.; Dives and Lazarus, xvi. 19 ff. Saying about fulfilment of duty without claiming reward, xvii. 7 ff. Healing of the ten lepers, xvii. 12 ff. The unperceived coming of the Kingdom of God, xvii. 20 f. Parable of the Pharisee and the Publican, xviii. 9 ff. Visit to the house of Zacchæus, xix. 1 ff. Jesus weeps over Jerusalem, xix. 41 ff. Sayings at the Last Supper, xxii. 15 f., 28–32, 35–38. Appearance of the angel in Gethsemane, xxii. 43. Trial before Herod, xxiii. 7 ff. Sayings on the way to Golgotha, xxiii. 27 ff. The words from the cross, xxiii. 34, 40–43, 46. Appearance to the disciples on the way to Emmaus, xxiv. 13 ff., and to the eleven at Jerusalem, xxiv. 36 ff.

How are we to explain the fact that alongside of so much that is common to both in the non-Marcan matter there is so much that is peculiar to each? It is hardly compatible with the use of one by the other. Least of all can we think of a use of Matthew by Luke. There is not one word in the Gospel of Luke which indicates dependence upon Matthew; in the parts common to both, the greater originality is almost always on the side of Luke, and even the proportionately rare exceptions can be explained by the independent, and in some cases less felicitous, handling of the source material by Luke, without any reference to Matthew. Moreover, an acquaintance with our Gospel of Matthew on the part of the author of the Gospel of Luke is excluded by his preface, which implies that among his many predecessors there had been no Apostle or eye-witness: all of them had received their knowledge at second-hand. That is incontestable evidence of the fact that at the beginning of the second century, when Luke wrote his Gospel, nothing was known of the Gospel of Matthew, any more than of that of John. In face of this authentic evidence, the legends of Church tradition regarding the Apostolic authorship of these Gospels have no claims to consideration. It would be much easier to think of Matthew's having used

Luke than of Luke's having used Matthew. I can, however, leave this question open the less reluctantly because in any case the Gospel of Matthew could not be explained as derived solely from Luke and Mark. The differences between Matthew and Luke in their common material, and especially in the matter peculiar to each, are much too considerable for that. There remains, therefore, no alternative but to assume another source besides Mark which was common to both.

What has been said above regarding this source in our discussion of Luke's Gospel (p. 284 f.) receives confirmation here, since the relation of Matthew to Luke can be most simply explained by means of the hypothesis that both have used, besides the Gospel of Mark, one or more of the Greek translations and redactions of the primitive Aramaic Gospel, while each has also used other sources in addition. From the original Aramaic Gospel, Mark, as we have found it to be probable, compiled his Greek Gospel, which accordingly betrays in its strongly Semitic style the most direct dependence on an Aramaic source. After him, many others (Luke i. 1) tried their hands at the translating and working up of this material, and by using their preparatory work Luke supplemented Mark and at the same time smoothed the latter's language into a more readable Greek, everywhere taking into account, as regards the subject-matter also, the interests and needs of his Greek readers. Meanwhile the use of these Gospels was confined to the Gentile-Christian churches of the West, while the Palestinian and Syrian churches continued to hold to the original Aramaic Gospel, expanding it, however, by the addition of legendary narratives or of discourses of Jesus drawn from the oral tradition current among them. Then, as these Jewish-Christian supplements to the original Gospel were translated for the use of the Greek-speaking Jewish Christians of Asia and Egypt, there arose that apocryphal Gospel literature which, according to the evidence of the Fathers, was widely circulated and used in the West during the second century under the titles Gospel of the Hebrews, Gospel of the Ebionites, Gospel of the Egyptians, Gospel of Peter. The more the breach was widened, however, between the Jewish-Christian Gospel-making on the one hand and the Gentile-Christian (Mark and Luke) on the other, the more pressing became the need in the Church, which was now drawing together into a unity, for a harmonising Gospel which should lead the two streams of evangelical tradition, which had hitherto followed separate courses, into a common channel, and should take from each what was best, that is to say, what was most useful to the Church, and omit what was less important or less useful.

Out of this need for an ecclesiastical combination of the Gospel-making activities which had hitherto taken different directions among the Gentile and Jewish Christians, there finally arose our Gospel of Matthew. To this is due its constant vacillation from one side to the other, even to the very style, which is less Greek than Luke and less Semitic than Mark, while of its quotations from the Old Testament some follow the LXX and some the original Hebrew. To this is due also, in its subject-matter, its affinity with Mark and Luke in the most outspoken universalism, and, on the other hand, with the Gospel of the Hebrews in its ingenuous preservation of many conservative traits of legalism and particularism which were found in the latter, and also of many legends of obviously Jewish origin. For this very reason—because, namely, it was specially adapted to meet the general needs of the Church—it naturally became at once the favourite Gospel of the Church. Here the Church found what belonged to each of its separate tendencies united in one, their inconvenient extravagances skilfully removed; in particular, the stormy and revolutionary character of early Christian enthusiasm and socialism was moderated to the proper mean of ecclesiastical practicability, in such a way that it no longer presented itself as a danger to the position of an organised Church which was now coming into amicable relations with ordinary social life. In this way is to be explained the combination in this Gospel of the earliest with the latest, of narrow with broad, of legal and spiritual, of Jewish and universalistic; it has not, in fact, been composed as a unity by a single author; many different hands, nay, many generations of early Christianity, have laboured at it; it has grown out of the primitive Gospel by a very complicated process of transformation, expansion, modification, and combination; it has grown up with and out of the Church. When and whence it acquired the title "According to Matthew" we do not know. It is possible that the Aramaic Gospel had already been brought into some kind of connection with the Apostle of this name, and that this was the basis of the claim which Jerome mentions as being made by the Palestinian

Jewish-Christians that their "Gospel according to the Hebrews" was the original of the canonical Matthew.[1] If this were the case, an ecclesiastical Gospel which combined the Jewish-Christian Gospel tradition of the East with the Gentile-Christian Gospel tradition of the West into a single whole might be called the "Gospel according to Matthew" with as good right as the third Gospel was called by Luke's name because the author had used Lucan traditions as sources. But it is also possible that, without any historical ground, the Church, which, according to the custom of the time, wanted an Apostolical authority for the harmonising presentation of the Gospel story which had only come to maturity comparatively late, affixed the name of Matthew as that of the Apostle who, from his previous occupation as a tax-collector, might be considered the most likely to be skilful with the pen. The earliest mention of the Gospel under his name occurs in the statement of Papias discussed above, which dates from the middle of the second century. The earliest "quotations" (Ignatius, Justin) are so inexact that it is impossible to tell whether they were taken from the canonical Matthew itself or from some apocryphal Gospel which preceded it or circulated alongside of it. The latter is the more probable.

[1] That it was not really so, but a collateral branch from the parent stem of the original Aramaic Gospel, will be shown later.

THE PREACHING OF JESUS AND THE FAITH OF THE FIRST DISCIPLES

CHAPTER XV

THE PROCLAMATION OF THE APPROACHING REIGN OF GOD

ACCORDING to Mark i. 15, Jesus began His ministry with the proclamation, "The time is fulfilled, the kingdom [reign] of God is at hand; repent ye, and believe the gospel." The content of His preaching is still more simply summarised in Matthew (iv. 17): "Repent, for the kingdom of the heavens is at hand." This expression, which Matthew uses almost uniformly instead of the "kingdom of God" which is customary elsewhere, has in essence exactly the same signification; it is the literal translation of the Jewish expression *Malkuth Shamayim* (Heb.) or *Malkutha Dishmaya* (Aram.), in which "Heaven" is only the then customary paraphrase for the name "God."[1] By this is meant, not a territory which has its locality or origin in heaven, but a "reign" of God who dwells in heaven—the rule which He, exalted above

[1] As the chief experts in Jewish theology, Dalman (*Worte Jesu*, pp. 75 ff. = E.T. 91 ff.) and Schürer (*NTliche Zeitgeschichte*, ii. 453 f. = E.T. ii. 2. 170), are agreed in this interpretation, it is to be preferred to the local interpretation, which is also possible, "the Kingdom which is coming from heaven."

the world, exercises over the world, and which His saints are to experience in a corresponding condition of happiness. As modern ideas are apt to associate themselves with the words "Kingdom of God" and confuse its original sense, it seems advisable to use instead the more exact rendering "Reign of God" (*Gottesherrschaft*).

If the traditional opinion were correct, that Jesus meant by the Kingdom of God, of which He proclaimed the approach, something entirely different from that which was understood by the Jews of His time, it would be natural to expect that He would explain exactly the new sense which He was giving to the old name, in order to obviate any misunderstanding of the meaning of His proclamation that the expected Kingdom was at hand. But neither Jesus nor John the Baptist, who already before Him had made the same proclamation (Matt. iii. 2), found it necessary to give such a definition, explanation, or correction of the meaning of the Reign of God. We have therefore no right to assume that they attached to the term a different connotation from that which was generally current among their nation. That Jahweh was the King of Israel is one of the oldest ideas of the Israelitish religion; for it was based upon the belief that Israel was the people of Jahweh, and Jahweh the God and King of Israel. In pre-Exilic times the exercise of this Divine Kingship was seen in the earthly rule of the Davidic kings, who, as the instruments of the Divine King, are called His "sons" (2 Sam. vii., Ps. ii., etc.). The well-being of the nation, its power in the world and its happy internal condition, such as obtained under the rule of David, seemed to later times to represent the realised ideal of the Reign of God in Israel. As later times always fell more or less short of this ideal, the prophets hoped for a better future, in which such a condition of Israel as seemed to be demanded by the idea of the Reign of God should come to realisation. And so long as the Davidic kingdom still stood, the realisation of the full ideal of the Reign of God might be conceived as about to be effected in the historical course of events, by a favourable turn of political affairs under the Divine guidance. Things were changed, however, in post-Exilic times, when the Jewish state passed from the domination of one foreign power to that of another, and still more so when the heathen power began to lay hands upon the most sacred possession of the Jewish people—its religion. From that time forward the actual state of things appeared to a seer like the author of the Book of Daniel so full of gloom that he could see in it only the direct opposite of the Reign of God—only the increasing hostility of the world-powers against God and His Kingdom. The Reign of God seemed to have withdrawn itself more or less completely into heaven, and to have abandoned the world to the hostile powers. But only until a fixed and not very distant period; then, so it was hoped, the present godless era would come to an end, and a new era would be miraculously introduced by God; the world-powers would fall, and the Reign of God would be made manifest from heaven, represented by the victorious rule of "the saints of the Most High," *i.e.* the Jews. This expectation—resting on a pessimistic estimate of the present and a dualistic background[1]—of a sudden introduction of the Reign of God by a miraculous catastrophe which should bring to an end the present world-era (æon) and open a new one, remained thenceforward the ruling temper and attitude of mind in the apocalyptic circles of Judaism. It was no longer from the world, and from the natural development of events, but only as a miracle of Omnipotence, issuing from above, that the promised deliverance from the present utterly corrupt condition of things could be hoped for. Thus, for example, the Aramaic prayer of Kaddish, which goes back to a remote period, closes with the words, "Exalted and glorified be His great name in the world which He has made according to His will. May He establish His kingship (and may His salvation put forth its blossom, and may His Messiah come near and deliver His people) in your lifetimes and in the lifetime of the whole house of Israel, speedily and soon!" The bracketed words are a later addition, but give a quite correct explanation of the sense which the author of the prayer attached to the establishment of the Kingdom of God, the redemption of Israel by the coming Messiah. In the "Midrash" on the Song of Solomon (ii. 12) we have the words, "The time is at hand for the Reign of God to be manifested"; and it is to take

1 Wellhausen and J. Weiss have rightly indicated the dualism of the Iranian religion as at least a contributory factor in throwing the apocalyptic hopes, since the time of Daniel, into a transcendental form. According to Dalman also (*Worte Jesu*, p. 124 = E.T. 152), the conception of the "age" = æon was introduced into Jewish thinking from Greek thought either directly or through the intermediacy of the Syrians; but the sharp antithesis of the future and the present æon is not of Greek but of Persian origin.

the place of the "Reign of Iniquity" (the world-power which is hostile to God), which is destined to destruction. Especially instructive is the apocalypse known as the Assumption of Moses, which probably originated shortly before our era,[1] where, in chapter x., it is said: "Then shall His [God's] rule appear over all His creatures, then shall the Devil be no more, and with him shall misery come to an end. The Heavenly One shall rise up from His throne and go forth from His holy dwelling in indignation and wrath because of His children. The Highest, the alone eternal God, shall visibly come forth in order to punish the heathen and destroy all their idols. Then shalt thou be happy, O Israel, and mount up on eagles' wings and look down upon thine enemies upon the earth." The conception of the seer appears to be that, up to the present, the Devil reigns upon earth and ill-treats the children of God, *i.e.* the Jews, but that in the immediate future, God, incensed at this, shall rise up out of His calm, come forth in His might, seize the reins of power, make an end of the Devil, punish the heathen, and exalt Israel to victory and happiness. This was the hope cherished at the time of the birth of Jesus in the circles of the "quiet in the land," who belonged neither to the Pharisaic party nor to the sect of the Essenes, but shared with the former their ardent Messianic hopes, and with the latter the inwardness of a pure and world-renouncing morality, who hoped not merely for the deliverance of Israel from external enemies, but also for the deliverance of the pious poor from the yoke of those proud and

[1] According to Clemen, in Kautzsch's *Pseudepigraphien des Alten Testaments.*

"ungodly" men who, under the cloak of an outward (legal) righteousness, gave themselves up to avarice, self-indulgence, and contentiousness.[1]

Now if, as we may with the greatest probability assume, it was just from this section of the Judaism of the time that both Jesus and John the Baptist sprang, everything suggests that they both shared the view which was cherished in those circles regarding the Reign of God which should bring deliverance. And this supposition finds an unmistakable confirmation in the testimony of our Gospels, which prove that "*for Jesus the Reign of God is always an eschatological conception*, and can only be spoken of as present because the end is already drawing near" (Dalman). If that is overlooked, and what was eschatological, apocalyptic, catastrophic, in Jesus' expectation of the Kingdom is subordinated to our modern ethical, evolutionary, philosophic conception of the Kingdom of God, the inevitable consequence is that the heroic enthusiasm of Jesus, which had its roots in these apocalyptic expectations, which inspired His actions, and which was the cause of His sufferings as well as of His successes, fails to be understood, and what is most characteristic in His mighty appearance on the field of history is painted over with an ideal picture of universal humanity until it becomes

[1] *Cf.* the polemic in Assumption of Moses vii. with the complaints in Enoch xciv.–civ., and with both Luke i. 51 ff., vi. 20–26, and Matt. xxiii. An interesting, if perhaps rather idealised, picture of these "quiet in the land" has been drawn by Cremer (*Paulin. Rechtfertigungslehre*, pp. 140–159). But I can scarcely admit that the antithesis which he there constructs between their attitude and that of the apocryphal and apocalyptic literature of the Judaism of the time is justified.

unrecognisable. Examples of this are found everywhere in the "Life of Jesus" literature; for the last decade, however, a wholesome reaction has set in in the direction of a strictly historical conception, which has, however, not yet been carried to its logical issue.[1]

In face of rationalising attempts to emphasise occasional sayings of Jesus which seem to indicate the actual presence of the Kingdom in such a way as to make it appear that this was the real meaning of Jesus in contrast to the Baptist and the Jews, it must, as Weiss rightly remarks, be emphasised once more that "the proclamation of the *coming* Kingdom is the normal, the sayings which speak of it as though it were present are exceptional. It is not only in point of numbers that the sayings which refer it to the future are predominant, they are also the most important in point of content. The fundamental character of the preaching of Jesus is, in point of fact, prophetic; its key-note is hope—hope, no doubt, which is certain of its goal, but, after all, simply hope." As Jesus from His first appearance repeated the Baptist's prophecy of the near approach of the Reign of God, so, later, when He sent forth His disciples, He charged them to proclaim, not the presence, but the approach, of the Reign of God (Luke x. 9, 11). He taught His disciples to pray, "Thy Kingdom come," which certainly implies

[1] Out of the very numerous treatises and monographs of this character I may single out as especially worthy of attention J. Weiss's *Predigt Jesu v. Reich Gottes* and Georg Schnederman's *Jesu Verkündigung und Lehre vom Reich Gottes*, and the relevant section in Dalman's *Worte Jesu*.

that it has not yet come. In the beatitudes of the Sermon on the Mount, or Sermon on the Plain (Luke vi. 20 ff.), He explains the promise to the poor that the Kingdom of God "is" theirs, by using the future tense in the sayings which follow: those who now hunger and mourn shall be satisfied, shall laugh for joy, namely, at the coming of the Reign of God, which shall introduce a new order of all things for the benefit of the saints who now suffer under the injustice of the world; they are pronounced blessed not because of what they now are, not because of the excellence of their inward character, or of the religious advantages which they now possess, but entirely because of the future happiness which they have reason to hope for in the near future from a manifestation of the power of God, who shall redress the injustices of the present. It was Matthew who first, from the point of view of altered circumstances and ecclesiastical interests, obscured and spiritualised the clear sense of the original Lucan beatitudes in such a way that we can certainly find in his beatitudes the thought of the inner blessedness which is now received by the spiritually poor, the humble and meek, the pure in heart, the merciful, and those who hunger after righteousness; yet even here, in the promise that the meek shall inherit the land, the original eschatological sense shows through clearly enough. And how could one fail to recognise this sense in that word of encouragement to the "little flock," "Fear not, it is your Father's good pleasure to give you the kingship" (Luke xii. 32)? This promise is repeated in a fuller form at the Last Supper: "As my Father has appointed unto me a kingship, so I appoint unto you, that ye may eat and drink at my table under my kingly rule, and sit on thrones judging the twelve tribes of Israel" (Luke xxii. 29 = Matt. xix. 28). In the same context is found also the noteworthy saying, "I will drink no more of the fruit of the vine until the reign of God be come" (Luke xxii. 18 = Mark xiv. 25: "until the day when I shall drink it new under the reign of God"). In the passages which have just been quoted we can hardly think of anything else than the approaching introduction upon earth by the intervention of the Divine power of a new order of things, in the interest of Jesus and His disciples—an era which, in spite of its being completely "new," is not to be thought of as so diverse from the present that there will not be eating and drinking in it. To force upon these words a reference to blessedness in another world is an entirely arbitrary proceeding. If we take into account also the question which Acts (i. 6) represents the disciples before the Ascension as addressing to their departing Master, "Wilt thou at this time restore the kingdom to Israel?" we may rightly see in this a true expression of the fundamentally eschatological temper of mind of the primitive Church; but how could that have been possible if Jesus Himself had taught nothing of the kind, or, indeed, the direct opposite? "Jesus was too wise to have spoken in imagery which set in motion all the national hopes and passions, if He had actually meant something quite contrary to these; and the Gospels are not so untrustworthy as to have turned Jesus' teaching into its exact opposite" (Keim).

That the unanimous testimony of these quite unambiguous eschatological utterances regarding the Reign of God could be invalidated by isolated sayings of an opposite tenor is *a priori* improbable, and can, as a matter of fact, be shown, by a careful examination of these alleged instances to the contrary, to be a mistake. The leading instance in favour of a present inward and spiritual Kingdom of God is, of course, Luke xvii. 20 f.: "The kingdom of God cometh not with observation; they shall not say, Lo here! or, Lo there! for, behold, the kingdom of God is within you." Now we have seen above (p. 167) that this saying is in flagrant contradiction with what follows, where the sudden, catastrophic, startling coming of the Messianic era is expressed with the utmost possible definiteness. Now as it is impossible that Jesus can have given in one breath such contradictory teaching, there remains only a choice between two hypotheses: either the saying had in its original form a wholly different sense, the exact opposite of that given above, a point on which the experts in Aramaic are not at present agreed; or (as is more probable) the saying was freely invented by the Evangelist, in consequence of the Pauline and Johannine spiritualisation of the primitive Christian idea of the Kingdom (*cf.* Rom. xiv. 17, John xviii. 36), and inserted in this passage in order to put a timely check upon the too ardent apocalyptic expectations to which the following sayings seemed to give too much countenance. In either case, Luke xvii. 20 f. can no longer be quoted as an argument against the eschatological sense of the "Reign of God"; on the contrary, the continuation of this passage (22–37) offers the strongest evidence in favour of this sense.

Again, in the saying of Jesus when defending Himself against the charge of being in league with Beelzebub (Luke xi. 20 = Matt. xii. 28) some have found a proof that Jesus had drawn from the success of His healing power over the demoniacs the conviction that the Reign of God had not only come nigh (ἤγγικεν), but actually arrived (ἔφθασεν), and was a present reality. But if we consider that immediately before the disciples had been commissioned to preach that the Reign of God was at hand (Luke x. 9, 11: ἤγγικεν ἐφ' ὑμᾶς), it appears very doubtful whether the Evangelist really meant, in altering the expression in xi. 20, to alter the thought in this way, or whether it was merely that the same word in the Aramaic source chanced to be translated in two different ways. Yet even assuming that the "coming" (ἔφθασεν) in xi. 20 really meant something more than the "coming nigh" (ἤγγικεν) which is elsewhere usual, it does not by any means follow from that that the thought of a present and inward Kingdom of God has been put in the place of the eschatological hope, which before as well as after, and up to the end of the Gospel, remains the ruling idea. It is not to be doubted that Jesus did see in the frequent success of His cures of demoniacs a sign and guarantee of the fact that the rule of Satan and his demons was coming to an end; that God was about to grasp the reins of government and exhibit His victorious might; that therefore the end of the old and the beginning of the new era was coming to pass. But "one swallow does not make a summer," even though it be welcomed as the harbinger of its approach; between isolated victories of the Divine spiritual power over diseases caused by demons and the realisation of the Reign of God in the redemption and renewing of the whole life of the nation there is, after all, a great difference. And since it was the latter and not the former which was the object of the hopes of all, therefore what Jesus preached from first to last was only the promise of an approaching eschatological good, which was to be brought about by a miraculous intervention of Divine power, not instruction about an already present social life of a moral and spiritual order which was to be "developed" by human effort. The difference in kind between these two views is too great to admit of their being reconciled by means of any kind of logical or psychological dialectic; it must simply be recognised as an historical fact and understood as the expression of the difference between the systems of thought of two different periods, between which lies a development of nearly two thousand years. But, as we know from experience, nothing contributes so much to make the understanding of this historical development of Christian thought difficult and obscure as the traditional habit of carrying back our modern ideas into the entirely different world of the faith and hope of Jesus and His contemporaries.

But, people ask, did not Jesus Himself teach an inner "development" of the Kingdom of God in the parables of the Sower, the Seed Growing Secretly, the Tares among the Wheat? This objection is only of weight so long as the parables are taken for allegories in which every single trait must have a symbolical meaning. But the parables, as has been generally recognised since B. Weiss and Jülicher, are no complex allegories, but simply aim at illustrating simple religious truths by means of familiar circumstances of daily life. Thus, even the parables about the seed do not, as we saw above (p. 16 f.), unveil doctrinal mysteries regarding the spiritual nature of the King-of God, but illustrate for the use and edification of those who look anxiously for the coming of the Reign of God, the practical truth that this coming cannot be forced or hastened by human interference; it can only be prepared for by the proclamation of the good tidings, but whether, and how far, this shall be followed by results, and how quickly or slowly the seed shall ripen to harvest, does not depend on our labour or anxiety; therefore we must wait patiently until God's time and hour comes. And we are not to be discouraged by the still imperceptible beginnings of the result of the preaching, nor by the, in some cases, unserviceable or unreliable character of the multitudes who flock to hear it: all these defects of the present time of preparation will disappear with the coming of the great day of the consummation of all things.[1] If we follow this principle of not allegorising in the interpretation of the parables about the seed, we find indeed present and future, preparation and fulfilment, seed and harvest more closely connected than elsewhere; but they do not on that account by any means fall out of the frame of the eschatological preaching of Jesus regarding the Kingdom. In particular, the modern thought that the Kingdom is already present in the ethical

[1] *Cf.* Jülicher, *Gleichnisse Jesu,* ii. 581; J. Weiss, *Predigt vom Reich Gottes,* 2nd ed., pp. 84 f.; Weinel, *Die Bildersprache Jesu,* pp. 22 f. and 44 ff.

ideals of human society, and is to be further "developed" by its moral action, is wholly foreign, nay opposed, to them. Its coming is still future, in the day of the harvest; and the harvest cannot be brought about by human effort, but can only be waited for with patience.

It is no less mistaken to draw from the parables of the Hidden Treasure and the Pearl of Great Price the thought that the Kingdom of God is to be won by some pious sacrifice, and is therefore an already present condition of blessedness consisting of forgiveness of sins, peace, and fellowship with God. These parables really embody only the practical lesson that we should stake everything, and shun no sacrifice, in order to win the supreme good of sharing in the blessings of the Reign of God; but of what this good consists, or when and how it comes, they do not say. But of this we are informed with all the clearness we can desire by the saying, "Everyone who has left houses, or brethren, or sisters, or father, or mother, or children, or lands, for my name's sake, shall receive manifold compensation and inherit eternal life" (Matt. xix. 29 = Mark x. 30, according to Cod. D; *cf.* above, p. 48 f.). That which is to be won, the good which is to be purchased by the sacrifice of self and the renunciation of the world, does not, according to this, consist in a present inward condition of mind, but in the future abundant reward and compensation which the Reign of God shall bring about at the renewal of all things (παλινγενεσίᾳ, verse 28). Only in so far as the *hope* of this future reward gives already in the present a certain foretaste of it, can it be said that the preaching of the Kingdom offers a present blessing; but in so far as hope is not identical with the thing hoped for (Rom. viii. 24), in so far the essence of the evangelical Kingdom of God does not consist in the present "religious blessedness." And still less does it consist in the present "ethical good," the virtuous frame of mind and conduct, as has been erroneously concluded from Matt. vi. 33. Righteousness, in the sense of human virtue, is, according to Matt. v. 20, the *condition* of entering into the blessedness brought about by the Reign of God; how then could it be identical with the latter? Rather, it is divided from it *toto cælo*; for it is human action, and the Reign of God is Divine action. Moreover, in Matt. vi. 33 there is no direct reference to the human virtue of righteousness; what is said is that the highest aim of our efforts should be the reign and the righteousness *of God.* These two terms, God's reign and God's righteousness, are exact correlates. The former describes the Divine rule and the resulting condition of the saints, their salvation and partaking in eternal life; the latter describes the Divine judgment and the resulting condition of the saints, their acquittal and their claim to eternal life. This partaking in the life of the Kingdom of God is conditional upon the sentence of God as Judge, declaring the saint to be righteous and worthy of entrance into life. To be recognised as righteous by God's judgment should therefore be the first care of men; the means to this is, of course, ethical righteousness of thought and life, change of heart, doing of the will of God (v. 20, vii. 21), of which we shall have more to say later. If, therefore, this moral conduct on man's part is the condition of the Divine recognition of his righteousness, and that in turn is the condition of his partaking in eternal life under the Reign of God, it is no doubt possible to say that the partaking of the individual in the blessedness of the Reign of God is bound up with his righteousness as an indispensable condition; but it is not possible to say that the Reign of God is brought about by the righteousness of men, still less that it essentially consists in the right conduct of men. In face of all such modernising interpretations, whatever confirmation they may have in present-day theological and ethical doctrine, the exegete and historian must insist that in the preaching of Jesus the Reign of God is always and exclusively an eschatological conception.

If we inquire, further, how Jesus thought of the realisation of the Reign of God in detail, we must be careful not to ascribe to Him an exact and rigidly defined programme of the future. This He had not, any more than His Jewish fellow-countrymen and contemporaries.[1] The same vacillation which runs through Jewish eschatology, between earthly and heavenly, material and spiritual, pictures of the future—a consequence of the intermixture of Hellenistic with ancient Jewish modes of thought—is found also in the Gospel pictures of the "last things." In addition to this uncertainty which is founded in the nature of the case, there is another source of uncertainty in the fact that we cannot

[1] Schürer (*NTliche, Zeitgeschichte,* ii. 440 ff. = E.T. ii. 2. 154 ff.) gives an instructive summary of "Messianic Doctrine" according to the Apoc. Baruch and 2 Esdras, but indicates that there was much uncertainty in regard to the details.

always definitely distinguish between elements which represent the eschatological beliefs of the primitive community, or of the Evangelists, and those which are derived from Jesus Himself. To the former doubtless belong (*cf.* above, p. 35 f., and further remarks below) the prophecies of the coming of the Son of Man, and the description of the afflictions which should precede the Messianic period in the apocalyptic discourse Mark xiii = Matt. xxiv = Luke xxi. But, at the same time, there are a few leading points which may be signalised as certainly belonging to the preaching of Jesus.

In the first place, as we have already seen, the Reign of God, or future age, will begin soon and suddenly, its appearing being visible to all. It will be a crisis, a terrible shattering and reversal of the present condition of the world, only comparable to such catastrophes as the Flood, or the rain of brimstone upon Sodom and Gomorrah (Luke xvii. 22 ff.). How soon this catastrophe shall occur is not more closely defined. On one occasion it is said that some of "those which stand here" shall see the Reign of God come with power (Mark ix. 1 = Matt. xvi. 28: "until they see the Son of man coming in his kingdom.") According to Matt. x. 23, the disciples will not have finished preaching the gospel in the cities of Israel before the Son of Man comes. In both passages, therefore, the time is fixed for the appearing of the Reign of God and of the Messiah within the lifetime of the generation of Jesus' contemporaries; even if the form of this prediction is secondary in Matthew, there is nothing against its genuineness in Mark. The suggestion has been made that later on, influenced by His disappointment at the dulness of the people, Jesus no longer expected so early a fulfilment of His hopes. Certainly a hesitation on this point corresponding to the changing experiences and circumstances of the Prophet would be intelligible enough. But there is much which tends rather to suggest that towards the close of His Galilæan period, and in Jerusalem, He even thought of the decisive moment as very much nearer than before.

That the Reign of God would be introduced by a great Day of Judgment was a standing assumption of the prophets, which uniformly prevails in Jewish apocalyptic also, sometimes in the form that the judgment of hostile world-powers and apostate Israelites shall be held by God Himself, before the coming of the Messiah (Enoch xc.), or without any reference to His coming (Assumption of Moses x.), sometimes in the form that Messiah, immediately upon His appearance, shall destroy the enemies of the people of God, whether by His might as a Warrior or by His sentence as Judge ("by the word of His mouth," Psalms of Solomon xvii.; similarly, 2 Esdras and the Similitudes of Enoch). The preaching of John the Baptist, too, proclaimed this approaching Judgment, but not as exercised upon the heathen nations while sparing the children of Abraham; on the contrary, at the Messianic assize it would profit a man nothing merely to be a child of Abraham unless he repented and brought forth the corresponding fruit of good actions. Here, therefore, in contrast to the usual Jewish hopes of national triumph, we have, as the principal point, the moral responsibility of individuals. And the same thing is found in the preaching of Jesus. At the threshold of the Reign of God stands the Judgment; not conceived, however, as the punishment of the heathen nations, but as the decision of the future fate of each individual, whether he should enter into life or be cast into hell, into darkness. "The Judgment thus acquires a quite different sense and a quite different result, coming to signify the rendering of one's personal account before God" (Wellhausen). It is not an exercise of God's power against the heathen, but the moral value of each individual life, which shall be made manifest. Prayers offered in secret, and quiet, unboastful beneficence, shall be openly rewarded by the Father in heaven, the faithful labourer shall enter into the joy of his Lord; but proud and self-satisfied sinners, the unmerciful and unforgiving, those who say "Lord! Lord!" but do not do the will of God, shall be excluded from the fellowship of the blessed; judgment shall separate the wheat from the tares, the good from the bad, consummating and making manifest distinctions which are already present in the moral character of individuals (Mark ix. 43 ff.; Matt. vi. 4–18, vii. 21 ff., x. 28, xiii. 41 ff., xviii. 34 f., xxv. 21–30, 31–46). There is some obscurity as to the relation of this future decisive separation to the division and reward which happens immediately after death. When the rich man in the parable (Luke xvi. 22 f.) goes immediately after death to the place of torment, and Lazarus to Abraham's bosom, or when the promise is given to the thief on the cross that he shall that day be with Jesus in Paradise (Luke xxiii. 43), that does not seem to refer to a merely provisional intermediate state, but to a definitive condition of blessedness or unblessedness. But if so, what place is there for the future judgment or for the future resurrection? However, both these passages, which are peculiar to Luke, are probably of secondary origin.

Jesus was at one with the Pharisees in teaching the resurrection of the dead, and defended it against the doubts of the Sadducees, appealing to Scripture and the Divine omnipotence (Mark xii. 24 ff.). The penetrating interpretation of the formula "the God of Abraham, Isaac, and Jacob," to the effect that God was not the God of the dead but of the living, would in itself prove rather the continued life of immortal souls as taught by the Essenes than the bodily resurrection of the dead. But Jesus spoke too clearly of a future resurrection of the dead to allow us to ascribe to Him the Hellenistic or Essene doctrine of immortality. It remains problematical in what form Jesus thought of the resurrection; whether as a restoration of the former earthly body, or the clothing of the soul in a higher super-earthly corporeity. A statement which appears to favour the latter view is, "When they shall arise from the dead, they shall neither marry nor give in marriage, but shall be as the angels in heaven" (Mark xii. 25), if this be understood to imply an angelic corporeity and not simply resemblance to the angels in the absence of marrying and giving in marriage. The other view is favoured by the presupposition that the risen patriarchs shall eat at the Messianic feast, which can hardly be understood in a non-literal sense, and that in general the scene of the Messianic glory and of the Kingdom of God is not the heavens above but the earth, more especially the land of Canaan; how super-earthly bodies are to be adapted to this earthly dwelling-place it is difficult to conceive. Further, it is not clear whether the resurrection is to be thought of as a universal resurrection before the Judgment and for the purpose of being judged, or only as the resurrection of the righteous to share in the Messianic glory? The latter is clearly implied in the Lucan version: "Those who shall be accounted worthy to obtain that world and the resurrection of the dead" (Luke xx. 35). The former, on the other hand, seems to be assumed in Matt. xii. 41, where it is said of the men of Nineveh in Jonah's day, that at the Judgment they shall rise up against this generation and condemn it; but in the Aramaic original the sense of this saying was probably only that if the men of Nineveh were to contend in judgment with this generation they would be victorious, *i.e.* that they were more righteous before God than the Jews, which does not necessarily imply a reference to the future Judgment (*cf.* Wellhausen, *Skizzen und Vorarbeiten*, vi. 188).

The condition of happiness under the Reign of God, to which the saints are to be admitted on the ground of the Judgment (while the godless are to be excluded from it and cast into outer darkness, or into the fire of Gehenna), is summed up in the conceptions Life and Joy. To enter into life, or eternal life, to receive it or inherit it, is equivalent to entering into, or inheriting, the blessings of the Reign of God. Since the future age will be of unending duration, life in it will be eternal, and to obtain it is to be delivered from destruction, from corruption. As regards the more detailed imagination of this eternal life, or life of partaking in [the blessings of] the Reign of God, Jesus simply shared the hopes current among the Jews of His time. As against the theological tendency to spiritualise the conception, Dalman is doubtless right in remarking, "Nor is there any call for peculiar speculations in regard to the conception of 'the life' as being . . . 'the sum total of all that constitutes life in its fullest sense—the true life.' The difference between the preaching of Jesus and Jewish views consists, not in the idea of 'the life,' but in what Jesus has to say of the theocracy (*Gottesherrschaft*) and of the righteousness without which life in the theocracy can never be attained" (*Worte Jesu*, p. 132 = E.T. 162). Naturally, it consists in a condition of perfect happiness, of complete joy and satisfaction. Therefore the loyal servant has held out to him as his reward the prospect of entering into the "joy of his Lord" (Matt. xxv. 21). Frequently this joy is represented as a partaking in the Messianic feast, the guest at which shall sit at meat with the patriarchs, or eat and drink at Christ's table (Matt. viii. 11; Luke xiii. 29, xxii. 30). Now as that is certainly not to be thought of as a mere figure,[1] and as the scene of this festal joy is

[1] Dalman, *ut sup.*, p. 81 (= E.T. 111): "Even for Jesus, this repast was no mere figure of speech." Joh. Weiss (*ut sup.*, p. 120) considers the arguments for the figurative interpretation of this conception "extraordinarily trivial"—meaning thereby, no doubt, superficial and untenable.

certainly the "land" of Canaan (Matt. v. 5; *cf.* Ps. xxxvii. 11, Enoch v. 7, xc. 20), Jesus seems to have thought of the condition of the partakers in the Reign of God, not as a supersensuous existence comparable to that of heavenly spiritual beings, but as an earthly existence raised to a higher power and freed from the evils of the present life. That was certainly the way in which the primitive community of His followers understood it, as may be concluded from the fact that they supposed the description which is found in Apoc. Baruch (xxix. 5) of the fabulous fruitfulness of field and vine (in the Messianic times) to be a prophecy of Jesus; and even though they were mistaken in this, the mistake would be unintelligible if Jesus had thought and taught the direct opposite—if He had represented the unending life under the Reign of God as completely freed from earthly conditions, and as the blessedness of heavenly spirits. This misunderstanding, which affects the whole conception of the Messianic movement, is based on the assumption that it is legitimate to carry back the later transcendental conception of "eternal life" into the older idea of the "future world" or period of Messianic salvation, whereas the latter, retaining the impress of its Old Testament origin, rests entirely on an earthly and realistic basis. It was this conflict of conceptions which, at a later period, led to the separation of this earthly Messianic time of salvation ("Days of the Messiah"), as a temporally-limited preliminary period, from the final heavenly consummation—the general resurrection and judgment of the world being placed between—and thus gave rise to the conception known as Chiliasm.[1] This was an expedient intended to reconcile the later transcendental view of "eternal life" with the view which came down from the prophets and was never given up either in Judaism or in early Christianity—the view of the Messianic time of salvation as of a life of blessedness under the Reign of God upon earth.

Only in one point have we hitherto found a material divergence between the hopes of the future cherished by Jesus and by the Jews: He makes no allusion to the victory of the Jewish nation over the heathen nations. This is certainly a difference of which the importance must not be underrated, but of which the true explanation can hardly be found in the traditional assumption that Jesus had separated the hoped-for Reign of God from any close connection with the Jewish people, and had thought of it as destined for all men. That is directly contradicted by the dialogue of Jesus with the Syrophœnician woman, in which He declared that He was only sent to the lost sheep of the house of Israel, and that it was not right to take the bread which was meant for the children of the house and give it to the dogs (heathen) (Matt. xv. 24 ff.). So, too, He commanded His disciples not to go into the "way of the Gentiles," nor to enter any city of the Samaritans, but only to the lost sheep of the house of Israel (Matt. x. 5). He never sought out the Gentiles; only when they came to Him unsought and asked His help did He, by way

[1] We shall recur later to this conception, which is found in the apocalypses of Ezra and Baruch and the canonical Revelation at the end of the first century.

of exception, answer their earnest petitions, as in the cases of the Syrophœnician woman and the centurion of Capernaum. When He expressed His joyful surprise at the faith of the latter (Matt. viii. 10), that only shows that He had not thought at all of the possibility of Gentiles believing. Matthew brings in here the saying which Luke inserts in another and no doubt a more correct connection (Luke xiii. 28 f. = Matt. viii. 11 f.): "Many shall come from the east and from the west and shall sit at meat with Abraham and Isaac and Jacob in the kingdom of heaven, but the children of the kingdom shall be cast out into outer darkness." That does not, after all, go beyond the expectation of the prophets that only a remnant of Israel should be saved, and that many Gentiles should come, along with this saved remnant, to pray at Zion; but the main stock of the people of God remains throughout always Israel, and its capital Jerusalem as the centre of its worship. This must have been Jesus' meaning too, when, at the Last Supper (according to Luke xxii. 29), He promised the Twelve that they should sit on thrones judging the Twelve Tribes of Israel, *i.e.* that they should have a share in His Messianic rule *over the people of Israel*; of a rule over the nations of the world there is, in the genuine sayings of Jesus, no mention. The passage about the Son of Man judging all the nations (Matt. xxv. 31 f.) does not come from Jesus but from the ecclesiastical Evangelist, as does the saying about preaching the gospel in the whole world (Matt. xxiv. 14) and the command to baptize all nations (xxviii. 18 f.), the origin of which from the later convictions of the Church is betrayed by the Trinitarian formula. The attitude of the older Apostles, too, towards the mission to the Gentiles is a sure sign that they knew nothing of any such command of Jesus. There are many traces in the version which the Evangelists give of the parables of Jesus that they had a tendency to put their own conviction of the universal destiny of Christianity into the mouth of Jesus (while in reality the thought of founding a new Church was foreign to His mind). Thus Luke in the parable of the Great Supper (xiv. 21 ff.), after the refusal of those who were first invited, represents two other invitations as being issued; not merely to the poor of the town, but also to those "in the highways and hedges," by which he doubtless meant the heathen. That is not found in Matthew; but, on the other hand, he has, in the parable of the Wicked Husbandmen (xxi. 43), the threat, "The kingdom of God shall be taken from you and given unto a people who shall bring forth the fruits thereof," by which the Evangelist doubtless means the Gentile Church. But in the parable in Mark (xii. 11) it is expressed in a still vaguer fashion: "He will take the vineyard [of the Israelitish theocracy] and give it unto others," by which is certainly meant not the Gentiles, but another section of the Jewish people, namely that "little flock" of the weary and heavy-laden, of the simple and poor, who, under the stress of deep poverty and religious neglect, longed for deliverance and eagerly accepted the message of Jesus; to them Jesus promised that His Father would give them the Kingship (Luke vi. 20, xii. 32; *cf.* x. 21). That means, "instead of a world-rule of the nation of Israel, a reign of these righteous men" (J. Weiss); instead of the national political ideal of the Pharisee, the socio-religious ideal of the "Quiet in the Land," the promise that the coming Reign of God would bring them deliverance from their present distress, comfort, joy, satisfaction, authority—these were the "glad tidings" that Jesus brought to the poor and to "sinners." The question regarding the relation of the Jews as a nation to the heathen nations was thus wholly relegated to the background—the subjugation of them by the Jews, which to the Pharisees was the main thing, never entered the mind of Jesus. One might, on the contrary, draw from the famous saying "Render unto Cæsar the things which are Cæsar's, and unto God the things which are God's" (Mark xii. 17), the conclusion that He held possible the continued existence of the outward political rule of the Romans alongside of the Reign of God, which should manifest itself in the establishment of new social and religious conditions within the nation. But about this we can have no certain knowledge; I hold it to be most probable that as regards these details of the realisation of the Reign of God Jesus did not form any exactly defined conception, but left the disposition of these matters in the hands of His God and Father.

"In all the points which have hitherto been discussed, Jesus did not come into any conflict with His nation as a whole—neither with the heads of it nor with the masses. No one, it is true, with the exception of the Baptist, had dared to go so far as Jesus had done. But it was possible for an Israelite to listen to Him, to let himself be led and carried away by Him, and look forward to the things which He was to bring, and yet remain all the time a thorough Israelite."[1] In fact, even the one point which we mentioned a moment ago in which Jesus was at variance with the Messianic expectations of the Pharisees, namely the subordination of the national, political side, was not wholly new, but corresponded to a certain under-current in the popular religion of the time, of which John the Baptist had already appeared as the spokesman, when he sharply attacked the racial arrogance of the Pharisees. If we ask, however, what it really was in Jesus' proclamation of the near approach of the Reign of God that was specially new and arresting, the answer can only be that it was not any kind of new content but *the new character of the preaching and the Preacher.* John had been a preacher of repentance, who, by proclaiming the nearness of the Judgment, sought to rouse, alarm, and sway the sinful masses—an endeavour with which his outward ascetic appearance was in keeping. But an ascetic is not a man of inspiration, and there is nothing inspiring in the preaching of penitence. It is therefore intelligible enough that no miracles are recorded of John, and that no legends of miracle gathered about his person; for that is always the expression of enthusiastic reverence on the part of the masses for a personality which powerfully lays hold upon them and fires their hearts and imaginations. This was the character of Jesus. He inspired others be-

[1] Schnedermann, *Jesu Verkündigung und Lehre vom Reich Gottes,* p. 127. How, out of this common ground of the Jewish idea of the Kingdom there grew up the opposition and the strife against the Pharisees, is excellently told by Schnedermann.

cause He was Himself inspired; He was a man of inspiration, of spiritual enthusiasm, whose preaching was not traditional scholasticism, and not the preaching of penitence, but good tidings of salvation for all who needed salvation. From His words, looks, and bearing men drew the impression that a higher, mysterious power worked in and through Him (Mark i. 27)—a Divine Spirit, as some felt; a demonic spirit, as others caluminously asserted—in any case, a wonderful power of touching hearts, of driving out evil spirits, of healing the body. Into the mystery of such a Spirit-filled Personality we can never, indeed, fully penetrate, because we can never wholly explain whence comes the Spirit, or how, or why (John iii. 8). Yet even here we may form some idea of the psychological conditions. The conviction inspired in Jesus by the Baptist of the near approach of the Reign of God did not give rise in His case to an awe-inspiring proclamation of judgment, but to a joyful proclamation of deliverance (Luke iv. 18); because He saw in the masses of His nation not so much guilt-laden sinners as a shepherdless flock, ill-treated and deserted, which was deserving of pity (Matt. ix. 36). With the eye of trustful love He recognised, beneath the obvious misery of the neglected religious condition, which stood in close causal connection with the miserable economic condition,[1] of the masses, a glimmering spark of pious hope and yearning after salvation and higher things—a spark

[1] On this, *cf.* Holtzmann, *NTliche Theologie,* i. 132 ff.; Joh. Weiss, *Predigt Jesu vom Reich Gottes,* 129 f.; Friedländer, *Zur Entstehungsgeschichte des Christentums,* 3rd Section, "Pharisäer und Amhaarez," pp. 37 f.

which must not be extinguished by arrogant exclusion and condemnation, but met with the tender succour of a seeking, merciful love. Therefore He did not separate Himself like the Pharisees from the masses, whom they despised as unclean (the *'am ha'arets*), nor retire like John to the desert and wait for the masses to come to Him, but Himself went to the people, sought them out in their synagogues on the Sabbath as well as at their work during the week, went into the houses that were open to Him, to the bedsides of the sick when His help was asked for, as well as to the guest-table at which the despised publicans sat. This welcoming love which sought and saved the lost was something new which had not been seen before, whether in the self-satisfied religious correctness of Pharisaism or in the anxious asceticism of the Essene order, or in the stern preacher of repentance, John the Baptist. It was a revival of the best spirit of the ancient prophets, of a Hosea or a Jeremiah; and yet different from theirs, because it had for background a different period—a time of feverish tension, in which despair of the present and expectation of the apocalyptic catastrophe had reached their highest point and had created the deepest unrest among the people. The union in the mind of Jesus of this glow of apocalyptic hope with the unfailing warmth and practical energy of pitying love to the poor, the distressed, the sinful, was the secret of the magical charm of His personality, of the enthusiam and heroism of His public life, of His irresistible influence over the masses, and of His power to attract and rivet the devotion of individuals, especially those of a gentle and sensitive nature: and it was that, too, which led to His collision with the ruling authorities both of His nation and of the foreign world-power—in short, it was the cause both of His success and of His fate.

It was not the proclamation of the approach of the Reign of God, in itself, which brought Jesus into conflict with the ruling party of the Pharisees, who shared the general Messianic hopes, and were not likely, in the early stages of Jesus' work, to notice the absence of the national, political element, and of enmity towards the heathen, from His teaching. But that Jesus should feel Himself urged by the impulse of merciful love towards the multitudes whom the Pharisees held to be "sinners," that is, profane people who did not keep the Law—that seemed to these legal zealots to be inconceivable and unpardonable in a prophet. When Jesus replied to these reproaches with the saying "They that are whole need not a physician, but they that are sick; I came not to call the righteous (to take part in the salvation which the Reign of God shall bring), but sinners" (Mark ii. 17), that seemed at first sight to imply the recognition of the righteousness of those who blamed Him; but on closer examination it contained the sharpest criticism on their kind of piety, and the denial of their conviction that the Messianic salvation was only destined for legally righteous people like themselves. But when Jesus further declared the forgiveness of the sins of the paralytic, in whose face He read humble penitence, the teachers of the Law found in this an encroachment upon the sovereign rights of God, who alone could forgive sins (Mark ii. 7). In truth, according to their opinion, God Himself could not forgive of free grace, but exacts the payment of every debt, or compensation for it in good works and expiatory suffering.[1] When Jesus, following the impulse of love, in which He recognised His divine authorisation, restored the soul of the penitent sinner, before healing his body, by the comforting word of forgiveness, His action was as certainly in full harmony with the religion of the prophets and the psalmists as it was completely opposed to the legal religion of the Pharisees. To this were soon added the various causes of offence which Jesus and His disciples gave to the legal zealots by their laxer observances of the Sabbath and their indifference in regard to the customary fastings and ceremonial purifications of the Pharisees. In the ensuing conflicts Jesus soon passed from defence to attack, which was finally intensified into a destructive criticism of the whole Pharisaic system of piety. In essence, all these conflicts turned on that opposition of spirit and letter which Paul afterwards carried to its logical issue in the sphere of dogma. This does not mean that Jesus went to the same lengths as Paul did in declaring the abrogation of the Mosaic Law—we shall see later how far He was from doing so—but by His zeal against the new-made ordinances of the Jewish Schools and the heartless fanaticism of the Pharisees He attacked in principle the legalistic spirit in religion. By His enthusiastic hope of the coming Reign of God, which should make all things new, He felt Himself raised above the pettinesses of the legalists who strained out gnats and swallowed camels; and His merciful love, combined with that boldness of genius which carries with it its

[1] Weber, *Altsynagogale palästinensische Theol.*, pp. 300 ff.

own justification, raised Him far above all the barriers which religious and social pride had set up. Thus from the combination of these two ruling motive-forces in the soul of Jesus there arose, by an inner necessity, the conflict of principle with Pharisaic Judaism, the tragic issue of which was to be the means to a fuller victory of His spirit than He Himself had ever expected.

THE PREACHING OF JESUS AND THE FAITH OF THE FIRST DISCIPLES

CHAPTER XVI

The Call to Repentance

"Repent, for the reign of God is at hand": that is the summary which the Evangelists give of the preaching of Jesus. The promise of a religious blessing, now nigh at hand, which should carry with it the highest happiness, was therefore the basis of this fundamental ethical demand of repentance. This basing of Jesus' ethical demands upon an ardent eschatological hope is to be noted as significant of the special character of His moral teaching; it was not derived from calm reflection on the conditions and needs of human nature and society, but from the enthusiasm of His faith in the approaching Day of God which shall make all things new and decide the fate of each individual for good or ill, for life or destruction. Since only those shall share in the blessings of the Reign of God who are pronounced "righteous" by the judgment of God, therefore the call to repentance is addressed to all. It is not merely gross sinners who are called on to turn from their evil way and give up their iniquities; even those who are counted righteous in their own eyes and in the eyes of the world are not "good" according to the standard and the judgment of God, who alone is truly good. For evil thoughts find a place in their hearts—evil passions, sinful lusts, earthly cares, and, as the worst despotism of all, the idolatry of "Mammon." A heart thus impure, oscillating between various interests, serving many masters at once, cannot please God, who desires to be loved with the whole heart and soul (Deut. vi. 5; Mark xii. 29). Therefore the natural mind, given up as it is to selfishness and worldly lusts, must change the direction which it has hitherto followed and give itself up to God without reserve; the heart must wrench itself free from the earth, in the perishable things of which it has hitherto found its treasure, in order to seek the Reign of God as the only true, or the highest (Matthew), good, and the righteousness of God, which is the sole condition of obtaining its blessings (Matt. vi. 33 = Luke xii. 31).

But that the righteousness which can be recognised by God as worthy to have a part in His Kingdom must be *better* than that of the Scribes and Pharisees, was, from the Sermon on the Mount onwards (Matt. v. 20), the constant theme of the moral preaching of Jesus. Wherein lay the distinction between righteousness, as Jesus understood it, and that of the Pharisees? The righteousness which Jesus demanded does not consist in the mere outward legality of what is done or not done, nor in the practice of good works done for appearance' sake, but in a purity and goodness of man's inmost spirit like to that of God. Not merely the deed of murder or adultery is guilty before God, but even the cherishing in the heart of the passion of anger, or revenge, or lustful desire. Alms-giving, prayer, and fasting are only valuable so far as they are the genuine expression of a corresponding attitude of mind and heart; if, on the other hand, they are mere external works (*opus operatum*), and seek honour from men in addition to merit before God, they have their reward in the former only. Similarly, Jesus condemns as mere hypocrisy the Pharisaic over-esteem for ritual correctness at the expense of moral duties; He frequently quotes the saying of Hosea, "I will have mercy, and not sacrifice"; He defends the doing of works of necessity and works of love upon the Sabbath, since the Sabbath was made for man, and not man for the Sabbath. Against the rigorous ordinances of purification insisted on by the teachers of the Law He utters a saying which logically carries with it the overthrow of legalism, viz. that external matters such as eating and drinking with unwashen hands do not defile a man, but only the sinful thoughts which proceed out of the heart. On the same occasion He reproaches the legalists because, while claiming to be defenders of the Law they rather make it of no effect by their "ordinances of men"—by teaching, for example, that the making of a gift to the Temple is a better thing than the fulfilment of duty towards parents (Mark vii. 6 ff.). In all this Jesus followed the footsteps of the ancient prophets, who emphasised, in contrast to the hypocritical religiosity of the popular worship, the true will of God as it is manifested in the fundamental order of human society and in the uncorrupted ethical consciousness.

But Jesus went beyond the prophets in teaching us to find an example and stimulus for our striving after true righteousness in God's fatherly love towards us. Of old, God had said to the people of Israel, "Be ye holy, for I am holy" (Levit. xi. 44), thus making the exaltation of Jahweh above the impure world the motive and example of Levitical holiness, that is, the separation of Israel from the heathen life of her neighbours. But now Jesus said, "Love your enemies, so shall ye be the children of the Highest, for he is kind to the unthankful and the evil. Be ye merciful as your Father is merciful" (Luke vi. 35 f. = Matt. v. 45 f.: "that ye may be the children of your Father in heaven; for he maketh his sun to shine upon the evil and upon the good, and sendeth his rain upon the just and upon the unjust. . . . So shall ye be perfect, as your Father in heaven is perfect"). The greatness of this saying is not diminished even if we must give up the traditional opinion that the application of the name Father to God by Jesus was a new thing. Even in the canonical Scriptures of the Old Testament, God is often called the Father of Israel,[1] and the Israelites are called His children —sometimes in reference to the relation of protection on the one side and defence on the other which subsists between God and His people, but sometimes also in the sense that God is the author of Israel's being, its creator. In the post-Exilic apocryphal writings, Father is used of the relationship of God to individual saints. Sirach calls God "the Father and Lord of my life" (xxiii. 1, 4, li. 10); the author of the Book of Wisdom calls not only the

[1] Deut. xiv. 1, xxxii. 5 f.; Hos. ii. 1; Isa. i. 4, xxx. 9, xliii. 6, xlv. 11, lxiii. 16, lxiv. 7; Jer. iii. 4, 14, 19, xxxi. 8, 20; Mal. ii. 10. *Cf.* Ps. ciii. 13.

people of Israel (xviii. 13) but also individual righteous men "sons" or "children" of God (Wisd. ii. 13, 18), and addresses God as Father (ii. 16, xiv. 3); so, in Tobit xiii. 4, God is called "Our Father," while in Enoch lxii. 11 and the Psalms of Solomon xvii. 30, pious Israelites are called "sons of God." Dalman quotes a number of sayings from the Rabbis of the early centuries of our era in which God is described as the "Heavenly Father," with the suggestion of a relationship of fatherly love and childlike trust. The designation "Our Father in Heaven" was, according to Dalman, "a popular substitute for the name of God, which was no longer used," and Jesus simply "adopted it from the popular usage of His time"; nor was it anything new in the Jewish religion for the Fatherhood of God to be spoken of in relation to individuals, and thought of as the ground of a pious trust in God.[1] It is the same here as with the conception of the Reign of God (*sup.*, p. 423): the content of the doctrine was not new; only the way in which Jesus preached and practically applied it. It was far from the mind of Jesus, as a true son of Israel, to proclaim a new God, in the sense in which Marcion thought He had put the loving Father-God in the place of the holy and righteous God of the Jews; Jesus, as well as the Jews, knew the God of judgment, who is to be feared more than men, because He can destroy both body and soul in hell,[2] and the Jews, on their part, were not un-

[1] Dalman, *Worte Jesu*, pp. 154 f. (=E.T. 188 f.).

[2] *Cf.* Cremer, *Paulin. Rechlfertigungslehre*, p. 231: "There is no suggestion of a new knowledge of God which had dawned on Jesus and was witnessed to by Him, by which God the Father was put in

acquainted with the thought of God as a merciful and loving Father.

The distinction, therefore, lay not so much in the conception of God in the one case and the other, as, rather, in the way in which feeling and will reacted upon that conception. In the case of the Jews, trust in the fatherly attitude of God could never attain all-pervading and dominant importance because the legal relation of king and subject, or master and servant, always formed the ruling centre of the national legal religion; for the mind of Jesus, on the other hand, it is precisely the fatherly goodness, which for others stood only alongside of, or behind, other attributes of God, which becomes the main point, the essential character, to which power and glory and righteousness are subordinated. And why is that? Manifestly because He could not help thinking of that which He recognised as highest in Himself as being also the highest in God, His essential being. His own heart, which, for all its purity and separateness from sin felt itself drawn out in tender pity and the saving energy of love towards the misery of sinners, was for Him the guarantee that this holy and saving love was also supreme in God. We may call this profound intuition of love which directly determined the content of His God-consciousness a religious "revelation," which, by arising in His heart, made Him the "First-born of the sons of God" (Rom. viii. 29), to whose likeness we are all to be conformed. But this

the place of God the Judge. On the contrary, just as the expectation of the Judgment cannot be dissociated from the idea of the *βασιλεία*, the Fatherhood by no means excludes the Judgment of God."

revelation need not be supposed to be a supernatural miracle, since it is just the outcome of the Divine endowment of reason which lies in our human nature, of that "Logos" which is "the light of men, which lighteneth every man" (John i. 4, 9). Because Jesus was merciful Himself, He thought of God as the merciful Father; and because He thought of God in this way He demanded of men that by becoming like God they should become true sons of God (Luke vi. 35 f.). Sonship to God is therefore, in the thought of Jesus, not a present reality, but an ideal standard; not a relationship of nature with God as the ground of our life which can be asserted of humanity as such, and which might serve as the presupposition of our moral effort, but a likeness of character to the perfect type of goodness which we see in God, and which every individual is to strive after by moral effort. From this there results an ambiguity in the thought of sonship to God similar to that which is found in Paul. In so far as it is an ideal which has still to be striven after—and that is for Jesus the leading thought—it is, strictly speaking, not yet actual, but has still to become so in the future. But, on the other hand, so far as it has not only its perfect type but also its basis and guarantee in the Father-will of God, he who believes in this fatherly will of God may feel himself even in the present a child of God—in process of becoming. Now the possibility of "becoming" implies a certain "being," and that not only on God's side but also on man's, and therefore the thought of sonship to God, in the sense of an ideal in process of realisation, needed the supplement which is supplied by the Pauline and Johannine teaching about the indwelling Spirit of God, which moreover only embodied in doctrinal form a truth which was given in Jesus' enthusiasm of faith and love as inner personal experience.

To the Father-will of God, in so far as it is the motive of the religious and ethical attitude of man, corresponds the twofold command to love God with the whole heart and our neighbour as ourselves. The first part is found in Deut. vi. 5 as the fundamental demand of monotheistic faith in God, the second in Levit. xix. 18 as the command to love one's fellow-countryman as oneself. Hillel had already extended this command to the love of mankind in general, and described this as the kernel, the quintessence of the whole Law. Here again, therefore, it has to be said that the content of the twofold command was not new, but Jesus' way of taking it in earnest certainly was so. In Judaism the higher insight of Hillel had not been able to produce its full effect, because not even this Pharisaic teacher himself, much less others, could get free from the fundamental mistake of all legalistic religion and morality, the splitting up of the Divine will into a number of positive commandments (the Pharisees counted 613) which at bottom were all equally obligatory because given by God; and the ritual ordinances, while theoretically at least of equal importance, were practically more important than the moral. It was this that condemned the religion and morality of Judaism to the torpor and externality which had begun in Pharisaism and was completed in Talmudism. Jesus broke the spell by the fact that He had not only theoretically recognised the love of God and our neighbour as the most important thing, but had practically experienced it as an overmasteringly powerful spiritual impulse, which raised Him far above all the pettinesses of the Scribes. And as for Him this experience united the love of God and love of man into one indivisible living impulse and motive, He combined the two commandments as of equal importance into the two-fold command in which the epitome of the whole Law is contained, the whole will of God for us, in its essential inner unity, included. By this, religion and morality, which in Judaism were always tending to fall apart, are bound together with cords that cannot be loosed; henceforth there should be no religion which manifested itself only in morally worthless ceremonies, in purely ritual "holiness." Even the ceremonies of the cultus come to be estimated in a different way; they are no longer a service to be rendered to God by which man may acquire merit in the sight of God or buy His favour, but the natural expression of pious feeling, and are only of value in so far as they are the outward embodiment of a corresponding inward frame of mind. Where this is wanting, prayer and fasting are mere empty show, hypocrisy (Matt. vi.). The keeping of the Sabbath, too, is not a service which man does to God, but a benefit intended by God for man (Mark ii. 28); therefore the best, the worthiest way of keeping the day is by doing good to one's neighbour (Mark iii. 4 and Luke vi. 9). Therefore ceremonial worship must never be preferred before the fulfilment of plain moral duties. "I will have mercy and not sacrifice," Jesus quotes from Hosea; and He most sharply condemns the practice of the Pharisees, which set a pious offering above duty to parents, and turned prayer into a means of satisfying vanity and avarice. In contrast with this, He commands that even the performance of an act of worship, such as sacrifice, shall be interrupted in order not to delay the more pressing duty of reconciliation with an offended brother for a single moment (Matt. v. 23 f.).

Thus, in place of the ceremonial worship of God there is to be substituted moral beneficence towards men. Service rendered to men, God looks on as though done to Himself (Matt. xxv. 40). Conversely, all moral action must spring from and be in accordance with the religious motive of whole-hearted love to God. It is to consist, on the one hand, of imitation of the absolute goodness of God in a faithful willing and doing of good to all, which perseveres in spite of provocation and enmity; and on the other hand of an unconditional surrender to the fatherly will of God in child-like trust and humble resignation. It is in a pure love of one's neighbour, free from all self-seeking, and a pure trust in God, free from all worldly anxiety, that the attitude of mind consists which is in conformity with the fatherly will of God, and which therefore makes a man a true child of God, or, to put it otherwise, constitutes his true "righteousness," which is certain to be accepted by God. In the detailed development of these two main thoughts, which run through the whole preaching of Jesus, there can be distinguished, however, two different tones—one of a cheerful and confident wisdom which combines its quiet and harmonious strain with an idyllic, optimistic view of Nature; the other a stern, ascetic rigorism, the heroic demands of which have as their dark background an ascetic, pessimistic estimate of the present world and an ardent expectation of apocalyptic catastrophies. According to Renan and Keim, these different moods belong to two different periods of the public life of Jesus—its beginning and its close. That is not indeed impossible, but it cannot be proved; for in the account given in our Gospels (which do not necessarily, of course, reproduce the historical order) the softer and the harder tone are found side by side from the first, and often pass into one another. However we may explain this, the fact must not be overlooked or concealed by the unprejudiced historian; he must not allow his judgment to be warped by apologetic or polemical motives into suppressing either of these different tones in the preaching of Jesus.

It is easy to understand why rationalism always preferred the cheerful, optimistic, harmonious strain in the preaching of Jesus, with which it naturally sympathised, and which, in fact, contains a rational truth suitable to all times, the universal human ideal. Of unequalled loftiness and imperishable value are those sayings of the Sermon on the Mount:—"Love your enemies, and pray for your persecutors, that ye may be the sons of your Father in heaven; for he maketh his sun to shine upon the good and upon the evil, upon the righteous and the unrighteous." "Take no thought for your life, what ye shall eat, nor for your body, what ye shall put on. Is not the life more than meat and the body more than raiment? Behold the birds of the air, they sow not neither do they reap nor gather into barns, yet your heavenly Father feedeth them. Are ye not of much more value than they? Which of you by taking thought can add a cubit to the length of his life? And why take ye thought for raiment? Behold the lilies of the field, how they grow; they toil not, neither do they spin, but I say unto you that Solomon in all his glory was not arrayed like one of these. But if God so clothe the grass of the field, which to-day is, and to-morrow is cast into the oven, shall he not much more clothe you, O ye of little faith? Therefore ye shall not be anxious, nor say, What shall we eat? or, What shall we drink? or, Wherewithal shall we be clothed? After all these things do the Gentiles seek. But your heavenly Father knoweth that ye have need of these things. Seek ye first the kingdom of God and his righteousness, and all these things shall be added unto you. Therefore take no thought for the morrow; for the morrow shall take thought for the things of itself. Sufficient unto the day is the evil thereof." In such sayings we see a tone of mind in which the inward piety and submission to God's will of the true Israelite seems to be united to the inward freedom and harmonious view of the world of the Hellenic sage; they sound like the primal utterances of human wisdom, like elemental truths, which Nature herself seems to reveal to the pure mind, and which are therefore as imperishable as the eternal laws of the world-order. But we must not forget that Nature, after all, is not really able to teach such truths; to cool reason she shows, in addition to this cheerful side, another and a very dark one—the hard struggle for existence, the unnumbered woes of the suffering creation, from which man himself is not by any means exempt; and if Nature showers her good things impartially upon righteous and unrighteous, she does the same with her evil things. The optimistic view of life is therefore always not so much read out of Nature as read into it. For Jesus, too, it was certainly the inner revelation of God, the intimate union with God of His trustful and loving heart, which enabled Him intuitively to recognise and gratefully to reverence in Nature, and in the lives of the simple and child-like souls who stand close to Nature, the loving care of the heavenly Father. The cheerful, optimistic outlook upon the world of Nature and on childhood (Mark x. 13 ff.; Luke x. 21) is incontestably a characteristic trait of the religious life of Jesus, an expression of His child-like trust in God and of the purity, freedom, and healthfulness of His mind. And because it springs from inward religion, this optimistic view of Nature does not remain a mere theory or an æsthetic mood, but becomes the motive of a corresponding ethical attitude. The confident faith that all that happens even in Nature is ruled by the will of God, who cares much more, even, for the good of His human children than for other creatures, frees us from the trammels of earthly care and fear (Matt. vi. 25 ff.). The thought of the unbounded goodness of God, which, raised far above human weakness, showers the abundance of its natural goods even upon the unthankful and the evil, becomes the motive for a similar magnanimity and patience in benevolence and beneficence towards even those who reward it with hostility (Matt. v. 44 f.). In so far as we understand the love to enemies which Jesus commanded as freedom from vengeful feelings, as a constant readiness to forgive and be reconciled, and as the persistent endeavour not to be overcome by evil but to overcome evil with good,—in short, as unconquerable faithfulness in love to one's neighbour,—we must recognise it as an exalted virtue which often, indeed, goes beyond our capacity, but not entirely beyond our comprehension and the approval of our understanding; the less so as similar teaching has been given by other sages (Buddha, Plato, Seneca, Epictetus).

But it must be admitted that this attitude is not constant; Jesus also gave commandments of so severe an ascetic rigorism that they cannot be thought of as universally applicable rules for an orderly condition of human society, but are rather to be thought of as corresponding to a special historical situation. A notable example is the saying which Luke records in connection with the command to love our enemies (vi. 29), but Matthew, perhaps more correctly, unconnected with this, as an independent antithesis to the old law of retaliation (v. 30 ff.), "I say unto you, resist not evil, but whosoever smites thee upon the right cheek, offer unto him the other also, and he who will go to law with thee to take thy cloak, let him have thy mantle also." It is clear that this saying could not be carried out in any society, for it would do away with all equitable order and play into the hands of brutal violence. It cannot, moreover, be reconciled with that other saying of Jesus, "Whatsoever ye would that men should do unto you, do ye also unto them" (Matt. vii. 12 = Luke vi. 31). According to this, no one is to treat another simply as a means to his ends, but each must regard the other as the possessor of similar ethical rights. From this it obviously follows that each may demand from the other the same respect for his own rights and personal dignity. The principle of mutual obligations and mutual rights which underlies the saying that we are to love our neighbours as ourselves, excludes the abandonment of our own rights by submitting to wrongs inflicted by others, not less than disregard of the rights of others by injustice on our part. But as man's natural instinct of self-defence is apt to react against wrong inflicted by others in passionate feeling (anger, revenge), and as in doing so the bounds between mere self-defence against the offered injustice and the doing of injustice on one's own part are very easily crossed, Jesus sets up, in contrast to the natural impulse of self-love, its opposite—unconditional abandonment of all self-love, the surrender of one's own rights, as the ascetic *radical cure.* It is only from this point of view of extreme ascetic rigorism, not from some idea of moral influence on one's opponent, that we are to understand the precept of non-resistance; it is not intended as a rule for the ordinary conditions of human society, but asserts the principle, in a time when the world is breaking up and all social values are cast into the fire of the Judgment, that, by heroic victory over self, the naked soul is to be saved, and, by complete contempt for honour or shame in this perishing world, the glory of the world to come is to be secured.[1] That it is only in view of

[1] *Cf.* Joh. Weiss, *Predigt Jesu vom Reich Gottes*, 2nd ed., pp. 150 ff. Also, on p. 139, the pertinent remark about the "useless trouble people give themselves to weaken these bold and forceful words by giving them an unnatural interpretation, *i.e.* by taking the heart out of them in order to be able to maintain their permanent and literal applicability to all periods."

this dark eschatological background that the bold paradox of non-resistance is to be understood is made clear by the two related sayings, "Be reconciled to thine adversary quickly, while thou art on the way with him (to the judge), in order that the adversary may not deliver thee to the judge and thou be cast into prison" (Matt. v. 25), *i.e.*, in view of the nearness of the Judgment, a man should extricate himself from all earthly quarrels as speedily as may be; and again, "He who will save his life shall lose it; but he who will lose his life for my sake and the gospel's shall save it. For what doth it profit a man to gain the whole world and lose his own life? Or what shall a man give in exchange for his life?" (Mark viii. 35 f. = Luke ix. 24 f. = Matt. xvi. 25). It is customary to interpret this saying in the sense that by giving up the natural life, *i.e.* by overcoming the lower impulses, the higher life, rich in all spiritual blessings, is to be won. But that is rather a practical application of it than an exposition of the original sense of the saying; this is rather, "Whosoever in this last critical time, through fear for his life, becomes cowardly or disloyal, shall certainly at the Judgment lose his life, and then whatever he has gained will profit him nothing; but he who is ready to stake his life upon the success of the Messianic cause is certain to receive in the world to come the eternal life (of the resurrection), and therewith all other blessings besides (Matt. xix. 29).

The same eschatologically coloured asceticism is found also in numerous passages in which Jesus demands of His followers a complete severance from all that binds them to this present world, even including family ties. There is the familiar story of the rich young man who, in answer to his query what he must do in order to inherit eternal life, received the commandment to sell all that he had and give to the poor, that so he might have treasure in heaven—a bond, so to speak, lodged in heaven, which assured his claim to eternal life. Matthew was no longer willing to understand that as a demand of general application, and therefore weakened it into an individual and conditional counsel, " If thou wilt be perfect," etc. But in Mark and Luke the command is quite unconditional, and that this was the original meaning is clear from the saying of Jesus which follows in all the Gospels—that it is as impossible for a rich man to enter into the kingdom of God as for a camel to go through the eye of a needle; so impossible, indeed, that it could only be effected by a Divinely wrought miracle. Obviously Jesus judged riches in themselves to be something corrupting—to be the greatest, the most irresistible danger to the soul of the possessor; to be, in fact, an idol (Mammon) which held men so completely bound in his service that it was impossible to serve God at the same time (Matt. vi. 24). For this reason riches are called in Luke (xvi. 9, 11) the " Mammon of unrighteousness," " unrighteous Mammon," not on the ground of the unrighteous manner in which, in that particular case, it had been obtained, but because it is itself a power hostile to God, which makes righteousness, in the gospel sense, impossible for the man who has it or is striving after it. Therefore Jesus commanded men not merely in individual cases and by way of test, but quite generally and literally, to jettison this soul-destroying cargo and run for shelter, along with the poor, into the safe harbour of the Kingdom of God. "Sell what you have, and give alms; make for yourselves purses that wax not old, a treasure in heaven, that fadeth not away, where no thief can break in and no moth destroy. For where your treasure is, there will your heart be also. . . . Whosoever of you forsaketh not all that he hath, he cannot be my disciple" (Luke xii. 33, xiv. 33). It is obviously to do violence to these words to give them the spiritualising interpretation that a man is merely not to set his heart upon wealth in an avaricious or miserly way, but, apart from that, may well retain it and prudently apply it to morally good ends. That is the view we modern Protestant Christians take, because we think of all earthly goods as a means to ethical action, equally capable of a good or a bad use; and we should therefore judge the renunciation of all one's possessions, which would deprive one of the means of all independent moral action, to be not ethically right. But Jesus thought in every respect quite differently on this point. In common with all antiquity, He saw in riches not a means of productive moral action but merely a means of enjoyment; and in common with the pious Jews of His time[1] He saw in the rich, as a class, born worldlings, oppressors of the pious poor, despisers and enemies of the Reign of God. Finally, He lived in the fixed conviction that He stood at the close of one era of the world and the beginning of another: in view of this impending world-catastrophe, this decisive day of the judgment of God, He could not think of giving rules for the

[1] *Cf.* the apocalypses The Assumption of Moses (vii.), and Enoch xciv., xcvi., xcviii., cviii. See above, p. 401.

moral use of wealth in a society organised upon a permanent basis. His object was that everyone, in order to prepare for the world to come, should free himself as speedily as possible from the fetters which bound him to the present passing world. "Let your loins be girded about and your lights burning, and be ye like servants who wait for their lord's return from the wedding, that they may open to him at once when he comes and knocks." This exhortation to be ready follows immediately upon the passage quoted above about selling one's possessions and laying up treasure in heaven (Luke xii. 33–36)—a clear proof that the apocalyptic expectation of the approaching end of the world is the simple explanation of Jesus' pessimistic estimate of earthly possessions. Instead of twisting round His rigoristic utterances upon this point and endeavouring to force them into accordance with our present social ethics, we should familiarise ourselves once for all with the thought that Jesus did not come forward as a teacher of the ethics of pure reason, but as an enthusiastic prophet of the approaching Reign of God, and that it was just by this means that He became the source and founder of the religion of redemption; but anyone who seeks to make eschatological prophetic enthusiasm a permanent authority and standard of social ethics is acting no more wisely than one who should attempt to warm his hearth and cook his dinner with the flames of a volcano.

But it was not merely upon earthly possessions that Jesus declared war: His demand for a radical breach with the present world did not stop short of the sacred ties of family, of piety towards parents, of the love of wife and children. When one who was called to follow Him wished first to go and bury his father, Jesus said to him, "Let the dead bury their dead; but go thou and preach the kingdom of God"; and another, who desired to take leave of his family, He forbade with the words, "Whoso putteth his hand to the plough and looketh back, is not fit for the kingdom of God" (Luke ix. 60 ff.). Naturally, here, too, the exegetical art of theologians has not lacked means of explaining and softening down these hard sayings: they were only intended to test those to whom they were spoken, Jesus foresaw that the delay would prove fatal to their good resolutions, and so forth. But the truth is rather that it was not a question of individual exceptions but of a general principle—the same principle which Jesus Himself followed in His conduct towards His mother and brethren, and to which He gave the sharpest and most unmistakable expression in the saying, "Whosoever cometh unto me and hateth not his father and mother, wife, children, brethren and sisters, yea his own life also, cannot be my disciple" (Luke xiv. 26 = Matt. x. 37 f.). Obviously, this saying is unsuitable to the Church's catalogue of domestic virtues and duties; accordingly, the ecclesiastical Evangelist Matthew already found it needful to give it the unexceptionable turn, "Whoso loveth father or mother more than me, is not worthy of me." In this weakened form it may of course be understood to mean that in case of a collision between family duties and the cause of Christ the latter must take precedence; and *we*, moreover, assume that such cases of painful conflict of duties can only be rare exceptions. But if that had been

Jesus' meaning it would seem to have been expressed, in the form recorded by Luke, which is doubtless the original form, in a way which invited misunderstanding. As the saying stands, it can indeed only be understood on the assumption that Jesus regarded family ties as an absolute hindrance to discipleship, and therefore tolerated no compromise between the two interests, but demanded on the part of His disciples as decisive a breach with all family ties as He had made in His own case (according to Mark iii. 33). That may certainly appear strange in the case of one who rated the sacredness of marriage so highly that He forbade its dissolution, who put the performance of filial duty above religious oblations (Mark vii. 10 ff.), and who often showed Himself a lover of little children (Mark ix. 36, x. 13 ff.). But we must never forget that "in His breast there dwelt two souls,"[1] and that the ardent expectation of a new world *must* involve a transposition of values in the present order of things. The enthusiastic prophet of the Reign of God, of the New Age in which there should be no more marrying or giving in marriage, in which all sacrifices of family happiness will be compensated a hundred-fold in new forms of social life (Matt. xix. 29, xxii. 30), could not but hold dependence on parents or children and husband or wife as, not less than gold and possessions, fetters from which one must free oneself by a heroic resolution, in order to gain a share in the eternal life of the age to come. Only from this point of view is it possible to

[1] An allusion to *Faust*:—

"Zwei Seelen wohnen, ach! in meiner Brust."

—TRANSLATOR

explain why Jesus gave no positive precepts regarding the relations of husband and wife, the bringing up of children, the exercise of one's earthly calling,[1] and the duties of citizenship.[2] This complete ignoring of all that makes the concrete content of social ethics would be unintelligible if Jesus had intended to be a teacher of humane morals for men in this present world, but it becomes quite intelligible on the assumption, which apart from this is quite clearly evidenced, that He believed in, hoped for, and proclaimed the approaching end of the old natural order of things and the commencement of a new order of things which was to be brought into existence by the exercise of supernatural power. For this reason, the often-expressed opinion is untenable, that Jesus had given no positive social rules because He desired to leave to the natural development of things the formation of a new, ethical, social order in the community of His disciples. This is to overlook the fact that He did not look forward to any natural development of things at all, but expected a catastrophe which should make all things new at one stroke. But even if the content of this hope, which Jesus shared with the men of His own race and time, has proved to be illusory, nevertheless the enthusiasm of faith and love which lived and worked in Him and in His disciples was a reality

[1] In the sayings in Matt. vi. 25 ff. religious idealism finds such bold expression that it does not seem easy to combine with it the assignment of a positive ethical value to work.

[2] No positive prescription in this respect is to be found in the saying in Matt. xii. 17, since the separation which is here enjoined between religion and politics, and the submission to the Roman administration, do not rest on any positive interest in political matters but rather upon its opposite.

of the highest order; it was, in fact, the beginning of a new ethical and religious spirit, out of which, moreover, new forms of society and a new social ethic have actually, in course of time, developed. The saying "He that will be great among you, let him be your servant; and he who will be first, let him be the servant of all" (Mark x. 43), in which the fundamental attitude of Jesus finds classical expression, became the positive principle of Christian social ethics, and gave the initial incentive to the transformation of human society, the driving and directing power of which still continues to exercise its influence, since this ideal is still far from realised. In this respect it is true that the whole historical development of Christian ethics stands in a relationship of cause and effect with Jesus' character and life-work. But we ought not to overlook the distinction between the later forms of development conditioned by many contributory factors and the actual original content of the personal consciousness of Jesus; and we ought not to make Him, without more ado, a moral law-giver for all time, which He neither desired to be, nor, in the nature of things, could be. His demand of a world-renouncing asceticism was the practical consequence of His apocalyptic belief in the approaching end of the world, which was to be brought about by supernatural means; since we no longer share this belief, the ascetic demands which rest upon it can no longer be for us of direct validity. But that does not hinder the temper of mind which lies at the basis of them from being of abiding and typical significance—the temper, namely, which consists in the suppression of all selfish desire, and in unconditional surrender to the will of God. But since for us the Divine will no longer manifests itself in the supernatural catastrophe of the Judgment but in the natural course of the history of the world, our submission to the Divine will does not show itself in breaking with the historical conditions of social life, but in the shaping of these in an ethical direction. This *transition from apocalyptic asceticism to rational ethics* was begun even by the Apostolic community; the Church completed it. The transformation of early Christian enthusiasm into the beliefs and morals of the Church forms the core of the history of early Christianity; and the way to the understanding of that history is barred whenever the later developments are wrongly dated back to the beginning.

In view of the apocalyptic foundation of Jesus' ethics, it was inevitable that the thought of reward should occupy a prominent place in them. The question of Peter, "Lo, we have left all and followed thee; what shall we have therefore?" (Matt. xix. 27 ff.), is not rebuked as unbecoming; instead, the prospect is held out to all the disciples of receiving as the reward for their present sacrifices a rich compensation in the world to come, and to the Twelve, in particular, a share in the Messianic Reign. The conversion of one's earthly possessions into alms is, especially, often recommended as the means of laying up treasure in heaven (*i.e.*, of securing a claim upon eternal life), or of ensuring for oneself a welcome in the eternal habitations by reason of the gratitude of the poor who have been the recipients (Matt. xix. 21; Luke xi. 41, xii. 33, xiv. 14, xvi. 9). It cannot be denied that in these sayings, as also in those regarding the reward for fasting and prayer (Matt. vi. 4, 6, 18), the Jewish view of the merit of "good works" of this kind is accepted without alteration. It is therefore the more worthy of note that these Jewish views, which in theory are retained, are sometimes inferentially contradicted or corrected by other sayings. In the parable of the Labourers in the Vineyard, the legal view of reward as a proportionate return for the service rendered is assumed at the outset, but is practically set aside by the fact that in the end all the workers receive the same payment (Matt. xx. 13 ff.); for when the payment is no longer in proportion to the measure of the service, it is no longer the legal equivalent of it, but becomes a free gift of grace which is given to all who follow the Divine command in willing obedience. And since the reward consists in the inestimable blessing of a share in the Kingdom of God, which is beyond all comparison greater than all human services and sacrifices, there cannot really be any question of the exact equivalence of service and reward, and all reward becomes, properly speaking, a matter of grace, so that in Luke vi. 32–35 the terms grace (χάρις) and reward (μισθός) are used interchangeably. According to Luke xvii. 7–10, we men have in God's eyes as little actual claim to reward as servants who have simply done their duty; at the same time, according to Luke xii. 37, the Lord will reward the faithfulness and watchfulness of His servants so richly that He will make them sit at His table and serve them Himself. The two representations are so far agreed that in both the thought of a legal due is rejected, and the idea of a gift of grace is substituted. Finally, the ethical and teleological version of the idea of reward, which has secured a place in all ethical systems, may be found in the parable of the Talents, inasmuch as the servants who have been faithful in a few things are made rulers over many things" (Matt. xxv. 21 ff.), *i.e.* their sphere of activity is extended in proportion to the capacity they have shown. This thought, that faithfulness shown in a narrow sphere leads on to a higher degree of power, or that social eminence is conditioned by social service (Mark x. 43), contains that element of truth in the idea of reward which society is concerned to maintain.

It is the same with the question of the Law as it is with the question of reward. The traditional Jewish view is not denied, but expressly accepted; but this conservatism is broken through by sayings in which a new spirit involuntarily betrays itself. An express declaration by Jesus of the permanent validity of the Mosaic Law, nay, even of every letter of it, is found in Matt. v. 18 f.: "Verily I say unto you, till heaven and earth pass away, one jot or one tittle shall in no wise pass from the law until all be fulfilled. Whosoever, therefore, shall break one of these least commandments, and shall teach men so, he shall be the least in the kingdom of heaven; but whosoever doeth and teacheth them, the same shall be great in the kingdom of heaven." It is, no doubt, possible to regard the second half of this verse (19), which is peculiar to Matthew, as a later, emphasising, addition; but the genuineness of verse 18 cannot well be doubted, since the same saying is found in a somewhat different form, and in an entirely different connection, in Luke xvi. 17. Moreover, in the polemic against the Pharisees, two sayings of a similar conservative character are to be found: "All that they (the Pharisees and scribes) say unto you, that hold and do; but do not according to their works, for they say, and do not. . . . Woe unto you, scribes and Pharisees; for ye tithe mint, anise, and cummin, and neglect the weightier matters of the law, righteousness, mercy, and faith: these ought to be done, without leaving the others undone (Matt. xxiii. 3, 23). Here, therefore, the current practice of the Jewish teachers of the Law is no doubt rejected, but not the Law itself, the observance of which is rather commanded. With this agrees the attitude of the primitive community, which could not have so confidently maintained the observance of the Law as a self-evident duty, and defended it against Paul, if Jesus had in any way taught His disciples to cast off the yoke of the Law. For these reasons the interpretation of Matt. v. 18 (= Luke xvi. 17), which makes them mean that permanent significance belongs to the spirit, not the letter, of the Law, is not tenable. It was, no doubt, in this sense that the Church, and probably even the Evangelists, understood them (*cf. sup.*, p. 324); but that cannot possibly have been the original sense of the saying, because it is in such striking contradiction with the literal sense. We cannot, therefore, help agreeing with the pronouncement of B. Weiss: "That Jesus described or treated the legal system of life and worship, the Divine origin of which He recognised, as in itself defective and not in accordance with His views, that He claimed the right freely to exercise authority over it, and used this right in order to release His disciples from its yoke, is, from the point of view of historical investigation, inconceivable and inadmissible." But Holtzmann is not less justified in his assertion that "while owning allegiance to, and submitting to the authority of, the Law with all the piety of a religious Jew, Jesus at the same time gradually outgrew the trammels of legalism, and attained without a struggle to an emotional certainty of the higher authority which He carried within Himself: in the first instance, no doubt, to a *practical* application of it. We can only ask whether, and how far, it subsequently worked out into an objective intellectual certainty. There are, in fact, stages on this road." In the first instance, it was not the commandments of the Mosaic Law, but only the ordinances of the Pharisaic schools, against which Jesus, with sound ethical insight, protested. Thus He repudiated the practice of ostentatious fasting, and defended His disciples for not fasting on the ground that it was inappropriate to the present joyful period. On this occasion, too, He uttered the significant saying about the new patch being unsuitable to the old garment, and the new wine to the old wine-skins (Mark ii. 21)—a saying of which the significance goes far beyond the actual matter of controversy, since it asserts nothing less than the impossibility of uniting the new content of life under the Reign of God, which was now commencing, with the old forms of life under the Law. In the same way Jesus rejected the rigorism of the Pharisaic Sabbath observance, on the ground that man was not made for the Sabbath, but the Sabbath for man, and therefore the son of man, *i.e.* man in general, was lord also of the Sabbath (Mark ii. 28). That asserts the relativity of the law of the Sabbath, compared with the unconditionality of the ethical end of man in himself, in a manner of which the logical consequence is to call in question the unconditional validity of the ritual Law as a whole, and not merely the treatment of it by the Jewish schools. The conflict came to a still sharper issue in regard to the Rabbinic ordinances of ceremonial purity (Mark vii. 8 ff.). In the first place, indeed, here also it is only the revealed Law of Scripture which is contrasted with the ordinances of tradition; but in the course of His polemic Jesus asserts a principle of much wider scope, which would also invalidate the Mosaic dietary and ceremonial laws: "Nothing that enters into a man from without can make him unclean, but that which comes forth from him (the evil thoughts of the heart), that it is which defiles him." In His treatment of the question about divorce Jesus goes still further (Mark x. 2–12); here it is not merely Scripture which is set against tradition, but Scripture against Scripture—namely, the revelation of God at the creation (according to Gen. i. 27, ii. 24) against the Mosaic Law of marriage which permits and regulates divorce. It is true that in the version of Matt. xix. 9 and v. 32, according to which the unfaithfulness of the wife forms an exception to the prohibition of divorce, Jesus would seem only to have taken up the stricter standpoint of the school of Shammai as against the laxer theory of Hillel; but according to the certainly more original version of the other Evangelists, His condemnation of divorce was unconditional, and in this case it is evidently a direct correction of the Mosaic Law, the appointment of which is declared to have been a concession to the weakness and the hard-heartedness of men, which did not correspond to the original intention of the Creator. Similarly, the permission of retaliation in the Mosaic Law is corrected by the ascetic command to submit to injustice, of which we have spoken above (p. 442). Finally, there is the very significant saying which is ascribed to Jesus, though, according to the Evangelists, only by false witnesses (Mark xiv. 58, xv. 29), "I will destroy this temple made with hands, and in three days will set up another made without hands." If this saying was really spoken by Jesus (which is, of course, not certain, though it is not improbable), it could hardly mean anything else than a prediction of the speedy end of the sensuous Temple service and its replacement by a more spiritual service of God. A saying of that kind might well be the outcome of Jesus' impression of the impossibility of reforming the Jewish hierarchy, which stood or fell along with the Temple service; and since it is derived from the last days of Jesus' life, it seems to favour the conjecture that Jesus, taught by experience and under the growing pressure of His struggle with the hierarchy, in the end abandoned more and more completely His original attitude of acceptance of the Law. It should not, however, be overlooked that the conservative sayings quoted above from the anti-Pharisaic polemic (Matt. xxiii. 3, 23) likewise belong to the last days of the life of Jesus, while the liberal saying about the new wine and the old wine-skins belongs to an earlier period (Mark ii. 21). There remains, therefore, nothing for it but to admit that, in judging the attitude of Jesus to the Jewish Law, various sayings not altogether without contradiction have to be taken into account. Such contradictions would find their most natural explanation in a change of mood, such as is found in other heroic pioneers, as, for example, in Luther. In lofty moments of prophetic inspiration, of enthusiastic hope of a new world, and of passionate struggle against the low reality, Jesus felt Himself raised more and more above the legal limitations of His nation, until He formed the impression that their end was at hand. But from that to a conscious breach with the Law is a long step, which Jesus Himself never completed ; its completion was reserved for His Apostle, Paul.

THE PREACHING OF JESUS AND THE FAITH OF THE FIRST DISCIPLES

CHAPTER XVII

The Messianic Beliefs of Jesus and His Earliest Followers

There can be no doubt that according to the view and the representation of our Evangelists Jesus was, from His first appearance, the Messiah; Himself testified that He was so by deed and word; and was acknowledged as such by human and superhuman testimony. That is self-evident in Luke and Matthew, whose narratives of the Childhood introduce Jesus with due solemnity as the Messiah and Son of God; whose narratives of the Temptation describe the victory of the Messiah over Satan; and in whose Gospels Jesus declares Himself at His first public appearance to be the fulfiller of the Law (Matt. v. 17 ff.) and of the promises (Luke iv. 17 ff.). But even in Mark the position is not really different. Although he has no story of the Childhood, he tells how at Jesus' Baptism He was made the Christ, or the Son of God, by receiving the Spirit which was sent down from heaven, and declared to be so by a heavenly voice; therefore the Baptism is to him the "beginning of the gospel of Jesus as the Christ."[1] He does not think of it merely as a subjective (visionary) occurrence in the consciousness of Jesus, but as a mysterious objective event by which Jesus became a vehicle of the Holy Spirit and entered into a mysterious relationship to the world of spirits, which immediately manifested itself in His being driven forth by the Spirit into the wilderness, tempted by Satan, and served by angels; but, further, also by the fact that the demonic spirits of the possessed recognised and acknowledged Him as "the Holy One of God," *i.e.* the Messiah (i. 24, 34).

In marked contrast with this conception of the Messiahship of Jesus, which is common to all our Gospels, stands the statement, which is also common to them, that Jesus at the close of His Galilæan ministry, in the course of a journey into the district of Cæsarea Philippi, asked His disciples whom the people took Him to be; whereupon they answered, "John the Baptist, or Elias, or one of the prophets." Then He asked them whom they themselves took Him to be; whereupon Peter answered, "Thou art the Christ" ("the Christ of God," Luke; "the Christ, the Son of the living God," Matthew). In connection with this narrative, several questions force themselves upon the unprejudiced reader; above all, the question how it was possible that the people did not yet recognise Jesus as the Messiah in spite of the many astounding miracles which He had already performed, and in spite of His, in some cases, quite clear Messianic self-witness, and in spite of the utterances of the demons, to whom

[1] The genuineness of the words υἱοῦ θεοῦ is doubtful; if genuine, they are to be understood in the same sense as the voice at the Baptism (i. 11).

a higher knowledge was universally ascribed. But the representation that the disciples now for the first time expressed their belief in the Messiahship of Jesus is also surprising. In Matthew they are certainly reported to have said at an earlier point, after the miracle of the walking on the sea (xiv. 33), "Thou art in truth the son of God"; but this notice, which is peculiar to Matthew, makes it even more difficult to account for the way in which this same Evangelist emphasises Peter's confession as something new and as derived from a Divine revelation (xvi. 17 ff.). In fact, we are here confronted by a dilemma. If all the preceding Messianic deeds and words are historical, the incident on the way to Cæsarea would hardly have been possible; if, on the other hand, the latter is historical, the representation of the Evangelists, who introduce Jesus from the first as the Messiah and Son of God, does not rest upon historical reminiscence, but only upon dogmatic or apologetic presuppositions and postulates. And this very circumstance — that it so strikingly contradicts the general presuppositions of the Evangelists—is the strongest proof of the historical character of the confession of Peter at Cæsarea Philippi, for which a further argument may be derived from the mention of this definite locality. However, new difficulties present themselves in the further course of the narrative, even if we leave out of account the wholly unhistorical exaltation of Peter in Matthew (*sup.*, p. 349 f.) and confine our consideration to the representation in Mark. Immediately after Peter's confession, he tells us, Jesus urgently charged His disciples that they should tell no man concerning

Him—namely, what had just been said, that He was the Messiah (as Luke and Matthew add by way of explanation). Thereupon He began to teach them about the necessity that the Son of Man must suffer and be rejected by the Jewish hierarchy, and be put to death, and after three days rise again. Peter then urged Him to avoid this fate, but Jesus rebuked him as a "Satan, whose thoughts were not the thoughts of God but of man."

Here there arises, in the first place, the question, Why did Jesus forbid His disciples to speak of His Messiahship? If He Himself claimed to be the Messiah, must He not have desired that the belief of His disciples should be made known to all the people and shared by as many as possible? In fact, it is so difficult to form a conception of a Messiah who only desires to be so in secret, that it is quite conceivable how critics like Martineau (*Seat of Authority*, pp. 349 ff.), Wellhausen, Lagarde, and Havet have concluded that Jesus did not really desire to be received as the Messiah at all.[1] Most expositors, however, think that the difficulty which presents itself here can be solved by supposing that it was owing to His wisdom and prudence as a teacher that Jesus forbade the making known of His Messiahship, because He feared that the people would take Him for a political Messiah, whereas He himself only desired to be a spiritual Messiah, or, alternatively, to become by His suffering and death a heavenly Messiah. Widely current as this view is, it seems to be beset with grave difficulties.

1 This opinion seems to have been adopted, although upon somewhat different grounds, by Wrede, *Das Messiasgeheimniss in den Ev.*, pp. 220, 229.

Would it not, we are compelled to ask, have been the simplest way to avoid being misunderstood by the people if Jesus had openly and clearly declared that He was indeed the Messiah—not, however, in the old Jewish sense, but in this or that new sense? But we nowhere find that He gave such a new interpretation of the traditional Jewish conception of the Messiah any more than of the traditional conception of the Kingdom of God. And yet there would have been an urgent necessity for doing so in both cases, not merely for the sake of the people but also for the sake of the disciples; for the Evangelists often allow us to see how completely the disciples shared the popular Jewish conception of Messiah and His Kingdom, *e.g.*, in the request of the sons of Zebedee for the places of honour at the right and left of the Messiah in His glory (Mark x. 37), or in the Messianic acclamations of the Passover pilgrims (among whom were included the disciples) who at the entry into Jerusalem greeted Jesus as the "son of David" and blessed the "coming kingdom of our father David" (Mark xi. 9 f. = Matt. xxi. 9). On the hypothesis that the motive of Jesus in forbidding the making known of His Messiahship was a wise and prudent avoidance of a teaching which was liable to be misunderstood, we should certainly expect that on occasions such as these Jesus would not have neglected the opportunity of giving His disciples an explanation which could not fail to be understood regarding the mistaken character of these expectations and the true meaning of His own idea of the Messiah. As He never did that, but on the contrary by His tacit acceptance of Peter's confession and of the Messianic ovation at the entry into

Jerusalem, and by many sayings, too, such as those at the Last Supper (Luke xxii. 18, 29 f.) seemed rather to confirm than to reject the popular Messianic opinions, the above hypothesis can hardly be considered tenable. But even the more radical hypothesis that Jesus did not believe Himself to be the Messiah or give Himself out to be so, which would no doubt provide the simplest explanation of the command not to speak of His Messiahship, seems to me to make shipwreck on the above-mentioned well-authenticated facts. If Jesus altogether refused and rejected the Messianic idea, why did He accept the confession of Peter? Why did He permit without protest the acclamations of the Passover pilgrims? Why did He speak of places of honour and thrones of judgment in His Kingdom? We may leave out of account His confession of His Messiahship before the Sanhedrin, because its historicity is uncertain (none of the disciples were present to hear it, and the apocalyptic prediction which is added in Mark xiv. 62 certainly reflects the conceptions of the Church). On the other hand, the controversy with the Scribes regarding the "son of David" is certainly one of the instances against the theory.

According to the original version in Mark (xii. 35 f.), Jesus asked how it was that the Scribes said that the Christ was the son of David, whereas David himself calls Him Lord (in Ps. cx.), how then could he be his son? The sense of this question is not doubtful: Jesus simply wishes to show that the assertion of the Scribes that the Messiah was the son of David was false, because it contradicted the utterance of David himself, who was inspired, and therefore infallible. It is a refutation of a hostile assertion by showing its inconsistency with something universally admitted, similar to that in the case of the Beelzebub charge. But what motive can Jesus have had in refuting the scholastic opinion regarding the Davidic sonship of the Messiah? Certainly not mere love of disputation, but a very practical and personal interest. He saw in that opinion a hindrance which stood in the way of belief in His Divine appointment to be the Messiah, since He Himself could not boast of Davidic descent. His anxiety to refute that opinion by Scriptural arguments certainly shows that at least the thought of His being destined to be the future Messiah or theocratic Head of the renewed people of God occupied Him seriously at that time. How could that have failed to be so after the Messianic acclamations at His entry into Jerusalem? When the belief in His destiny to be the Messiah in the coming Kingdom of God (for it could be a question of that only) met Him for the first time in Peter's confession, this thought was still so new to Him, the greatness of the gift and of the task was so awe-inspiring, that He shrank back in terror from it and sought, like Jeremiah of old, to escape His prophetic calling; a condition of surprise and alarm such as this would naturally explain the command not to make known their belief. When, however, on the way to Jerusalem the company of His enthusiastic adherents became ever larger and larger, when His passing through Jericho, and from there onwards the whole journey up to Jerusalem, took the form of a triumphal progress, till finally the enthusiasm of the companies of pious pilgrims could no longer be restrained but broke out into cries of jubilation which hailed Him as Messiah, He could not and would not any longer resist; He no longer forbade the Messianic salutations, but let the joyful enthusiasm take its course; nay, when His opponents pointed out to Him the danger of these acclamations He is said to have answered, "If these should be silent, the very stones will cry out" (Luke xix. 40); He held this popular enthusiasm to be an elemental power, not to be hindered by any human opposition. Whether the belief in His Messianic destiny became from that time forward a fixed and abiding conviction, or whether He did not up to the last attain to full certainty,[1] but in pious resignation left the decision of that question to the heavenly Father who guides the destinies of men—who can tell? All that we can clearly recognise is, as it seems to me, that Messianic ideas strongly influenced the mind of Jesus during the last days at Jerusalem, and form the presupposition upon which we have to understand His speech and action: the cleansing of the Temple, the parable of the Wicked Husbandmen and the other discourses directed against the hierarchy, the controversies regarding the tribute-money and the son of David, the promises and exhortations addressed to the disciples, and, not least, the anointing at Bethany, in which we recognise as the historical basis, underneath the legendary embellishment of the scene, an anointing as Messianic King, the complement and continuation of the homage paid to Him as Messianic King at the entry into Jerusalem (*cf.* p. 71 f.).

But because the thought of His Messiahship in the

[1] The latter is the view of W. Brandt, *Ev. Gesch.*, pp. 475 ff., whose discussion of the above question is marked by exceptional sobriety and clearness.

simple original sense in which the historical Jesus shared it with His disciples and friends was immediately afterwards robbed of its content by His death, but then, by the Easter visions, carried over into the higher level of apocalyptic ideas, undergoing at the same time a change of form, it meets us in the Gospels for the most part only as theologically transformed by the later consciousness of the community, and the substitution of this conception for the historical consciousness of Jesus leads to endless confusion. Even criticism has been largely led astray by the presupposition that Mark because he generally (though not always) gives a more original version of events than the other Evangelists therefore gives the absolutely original or really historical account. How far he is in reality from doing so, how far his representation is already influenced, in the principal points with which we are now concerned, by theological considerations, has been seen above in connection with his story of the baptism of the "Son of God," and will be seen still more clearly below in connection with the predictions of the passion and resurrection of the "Son of Man." The practice of taking Mark's account in all these cases for pure history, and of overlooking completely his theological, apologetic tendency, or of reducing it to a minimum, has laid an embargo upon sound and methodical criticism of the Gospels from which we ought now at last to free ourselves. It must be recognised that in regard to the theological transformation of history *all* our Gospels stand in principle upon the same footing, and that the distinction between Mark and the other two Synoptists, and between them and John is only *a difference of degree* between the different strata of theological reflection and ecclesiastical ideas.

That there certainly is such a difference between the doctrine of Christ's person in Mark and Matthew may be recognised—to return to the question with which we were lately occupied—in the different forms which they respectively give to the question about the son of David. The original aim of this question, which can still be recognised in Mark's account, was to refute the opinion of the Scribes regarding the Davidic sonship of the Messiah; this was no longer understood by Matthew, because for him, as his genealogy (i. 1–17) suffices to show, the Davidic sonship of Jesus was a fixed assumption; the quite new sense given to the question, then, in Matthew's version, is how, on this assumption, David can call the Messiah his Lord. And to this form of the question the Evangelist can only have had in mind the answer which has thenceforth been current in the Church; that, namely, Jesus the Messiah was, according to His human nature, David's son, but, according to His divine nature and origin as Son of God, was at the same time David's Lord. This is the Church doctrine of the two natures, the foundation for which was laid by Paul (Rom. i. 3 f.), and which is found in Matthew already in the first stage of its ecclesiastical development. The same view has probably given rise to the divergent form of the question of Jesus in Matt. xvi. 13 and the answer of Peter in verse 16. Jesus asks, "Who do men say that the Son of man is?" and receives for answer, "Thou art the Christ, the Son of the living God." That is, in Matthew's meaning, not, as in Mark and Luke, merely an acknowledgment of the theocratic Messiahship of Jesus, but also of His supernatural being, derived from His miraculous birth, as Son of God, in contrast with His outward manifestation as Son of Man. The supernatural character of Christ's person is emphasised elsewhere in Matthew in a way which goes decidedly beyond Mark and Luke. Whereas the two latter found no offence in the saying of Jesus recorded by tradition, "Why callest thou me good? None is good, save God only," Matthew found the human modesty of this self-estimate no longer suitable to the supernaturally begotten Son of God, and therefore gave to the saying the artificial turn, "Why askest thou me about that which is good? One there is who is good" (xix. 17). And as he removes the limitations of His ethical perfection, so he does also with the conditionality of His miracle-working power, and therefore alters the Marcan statement that Jesus *could not* do any miracle in Nazareth because of the unbelief of His countrymen into the statement that He *did* not do any miracle there (*i.e.* intentionally, in punishment for their unbelief) (Matt. xiii. 58 = Mark vi. 5). How could it be otherwise in a Gospel in which Christ takes leave of His followers with the majestic words, "All power is given unto me in heaven and on earth" (xxviii. 18). To this advanced stage of the doctrine of Christ Mark has no parallels; Luke has, however, in the passage common to him with Matthew (x. 21 f. = Matt. xi. 25 f.), which puts into the mouth of Jesus a Christological hymn which betrays its ecclesiastical origin even in its artistic metrical form :[1]—

"I thank thee, O Father, Lord of heaven and earth,
  That thou hast hidden this from the wise and prudent,
  And hast revealed it unto babes :
Yea, Father, so it has seemed good in thy sight.

"All things have been delivered unto me by my Father :
  And none hath known the Father save the Son ;
  Nor hath any known the Son save the Father,
And they to whom the Son willeth to reveal.

"Come unto me all ye that labour and are heavy laden,
  And I will give you refreshing.
Take my yoke upon you, and learn of me ;
For I am meek and lowly of heart :
  So shall ye find refreshing for your souls.
For my yoke is easy, and my burden is light."

We can hardly fail to recognise that this artistic arrangement of strophes in something like a sonnet-form points to the moulding hand of the Church. But even the contents of the strophes are, as was shown above (pp. 144, 339), partly dependent upon Paul, partly upon Jesus the Son of Sirach (li. 1. 13 ff., 23 ff.), partly upon Jeremiah (vi. 16). That a composition such as this, with its artistic form and content, was directly derived from Jesus, I hold to be extremely improbable. Brandt pertinently remarks :[2] "Since the historic Christ is not likely in one hymn to have first thanked the Father, then asserted His peculiar relation to God, and finally called the

[1] According to Brandt, *Ev. Gesch.*, pp. 562 and 576. Upon the divergences of reading, the importance of which has been much exaggerated by the defenders of the historical genuineness of this hymn of the Christ, see above, p. 144, note.

[2] *Ev. Gesch.*, p. 562.

afflicted to Himself, this hymn can only have been put into His mouth later. And for those who have given up the Gospel of John as an historical source, the assumption of the unique God-consciousness of Jesus must stand or fall with the genuineness of this logion." This last point is without doubt the reason why historical criticism has here spoken so hesitatingly and the apologists have been so zealous. We ought not, at least, to refuse to recognise that the words of this hymn, if they are allowed to mean what they say without arbitrary softening down, really imply a superhuman personality, such as the Christ of the Church is, and the historical Jesus was not. Only of the exalted Christ could men say, and the Church from Apostolic times onwards did say, that all things were delivered unto Him, all power over heaven and earth (Matt. xxviii. 18; 1 Cor. xv. 27). The earthly Jesus could not so speak, and never did so speak, even when He gave the boldest expression to His Messianic hopes, as in Luke xxii. 19, where He says that, as His Father has granted unto Him the Kingship, He grants to His disciples that they shall sit at meat with Him and bear rule over the Twelve Tribes of Israel. In saying that, He expresses, indeed, His belief that the Messianic rule over the people of Israel is destined, designed, for Him; but He does not assert that now, already, all things, the whole world, is delivered unto Him. The former assertion stands on the historical basis of the Jewish Messianic beliefs which Jesus shared; the latter soars into the transcendental regions of apocalyptic and dogmatic speculation about Christ, in a way which only became possible to the Christian community after His death and the occurrence of the Easter visions. It has indeed lately been proposed to understand the words "All things are given unto me of my Father" as meaning that all truths of the gospel were delivered, *i.e.* revealed, to Him by His Father. But, in the first place, that would be a strange use of the word, which elsewhere is used of human tradition *in contrast with* Divine revelation, but is never used of the latter; and even if it were so, that would not help much. For, even so, the relation of Christ to God as His Father would remain something quite unique, and exclusive, such as is, of course, self-evidently appropriate in the case of the supernatural being of the Church's Christ but can hardly be accepted in the case of the historic Jesus. That the latter needed a unique, mysterious revelation in order to recognise God as His Father will be difficult to prove, seeing that so thorough an expert in the Jewish religion of the time as Dalman has expressly asserted that "Jesus took this designation of God from the popular usage of His time," and that even the reference of the fatherly relation to individuals within the Jewish nation was nothing new.[1] When, however, the same scholar maintains that Jesus drew a sharp line between Himself and the disciples, and prescribed for them the customary Jewish "our Father in heaven," but Himself deliberately avoided it, I can find nothing of the kind in the Synoptic Gospels; here Jesus speaks in so exactly the same way of "our Father," "thy Father," "your Father," and "my Father," that there is no reason to suppose that the latter is not to be understood in precisely the same sense as the former expressions,

[1] Dalman, *Worte Jesu,* p. 154 (E.T. 188).

namely, as indicating an ethico-religious relation of trust in the fatherly goodness of God, and of imitation of it in our own moral attitude. If Jesus is the pattern for His disciples of this relation to God, that very fact implies the essential likeness of the relationship, and therefore excludes that uniqueness which is asserted in the Christological hymn. Moreover, Dalman only finds it possible to rescue the genuineness of this saying by means of the daring hypothesis that this way of speaking was originally used figuratively of the relation between father and son in general, and that then this figure was applied to the relation of Jesus to His heavenly Father. Apart from this (extremely problematical) figurative use, "the Father" and "the Son" would have to be understood as theological terms which had already attained to fixity, as in Mark xiii. 32 (= Matt. xxiv. 36), and "we should therefore have to suppose that the text had been influenced by the language of the Church." In the baptismal formula also in Matt. xxviii. 19, Dalman admits that "this use of the name of the Son, which is not found elsewhere in the sayings of Jesus, is determined by the phraseology of the Early Church."[1] What Dalman himself admits in this last case must equally apply, as it seems to me, to xi. 25 ff. From whatever side one looks at this hymn, one comes back to the same result, that it is so far apart in thought and expression from Jesus' way of speaking elsewhere in the Synoptic Gospels, that it can as little be ascribed to the historical Jesus as can the Johannine discourses. The historical Jesus can have called God His Father in no other sense than that

[1] *Worte Jesu*, pp. 235, 232, 159 (E.T. 288, 283, 194).

in which He called Him "our Father." He never claimed a unique, metaphysical, superhuman relation of sonship to God, but acknowledged all those who do the will of God as His brethren and sisters (Mark iii. 35), thus including Himself in the family of the human children of God.

Jesus' customary way of speaking of Himself in the Gospels is as "the Son of man" (*ὁ υἱὸς τοῦ ἀνθρώπου*); and the Evangelists have certainly everywhere understood this as a Messianic self-designation. But could it have been so in the mouth of Jesus Himself? In the Aramaic, which was the mother-tongue of Jesus, the corresponding word *barnasha* never denotes anything else than "man" in general.[1] The question therefore arises, How came a general expression of this kind to have the special sense of a Messianic title, as it doubtless has in the Gospels? Is it possible to suppose that Jesus Himself used the term in this special sense? Or, if not, how came the Evangelists to put this self-designation into His mouth? It has been held that Jesus called Himself the Son of Man, *i.e.* man in an emphatic sense, in order to indicate, on the one hand, that nothing human — misery, suffering, death — was foreign to Him; or, again, that He is the true man, the realisation of the ideal of humanity. This is a useful theological conception, but little probable in the mouth of Jesus, who was neither a Greek philosopher

[1] *Cf.* A. Meyer, *Die Muttersprache Jesu*; Lietzmann, *Über den Menschensohn*; especially Wellhausen's *Aufsatz über den Menschensohn* in the *Skizzen und Vorarbeiten* of 1899, where, also, the philological objections of Dalman (*Worte Jesu,* pp. 191 ff.) are answered.

nor a modern humanist, and also was not speaking to philosophers or humanists. And how could His hearers have understood an enigmatic saying of that kind? Would they not sometime or other have asked Him what it really meant? But there is no trace of any such question, nor of any explanation on the part of Jesus. Hence others have supposed that the title was no riddle to the hearers, because "Son of Man" was already a traditional designation of the Messiah in the apocalyptic terminology of the Jews of the time. In explanation of it they point to Dan. vii. 13, "Behold, there came upon the clouds of heaven one like unto a son of man." The seer, it is true, understood by that, not a personal Messiah, but a symbol of the ideal theocracy, which appears in human form in contrast to the animal forms which symbolised the heathen empires; but that did not prevent the symbolical human figure from being understood in later Jewish apocalyptic as representing the personal Messiah. Hence we find "Son of Man" used, not indeed as a standing expression, but as an occasional title for the Messiah in the Similitudes of Enoch and in 2 Esdras, but always only with reference to the Messiah as pre-existing in heaven and to be expected thence, never for the earthly Messiah. Is it then probable that Jesus would have chosen as His self-designation an expression which in apocalyptic language did not mean an earthly Messiah but a miraculous Messianic being, coming on the clouds of heaven? As the self-designation "Son of Man" is found from the beginning of the Gospels it must, in this case, be supposed that Jesus from the first looked forward to a transcendental

Messiahship, to be attained by suffering and death; that is, however, inherently very improbable, and, moreover, in contradiction with the Gospels, according to which He first began to predict His death and resurrection at the end of His Galilæan ministry, after Peter's confession. In view of these considerations, it has been conjectured that Jesus first adopted this apocalyptic self-designation at that time, in order to indicate the transcendental character of His Messiahship, when it first dawned upon His mind in consequence of His presentiment of death, and that the carrying back of this expression to His earlier discourses is due to the Evangelists. Ingenious as this hypothesis appears, I cannot hold it to be satisfactory: it seems to me too complicated to be true, and it presupposes the historicity of the predictions of the death and resurrection, which, in view of critical considerations, cannot be maintained; but if we are to admit an anticipation of the Messianic self-designation "Son of Man" in the Gospels, why should we not take a short step farther and find the source of this Messianic title, not in the reflection of Jesus upon His future death, but in the reflection of the Church upon the past catastrophic death and exaltation of her Lord? Another consideration which points to this simplest solution of the problem, is that the absence of the Messianic title Son of Man in Paul's writings would be quite inexplicable if it had really been familiar to the disciples from the first as the historical self-designation of Jesus. Moreover, the way in which the seer of the Johannine Apocalypse (i. 13 and xiv. 14) sees "One like unto a son of man"[1] sitting upon the clouds reminds us much more directly of the Jewish apocalypses than of the Gospel terminology. But if this was unknown both to Paul and to John the author of the Apocalypse, it cannot be derived from a reminiscence of the real linguistic usage of Jesus, but must have been made a designation of Jesus at a later period, especially from the time when Greek Gospels began to arise, and then attributed to Himself.

This procedure can easily be explained. When the belief of the disciples in Jesus' Messianic destiny appeared to be destroyed by His death on the cross, but soon afterwards was revived by the Easter visions in such a way that Jesus was now thought of as exalted to heaven but soon to come thence again to establish His Kingdom, they could find no more suitable expression for their new faith in Christ than Daniel's figure of the coming of a Son of Man from heaven to assume the kingship over the people of God. "In the whole Old Testament there was no Messianic conception to be found which corresponded so exactly as that of Daniel to the Christian belief regarding the character of Jesus' Messiahship. Elsewhere in the Old Testament the Messiah was always a rising star, one who raises himself out of the dust and stands up among men; but Jesus was expected to come back from heaven, where they had seen Him since His death. Now in the vision of Daniel there was mention of a human figure which should come amid the clouds of heaven; whence, is not said, and, strictly speaking, what is suggested is some distant

[1] *ὅμιον υἱὸν ἀνθρώπου*, a verbal imitation of כְּבַר אֱנָשׁ in Dan. vii. 13 but not, as in the Gospel, *ὁ υἱὸς τοῦ ἀνθρώπου*.

region where it had hitherto existed inactive, like other things which in the Jewish view pre-existed in the Divine wisdom; further, he is immediately carried away by the clouds into the presence of God. But that did not concern the Christian; for him the representation of the coming in the clouds of heaven was sufficient to enable him to find his expectation of the return of Jesus expressed in the whole passage. If this apocalyptic view had taken possession of the imagination of many at that time, if it had perhaps only lately attained a specially wide circulation among the Jews and the Christians of Jewish nationality (it has, as is well known, been taken up into the New Testament apocalypses—Apoc. i. 7, 13, xiv. 14; 1 Thess. iv. 16 f.; Mark xiii. 26, and parallels), the Christian Evangelist could not fail to indicate with all emphasis, in the interests of his faith and its propagation, that it referred to Jesus."[1] It is, however, to be noticed that the oldest Evangelical tradition shows a certain shrinking from representing the expectation of the Parousia as expressed quite directly and plainly by Jesus Himself. At first it was only the Daniel passage which was put into His mouth—the Son of Man shall appear in the clouds of heaven (Mark xiii. 26, xiv. 62)—in which the reference of the expression is still left vague—Wellhausen's word is "furtive" (*verstohlen*)—and needs a specifically Christian interpretation to affix it to the person of Jesus: a Jew might think of this Son of Man only as Messiah, without thinking of Jesus in connection with it; and, indeed, the Evangelical apocalypse to which Mark xiii. 26 belongs probably has a Jewish basis.

[1] Brandt, *Ev. Gesch.*, p. 567; *cf.* Wellhausen, *ut sup.*, pp. 208 ff.

From this practice of at first attributing to Jesus only the traditional apocalyptic way of speaking of the "coming of the Son of Man" there arose later the custom of regularly avoiding the "I" in those predictions of His fate which were ascribed to Him with ever greater definiteness, and of always making the Son of Man the subject of them. In this way it naturally lost its originally "furtive" connotation, and became a mere equivalent in the mouth of Jesus for the first person singular, the standing expression for His Messianic self-designation. As men grew accustomed to see in Jesus not merely the Messiah who was to come from heaven in the future, but also to presuppose even in His earthly life a present Messiah, latent indeed, but conscious from the first of His higher dignity and destiny, a definite expression was needed for this Messianic consciousness of the earthly Jesus; and as there was no traditional reminiscence of such an expression—for a very obvious reason—the omission was readily supplied by the apocalyptic title which had at first designated only the Messiah as to come from heaven in the future. In this respect it may be said that the Gospel use of the Messianic term Son of Man includes in embryo the whole history of the early Christian doctrine of Christ. Its transference from the apocalyptic future back into the historical past is reflected in the gradual development of the usage of the title Son of Man. This is at first only referred to the heavenly Jesus as the Christ who is to come (not come again) at the Parousia, then to the earthly Jesus when predicting the path of suffering and death by which He was to reach His

Messianic throne (predictions of the Passion in Mark viii. 31 f., ix. 12, 31, x. 33 ff., 45, xiv. 21, 41), finally, used in all passages in which the earthly Jesus bore witness to His Messiahship, whether they were of eschatological import or not. There are, moreover, in Mark only two passages (ii. 10 and 28) in which the title Son of Man occurs prior to Peter's confession, and without reference to His sufferings and what lay beyond. In these two passages the Evangelist may indeed have understood the word in the same sense as elsewhere, but that was not here the original meaning, since in both passages (*sup.*, pp. 8, 12) the context requires the sense "man" in general, which was doubtless what was meant by the *barnasha* of the underlying Aramaic text. The fact, however, that the literal translation of *barnasha* coincided with the apocalyptic Messianic title, of which the usage had become fixed, may have contributed to efface, in Greek linguistic usage, the original eschatological limitation of the use of the term Son of Man, and to extend it into a general Messianic self-designation of Jesus. In the later Gospels we find it in this wider sense. Since in several passages one Evangelist speaks of the "Son of Man" where the parallels have the simple "I,"[1] the possibility must be left open that in other passages also in which both Evangelists have "Son of Man" this Messianic term has been substituted in the Greek Gospels for an original "I" or indeterminate "man" (*barnash*).[2] We cannot, however, expect to arrive at

[1] *Cf.* Matt. v. 11 with Luke vi. 22; Matt. x. 32 with Luke xii. 8; Matt. xvi. 13 with Luke ix. 18 and Mark viii. 27.

[2] So, perhaps, in Matt. xi. 19 = Luke vii. 34, and Matt. viii. 20 =

complete certainty with regard to every single passage in our Gospels where the term Son of Man occurs. So much, however, I hold to be certain, that all sayings with which the use of the title Son of Man as a Messianic self-designation is inseparably connected are not derived from Jesus Himself, since this self-designation cannot possibly be supposed to have been used by Him.

This result finds an illustration, and at the same time a fresh confirmation, in the Gospel predictions of the suffering, death, and resurrection of the Son of Man, which are often repeated from the time of Peter's confession onwards. The threefold repetition with progressively increasing exactitude of detail (Mark viii. 31, ix. 31, x. 33 f.) is sufficient to show that here the moulding hand of the Evangelist has been at work in the interests of primitive Christian apologetic. It was of the utmost importance to reconcile the contradiction—full of offence for Jewish minds, and, indeed, for those of all men—between the tragic end and the Messianic dignity of Jesus, by explaining His death as a means determined from the first in the counsel of God for His exaltation to heaven; from this apologetic interest sprang the Gospel predictions of the Passion as *vaticinia post eventum.* Before the events came to pass, no one either in the wider or narrower circles of the discipleship of Jesus had any inkling of the tragic fate which lay before Him, nor of the resurrection which should follow. The catastrophe came on them so unexpectedly, and shattered all their hopes so com-

Luke ix. 58. In Matt. xii. 32 = Luke xii. 10, ὁ υἱὸς τ.α. may be derived from οἱ υἱοὶ τ.α. in Mark iii. 28. *Cf.* Wellhausen, *ut sup.*, pp. 204 ff.

pletely for the moment, that they all, dumbfounded by the sudden blow, took to flight. It was only afterwards that they learned from the prophetic Scriptures what they must long since have known from the prophetic words of Jesus, if they had ever really heard them, that the Son of Man must, according to the Divine decree, suffer such things in order to enter into His Messianic glory. Moreover, the Evangelists themselves give a hint that the disciples had no knowledge beforehand of the resurrection of Jesus. After the Transfiguration, Mark declares, Jesus bade His disciples say nothing to any man until the Son of Man should be risen from the dead; "and they kept that saying to themselves and questioned one with another what the rising from the dead should mean" (ix. 9 f.). Similarly, after the second prediction of the Passion it is said, "They understood not that saying, and were afraid to ask him" (ix. 32). In Luke this failure to understand the prediction of the passion is even represented as a Divinely imposed disability: "But they understood not this saying, and it was hid from them, that they might not perceive it; and they feared to ask him of that saying" (ix. 45). How are we to explain so obstinate a misunderstanding of the most unambiguous predictions? The rationalising compromises (Jesus did not speak quite so clearly, the disciples did not so completely fail to understand Him, and the like) will not do here; in this case, as in many others, they only serve to prevent any clear insight into the facts. The contradiction between the unambiguous predictions of the Passion by Jesus which the Evangelists report and the absolute unintelligence and ignorance of the whole of the disciples in regard to them, is to be explained as solely and simply due to the contradiction between the theological apologetic *postulate* that Jesus the Messiah must have foreknown and foretold His paradoxical fate as determined by the Divine decree, and the historical *fact* that before the arrest of Jesus no one in His following had any apprehension of the catastrophe, all expected the very opposite—victory and glory—and similarly after His death and before the Easter visions no one expected His resurrection; on the contrary, the women who came to the tomb had intended to embalm His body. If, then, the predictions of the Passion and Resurrection are only evidence of a theological apologetic postulate which stands in absolute contradiction to historical facts, they were neither wholly nor partly, neither clearly nor obscurely, spoken by Jesus, but were simply not spoken by Him at all, but rather, in every case, put into His mouth by the Evangelists.

Against this inevitable result of a logical and methodical criticism the theological prepossessions of exegetes have struggled vehemently, doubtless because the doctrinal utterances regarding the redeeming power of Jesus' death which are similarly ascribed to Him stand or fall with the predictions of the Passion. But if we examine these more closely—those in question are Mark x. 45 and xiv. 24 with the parallels—we shall find that they do not contradict, but confirm, the result arrived at above. In rebuking the disciples who were disputing about precedence Jesus is reported by Mark, whom Matthew follows, to have said, "The Son of man is not come to be served, but to serve, and to give his life a ransom for many." This saying is not to be explained away in the sense that Jesus, as the friend of humanity, had dedicated His life to the service of many, had rendered service to many. What is meant is undoubtedly nothing else than the surrender of His life to death as an expiatory offering, to purchase the deliverence of many (namely of all believers) from eternal death. It therefore expresses exactly the same thought of a representative atonement as is expressed in 1 Tim. ii. 6, 1 Cor. vi. 20, Rom. iii. 25, etc. Now this view of the death of Christ as a means of redemption is found only once elsewhere in the Synoptic Gospels, namely, in the words of the institution of the Supper, the derivation of which from the Pauline theology is, for many reasons, highly probable, as we shall see below. Is it not likely that the same is the case here? The thought of a redemption through the atoning power of the death of Jesus the Messiah could not well arise until the fact of this death had become the subject of apologetic reflection with a view to removing the offence of the cross. The most obvious explanation was to suppose that the suffering and death of Jesus were determined beforehand by the Divine decree, and were either permitted or brought about by the Divine providence in order to test Him and to prepare the way to His Messianic exaltation; this is the point of view from which the death of Jesus is explained in the sermons of the Apostles in Acts, and it is very probable that the primitive community was satisfied with that. But the further question regarding the purpose of this paradoxical fate of the

Messiah in relation to the work committed to Him by God soon forced itself upon them. And to this a satisfying solution offered itself in the doctrine—founded on Isa. liii. and current in the Pharisaic theology—of the atoning power of the innocent sufferings of the righteous to wipe out the guilt of their adherents; the application of this doctrine to the death of Jesus made it appear an atonement bringing salvation to His followers. It is possible that even in the primitive community this thought had occasionally been made use of as an apologetic resource, but it was only by Paul that it was made the centre of the Christian faith, the foundation and corner-stone of the doctrine of redemption. But it must not be overlooked that this Pauline doctrine of redemption was far removed from the thoughts of Jesus. The salvation which He promised consisted in the speedy coming of the Reign of God—looked forward to by the ancient prophets and made by John the Baptist a subject of immediate expectation—with its miraculous consolations and blessings in which all those should share who did the will of God, loved God and the brethren, renounced the world and self; especially, renounced Mammon, and shrank from no sacrifice for the cause of God. In this preaching of a salvation which is through and through apocalyptic and ascetic there is no room for a representative atoning sacrifice of which the merits are imputed to those who believe. Everywhere Jesus has made the forgiveness of sins dependent only on the penitent and humble attitude of men and their willingness to forgive one another, without anywhere indicating that the Divine forgiveness has as its prerequisite a propitiation of God by a representative atonement; the parable of the Prodigal Son is in this respect especially instructive.[1] If, therefore, Jesus only expected salvation to be brought about by the coming Reign of God over a renewed society, and by the pious attitude of its individual members, He can have known nothing of a redemption by representative expiation, and cannot therefore have looked upon His own death as a means to that end. An indirect confirmation of this is furnished by the consideration that if Jesus had (like Paul) regarded His own death as the Divinely willed means of atonement and as the essential purpose of His Messianic mission, He could not possibly have recommended His disciples to buy swords,[2] the only object of which could be to defend Him against the attacks of enemies; nor is it possible that in Gethsemane He could have prayed that the cup might pass from Him, and least of all could He have uttered the cry of lamentation from the cross, "My God, my God, why hast thou forsaken me?" The striking contrast between these three facts which the Evangelists record and their theological postulates and apologetic constructions elsewhere, is in favour of the historical character of the former, and confirms the doubt, which is also suggested by internal grounds, regarding the authenticity of all the utterances which are put

1 *Cf.* the remark of Jülicher cited above, p. 159.

2 Luke xxii. 36 ff. *Cf.* my essay "Jesus' Foreknowledge of His Death" in *The New World* for September 1899 (and also in the essays collected by Orello Cone under the title *Evolution and Theology,* pp. 178–203).

into the mouth of Jesus by the Evangelists concerning His predetermined death and its redemptive effect.

The sayings at the Last Supper form no exception, since it can be shown that these, so far as they are to be considered historical, do not refer to Jesus' death, and, on the other hand, that so far as they refer to His death and its consequences they are derived not from Jesus but from Paul, or from the Evangelists who had been influenced by him. The words preserved by all three Evangelists — and therefore doubtless genuine—which Jesus spoke in distributing the bread, "This is my body (Mark xiv. 22 = Matt. xxvi. 26 = Luke xxii. 19), do not contain *in themselves* any reference to Jesus' death, but admit of a quite different interpretation, as is clear from 1 Cor. x. 17. They are certainly made to refer to His death by the supplement which Luke, following Paul (1 Cor. xi. 24), adds, "which is given for you." At the giving of the cup, Mark and Matthew both make Jesus say, "This is my blood of the covenant which is shed for many (Matthew adds, "for the forgiveness of sins"). In Luke, we find in this passage (at least in a part of the MSS.) a phrase which combines Paul (1 Cor. xi. 25) with Mark (xiv. 24): "This cup is the New Covenant in my blood, which is shed for you." In spite of the divergences in the form of the phrase, its sense in the three Evangelists and in Paul is essentially the same: the cup denotes the new covenant which is established by means of the blood, *i.e.* the atoning death, of Jesus. From this the celebration of the Supper receives the significance of an ever-renewed memorial of the death of Jesus—as Paul and Luke say, "Do this in remembrance of me." While there can be no reason to doubt the meaning of the words of institution in Paul and the Evangelists, there is every reason to raise the question whether these words were originally spoken by Jesus or not. It has lately been remarked, with good grounds, that, apart from the words in question, the description of the Last Supper in the Synoptic Gospels by no means makes the impression that thoughts of the imminent tragedy, or the sadness of a final separation, ruled the hearts of the participants. On the contrary, a tone of joyful confidence and the hope of the approaching victorious issue of His cause is expressed in the saying of Jesus, which all the Synoptists report, "I will drink no more of the fruit of the vine until the day when I drink it new (Matt.: "with you") in the kingdom of God" (Luke: "until the kingdom of God be come"). So it is also in the words reported by Luke (xxii. 29 f.), "As my Father hath appointed unto me the kingship, so I appoint unto you, that ye may eat and drink at my table in my kingdom, and sit on thrones judging (ruling) the twelve tribes of Irsael." The traditional opinion of exegetes, that these words are to be understood as a pictorial expression of the super-earthly blessedness which is to be founded on Jesus' death and resurrection, has no point of attachment in the text. The disciples certainly did not understand them in that sense, as their very earthly dispute about position and precedence shows, and also their complete discouragement after the catastrophe. If Jesus had had an entirely different, spiritual conception of the coming Kingdom of God, He would certainly, on earlier occasions and especially at this last opportunity of converse with them, have earnestly endeavoured to enlighten them as to their mistake, instead of confirming them in it by the saying about drinking the new wine with them in the Kingdom of God. This saying has no meaning if we accept the traditional assumption of transcendental hopes. It can only have an intelligible meaning if it was meant by Jesus in the sense in which His disciples could not fail to understand it, namely, as referring to an immediate victory of His reforming efforts to set up the true theocracy, in which the leadership of a renewed people of God should fall to Him and to His disciples. It is obvious to everyone that such hopes are far removed from the conviction of His approaching death which is presupposed in the words of institution in the Gospels. How is this contradiction to be explained?

The key to the explanation must be sought, not in theological dialectic and not in psychological subtleties, of which a rank crop has lately sprung up, to the great detriment of a plain, historical interpretation, but simply in textual criticism. It was remarked above (p. 178 f.) with reference to Luke xxii. 19b and 20, that this verse and a half was held to be spurious by some of the leading modern authorities in textual criticism, because it is wanting in many codices (D, it. Syr. Cur.). Others, however, defend the originality of this verse in the Gospel of Luke, but admit that the Evangelist did not derive it from his source, but formed it by combining Paul and Mark. I hold the former view to be the more probable, but am of opinion that for the question in hand it does not much matter which of the two views is correct; for in either case, whether the Evangelist himself or some later interpolator filled in the gap with this skilful combination, it must be assumed that in the original source used by Luke verses 19b and 20 were not present. This text, therefore, only recorded one giving of the cup, at the beginning of the meal (xxii. 17), without any reference whatever to blood or death or the New Covenant, but with the addition of the saying (verse 18) that Jesus would not drink again of the fruit of the vine until the coming of the Kingdom of God. Then followed (verse 19a) the giving of the bread, with the simple explanation, "This is my body"; here, too, without a syllable of reference to a body broken in death or delivered over to death, for the reference in verse 19b belongs to the interpolation taken from Paul. I hold it to be very probable that we have in this shorter Lucan text, as preserved by Cod. D, the oldest account of the Last Supper; for the deliberate omission of the second, symbolical cup, which was so important for the Church's view of the Supper, is inconceivable; while, on the other hand, it is quite conceivable that in later times the omission of this raised so much difficulty that an endeavour was made to fill in the gap by means of a skilful combination. But if we are to see in the shorter Lucan text of Cod. D the most original form of the report of the Lord's Supper, there follows the further consequence that the words in Mark also, who is followed by Matthew, "This is my blood, which is shed for many," do not belong to the oldest tradition, and do not therefore contain a reminiscence of what was then spoken by Jesus, but are an addition derived by Mark, the disciple of Paul, from the Pauline theology. A consideration which points in the same direction is that Jesus, even supposing He had at that time foreseen His death, could not possibly have described it as a means of establishing a new covenant which should take the place of the old covenant of the Law made with the fathers at Sinai; His intention was to fulfil, not to destroy, the Law and the Prophets—not to put a new religion in the place of that revealed by God through Moses, but to establish the old prophetic ideal of the theocracy in new splendour. It was Paul who first won from reflection on the accursed death of the Messiah upon the cross, the conviction that this death had been appointed in the counsel of God to be the end of the covenant of the Letter and the beginning of the new covenant of the Spirit. It was natural for the Apostle, to whom the crucified Christ had become the keystone of his faith, to give to the Lord's Supper a mystical reference to His atoning death, and to seek support for this new mystical conception in a corresponding re-interpretation and extension of the traditional words by which Jesus had originally made the common meal a symbol of the inner fellowship, the covenant of brotherhood, among His followers. Moreover, Paul has also preserved a reminiscence of the original meaning of the "breaking of bread" together, as the love-feast of the Christian brotherhood is named in Acts, in interpreting, as he does in 1 Cor. x. 17, the "one" bread as the symbol of the "one" mystical body of Christ, or of the Christian community. On the other hand, in 1 Cor. xi. 24 f.

he has made the bread the symbol not of the mystical body but of the actual body of Christ, and added the interpretation of the cup as symbolising the poured-forth blood of the New Covenant, and has thus given to the whole celebration of the Lord's Supper the character of a mystical commemoration of the death of Christ. This *new* conception of it then found its way, through Mark the disciple of Paul, into the Evangelical tradition, and has carried with it the alteration of the original version which is still preserved in the shorter text of Luke. This did not, however, everywhere displace the older form of the "Holy Communion," for that this long maintained itself in wide circles in the Church is proved by the Communion prayers in the "Teaching of the Apostles," which have no reference either to the Gospel text or to Paul.

As the Gospel of Luke has preserved for us in its shorter text the oldest, ante-Pauline, form of the words of institution, so too, among the last discourses of Jesus in the same passage, it has preserved a peculiar saying which deserves more attention than it has usually received from exegetes. At the close of the Last Supper, before they went out to Gethsemane, Jesus is reported in Luke xxii. 36 to have said to His disciples, "But now, he that hath a purse, let him take it, and likewise his scrip; and he who hath not these, let him sell his cloak and buy a sword."[1] That is to say, the possession of a sword is now a pressing necessity to you—more so than purse, or scrip, or cloak. Most expositors remark upon this that Jesus did not seriously mean to command them to buy swords, but only spoke of doing so metaphorically,

[1] For the rendering, *cf.* p. 181.—TRANSLATOR.

meaning that they must be prepared for a struggle with the hostile world. But this interpretation is beset with serious difficulties. Anyone who reads these words without a preconceived opinion receives the impression that they are not the pictorial expression of a general truth, but contain a literal and urgent command to His disciples to provide themselves with arms. It was certainly in this sense that the disciples understood them, for they immediately pointed to two swords which were at hand, whereupon Jesus answered, "It is enough" (verse 38). The exegetical theory that this was cutting irony directed against the misunderstanding of His words by the disciples is not suggested by the text. There the command to buy swords (verse 36) *could not* be understood by the disciples otherwise than literally, so there was no reason for irony, and Jesus would have been obliged to explain to His disciples clearly and convincingly that He was not speaking of literal arms but only of spiritual weapons; instead of that, He only says, "It is enough," and thus obviously confirms His hearers in the supposition that they are to provide themselves with weapons wherewith to defend themselves against the literal attacks of enemies. How could Jesus have left His disciples under an impression the consequences of which might have been foreseen (Peter's sword-stroke), if this had not really been His own meaning? I believe that any reader of Luke xxii. 36–38 who lays aside his preconceived opinion will gain the impression that Jesus quite seriously commanded His disciples to provide weapons as speedily as possible. But men provide themselves with weapons with the intention of using them if need be, and therefore with a view to resisting the attacks of enemies. If, therefore, Jesus spoke the words which Luke reports, He must have had the intention, on that last evening, of offering an armed resistance to His enemies. And that is quite conceivable. He had had opportunities enough during the preceding days to convince Himself of the deadly hatred of the hierarchy, and might have received warnings from many quarters of attacks upon His life which were being planned in these circles. Naturally, what He expected was an assault of hired assassins; against this He intended His disciples to defend Him, and for *this* purpose—defence against assassination—two swords might well be enough. Of an arrest by the servants of the Jewish (or Roman?) Government, Jesus had apparently never thought. That is the more easy to understand if we remember that the spiritual rulers of the Jews had been deprived of their criminal jurisdiction by the Roman Government; therefore it was quite natural that Jesus should expect, on the part of the hierarchs—and it was only from them that danger seemed to threaten Him—the sending out of ruffianly assassins, but not an official arrest. In this way the intention of armed resistance which unmistakably appears in the command to buy swords, can quite well be reconciled with the fact that after a feeble attempt on the part of a single disciple the resistance to the servants of the authorities was at once voluntarily abandoned at Jesus' command ("Hold! No more!" Luke xxii. 51).

If we accept this, as it seems to me, simplest explanation of Luke xxii. 36 ff., it throws a significant light upon the situation of Jesus immediately before the catastrophe. In the first place, it contains a remarkable confirmation of the result which we have arrived at in examining the various predictions of the Passion; namely, that Jesus never thought of a criminal trial and death on the cross as lying before Him. Just as He journeyed to Jerusalem not to die there but to overthrow the hierarchy, those "Wicked Husbandmen," and establish the true theocracy by means of a religious and social reorganisation of the people of God, so in the last days, in face of the deadly enmity of the hierarchs, He never abandoned His joyful confidence that God destined the kingship for Him and His "little flock" (Luke xii. 32, xxii. 29). He might well believe that by God's help He would succeed in winning the people, who indeed heard Him gladly (Mark xii. 38), for a reforming movement which would lead to the removal of the hierarchy. That this would not be accomplished without resistance, struggles, and dangers, He might well expect, and therefore His confidence of victory may have alternated with darker moods of anxious despondency, such as are expressed in the prayers in Gethsemane, but also earlier, in words which are certainly genuine: "I am come to kindle fire upon the earth, and how fain would I that it were already burning! But I have a baptism to be baptized with, and how am I oppressed till it be accomplished! Think ye that I am come to bring peace upon earth? I say unto you, Nay; but rather division!" (Luke xii. 49 ff.). That is the authentic language of a hero who is facing a hard struggle and is resolved to stake all, even to his life, upon the cause of God, but who, although he cannot quite conceal from himself the *possibility* of his own defeat, is far from thinking of it as a *necessity*. That Jesus was well aware during those days in Jerusalem of the dangers of His position is most clearly shown by the command to buy swords in order to ward off attempts at assassination. But the fact that He only thought of attacks of that kind shows that He had not taken into account the whole difficulty of the position. It is no diminution of His heroic greatness that He underrated, as heroes are wont to do, the forces of the actual world. To the pious Galilæan the relation of the Reign of God to the Roman rule seemed of slight importance; He believed it possible to realise the former without coming into collision with the latter ("Render unto Cæsar the things which are Cæsar's and unto God the things which are God's"). Upon this mistake, which does no discredit to the heart of the Greatest of Idealists, His plans of religious and social reform made shipwreck. That He Himself thought of His fate in this way, as the shattering of His dearest hopes, is proved by His last word from the cross, "My God, why hast thou forsaken me?"

Nothing could reconcile us to the awful tragedy of such a death of Jesus but the thought that, in the providence of God, it was the dawn of a higher life. The corn of wheat must fall into the ground and die in order to bring forth fruit; the Jewish Messiah, the Reformer of a single nation, must perish, in order that in the faith of the community of His followers "Christ after the Spirit" might arise, who should become the Saviour of the world and the King of the Kingdom of Truth. All that in the former lay under individual and human, temporal and national, limitations, perished in the unequal struggle with the forces of this world. But that which was the Divine essence of His being and work—the ideal of the reign of the heavenly Father in the hearts of His children and in the social life of His Kingdom—remained alive and marched victoriously forward over the world; it is alive to-day, and it will live for ever.

The first stages of the development by which the Jesus of History became the Christ of Faith can still be clearly traced in the Synoptic Gospels, and we may in conclusion glance rapidly over them. That which reanimated in the disciples, who had at first fled in fear, their belief in the Messiahship of their Master, who had died upon the cross, was the visionary experience which occurred sometimes to individuals (first to Peter), sometimes to a number of persons together—experiences similar to those which have occurred at all periods, and still occur, in circles where religious excitement is prevalent. For all their extraordinary character, they are nevertheless not, strictly speaking, miracles, for they have their sufficient cause in the psychical condition of the persons to whom they occur; they are the effects of psychic forces, the tension of which discharges and relieves itself in them. They therefore fall under the general category of the "enthusiastic" (spiritualistic[1]) phenomena which characterise primitive Christianity from its commencement, and which must be

[1] The word *pneumatisch* which Pfleiderer here uses—the brackets are his—carries no specific reference to "Spiritualism" in the narrower, modern sense. See vol. i. chap. xvii., "Life in the Spirit."—TRANSLATOR.

assumed to have been an important factor in the work of Jesus and in the results produced by Him. His personal enthusiasm of faith and love, which from the first had firmly attached His followers to Him, now continued to work with life-giving power in their souls, and manifested itself in the form of visions in which they supposed they saw Him again in person, no longer in earthly and human weakness, but as the Messiah exalted to the life and light of heaven. "So extraordinary was the impression which He had made on them, so real was the fellowship in which they stood with Him: He did not let go of His own" (Wellhausen). On the ground of these visions experienced by many persons, and repeatedly (1 Cor. xv. 5 ff.), they were henceforth convinced that their crucified Master had been raised up by God by an act of omnipotence and exalted to the Messianic throne upon the right hand of the Father (Ps. cx.), installed into the dignity of "Lord" and "Christ" (Acts ii. 36), and appointed to come again in the near future to judge both living and dead, to deliver Israel from her enemies, and to restore the Kingdom to Israel (Acts i. 6, x. 42; Luke xxiv. 21). The importance of the resurrection of Jesus consisted for the primitive community mainly in the fact that it was the guarantee of His speedy visible return upon the clouds of heaven to carry out His Messianic work upon earth. The primitive community did not suppose His Messiahship to be realised in His earthly life; He there appeared only as the Messiah designate. He became the true Messiah, or indeed, more exactly, the heavenly Son of Man in the sense of the Apocalypse, only in consequence of His resurrection and exaltation. In this respect the belief of the community of disciples appeared to be the same as that of the Jewish apocalyptic, which likewise looked for a Messiah descending from heaven. Nevertheless, there was from the beginning, in the very fact of the identification of the heavenly Messiah with the crucified and risen Jesus, a significant distinction between them. The vague conception of a human personality existing in heaven was filled in, through the identification with the historical Jesus, with a definite religious and ethical character with familiar and winning traits; and, in addition, the time of His "coming in glory" (Parousia) was brought into the near future, because the Resurrection was regarded as, in a sense, the prelude to it, and it became the object of the most fervent hope. The mood of enthusiastic eschatological expectation—of aversion from the present transitory world and eager longing for the coming New World which would bring to the followers of the Messiah a miraculous deliverance from all evils, victory over demonic and human enemies, and establishment of the ideal condition of the perfect Reign of God—now became, much more distinctly than ever before, the key-note of religious faith and life.

But it was inevitable that from this centre of hopeful faith reflection should be directed back upon the earthly life of Jesus, in order to find even here premonitions and pledges of His future appearance in Messianic splendour. All that in the past seemed to contradict this—suffering, shame, and death—must receive an interpretation which would satisfactorily reconcile the contradiction. For this line of apologetic reflection the Old Testament offered material of inestimable value. The Sacred Scriptures were now read with new eyes; types and predictions of the fate of the Lord Jesus were sought everywhere in them, and were naturally found. Thus there soon grew up in the assemblies of the Christian brotherhood a new understanding of the ancient Word of God; interpretations of passages in the Prophets and Psalms came to light, of which the schools of the Jewish Scribes had known nothing—interpretations which were sometimes simple and sensible, sometimes artificial and fantastic, always, however, tending to the edification of Christian hearers and readers, a mighty weapon of faith, both for attack and defence. Above all, it was the story of the Lord's sufferings which occupied attention from this point of view; types were found for every detail in the fate of righteous sufferers and in the complaints of pious psalmists. Conversely, some features of the Passion story were freely invented on the basis of supposed prophecies of this kind, and the traditional material thus received a more graphic and more edifying character. But even apart from the Passion story the mythopœic energy of religious imagination made itself felt from the beginning. The expected miracle of the Parousia threw back a glamour upon the earthly life of Jesus, and filled the gaps in historical knowledge with the pictures of pious imagination. The guiding principle was, that whatever miraculous acts and experiences the Old Testament had narrated of its greatest men of God, such as Moses and Elias, must be fulfilled, nay surpassed, in the Messiah. It was not cool reflection but prophetic enthusiasm, reading the Old Testament throughout in the light of its fulfilment by Jesus the Messiah, which gave rise to this imitation of the Old Testament legends in the Gospels. Yet in this process, alongside of unconscious poetic inventions, theological ideas, especially apologetic motives, from the first exercised an influence upon the formation of the Gospel tradition. Faith desired to see even in the earthly life of Jesus premonitions and pledges of that which the exalted Christ had come to mean for it in the present and future. He who was to come again as King and Judge must already in His earthly life—that was the self-evident postulate of faith—have proved Himself by many miraculous works to be the Lord of Nature, the conqueror of the demons, and the lawgiver of the new People of God, must have been authenticated by Divine voices as the Son of God and endowed with the miraculous power of the Spirit. From the large number of such ideal narratives we may here particularly notice three, because in them the progressive ante-dating and concomitant heightening of the Messianic dignity and Divine Sonship of Jesus may be clearly recognised. These are, the Transfiguration, the Baptism, and the miraculous Birth.

The story of the Transfiguration is, in its original sense, which is still recognisable in Mark, the symbolic anticipation of the glorification of Christ at His resurrection. As Paul had previously (2 Cor. iii.) represented the Old Testament legend about the glory of God being reflected in the face of Moses at the giving of the Law on Sinai as being surpassed in Christ as the forth-shining of the Divine glory, so Mark the Evangelist, the disciple of Paul, represents

Jesus as transfigured into a glorified form such as is appropriate to the heavenly beings. Thereupon appeared Moses and Elijah, as representatives of the Law and the Prophets, in order to do homage to Jesus as the Lord of the New Covenant. But when Peter proposed to build tabernacles for these three together—therefore to retain the old authorities side by side with Christ—there came a voice from heaven saying, "This (Jesus) is my Son, the beloved, hearken unto Him." Then Moses and Elias disappeared, and Jesus alone remained with the astonished disciples. That signifies that Christ has been appointed by God as the sole Lord and mediator of the New Covenant, and before Him even the authorities of the Old Covenant give away. Then Jesus forbids His disciples to make this known until the Son of Man should have risen from the dead; whereupon they asked one another in amazement what this rising from the dead could mean. This suggests that until the resurrection of Jesus no one knew anything of what is here narrated, and therefore that it is a mysterious story from the spiritual world, which was first revealed to the minds of the disciples after the death and resurrection of Jesus, when they were meditating upon the significance of these events. The purpose of the narrative is therefore to illustrate the significance of the resurrection of Jesus, to show that He was thereby made manifest as a heavenly, glorious Being, exalted to be "the Lord who is the Spirit" and the Lord of Spirits, declared to be the Son of God, the object of the special love of God, and the highest authority for the people of God. That is precisely the content of the doctrine of Christ as held by the primitive community, for whom Jesus was first "made Lord and Christ" by the Resurrection (Acts ii. 36, x. 42, xvii. 13; Rom. i. 4).

Before long, however, the Christian community was not content to see only in the Jesus of the Exaltation and the Parousia the Son of God and Messiah; He must have been so from the beginning of His public life, for—the reflection naturally suggested itself—how else could He have done so many miracles, how, especially, have healed so many possessed by demons, unless "God had been with Him," unless He had been "anointed by God with the Holy Spirit and with power"? (Acts ii. 22, x. 38). But when could that have taken place? What moment of His known life was more appropriate to fix on as that of His being thus equipped with the spirit and power of the Messiah than the moment of His baptism by John? Thus the appointment of Jesus to be the Messianic Son of God was pushed back from the end of His Galilæan ministry (the Transfiguration) to a point before the beginning of it, and brought into connection with the baptism of John. In both cases the accompaniments of the supernatural act of adoption are similar; as at the Transfiguration there appear heavenly light and heavenly spirits, so here the heavens are opened and the Holy Spirit descends upon Jesus in the form of a dove. In an extra-canonical but very old version of the legend there is also mention of an appearance of fire which at the moment of the Baptism shone round about Jesus, just like the light at the Transfiguration. Similarly, there follows a voice from heaven which speaks the same words as there: "This is [or 'Thou art'] my Son, the beloved, in whom I am well pleased." The words are partly from Ps. ii. and partly from Isaiah xlii. Moreover, it is to be noticed that in Luke, according to the text of Cod. D, which has patristic attestation, the voice at the Baptism follows exactly, without abbreviation, the words of Ps. ii., "Thou art my Son; this day have I begotten thee." It is highly probable that this was the earliest form of the words, and that the altered form of the received text is due to dogmatic reasons. If so, the significance of the miracle at the Baptism is the more clear; it is the solemn installation of Jesus as Son of God and Messiah by the reception of the Divine Spirit, whose instrument He henceforth is. Thus, whereas at first the resurrection of Jesus, the moment of His exaltation to the world of heavenly spirits, was held to be the moment of His installation into the dignity of Sonship and Messiaship, this is now transferred to His baptism as the moment at which the heavenly Spirit-Being entered into the earthly Jesus. That this long remained the prevailing conception is proved by the custom which grew up in Gnostic circles in the second century, was accepted by the Church, and was maintained down into the fourth century, of celebrating the baptism of Jesus as the "Epiphany" of the Divine Christ-spirit and the birthday of Christianity.[1] It was only in the fifth century that this significance of the feast of Epiphany was taken over by the feast of Christmas, a change which gave cultural expression to an advance in Christian belief which had doubtless been completed much earlier.

In time, however, it no longer seemed satisfactory

[1] *Cf.* Usener, *Religionsgeschichtliche Untersuchungen,* i. 69 f., 187.

to think of the baptism of Jesus as the beginning of His Messianic Sonship to God, since this implied a too external, accidental, and separable relation of the Divine to His human person; and, indeed, according to many of the Gnostics, the Christ-spirit which descended upon Jesus at His baptism was supposed to have left Him again before His sufferings. The only way of satisfying the need which was felt by faith of thinking of the Divine element as inseparably connected with Christ's human person seemed to be to think of the heavenly Spirit as not first descending upon, or entering into, Him at some point during His earthly life, but as being the constitutive principle of the earthly life of Jesus from His mother's womb. The narrative of the supernatural conception of Jesus, through the power of the Holy Spirit, in the womb of the Virgin Mary, is found only in the two Gospels of Luke and Matthew; and in the Gospel of Luke, indeed, it is only asserted in the two verses[1] i. 34, 35, while in the whole of the remainder of the Gospel and in the Acts of the Apostles there is no reference to it. This gives ground for the very probable conjecture that those two verses were interpolated later (although still very early) into the text of the Gospel, and that this did not therefore originally contain any story of the miraculous birth. In Matthew's Gospel, on the other hand, it forms an integral part, and is the presupposition of the higher Christology which he implies throughout. Besides the doctrinal need, which we have already indicated, of conceiving the divine and human in Jesus' Person as an original

[1] With the exception of the two words ὡς ἐνομίζετο, iii. 23, which are of a similar origin with these two verses. *Cf. sup.*, p. 103.

and inseparable unity, there have contributed more or less directly to the formation of this legend, which cannot be placed earlier than the second century,[1] several motives found in analogous legends. Certain indirect resemblances to it are offered by the Old Testament legends of the birth of Isaac, of Samuel, of Samson, who were born to their aged parents, after long, unfruitful marriage, in consequence of Divine enablement, and might therefore be considered as in some degree miraculously conceived. Another contributory influence was derived from the figurative language of Hebrew poetry, which was the more likely to be understood literally by the Greek-speaking Christian communities because these were unfamiliar with the pictorial character of Hebrew idiom. When, in Psalm ii. 7, God says to the Israelitish king, "Thou art my son, this day have I begotten thee," what was originally meant was only installation into the dignity of the theocratic kingship; but that was no longer understood by the Gentile Christians, and the words were therefore referred to the supernatural begetting of the literal Son of God, Jesus Christ. And since His Sonship was thus transferred from the baptism to His origin in His mother's womb, the voice from heaven at the Baptism, which was originally in the form of Psalm ii. 7, had, naturally, to be altered into the form of the received text. Again, when the prophet Isaiah (vii. 14) said of a child which was about to be born of a young

1 According to the view of Usener (*ut sup.*), it belongs to the very latest portions of the New Testament. This would seem to be worth taking into account in connection with the question regarding the age of the canonical Gospel of Matthew.

mother that His name should be called Immanuel as a symbol of the help which God would speedily give, he was not thinking of a miraculous birth or of a future Messiah; but since the name Immanuel was excellently suitable to the Messiah, it was natural to understand the passage Messianically, and then it was very easy for a Christian who was not skilled in Hebrew to understand the word *almah*, which in the passage in Isaiah means a young woman, in the sense of *virgo intacta*, and so to read into the passage the miraculous birth of Jesus the Messiah. Of course such bold interpretations were only possible to men who were inclined on other grounds to take such a view of the origin of Jesus. These were certainly not, however, originally the Jewish Christians, for whom the idea of a begetting by the Holy Spirit was difficult to conceive, because in Hebrew, spirit (*ruach*) is feminine, and therefore is not naturally thought of as mediating the fatherhood; indeed, in the Gospel of the Hebrews (xvii. 1) the Holy Spirit is actually called the "Mother" of Jesus. It is therefore to be taken as certain that the legend of Jesus' miraculous birth grew up on Gentile-Christian soil. And here we have not far to look for analogies. The idea of sons of gods belongs to the oldest and most widespread elements of all mythology; it lies at the basis of the worship of heroes in all its different shapes and forms. It was not merely the mythical heroes of Greek, Indian, and Persian epic who were directly or indirectly referred to a divine origin; in the case of men of conspicuous greatness, also, who had lived in the clear daylight of history, and had in one way or other made a powerful impression upon their contemporaries and successors, it was thought necessary to assume their supernatural origin as the sons of some god. Of the Indian founder of Buddhism, Gautama Buddha, legend tells that he came down from heaven in the form of a beam of light, or, in another version, in the form of a white elephant, entered into the womb of the Queen Maia who was living apart from her consort, and "without giving or receiving any stain" became the fruit of her womb. In reference to Plato the philosopher, a legend is mentioned in the funeral oration pronounced by his nephew Speusippus, which had grown up even in his lifetime, that he had been begotten of his mother Perictione, not by her husband but by the god Apollo, for which reason the Academy at Athens celebrated the memory of Plato on the birthday of Apollo. Of Alexander the Great, too, legend ran that he had Zeus for his father. Similarly, Scipio Africanus was held to be a son of Zeus; Augustus, a son of Apollo. Apollonius of Tyana, who was celebrated among the Neo-Pythagoreans as a saint and wonder-worker, was held by his countrymen to be a son of Zeus. The motive of all such legends is accurately assigned by Origen: "The impulse which led to such a legend being invented about Plato was the belief that a man of greater wisdom or power than average men must have had his physical origin from a higher and divine seed." Origen has left it to his readers to add the reflection that exactly the same is true of the Christian legend. While the Jews were accustomed to associate with the term Son of God only the idea of the Messianic theocratic dignity, it was much more natural for the Gentile

Christians, to whom this extended and figurative idea of sonship was not familiar,[1] to think of Christ the "Son of God" as a superhuman or divine Being, whether the conception took the form that a spiritual or divine being had come down from heaven and united itself in the most intimate fellowship with the human person of Jesus, or that the person of Jesus had been originally produced by the creative power of the Divine Spirit. The former was the older conception, early embodied in the legend of the miracle at the Baptism and widely accepted, and further elaborated by the Gnostics, with many variations; the latter, the essential sonship, which is only represented by Matthew's Gospel (leaving out of account the interpolation in Luke), is of later origin, and seems to presuppose a stronger influence and influx of the strictly mythical element upon and into the legend and doctrine. But it served the Church from the first as an excellent popular illustration of the religious idea that in the redeeming work of Jesus a divine-human Being is revealed, and that the true revelation of God which brings salvation does not consist so much in single miraculous acts as in the whole character of a man who is born of the Spirit. In this thought the Gospel legend of Christ's birth meets and harmonises with the Christological speculations of the Pauline and Johannine theology.

[1] *Cf.* Dalman, *Worte Jesu*, p. 236 (E.T., p. 288): "It was not natural to a Greek to employ the word 'son' in the same way that the Hebrew did to designate a great variety of relationships. He would always be inclined to understand ὁ υἱὸς τοῦ θεοῦ in the strictest sense."